COMPUTERS IN EDUCATION

Eighth Edition

Editors

John J. Hirschbuhl
University of Akron

John J. Hirschbuhl is the founder of the Center for Computer-Based Education, an assistant to the associate vice president for Information Services, and Professor of Education at the University of Akron. He is currently a Consulting Scholar for the IBM Corporation and a Senior Vice President of Development and Operations at Computer Knowledge International, Inc. He received his Ph.D. from Pennsylvania State University and his B.S. and M.A. from Temple University. Dr. Hirschbuhl has published over 100 articles in professional journals on Computer-Based Education and Training, and he has consulted with many of the FORTUNE 500 companies and academic institutions.

Dwight Bishop
University of Akron

Dwight Bishop, primary developer in the University of Akron's Multimedia Lab, has created commercial and academic software. He has instructed courses in computer-based education, multimedia authoring, multimedia screen design, and statistics. Mr. Bishop has 7 years of experience as a personnel consultant (training and selection). He received his B.A. from the University of North Carolina, his M.S. from Purdue (I/O Psychology), and his M.A. (Computer-Based Education) from the University of Akron.

A Library of Information from the Public Press
Dushkin/McGraw·Hill
Sluice Dock, Guilford, Connecticut 06437

Visit us on the Internet—http://www.dushkin.com/

The Annual Editions Series

ANNUAL EDITIONS, including GLOBAL STUDIES, consist of over 70 volumes designed to provide the reader with convenient, low-cost access to a wide range of current, carefully selected articles from some of the most important magazines, newspapers, and journals published today. ANNUAL EDITIONS are updated on an annual basis through a continuous monitoring of over 300 periodical sources. All ANNUAL EDITIONS have a number of features that are designed to make them particularly useful, including topic guides, annotated tables of contents, unit overviews, and indexes. For the teacher using ANNUAL EDITIONS in the classroom, an Instructor's Resource Guide with test questions is available for each volume. GLOBAL STUDIES titles provide comprehensive background information and selected world press articles on the regions and countries of the world.

VOLUMES AVAILABLE

ANNUAL EDITIONS
Abnormal Psychology
Accounting
Adolescent Psychology
Aging
American Foreign Policy
American Government
American History, Pre-Civil War
American History, Post-Civil War
American Public Policy
Anthropology
Archaeology
Astronomy
Biopsychology
Business Ethics
Child Growth and Development
Comparative Politics
Computers in Education
Computers in Society
Criminal Justice
Criminology
Developing World
Deviant Behavior
Drugs, Society, and Behavior
Dying, Death, and Bereavement
Early Childhood Education

Economics
Educating Exceptional Children
Education
Educational Psychology
Environment
Geography
Geology
Global Issues
Health
Human Development
Human Resources
Human Sexuality
International Business
Macroeconomics
Management
Marketing
Marriage and Family
Mass Media
Microeconomics
Multicultural Education
Nutrition
Personal Growth and Behavior
Physical Anthropology
Psychology
Public Administration
Race and Ethnic Relations

Social Problems
Social Psychology
Sociology
State and Local Government
Teaching English as a Second
    Language
Urban Society
Violence and Terrorism
Western Civilization,
    Pre-Reformation
Western Civilization,
    Post-Reformation
Women's Health
World History, Pre-Modern
World History, Modern
World Politics

GLOBAL STUDIES
Africa
China
India and South Asia
Japan and the Pacific Rim
Latin America
Middle East
Russia, the Eurasian Republics,
    and Central/Eastern Europe
Western Europe

Cataloging in Publication Data
Main entry under title: Computer Studies: Computers in Education. 8/E
"An Annual Editions Publication"
    1. Computer-managed instruction—Periodicals. 2. Computer-assisted instruction—Periodicals. 3. Computers and civilization—Periodicals. I. Hirschbuhl, John J., *comp.* II. Bishop, Dwight, *comp.* III. Title: Computers in Education.
ISBN 0-697-39303-8   371.3'9445'05   87–654373

Eighth Edition

Cover image © 1996 PhotoDisc, Inc.

Printed in the United States of America

Printed on Recycled Paper

Editors/Advisory Board

Members of the Advisory Board are instrumental in the final selection of articles for each edition of ANNUAL EDITIONS. Their review of articles for content, level, currentness, and appropriateness provides critical direction to the editor and staff. We think that you will find their careful consideration well reflected in this volume.

EDITORS

John J. Hirschbuhl
University of Akron

Dwight Bishop
University of Akron

ADVISORY BOARD

George M. Bass
College of William and Mary

Curtis Bring
Moorhead State University

Anthony A. DeFalco
*C. W. Post Center
Long Island University*

Mary Janet Henry
Indiana University East

Richard D. Howell
Ohio State University

John E. Jacobson
*University of Texas
Arlington*

Sandra L. Leslie
Belmont Abbey College

Fredric Linder
*Virginia Commonwealth
University*

Thomas E. Love
Malone College

John Mitterer
Brock University

Landra L. Rezabek
University of Wyoming

Bonnie L. Shapiro
University of Calgary

Rosemary W. Skeele
Seton Hall University

Sharon E. Smaldino
University of Northern Iowa

John E. Splaine
*University of Maryland
College Park*

Stephen J. Taffee
The Learning Company

Susan B. Turkel
Queens College

Marvin Westrom
University of British Columbia

Staff

Ian A. Nielsen, Publisher

EDITORIAL STAFF

Roberta Monaco, Developmental Editor
Dorothy Fink, Associate Developmental Editor
Addie Raucci, Administrative Editor
Cheryl Greenleaf, Permissions Editor
Deanna Herrschaft, Permissions Assistant
Diane Barker, Proofreader
Lisa Holmes-Doebrick, Program Coordinator

PRODUCTION STAFF

Brenda S. Filley, Production Manager
Charles Vitelli, Designer
Shawn Callahan, Graphics
Lara M. Johnson, Graphics
Laura Levine, Graphics
Mike Campbell, Graphics
Joseph Offredi, Graphics
Juliana Arbo, Typesetting Supervisor
Jane Jaegersen, Typesetter
Marie Lazauskas, Word Processor
Kathleen D'Amico, Word Processor
Larry Killian, Copier Coordinator

To the Reader

In publishing ANNUAL EDITIONS we recognize the enormous role played by the magazines, newspapers, and journals of the *public press* in providing current, first-rate educational information in a broad spectrum of interest areas. Many of these articles are appropriate for students, researchers, and professionals seeking accurate, current material to help bridge the gap between principles and theories and the real world. These articles, however, become more useful for study when those of lasting value are carefully *collected, organized, indexed,* and *reproduced* in a *low-cost format,* which provides easy and permanent access when the material is needed. That is the role played by ANNUAL EDITIONS. Under the direction of each volume's *academic editor,* who is an expert in the subject area, and with the guidance of an *Advisory Board,* each year we seek to provide in each ANNUAL EDITION a current, well-balanced, carefully selected collection of the best of the public press for your study and enjoyment. We think that you will find this volume useful, and we hope that you will take a moment to let us know what you think.

Computers in Education, Eighth Edition, is part of the *Annual Editions* subseries called *Computer Studies.* This unique series is designed to provide you with the latest information and trends regarding computers and the role they play in people's lives. One of today's trends is the mass move toward the Internet, whose World Wide Web carries digital technologies, including phone mail systems, bulletin boards, teleconferencing systems, and interactive networked multimedia systems. These technologies provide an electronic pipeline that can reach students anywhere on Earth.

Multimedia and interaction have become part of the education and entertainment industries, and a new product has taken the name "edutainment." The business world has recognized the value of edutainment and has responded with megamergers such as Disney and ABC, Westinghouse and CBS, and Time Warner and Turner Broadcasting. These megacorporations are betting billions of dollars on the future of networked, interactive edutainment. Within the next few years, we will be zipping our way along the worldwide digital highway on our way to edutainment that will stimulate us to interact with realistic simulations and key information that will enable us to conceive new and more powerful ways of thinking about and solving sophisticated problems. This edutainment highway will link all homes, schools, universities, and businesses with a wide broadband communication cable system. In the very near future, we will have the needed links to bring the community, home, school, and business together in a lifelong interactive educational experience.

However, today we can almost do the same thing with current technology. A computer with a modem, speakers, and a CD-ROM player is a dynamic and capable machine for delivering excellent interactive educational packages. There are many excellent educational and business titles available for networked use. We are now realizing the long-sought benefits of technology within the education and training systems of the United States.

This volume addresses the question, "How are the U.S. education and training communities riding the back of current technologies to make us a better edu-cated and more competitive nation in today's global economy?" We have reviewed the literature and selected key statements that respond to the issue.

In addition, there is an abundance of articles dealing with distance learning, networking, the Internet, and interactive multimedia applications for classroom, laboratory, and home. There is a pressing need for a publication that brings together this wealth of pertinent information on the successful implementation of current technology into schools, homes, and businesses as well as the new hardware/software applications that have made this possible. The *Annual Editions/Computer Studies* format uniquely meets this need.

This anthology addresses the current issues confronting computer-using educators and trainers. Both need to know about current classroom applications and software evaluations. It also provides a close-up look at integrating technology into the curriculum, teacher training, interactive multimedia, the Internet, and distance learning applications.

This volume is designed for use by educators involved in preservice and inservice education of educators, trainers, and administrators. It is also intended for parents, students, school board members, and others concerned about the use and impact of computers on today's education and training activities. Efforts have been made to include articles without references to specific hardware or software that may become quickly outdated.

As always, it is expected that you will have suggestions for improving future editions of *Computer Studies: Computers in Education.* You can help shape the next volume by completing and returning the postage-paid article rating form located on the last page of this book.

John J. Hirschbuhl

Dwight Bishop
Editors

Contents

The concepts in bold italics are developed in the article. For further expansion please refer to the Topic Guide, the Glossary, and the Index.

UNIT 2

Curriculum and Instructional Design

Four articles provide information on employing microcomputer-based software in the classroom.

UNIT 3

Classroom Applications and Software Evaluations

Five selections provide criteria for the selection and implementation of instructional software in the classroom.

UNIT 4

Teacher Training

Five selections examine the problems associated with staff development and teacher education to ensure teacher computer competency in the classroom.

The concepts in bold italics are developed in the article. For further expansion please refer to the Topic Guide, the Glossary, and the Index.

UNIT 5

Multimedia

Six selections demonstrate how educators have harnessed the power of multimedia to improve their students' education.

UNIT 6

Special Issues

Six selections discuss
the newly discovered
potential of computers in
educational applications.

The concepts in bold italics are developed in the article. For further expansion please refer to the Topic Guide, the Glossary, and the Index.

ix

UNIT 7

The Internet and Computer Networks

Five articles address several issues about the Internet and other networks: using the Internet for interactive field trips; how to use the Internet for bilingual studies; using the Internet as a ready-reference resource; how to plan for local area networks.

The concepts in bold italics are developed in the article. For further expansion please refer to the Topic Guide, the Glossary, and the Index.

x

UNIT 8

Distance Learning

Six articles discuss the value of interactive technologies within a distance learning environment.

The concepts in bold italics are developed in the article. For further expansion please refer to the Topic Guide, the Glossary, and the Index.

1

Selected World Wide Web Sites for *Computer Studies: Computers in Education*

All of these Web sites are hot-linked through the *Annual Editions* home page: http://www.dushkin.com/annualeditions (just click on a book).

Some Web sites are continually changing their structure and content, so the information listed may not always be available.

Internet Search Engines and Directories

Search the Internet—*http://www.isleuth.com/*—The Internet Sleuth is not a well-known search engine, but it offers a wide variety of specialized searches by category.

WebCrawler—*http://webcrawler.com*—This is a fast and weighty search engine that analyzes the full text of documents, allowing the searcher to locate keywords that may have been buried deep within a document's text.

WebCrawler Guide—*http://webcrawler.com/select/*—This search engine to the "best on the Net" is organized in categories, such as arts, business, chat, kids, life, games, entertainment, health, and so on.

Yahooligans! The Web Guide for Kids—*http://www.yahooligans.com/*—An excellent site for children, this resource can be used if you wish to limit access by your students but still allow independent searching.

Internet How-To Resources

Beginner's Guide to HTML—*http://www.itc.univie.ac.at/docs/html-primer.html*—This is a primer for producing documents in HTML, the markup language used by the World Wide Web.

Consortium for School Networking—*http://www.cosn.org*—This site provides information and discussion on how to implement networks in schools and updates on legislation affecting education and networking. It offers online resources and forums.

Getting U.S. Teachers Online—*http://quest.arc.nasa.gov/online/table.html*—This NASA resource provides online service providers, listed by state, as well as other access options for K-12 teachers.

Teaching with Electronic Technology—*http://www.wam.umd.edu/~mlhall/teaching.html*—This collection of World Wide Web sites addresses the use of electronic technologies in the classroom, which range from general and theoretical resources to instructive examples of specific applications to teaching and learning.

Web66—*http://web66.coled.umn.edu/*—The Web66 project is designed to facilitate the introduction of Web site development into K-12 schools. The site includes a directory of schools on the Web.

Writing HTML—*http://www.mcli.dist.maricopa.edu/tut/index.html*—Here is a tutorial for creating World Wide Web pages, which will allow an educator to create classroom home pages.

General Education Sites

Educational Resources Information Center—*http://www.aspensys.com/eric/index.html*—At this site there are links to all ERIC sites: clearinghouses, support components, publishers of ERIC material. You can search the ERIC database, find out what is new, or ask questions about ERIC.

ERIC Clearinghouse on Reading, English, and Communication (ERIC/REC)—*http://www.indiana.edu:80/~eric_rec/*—This site is dedicated to providing educational materials, services, coursework, and exemplary lesson plans to everyone interested in the language arts. Links to many other educational sites.

Goals 2000—*http://www.ed.gov/pubs/goals/progrpt/index.html*—The reform initiative started by the U.S. Department of Education has a progress report to share.

National Regional Educational Laboratories—*http://www.nwrel.org/national/regional-labs.html*—The Regional Educational Laboratories are organizations across the country that provide research on resources for education.

Online Internet Institute—*http://www.oii.org/*—A collaborative project between Internet-using educators, proponents of systemic reform, content area experts, and teachers who desire professional growth, this site provides a learning environment for integrating the Internet into educators' individual teaching styles.

Teachers Guide to the Department of Education—*http://www.ed.gov/pubs/TeachersGuide/*—Government goals, projects, grants, and other educational programs are listed here as well as links to services and resources.

Instructional Planning Resources

Boulder Valley School District Home Page—*http://bvsd.k12.co.us/*—This is the site of a district-developed home page containing planning ideas and links to educational resources for teachers and students.

Canada's Schoolnet Staff Room—*http://www.schoolnet.ca/adm/staff/*—Here is a resource and link site for anyone involved in education, including special-need educators, teachers, parents, volunteers, and administrators.

Classroom Connect—*http://www.classroom.net/*—This is the premier Web site for K-12 teachers and students, with links to schools, teachers, and resources online.

ENC Online—*http://www.enc.org/*—The Eisenhower National Clearinghouse includes science and math resources, lesson plans, a search engine, and more.

Mighty Media—*http://www.mightymedia.com/*—The mission of this privately funded consortium is to empower youth, teachers, and organizations through the use of interactive communications technology.

Mustang List of Lesson Plans—*http://mustang.coled.umn.edu/ lessons/lessons.html*—This source leads to many other sites that contain electronic lesson plans, including online interdisciplinary projects.

NASA Aerospace Education Services Program—*http://www.okstate.edu/ aesp/AESP.html*—This site leads to cross-curricular projects, science, technology, space, literature, math, language, astronomy, writing projects, museum links, and space image libraries.

Teachers Helping Teachers—*http://www.pacificnet.net/~mandel/*— Provides basic teaching tips, new teaching methodology ideas, and forums for teachers to share. Download software and participate in chat sessions. Features educational resources on the Web, with new ones added each week.

The Teachers' Network—*http://www.teachnet.org/*—Bulletin boards, classroom projects, online forums, and Web mentors are featured, as well as the book, *Teachers' Guide to Cyberspace,* and an online, 4-week course on how to use the Internet.

Teacher Talk Forum—*http://education.indiana.edu/cas/ttforum/ lesson.html*—Electronic lesson plans from Indiana University's Center for Adolescent Studies cover a variety of topic areas.

Curriculum Sites

Classics for Young People—*http://www.ucalgary.ca/~dkbrown/ storclas.html*—A growing number of children's literature classics are out of copyright and are among the books available in full text here.

Education Place—*http://www.hmco.com/hmco/school/School.html*— Houghton Mifflin's home page contains activities for students, parents, and teachers, which include weekly author interviews and child-written book reviews. Has links to excellent education topics and organizations with synopses of research (for instance, phonics instruction).

Electronic Field Trip to the United Nations—*http://www.pbs. org/tal/un/*—This trip to the UN includes seeing the UN in action, classroom activities, and links to other sources.

The Exploratorium—*http://www.exploratorium.edu/*—Here is a hands-on interactive learning experience that covers a broad spectrum of subjects.

MECC on the Internet—*http://www.mecc.com/*—MECC's page includes a demonstration of a variety of MECC software, including Oregon Trail.

NASA Spacelink—*http://spacelink.msfc.nasa.gov/home.index.html*— This aeronautics and space resource for educators contains a variety of space travel information, including travel throughout the galaxy with information and images.

The Nine Planets—*http://seds.lpl.arizona.edu/billa/tnp/*—This planetary tour through the solar system has sound and video clips and links to related sites.

Project Gutenberg—*http://www.promo.net/pg/*—At this site there is an ongoing attempt to make the texts of public domain books

and other materials available on the Net. The listings are provided by author and by title.

Scholastic Network—*http://www.scholastic.com/*—Here is a selection of Scholastic products, including Global Community, Magic SchoolBus, contests, Scholastic publications, and new school-home Software Clubs for Grades PreK-8.

SchoolNet Ocean Site—*http://schoolnet2.carleton.ca/english/manuals/ virtualprod/ocean/*—This site offers educators resources for developing a thematic unit on oceans with links to many interesting sites.

The Science Learning Network—*http://www.sln.org/*—This collection of museum sites includes movies, teachers' projects, news, and links to other science education material.

The TeleGarden—*http://www.usc.edu/dept/garden/*—Interact and view a remote garden filled with living plants. Members care for the garden through a robot arm.

Texas Center for Reading and Language Arts—*http://www.tenet.wsu/ teks/language_arts/*—The Center, an example of a state site, offers a wide range of resources and contact information for Texas teachers and teacher educators.

Virtual Tourist—*http://www.vtourist.com/webmap/*—This geographic directory connects you to all of the World Wide Web servers in the world.

Virtual Whales—*http://fas.sfu.ca/cs/research/projects/Whales/*—Here is an example of a virtual learning project: the feeding behavior of Pacific humpback whales.

Volcano World—*http://volcano.und.nodak.edu*—Study historic and live volcanoes worldwide. There are activities for children and adults, and lesson plans for teachers.

Media Sources

CNN Interactive—*http://cnn.com/*—The latest news, including pictures and archival links, is available here, along with the Infoseek search engine.

National Public Radio—*http://www.npr.org/*—At this site you can hear NPR's daily reports using RealAudio.

PBS Online—*http://www.pbs.org/*—Here you will find PBS programming, stations, and teacher resources (for example, The Donner Party or Pyramids: Inside Story).

We highly recommend that you review our Web site for expanded information and our other product lines. We are continually updating and adding links to our Web site in order to offer you the most usable and useful information that will support and expand the value of your *Annual Editions.* You can reach us at: *http:// www. dushkin.com/annualeditions.*

Topic Guide

This topic guide suggests how the selections in this book relate to topics of traditional concern to students and professionals involved with computers in education. It is useful for locating articles that relate to each other for reading and research. The guide is arranged alphabetically according to topic. Articles may, of course, treat topics that do not appear in the topic guide. In turn, entries in the topic guide do not necessarily constitute a comprehensive listing of all the contents of each selection.

TOPIC AREA	TREATED IN	TOPIC AREA	TREATED IN
Instructional Design	7. Interactivity and Computer-Based Instruction 8. Relevance of HCI Guidelines 9. Designing Interactive Learning Environments 10. Design and Application of Teaching Software 26. Strengthening the Visual Element 28. Making Most of Slow Revolution 40. Seven Principles for Good Practice in Distance Learning 42. Challenge of Distance Education	**Software**	9. Designing Interactive Learning Environments 10. Design and Application of Teaching Software 11. NAEYC Position Statement
Internet	24. Video to Desktop 28. Making Most of Slow Revolution 30. Computing Our Way to Educational Reform 33. Journey into Unknown 34. Traveling the Internet in Chinese 35. Ready Reference on Internet 36. Monster Job! 38. Distance Learning, Internet, and World Wide Web 39. Distance Learning's Explosion on the Internet	**Teacher Education**	16. Structuring Telecommunications 17. Six Stages for Learning to Use Technology 18. Dimensions of Knowledge Support System 19. Interactive Video Cases 20. Stage Well-Designed Saturday Session 27. Factors Facilitating Teacher's Use of Computer Technology
		Telecommunications	6. Unfilled Promises 30. Computing Our Way to Educational Reform 36. Monster Job! 42. Challenge of Distance Education
Multimedia	18. Dimensions of Knowledge Support System 19. Interactive Video Cases 21. Interactive Multimedia 22. Converting Traditional Multimedia Kit 23. 21st Century Classroom-Scholarship Environment 24. Video to Desktop 25. Multimedia and Cultural Diversity 41. Teaching at a Distance	**Tools**	13. Software Evaluation 21. Interactive Multimedia 24. Video to Desktop and Classrooms 29. Coming Ubiquity of Information Technology 40. Seven Practices for Good Practice in Distance Learning
		Video	19. Interactive Video Cases 22. Converting Traditional Multimedia Kit 24. Video to Desktop and Classrooms 26. Strengthening the Visual Element
Networking	16. Structuring Telecommunications 17. Six Stages for Learning to Use Technology 28. Making Most of Slow Revolution 33. Journey into Unknown 34. Traveling the Internet in Chinese 35. Ready Reference on Internet 36. Monster Job! 37. Tips & Tricks For K–12 Educational LANs 38. Distance Learning, Internet, and World Wide Web 39. Distance Learning's Explosion	**Videodisc**	19. Interactive Video Cases
		Virtual Classroom	5. 21st Century Classroom

Introduction

There is a conflict growing within the education establishment. The forces driving the Information Age are colliding with educators who are resisting change. The onrush of telecommunication technologies is forcing educators to understand and tentatively accept these new technologies and their impact. What has happened is that the telecommunications infrastructure has grown to include computers, broadcast, cable, and other electronic networks. At the heart of the conflict is the education establishment's commitment to nineteenth century instructional practices, and the push from Information Age students, behaving like barbarians at the gates, who are demanding a transformation of the college campus and the way they learn. The Internet, interactive multimedia, and teleconferencing are at the center of the Information Age learning explosion. There is currently a flood of multimedia educational products that increase the instructional options for the on-campus or at-a-distance classroom. Many of the networked computer-based multimedia applications are designed to make learners more self-reliant and willing to accept challenging material both on campus and at a distance. Teachers are beginning to utilize innovative forms of learning to provide alternate instructional delivery systems, but the pace needs to be accelerated. It is hoped that these alternate delivery systems will meet the learning needs of Information Age students who are both on and off campus.

The articles selected for this unit track how education, the "immovable object," is beginning to meet Information Age technology, the "irresistible force." This collision is causing a revolution with respect to how and where instruction is delivered in today's schools.

In the unit's first article, Howard Mehlinger reports on the forces driving the Information Age technologies and their impact on education. Mehlinger is certain that schools will be unable to resist the new technology. Next, Andrew Weiss suggests guidelines for implementing and supporting technology-rich education and describes the administrative organization that these systems will require.

The article, "Modern Land of Laputa: Where Computers Are Used in Education," by Chris Morton, describes how schools often use technology in a misguided effort to support nineteenth century instructional practice. He rejects the idea of the computer as a tool and makes a case for computer environments that shape and support the educational structure and lifelong learning. In the following article, "Education Wars: The Battle over Information Age Technology," James Snider provides a description of how new information technologies will transform education. He believes new education economics suggests a power shift away from regional educators to national educators. Vance Viscusi then conjures up a virtual classroom experience in which students maximize their learning potential in virtual environments. The author believes that the innovative technology of the next century will be Introspective Machines, which will give students the answer to the question, "How does what I am learning relate to me?"

Finally, William Lynch, Jane McDonald, and Greg Kearsley, in "Unfulfilled Promises," show that many school leaders are betting on advanced telecommunications as the best way to give all students an equal education opportunity. The article discusses the need for school districts to revitalize their skills in planning for technological change, and the authors provide a blueprint for doing it.

Looking Ahead: Challenge Questions

Where do you think technology will have its biggest impact—in K-12 schools, the undergraduate college, or university graduate schools? Why?

What social and economic factors are causing educators to rethink how and where instruction should be delivered?

What effect will the Internet/Intranet have on schools and learning? At what levels?

What is the greatest obstacle to integrating technology and education?

School Reform in the Information Age

The exact shape of future schools is unclear, but of this Mr. Mehlinger is certain: schools will be unable to resist the new technology. And they will be profoundly changed thereby.

BY HOWARD D. MEHLINGER

Give me a place to stand, and I will move the earth.—Archimedes

ARCHIMEDES was a great fan of the lever, a piece of technology that was presumably state-of-the-art when he lived. While not every person exhibits Archimedes' enthusiasm for technology, before and since Archimedes and throughout all regions of the world people have used technology to make their lives richer and more comfortable. Indeed, the ability to make and use such tools as the fulcrum and the lever is one of the ways we distinguish human beings from other animal species.

Technology is not only a product of a given culture; it also shapes the culture that created it. The automobile is not merely an American artifact; it influences where we live, where we work, and how we entertain ourselves. It stands as a statement to others about who we are. The automobile has affected courtship patterns and relationships between races and social classes. Getting a driver's license and acquiring a car have become rites of passage in American society. While we make our tools, to a remarkable degree our tools also make us.

HOWARD D. MEHLINGER is director of the Center for Excellence in Education and a professor of education and history at Indiana University, Bloomington. This article is adapted from School Reform in the Information Age *(Center for Excellence in Education, Indiana University, 1995), which can be ordered from Media Management Services, Inc., Newtown, PA 18940-3425. Ph. 800/523-5948.*

Consider an example of how technology affects our lives. The changes that occurred in the manufacture of cloth in England are part of the history of the Industrial Revolution. At one time, the spinning and weaving of wool were cottage industries. A middleman bought the wool, took it to cottages where the raw wool was spun into thread and woven into cloth, and then transported the cloth to tailors and seamstresses who manufactured the finished products.

With the advent of water power and, later, steam power, it was possible to erect large factories near the sources of power and labor and to install huge spinning wheels and looms capable of producing cloth much more quickly and cheaply. Moreover, the cloth produced in these factories was of a more dependable quality than that which hundreds of cottage workers could produce.

Today we are witnessing the return of another kind of cottage industry. It's called "telecommuting." In ever greater numbers, white-collar employees are working out of their homes and cars, with the encouragement of their employers. A 1993 survey found that, of 200 companies contacted, 30% had some type of telecommuting already in place. Large firms find it advantageous to reduce the number of offices they must maintain in expensive downtown locations; with the use of modern electronic tools that permit communication by voice, fax, and modem, workers can carry their offices with them and be closer to their customers. Today, some of us can truly say that, if there is something really important to get done at the office, it's best to stay at home.

It seems rather simple today to mark the changes that led to the Agricultural Revolution and the Industrial Revolution. But when one is in the midst of rapid change, it is more difficult to know how and when things started, when they have peaked, and when they have ended. The Industrial Revolution was named and described by 20th-century historians, not by those who lived through it.

The pace of change is even faster today. For example, from the invention of the wheel through the 17th and 18th centuries, people had no means of land transportation other than walking, riding an animal, or being carried in a wagon pulled by an animal. In the 19th century, steam engines provided wagons with power. They were soon followed by gasoline-powered internal combustion engines — and they, in turn, were followed by all the forms of powered vehicles we have today. In a single generation, Americans who once depended on horses and walking for transportation learned to drive cars, flew on airplanes, and watched as rocket propulsion took men to the moon.

Technology and Schooling

Technology has always been an important part of schooling in America, but until recently the technology employed was rather simple and changed slowly. No one reading this article can remember when there were no textbooks, but the kind of textbooks we have today are largely products of the 20th century. Nor did teachers always have their primary tools — the blackboard and chalk. Slate blackboards did not appear in urban schools until the 1830s.

When I was a young boy, one of the rituals at the start of the school year was a trip to the local department store to purchase school supplies: a "Big Chief" tablet, pencils, rubber erasers, pens with re-

Schools are beginning to meet the "irresistible force" — Information Age technology.

movable points (they became dull quickly), and a bottle of ink. Sometimes a pencil box would be added so that I could keep track of my personal supplies. Parents and students today go through similar shopping rituals each year. The technology has changed somewhat (ball-point pens have replaced ink and straight pens, pencil boxes have given way to backpacks), but it is essentially the same.

There have been many attempts to change the technology of schooling. They have each appeared with great fanfare and expressions of optimism by advocates. In the 1920s, radio was expected to have a major impact on schools; in the 1930s, it was to be film; in the 1950s, television; and in the 1960s, teaching machines. The one piece of new technology from those bygone years that truly found a place was the overhead projector. Introduced in the 1940s by the military, it gradually found its way into the schools. The overhead projector is easy to use and relatively inexpensive, it permits the teacher to prepare notes in advance of class and to project them onto the screen for all to see, and it can be used without darkening the room or turning one's back to the students. In many ways it is the perfect technology for supporting the kind of instruction that takes place in most classrooms today.

More advanced technology has hit the schools at about the same time as have ideas for school restructuring and findings from the cognitive sciences. According to Karen Sheingold, "The successful transformation of student learning and accomplishment in the next decade requires effectively bringing together three agendas — an emerging consensus about learning and teaching, well-integrated uses of technology, and restructuring. Each agenda alone presents possibilities for educational redesign of a very powerful sort. Yet none has realized or is likely to realize its potential in the absence of the other two."[1] I agree.

Skeptics will argue that we are merely going through another cycle of reform. School reforms come almost every decade; the schools absorb as many of the new ideas as they want and reject the rest. The result is that schools change very little where it truly counts — in the classroom. But the synergy of school restruc-

turing, new forms of learning and teaching, and new technology will make the difference this time.

The forces driving the Information Age seem irresistible. It is impossible both to participate fully in the culture and yet resist its defining features. Thus, if the schools are an "immovable object" (and I don't believe they are), they are beginning to meet the "irresistible force" — Information Age technology.

The analogy I carry in my head is that of a volcano erupting in Hawaii, spewing forth ash and lava. We have all seen pictures of such eruptions and what follows. The lava slowly oozes its way down the mountain toward the sea. No device or structure raised by human beings can block it. It either consumes all obstacles in fire or rolls over them. Finally, the lava reaches the sea — nature's immovable object. Throughout the process there is a lot of noise, smoke, and steam that can distract one's attention from the fundamental process that is taking place: the transformation of the landscape. In the most dramatic cases, entirely new islands appear. A volcanic eruption changes the environment in unpredictable ways; it is also irresistible.

Information Age technology is like that volcano. It is changing the landscape of American culture in ways we either take for granted or scarcely notice. There are holdouts. Many of us see no need for placing telephones in our cars or buying mobile telephones. Some believe that television is a corrupting influence and refuse to have a set in their homes. I know such people; I am largely sympathetic to their views. But most people who think television can be corrosive buy one anyway and try to control its use.

I cannot predict how schools will accommodate themselves to the force of computers and other electronic technologies. Some schools will move more quickly than others; some teachers will not change at all. The process may be slow enough that many teachers will be able to retire before they are forced to change. Some will quit teaching, and it is likely that some will remain anachronisms in a greatly altered school environment — antiques of a sort, surrounded by modernity but refusing even to use the telephones in their classrooms.

But schools will change! I don't know whether teachers will use the new technologies in the ways constructivists anticipate; other reformers have urged teachers to adopt similar progressive ideas in the past with mostly negative results. Perhaps technology will support constructivist approaches and make learner-centered instruction a practice as well as a theory this time. I don't know whether schools will have site-based management or some other kind of organizational structure. Other theories of learning and school organization will certainly appear. The exact shape of future schools is unclear, but of this I am certain: schools will be unable to resist the new technology. The new technology will be used in schools because it appeals to students and may enhance learning and because the schools can offer no reasonable defense for rejecting it.

The use of the new technologies will have a profound effect on schools. The very relationship between students and teachers will be challenged because the technologies enable learners to gain control of their own learning. In the past, schools have been places where people in authority decided what would be taught (and possibly learned), at what age, and in what sequence. They also decided what would *not* be taught — what would not be approved knowledge. The new technologies provide students access to information that was once under the control of teachers.

Years ago, as a high school teacher, I received a note from a colleague who was teaching a course in American history for the first time. He had given students reading assignments from one set of books while he turned to other books as sources for his lectures. The note said, "The game is up. The students know where I am getting my information." That is happening everywhere today, and the game is truly up. No teacher can compete with the power and the capability of the new technology as a presenter of information. If teachers and schools try to sustain that role, they will be whipped. On the other hand, no teachers will be replaced by a machine unless they attempt to do only what the machine can do better.

It may be that the technology will be used most extensively first by privately financed schools, such as Sylvan Learning Systems, Kaplan Educational Centers, or the schools of the Edison Project. Privately financed schools that successfully demonstrate the value of technology may provide the incentive to persuade public institutions of the instructional value of technology. Perhaps public schools that employ the new technologies successfully in restructured environments will begin as magnet schools or even charter schools; if they succeed, then the use of technology may spread to the remainder of the schools in a district. Possibly the technological challenge to public education will come from home schooling, when parents discover that through technology they not only retain the current advantages of home schooling but also gain access to the academic resources of the public schools and of the world.

The genie is out of the bottle. It is no longer necessary to learn about the American War of Independence by sitting in Mrs. Smith's classroom and hearing her version of it. There are more powerful and efficient ways to learn about the Revolutionary War, and they are all potentially under the control of the learner. Either schools will come to terms with this fact, or schools will be ignored.

It has never been easy for schools to change, and it is not going to be easy now. The current reform effort has been compared to changing a tire on a car that is continuing to speed down the highway. The job is actually much harder than that, because it is not repair but transformation that is required. It is more akin to changing a car into an airplane while continuing to drive the car. We are asking schools to become something different, without a clear picture of what the new institution should look like, even as we continue to satisfy the public that the old purposes of schooling are being served as well as or better than in the past.

Availability and Use of Technology In Schools Today

No one knows for certain what kind of technology exists in schools, how it is used, how much it is used, whether what exists is actually available to teachers, and whether what exists is broken, worn-out, or still in unopened boxes.[2] It is hard enough to maintain an up-to-date inventory within a given school district without trying to do the same for the nation. Various individuals and organizations have conducted surveys on technology use, and these provide some clues as to the situation generally.

Computers. We know that the number of computers in schools has grown enormously since 1983. At that time it was estimated that there were fewer than 50,000 computers in the nation's schools; by 1994 the estimate was revised to 5.5 million. In 1981 only about 18% of schools had one or more computers for instructional use; by 1994 this figure had risen to 98%. There is hardly a school in America today without at least one computer.

These figures tell us very little about student access to computers, however. In 1985 the median number of computers in K-6 elementary schools that used computers was three; that number rose to about 18 in 1989. In high schools for the same two years the numbers were 16 and 39 respectively. By 1994 the ratio of students to computers across all grades was 14 to 1. Thus, while there has been rapid growth in the number of computers in each school, the opportunity for a typical student to have access to a computer is still limited. For example, as late as 1989 a student might have had access to a computer for one hour per week — about 4% of instructional time.

A second issue concerns the location of computers and how they are used. The most common pattern in schools is to cluster 20 or so machines in a single laboratory and then to schedule classes for time in the lab once a week. A decade ago computers were used mainly to teach program-

> *It is no longer necessary to learn about the War of Independence by sitting in Mrs. Smith's classroom and hearing her version of it.*

ming, to teach about computers (computer literacy), and to run drill-and-practice exercises. More recently, computers have been used for enrichment, as work tools, and — less frequently — for purposes of computer literacy. However, computers in elementary schools continue to be used heavily to teach basic skills, and this pattern is growing in high schools. Federal funds for at-risk children have been a major source of school funding for computers, so it is hardly surprising that schools rely on them primarily for teaching basic skills and for remedial instruction. The use of computers to support instruction in the academic areas or to allow students independent exploration is sharply limited. Indeed, many American students have more access to a computer at home than at school.

Most computers are purchased as stand-alone machines. It is possible to connect computers, either through a local area network (LAN) or through a wide area network (WAN). The advantage of networks is that people can work together and share information. Computer networks are common in business and higher education; the use of networks in schools, though it is growing, is still small. Moreover, school LANs are used mainly to support integrated learning systems (ILSs) within a school. Thus far, relatively little has been done to foster communication among classrooms. Schools with modems have access to commercial network services, such as Prodigy, CompuServe, Apple Link, or America Online. And a rapidly increasing number of schools are beginning to use the Internet, a service originally created by the U.S. Department of Defense to connect researchers at labs and universities and that now connects many kinds of groups worldwide. The Clinton Administration wishes to build a national electronic infrastructure that would increase opportunities for schools to be connected to outside resources.

Video. Video use in schools seems to be growing and taking different forms. Instructional television, in which a program is broadcast to schools at scheduled times during the day from a state-operated or district-run studio, continues to exist, but it is not as significant as in the past. Many of these broadcasts were developed nationally through a consortium led by the Agency for Instructional Technology. The programs were designed to fit the school curriculum as determined by the state departments of education that were the most prominent consortium members.

As a result of federal financing through the Star Schools program, many schools are able to use courses delivered nationwide by satellite and originating from a single source at a predetermined time. These programs typically feature courses that are difficult for small schools to offer on their own, e.g., courses in German or Japanese or advanced courses in mathematics and the sciences. Rural schools in particular have taken advantage of these offerings; about one-third of all rural schools have the capability of receiving satellite broadcasts.

Commercial sources also provide programming to schools. In 1994 Whittle Communications, Inc., reportedly offered its programs to more than 12,000 schools and reached eight million students. The principal program offering was a 10-minute news show called Channel One. The program and all the equipment provided to the schools were paid for by the two minutes of commercial advertising that accompanied each show. CNN offers a rival news program called *CNN Newsroom*. This 15-minute news show is broadcast early in the morning over the regular CNN cable channel. Schools are permitted to tape the program and use it as they please.

The Corporation for Public Broadcasting is developing new programming for schools, and the Learning Channel and the Discovery Channel both provide programs that offer useful information for schools.

As a result of this proliferation of educational programming, the VCR has become a nearly ubiquitous piece of school technology. Virtually every school in the United States has at least one, and many teachers routinely collect tapes to use with their classes. Because it is more flexible and user friendly, the videotape has taken the place of film for instruction.

CD-ROM and videodiscs offer other ways for schools to employ video. The use of these media, while still limited, is growing rapidly. According to Quality Education Data, Inc., 26% of all school districts had videodisc technology in 1994, as compared to 18% in 1992-93.

Results. It would be wonderful if we could point to specific data that would demonstrate conclusively that the use of one technology or approach produced better results than the use of some other technology or approach. Alas, the problem is not so simple.

First, the existence of a particular technology does not prescribe the way in which it will be used. Yet how a technology is actually used is critically important. One English teacher might use computers mainly for drill on grammar and spelling, while another English teacher might allow students to use the computers for word processing.

Much of the evaluation research on media use is based on a specific intervention and focuses on short-term results. It seeks to determine, for example, whether the students receiving computer-assisted instruction (CAI) perform better on short-answer examinations than do those in a control group. In studies of this kind, the experimental group nearly always wins, but seldom does the investigator study the two groups a year or two later to find out if the gain has survived. Studies of short-term results, though interesting, are of marginal value to policy makers.[3]

What we need are studies of an altogether different order. When students and teachers are immersed in technology *over time*, will we detect changes in how students learn and how teachers teach? While it may be important to see some gain on a particular test, those who are trying to reform schools have larger goals in mind. Before we spend billions of dollars to equip every student with a computer at home and one at school and before we spend millions to equip teachers and to provide them with the necessary training, we need to know whether such a colossal investment of public funds makes sense. We cannot be certain, but the study reported below should encourage us.

A Suggestive Experiment

In 1986 Apple Computer, Inc., launched a project called Apple Classrooms of Tomorrow (ACOT).[4] The project began with seven classrooms representing what was intended to be a cross section of K-12 schools. Each participating student and teacher received two computers: one for home and one for school. The goal of the project was to see how the routine use of computers would affect how students learn and how teachers teach.

One issue the project hoped to confront was the possibility of any negative effects from prolonged exposure to computers. Some critics have worried that students who use computers extensively will become "brain dead" or less social from looking at the computer screen all day. At the end of two years, the investigators learned that some of their worst fears had been groundless.

• Teachers were not hopeless illiterates where technology was concerned; they could use computers to accomplish their work.

• Children did not become social isolates. ACOT classes showed more evidence of spontaneous cooperative learning than did traditional classes.

• Children did not become bored by the technology over time. Instead, their desire to use it for their own purposes increased with use.

• Even very young children had no problem becoming adept users of the keyboard. With very little training, second- and third-graders were soon typing 25 to 30 words per minute with 95% accuracy — more than twice as fast as children of that age can usually write.

• Software was not a major problem. Teachers found programs — including productivity tools — to use in their classes.

Standardized test scores showed that students were performing as well as they might have been expected to do without the computers; some were doing better. The studies showed that ACOT students wrote better and were able to complete units of study more rapidly than their peers in non-ACOT classrooms. In one case, students finished the year's study of mathematics by the beginning of April. In short, academic productivity did not suffer and in some cases even improved.

What I find most interesting, however, is that classroom observers noticed changes in the behavior of teachers and students. Students were taking more responsibility for their own learning, and teachers were working more as mentors and less as presenters of information.

By the end of the fourth year, ACOT classrooms had changed; teachers were teaching differently, though they did not all teach alike. Each teacher seemed to have adjusted his or her own style to the computer-rich environment, but all the teachers were aware of the changes that had occurred in their own professional outlooks.

The students had also changed, especially the ACOT students at West High School, a school serving urban, blue-collar families in Columbus, Ohio. Twenty-one freshmen were selected at random from the student body to participate in a study of ACOT. They stayed with the program until their graduation four years later. All 21 graduated, whereas the student body as a whole had a 30% dropout rate. Nineteen of the ACOT students (90%) went on to college, while only 15% of non-ACOT students sought higher education. Seven of the ACOT students were offered full college scholarships, and several businesses offered to hire those who did not intend to go on to college. ACOT students had half the absentee rate, and they had accumulated more than their share of academic honors. But perhaps the most important finding was the difference exhibited by these students in how they did their work. The ACOT students routinely and without prompting employed inquiry, collaboration, and technological and problem-solving skills of the kind promoted by the school reform movement.

This is only one study, of course, and it would be unwise to place too much weight on its findings. But those who believe that technology is the key to school reform and to more powerful learning by students can take hope from this investigation.

They may also find encouragement in the results of a 1994 study commissioned by the Software Publishers Association and conducted by an independent technology consulting firm, Interactive Educational Systems Design, Inc.[5] The study reviewed research on educational technology that had been conducted from 1990 through 1994. The report was based on 133 research reviews and reports on original research projects. Some of the conclusions of that study follow.

• Educational technology has a significant positive impact on achievement in all subject areas, across all levels of school, and in regular classrooms as well as those for special-needs students.

• Educational technology has positive effects on student attitudes.

• The degree of effectiveness is influenced by the student population, the instructional design, the teacher's role, how students are grouped, and the levels of student access to technology.

• Technology makes instruction more student-centered, encourages cooperative learning, and stimulates increased teacher/student interaction.

• Positive changes in the learning environment evolve over time and do not occur quickly.

While this study was commissioned by an organization that had a stake in the results, the conclusions seem consistent with other research findings, especially with those of the ACOT study.

The Future of Technology In the Schools

Thus far I have focused on the technology available to schools today. What about the future? We are only at the threshold of the Information Age. Tools we now treat as technical marvels will seem primitive in five years. Commodore Pets, IBM PC jrs., and the first Apple machines are throwaway items today. We can predict with certainty that technology will become faster, cheaper, more powerful, and easier to use. We can also predict that new devices that we can scarcely imagine today will be on the market before the end of this decade. Schools that expect to invest in a single computer system and then forget about technology purchases for several years will be surprised and disappointed. Schools must make decisions regarding additions and/or upgrades to their technology every year, in line with their own strategic plans.

Without going into detail regarding specific pieces of hardware, I can say with confidence that schools should expect more *integration*, *interaction*, and *intelligence* from future technology. In their early days in school, computers and video were regarded as separate entities, and it was assumed they would stay that way. In fact, we can expect a continuing *integration* of these technologies. Voice, data, and images will be brought together into one package. One current example of this process is desktop video. In a single, relatively inexpensive unit, one has telephone (voice), computer (data storage and manipulation), and video (sending and receiving moving images) capabilities. Those who use the machine can talk to people at a distance, exchange documents, work collaboratively, and even see their collaborators on screen.

Technology will also become more *interactive*. In the field of distance learning, rather than rely strictly on one-way video and two-way audio communication, teachers and students will see one another simultaneously, thereby making distance learning more like face-to-face classroom interaction. Computer-based instruction will also be designed to respond to learners' interests and abilities, giving them greater control over what they need to learn and the pace at which they learn it. And computer searches, which can now be bewildering to the casual user, will become easier and more responsive to what a user needs. Greater interactivity will make instructional programs even more powerful than they are today.

Finally, technology will have greater *intelligence*. This intelligence will be displayed in several ways. First, the technology will have more features and greater capacity. Second, it will have the capability to learn from the user, so that it can customize its services to fit the user's learning style and interests. Future technology will provide not only databases but knowledge bases. And the technology will be able to stay abreast of that information most valued by the user and to alert him or her to its availability.

Integration, interaction, and intelligence. These are three features we can expect of technology in the future. And they will change the way technology is employed in schools.

Technology Revolution in Schools

What is this revolution? It is the transformation of schooling through the use of technology, and it is occurring in classrooms all over the country. The seeds of the revolution are being planted everywhere, though seldom dramatically. Occasionally, there is an announcement that District A has received a major grant that will lead to the installation of Brand X equipment in all its schools. But these are the exceptions.

What is occurring nearly every week is that one school board has approved the purchase of 10 or 20 computers for use in a school to improve writing skills; another board has approved the high school's use of Channel One; still another has set aside funds so that a high school or middle school can subscribe to online, commercial information services, and so on. This revolution is not characterized by a major assault leading to the rapid sweeping away of every custom and practice of the past. This is a slow but steady revolution. Each decision by a school board, each act of support by a principal, and each initiative by a teacher is changing the nature of schooling.

This revolution is not like any other

When access to computers has been sufficient, the results have been positive for student learning.

school reform movement that I have observed, and I have been in the profession for more than 40 years. First, it is a grassroots movement. Actions by state and federal governments and by business and industry have helped fuel the revolution, but they did not provide the spark. Teachers and local school administrators are leading this revolution, and they are not leading it in order to save American business or to prove a new theory of learning. They are buying, installing, and using technology simply because they believe that students will be less bored and will learn more through the use of the technology than without it. In short, they are using technology to make schools better.

This revolution is eclectic and largely devoid of ideology; therefore, what schools do with the technology varies widely. Much technology is used for remediation, especially in the elementary grades; it provides drill-and-practice exercises that are boring for teachers to teach. School officials hope that computers used in this way will hold pupils' attention longer and save wear and tear on teachers. This approach to learning may irritate the constructivists and many others, but as long as society emphasizes mastering basic skills we need not be surprised if some schools use technology to meet these goals and to help students pass required tests.

Other schools are using the technology primarily to provide students with productivity tools, such as word processing and spreadsheets, to inspire students to make their work more professional in quality and appearance. In other places, such technology as compressed, interactive video is used to share an instructor across one or more school sites. Technology has its foot in the door of classrooms all across America, and the schools will never be the same.

Some people will be annoyed to learn that there is a revolution under way and that they have not been informed of it or invited to participate. While they may know that millions of dollars have been invested in computers and other technology during the past decade and a half, they have assumed that most teachers have been resisting the technology. They may also believe that these investments have accomplished little because there has been no

evidence of sharp improvements in scores on the SAT I or on national achievement tests.

In response to the first point, I agree that many teachers do not yet employ instructional technology and probably will not do so for some time. As in every revolutionary movement, those teachers in the vanguard are the dedicated ones with a special interest in the cause; the rest must be persuaded that the revolution is in their own interests. In the case of technology, we don't make it easy to convince them. Few schools currently provide computers for each teacher, so the computers they do have must be shared. Teachers are provided little training in how to use the new technology, and seldom is there adequate technical support when something breaks down. In such a situation, it makes sense to some teachers to continue doing what they have always done rather than to spend time learning to use technology with all the attendant frustrations.

With regard to the second point, we have considerable evidence that the appropriate use of technology *does* contribute to student learning. These small-scale experimental results, however, are often overlooked when national results are reported. On a national scale, despite major investments to date, we have only begun to provide schools what they need. Except in a few cases, students have access to a computer for only a short time each week and then often for the purpose of working on preselected exercises. Imagine the outcry if students had access to a textbook only one day a week or if they had to share a pencil with 15 other students. Imagine a business, say an insurance company, that had only one computer for each 15 workers and made them take turns entering their data. When access to computers has been sufficient, the results have been positive for student learning.

We cannot blame teachers or students if technology has failed to transform all schools. There has not been enough time or enough money for the purchase of equipment, for training, or for support. Transforming schooling through technology will work; we have evidence that it does. But it will take time, and it will be expensive.

There are also people who do not want the technology revolution to succeed. Some are offended that this reform is truly a grassroots effort. While the technology revolution is certainly abetted by business and government, unlike most education reforms it has not been a top-down effort. This is not a reform hatched in universities or think tanks and handed on to schools to implement. Indeed, universities and most think tanks are largely unconnected to this reform. Obviously, specific professors and researchers are deeply involved, but institutional responses have been erratic: sometimes positive, occasionally negative, usually absent.

Other people want to improve schools, but they want to do it on the cheap. They hope that more regulation, stiffer accountability measures, and stirring speeches, alternating with scolding lectures when results do not improve, will do the job. They are wrong, and they are cheapskates.

A few, mainly in universities, are offended by the thought of linking technology to learning. For ideological reasons they wish to keep technology out of schools because it might "de-skill" teachers. Technology might place schools in the service of business and industry; it might exacerbate equity problems. These issues are fundamentally important to some college professors, but few teachers are listening. What may be most threatening to university professors is that they have spent their lives becoming experts in narrow areas, and now technology threatens to make their hard-won knowledge available to everyone. Much is made of the threat that the computer poses to K–12 teachers because the computer challenges their role as keepers and presenters of knowledge. If that threat disturbs some K–12 teachers, it is all the more frightening to many college professors.

What Are the Chances For Success?

The likelihood of success for the educational technology revolution cannot be judged in the same way as chances for the success of other educational innovations. First, the movement is driven by teachers rather than by outside experts. Second, teachers are not required to use the technology in prescribed ways; they use it as they choose or reject it if they wish. Third, their students are eager to use technology, and parents want their children to have access to technology in school. Fourth, once teachers have overcome their initial concern about feeling stupid while they learn to use a new tool, they find themselves using the technology in various instructional situations. They are pleased to have learned a new skill, and they gradually change the way they teach. Because of these factors, I cannot imagine that this reform will fail for the same reasons as previous reforms.

The progress of technology in the schools will surely proceed more slowly than its proponents would prefer. The reasons are mainly lack of time and lack of money. While Americans talk expansively about creating "break the mold" schools, by and large they want cheap reforms. They hope that by reorganizing the administration of schools (leading to "site-based management") or by allowing parents to choose schools for their children, school reform will be successful. They are wrong. These cheap solutions will have little impact. In contrast, enormous amounts of money will have to be spent on rewiring and equipping schools, and still more money must be devoted to staff training. It is not yet clear that Americans want new kinds of schools badly enough to pay for them.

Lack of money will slow the revolution — making it seem more like evolution — but it won't stop it. If you believe that schools are a part of the American culture, that the American culture is increasingly influenced by Information Age technology, and that teachers participate in the American culture as much as other Americans, then you cannot also believe that teachers will use the technology outside of school but fail to employ it in their classrooms. Technology will be used extensively in schools. That much is inevitable.

1. Karen Sheingold, "Restructuring for Learning with Technology: The Potential for Synergy," in Karen Sheingold and Marc Tucker, eds., *Restructuring for Learning with Technology* (New York: Center for Technology in Education and National Center on Education and the Economy, 1990), p. 9.

2. Establishing precise figures regarding the availability and use of technology in schools is a reckless enterprise. Even when data are gathered carefully and systematically, the numbers are quickly out-of-date. Readers should judge my figures as "best estimates." In arriving at these estimates, I drew heavily on data compiled by Barbara Means et al., *Using Technology to Support Education Reform* (Washington, D.C.: U.S. Department of Education, 1993), and on data assembled for me by Media Management Services, Inc., which drew upon several databases available to the firm.

3. "Integrated Learning Systems: What Does the Research Say?," *Computing Teacher,* February 1995, pp. 7–10.

4. My description of the ACOT project was based on an article by David Dwyer, "Apple Classrooms of Tomorrow: What We've Learned," *Educational Leadership,* April 1994, pp. 4–10.

5. *Report on the Effectiveness of Technology in Schools, 1990–1994* (Washington, D.C.: Software Publishers Association, 1994).

System 2000
If You Build It, Can You Manage It?

BY ANDREW M. WEISS

Districts are increasingly building complex computer systems to meet changing requirements for technology-rich education. Mr. Weiss suggests guidelines for implementing such systems and describes the administrative organization that these systems will require.

I N SOME ways the year 2000 has no greater significance than any other year. We know intellectually that it will be little different from those that precede it and those that follow it. In that sense we plan for 2000 as if it were simply one year past 1999. We estimate budgets, revise time lines, and plan vacations as if nothing more were at stake than a simple turn of a calendar page.

But the milestone that is the year 2000 has an almost mystical quality for many of us. We can't help but respond emotionally to the roundness of the number. We behave as if it punctuates man's existence

ANDREW M. WEISS has a private consulting practice and is technology plan manager for the Chappaqua Central School District, Chappaqua, N.Y. His articles have appeared in several publications, including Multimedia Schools. *He can be contacted at the following e-mail address: 75352.2462@compuserve.com.*

Illustration by Brenda Grannan

From *Phi Delta Kappan*, February 1996, pp. 408-415. © 1996 by Phi Delta Kappa, Inc. Reprinted by permission.

1. INTRODUCTION

on Earth. We expect to look back in time from the lofty perch of 2000 years of the common era and realize that we are meaningfully different from our ancestors of the prior millennium and the prior century. We want and need to compare ourselves to the generations that preceded us. We hope to see growth, change, and progress.

Few analysts of the millennial shift will underestimate the computer's pivotal importance in altering the way humans do business. While the dramatic changes of the last 120 years cast a long shadow over the claims for the primacy of any one invention, many view the computer as both the culmination of that fecund age of discovery that began with atomic theory and the herald of a new epoch. Strictly speaking, the computer is not a true descendant of the mechanical or even of the electrical age (at least not in the way that the telephone and the battery are). Fundamentally, it is a tool for creating and transforming an electronic metaphor of reality. By engaging ourselves with that metaphor, instead of with the reality, we save space and time. The computer is the culmination of mankind's engagement with the ability to manipulate symbols.

Schools and teachers have served as faithful governors of information and knowledge for 500 years, and for them this new tool is both exciting and frightening. It offers enormous power and flexibility, but at the same time it threatens the time-honored dialectic of teacher and pupil, master and student. While some educators view computers as the instruments of a new approach to knowledge, those of a more suspicious nature believe them to be sinister and unwelcome invaders. The climate in many schools is ambivalent — as much characterized by fear and doomsaying as it is filled with excitement and anticipation.

By now, all but the poorest of school districts are facing the exciting but intimidating consequences of a rapidly changing technological landscape in education. While some administrations have plunged ahead — wiring buildings and installing pods of computers — others have carefully planned their strategies and are only now working out funding solutions. Still others act as if they hope technology will just go away. In any case, it is becoming increasingly clear that, for most communities, the goal of all this activity is a concept of education very different from the one we knew as children.

For some districts, this evolving concept of technology-rich education may be the private province of a single adminis-

trator or school board member. For others, it is the subject of a lengthy analysis and formal design by a multidisciplinary team of teachers, administrators, and community members. Many districts have established — or are in the process of convening — a technology committee to articulate a vision of the future. Such committees are pivotal in building consensus, identifying key issues, supporting funding requests, educating the community, and shaping the collective imagination. They serve the crucial roles of arousing, informing, guiding, and persuading members of the school community.

Still, even a formal technology plan tells us only some of what we need to know to understand what I call "System 2000," the kind of technology system that the school district of the 21st century will require. With few exceptions, the products of technology committees are less working documents than wish lists with timetables attached. The real work—not only of specifying and choosing computers and software, but also of developing policy and setting standards — is typically omitted from the formal process of technology planning. It is too often left to the implementers, the general contractors of the technology infrastructure, to grapple with the real world and its very real limitations.

Some of the omissions in collaborative technology plans are simple to remedy, either during or just after the planning process. Merely mentioning the need to calculate the cost of computer furniture or the need to estimate separately the infrastructure wiring and hubbing or the need to obtain a costed-out electrical design will suggest to many the obvious solutions that apply. Other omissions, however, are of a more systemic nature and are more difficult to address.

One important item that is often omitted from many technology plans is a position statement on issues related to standardization, especially the choice of a standard computer platform. While experts agree that the adoption of a set of realistic and responsible standards is pivotal in controlling costs, few committees include such wording in their formal plans. Even in mission statements, which are intended as abstract policy declarations and in which one would expect to find a statement of direction, the notion of standardization is conspicuously absent.

Probably the most striking omission from technology plans has been a realistic model of technical staffing. While administrations maintain modern staffs for business

operations, purchasing, curriculum, human resources, buildings and grounds, and so on, few superintendents or planning teams have recognized that a large network of computers will require a substantial group of trained professionals to cope with its many demands. It is truly startling to examine a plan, developed through extensive collaboration involving dozens of well-meaning individuals, and find that it ignores or grossly underestimates the expert staff that a new system will require. In fact, it is not uncommon for technology plans to include no mention of an administrative model at all.

Technology plans are doubly cursed when staff needs are underestimated *and* a standards policy is not articulated. No step can do more to control the proliferation of new staffers than an effective set of standards. Districts that choose to adopt a freewheeling systems policy will see their staffing requirements grow uncontrollably as their projects increase in size. Such districts will then have to choose between two equally unattractive options: either to understaff or to pay the price, no matter how high. Most districts in these circumstances will choose to understaff, thereby hamstringing their system far into the future.

While at first glance the lack of a realistic staffing model for technology proposals seems surprising, a familiarity with school district biases suggests reasons why the lack is all too common. First, many school boards assume that proposed increases in administrative staff will make a new budget less attractive to voters. Administrators themselves do not want to seem self-serving or to appear incompetent by increasing their management costs. Beyond these reasons, however, one factor stands out above all the others as contributing to the underestimates of technical staff requirements: the inability of most technology planners to recognize the size and complexity of the system they are designing.

A Model of the Proposed System

The first step in moving a technology plan from proposal to real-world project is that of full-scale modeling. This process entails developing a reasonable picture of the eventual system being designed. A model anticipates the size, shape, and complexity of a planned system and permits extrapolation of staff, materials, and expenses that the system will ultimately require. Such a step has extraordinary benefits in highlighting crucial, systemwide issues that technology planners might otherwise ignore.

Modeling of this kind also allows comparison to other, similar institutional projects already in place. A planning team can draw on a wide literature and history of institutional practice. By recognizing the missteps of others and appreciating the knowledge of their predecessors in similar circumstances, system planners can steer a steadier, smarter, and less expensive course than those without knowledge of prior experience.

What Kind of System?

Many of today's school projects are impressively large and complex, even when compared with other institutional systems, such as universities, public library systems, and medium-sized regional corporations. Our systems will be, typically, multi-site and many-faceted, involving large concentrations of machines and small remote groups of workstations, as well as dozens of printers, scanners, and other devices. Our networking will be multidimensional and sophisticated and will often extend over a wide area (67% of planned systems, according to the U.S. Department of Education, are multi-site configurations). Such systems require complicated hubbing, routing, and internetworking solutions.

For example, a typical school computer system will need to be capable of supporting thousands of end-users of widely differing skill and ability levels. Staff development initiatives, part and parcel of any technical project, will involve thousands of hours of training and support. Student training, even for basic literacy, will clearly be an enormous and costly undertaking.

The requirement for system performance will be monumental. As the speed and power of workstations have increased over the past 10 years, there has been a corresponding geometric increase in the capabilities and comprehension of software programs. To meet routine instructional goals, departments are increasingly requesting new applications that use graphics and multimedia. These programs gobble up resources and soon make today's fantastic performance into tomorrow's just barely sufficient capability.

System 2000 will support at least one computer for every five students. For every six computers, there will be a printer or some other adjunct. Aside from computing

devices, the network itself will have numerous special devices of its own, working transparently in many locations. These components will operate under a variety of arcane communications protocols, none of which will be known to the average user at a workstation. Internetwork links permitting access to the outside world, as well as school-to-school contact, will add to the complexity.

Hundreds of computer programs will be installed on a system, each with its own quirks and exigencies. New versions will appear regularly, as software vendors compete to deliver bigger, brighter, and better products. Each new version will use more and more resources and will raise the minimum standard in lockstep with the new features.

New media types are guaranteed — not just expected. High-density floppies and super CDs are only two of the known forms that we will surely see before long. Back-up techniques will continue to evolve, and they will become more centralized.

The system itself will be engaged in a fevered battle to ward off obsolescence. Every computer, including the file servers, will need to be replaced at least every five years. Printers will need to be replaced on roughly the same schedule, as manufacturers lose interest in servicing old models, software drivers disappear from bulletin boards, and new machines offer exciting new features. As the number of workstations increases, the ever-increasing need for bandwidth and speed will grind up old network solutions in favor of new technologies. Leading-edge network hardware, in precious little time, will become just so much ballast, as systems struggle to perform well and stay vital.

Can Such a System Be Managed?

Along with a hardware and software infrastructure, computer systems will require a number of parallel infrastructures in order to function at all. Skilled individuals will be needed to repair the machines when they break. And this repair includes more than the desktop machines out in the open; it also includes the array of networking devices hidden in closets. Other individuals will need to be available to diagnose systems in order to determine whether they need repair. Staff developers will be necessary both to train staff members in the use of computers and to model new teaching methods that can be integrated into the curriculum. A "help desk" system will be needed to answer users' ques-

tions over the telephone and to offer field support when necessary. Technicians will be required to install new equipment and transfer files as obsolete models are replaced. Specially trained network experts will be needed to solve problems arising beyond the individual workstations. New software and hardware will have to be tested for appropriateness and compatibility with the existing equipment.

The enterprise will require uniquely skilled administrators who understand technology and stay current with all its vagaries. These administrators will need to be capable of managing computer personnel, advising the staff on rapidly changing products, providing vision in a changing technological landscape, and managing a large budget. Moreover, the budget will grow steadily, as textbooks, office equipment, audiovisual products, and research/library equipment all become subsumed under the umbrella of Information Management.

Staffing Patterns

Regional and national companies, universities, and libraries have amassed considerable experience in staffing increasingly complex technical infrastructures not unlike those anticipated by most school planners. While not all examples are appropriate for a K-12 setting, much can be learned by examining the various administrative models that have developed out of the progress and missteps of other institutions facing a similar period of growth.

History of Network Management

Corporations started building networks of desktop computers in the early 1980s. The first model for technical staffing, which I call the "workgroup-coordinator model," began informally as users needed on-site support to integrate new ways of operating. In this model an insider, usually an employee who showed unusual computer skills, was given the job of understanding and managing the technology and fostering its growth. While these de facto technology coordinators took on policy and management functions, they were seldom offered full-time positions as managers.

By the middle of the decade, however, as networks flourished, workgroup-coordinator management fell out of favor. There were several reasons for this change. First, the costs of the systems multiplied, and demand for support grew as more and more work groups installed computers. De facto

1. INTRODUCTION

coordinators were overwhelmed by the sheer volume and increasing complexity of the requests for their assistance. Companies became dependent on outside vendors for critical support. Second, systems became stuck in time and reflected the personal preferences of these unofficial site-based managers. No organized policy was being followed as autonomous work groups chose their own directions. Institutions were overspending because information was not being shared and because buying power was not being leveraged. Advantageous purchasing relationships could not be forged without a coordinated voice speaking for the entire institution.

Another reason for the failure of the workgroup-coordinator model was the growth of networks to encompass workstations at a variety of locations, first on entire floors and then on multiple floors. The greater number of machines and the burgeoning demand for new applications, greater power, and increased bandwidth required increasingly sophisticated technical solutions. Special training and experience became crucial to the competent management of systems. Part-time coordinators were simply too busy to become proficient in the broad array of emerging technologies necessary for advanced networking.

An improvement on the workgroup-coordinator model emerged in the mid-1980s. The Management Information Systems (MIS) model, which stressed central administration, developed with the establishment of coordinated technology departments. All technical staff members were gradually organized into these new divisions. Each MIS department was led by a director who served at the supervisory or middle-management level in the institution.

MIS departments offered significant advantages over workgroup-coordinators in that they provided superior technical support and maintenance. Specially trained providers could be employed and shared by all an institution's work groups. These individuals could offer a higher level of knowledge and experience than that provided by site-based coordinators. Central administration led to the development of standards, which resulted in a more stable system that could be managed for less cost. Purchasing power could be consolidated. Software could be purchased on a per-site basis, reducing overall expenditures.

The MIS model, however, still had several weaknesses. Principal among these was that the MIS director was not a policy maker but served in an advisory capacity to senior staff members. As a result, the ultimate decision-making authority was still vested in administrators who were untrained to make technical distinctions. Because of companies' growing demand for computing power and for increasingly sophisticated internetworking configurations consisting of hundreds (even thousands) of workstations, technical choices became high-tech gambles that required extraordinary skills, knowledge, and nimbleness to navigate successfully. The indirect and sluggish decision-making apparatus whereby the MIS manager advised senior staff members became, at the very least, an impediment to growth. For many companies, the impractical structure undermined morale and led to costly and crippling missteps.

Another problem with the MIS model grew out of the increasing dependence of institutions on their information services. As technology became inextricably linked with the way companies functioned, basic operations came to include the management of information. Gradually, in many companies, distinctions between information management and basic operations blurred. This led to confusion, overlapping responsibilities, and, in some cases, turf battles. As MIS came to require an increasing portion of the capital and operating budgets, its continued status as a cottage department housed in finance or operations became untenable.

As the 1980s gave way to the 1990s, institutions chose a management model that permitted MIS to take on a management status equal to that of other departments. In this way institutions were able to be more responsive to users and more sensitive to the rapidly changing technology landscape. Organized in three tiers, rather than the two of the original MIS model, the Information Technology or Information Systems (IS) model has almost completely replaced its predecessor in modern institutions.

Today, in most institutions, there are three levels of administration in an IS Department (ISD). The CIO (Chief Information Officer) or IS manager (assisted by a network architect in larger organizations) functions in an overall policy and planning role. Network specialists, one level lower in the hierarchy, include network administrators and analysts. They are the hands-on managers of network installations. At the lowest of the three levels are support providers, a category that includes those who staff the help desk, repairpersons, installers, curriculum integrators, and on-site support personnel.

What Can Be Done in Schools?

School districts generally follow one of the two mid-1980s institutional models for technical staffing. When districts have accumulated a large number of computers, they have grown their own MIS-style organizations. Other, less progressive districts have continued to use the workgroup-coordinator model.

In order for school districts to plan, build, and manage large internetworking systems while avoiding the mistakes of the past, an IS staffing model should be adopted as soon as possible. This approach will provide the district with the sophisticated planning needed to design a wide-area network system and a knowledgeable administrator to shepherd its growth. It will also put into place a decision-making apparatus that will be flexible enough to respond to changing technology without being hampered by chain-of-command and turf issues that may make growth difficult or impossible.

An IS manager will have the time to champion systemwide issues — such as choice of platform, standards, and obsolescence — and remain current on high-technology configurations. He or she will also be able to help in the revamping of the curriculum to include technology at all levels. During the initial phase the IS manager will offer expertise with regard to networking and computer operation and be able to supervise the burgeoning technical operations. Hardware maintenance can be outsourced for small districts, but moderate-sized districts should consider hiring an in-house technician under the direction of the IS manager as a desirable alternative.

Once a large network is in place, a hands-on network administrator will have to be added to fill out the three levels of IS management and provide a link between the site-level support system and the administrative level. The number of employees at each of the three levels will be determined mostly by the number of workstations installed and by the current phase of automation. For example, if a district needs to make a great effort toward staff development, it will require a number of curriculum integrators. After four or five years, other job titles may be more important. Factors such as the degree of standardization of the system as a whole will enter into this equation as well.

Staff Responsibilities

The responsibilities of the IS manager are many. They include advising the faculty on technology plans and changes; advising the administration and the school board on new directions (including budget considerations); establishing and maintaining all technical policy and procedures; assessing the performance of the system and of the staff; supervising the technical staff; overseeing the budget; overseeing all technology testing; preparing and scheduling upgrades; evaluating new technologies; planning the least disruptive integration of new equipment into the system; selecting vendors; selecting equipment and software; negotiating with vendors for price, delivery, and availability; preparing and maintaining written system specifications; and so on.

The IS manager is the chief architect of the system. He or she must maintain the system at a high state of performance and must integrate new technologies on an ongoing basis. The IS manager also serves in an advisory capacity for all levels of the school community: managing all the related infrastructures that grow up around a system, seeing that all technical support is delivered promptly and efficiently, ensuring that adequate spare parts are always available and that technical personnel perform repairs professionally and quickly, ensuring that staff development is integrated into the faculty's schedules, and monitoring the effectiveness of staff development. The IS manager must make the critical decisions to formulate the district's response to obsolescence. He or she must assess the impact on the installed technology of proposed physical changes to buildings and must support the district's special education programs through evaluation and integration of assistive technologies.

The network administrator is the principal hands-on service provider for problems at the system level. Often, this person is a certified engineer with an in-depth understanding of the exact physical configuration of the district's wide-area network. He or she is intimately familiar with all the district's wiring closets and with the setup and capabilities of all communications and distribution equipment therein. The network administrator also understands the language of all supported protocols and is intimately familiar with all routers, hubs, switches, and the like that support the wiring. Moreover, the network administrator is capable of using sophisticated hardware and software to diagnose network problems from a central station. In short, the network administrator speaks the language of the network.

On the software side, the network administrator must deal with all issues involving file servers and communications. He or she must be very familiar with all software installed on the servers, as well as with the network operating systems that support them. The network administrator must be sensitive to the often delicate interfaces between hardware and software and between software and other software. He or she must have superior diagnostic capabilities and be able to sort through the contributions of each element of a large system. Once the network administrator has recognized the source of a problem, he or she must think of a judicious, practical, and nondisruptive solution and recommend changes in the system's overall design to prevent recurrences.

The network administrator must operate a testing facility where new hardware and software can be evaluated before being taken "live" on the system. Using systemwide criteria established by the IS manager, the network administrator must determine that new products are efficient and well-designed. He or she must also evaluate each product in the context of its fit with other parts of the existing system. The network administrator must establish standards of performance and keep careful records in the event that future samples of a product fail to meet established criteria.

The individual service providers are the third level of IS support. They are the frontline workers of the technology infrastructure, but they are hardly drones. Service providers include technicians, curriculum integrators, help-desk support personnel, and installers.

Technicians install new hardware and repair existing equipment. They are responsible for configuring software on computers and for connecting hardware together to ensure that it functions properly. They make field diagnoses and replace defective parts. Technicians also provide a channel of communication between the faculty and the ISD. Suggestions, complaints, requests for changes, and so on are often first delivered to technicians.

Curriculum integrators work with professional staff members and provide training, software evaluation, and inside support. They develop and refine programs for staff development and educate the faculty on new curricular offerings. Curriculum integrators are available on-site to support the various instructional initiatives and to assist in diagnosing problems and bringing them to the attention of technicians. While they are involved in significant ways

with the curriculum, curriculum integrators can be a tremendous asset to an ISD by providing feedback on equipment, policies, and programs.

Support, installation, and maintenance personnel are generally qualified to work on both hardware and software, but an institution may wish to have individuals on staff with specific talents. Software technicians can help diagnose workstation problems because of their familiarity with the delicate changes in system configuration that are sometimes required in installing new programs and equipment. Hardware specialists may be needed to provide meticulous attention to detail and an understanding of mechanics. Each offers advantages, and, together, they potentially offer a synergy unavailable with only one kind of provider.

Can Costs Be Controlled?

The cost of designing System 2000 can be a daunting obstacle for any district. The size and cost of an information management infrastructure can be controlled in two ways: through *outsourcing*, i.e., hiring expertise and contracting for technical assistance from outside agencies; and through *standardization*, which can control costs significantly by limiting the complexity of the system and increasing its predictability.

Outsourcing

For some districts, hiring salaried individuals for administrative tasks is not a desirable alternative, and in other districts it can be politically impossible. These institutions may find it useful to hire individuals from outside on a contract or consulting basis. This practice is known as outsourcing, and it can be a reasonable way of controlling costs and avoiding the commitment of hiring a full-time employee.

When considering outside sources for technical staff, the three levels of the IS model described above should be respected. While competent providers should be available at all three levels (at least near large metropolitan areas), not every individual can provide service at all levels. For the top level, IS manager, consider an individual with experience as a network architect. Educational consultants will serve your needs, but some may have experience only with the current practice in schools (which could be as much as 10 years behind current practice in corporations and universities). Knowledge of education is important, but it is not crucial. A competent individual from a corporate or university background will already have considerable experience serving a varied and demanding user base.

For hands-on network administration, choose an individual or company that can respond quickly. If your outside source is highly knowledgeable but doesn't call back for hours, then your network will suffer unnecessary downtime. Communication skills should also be examined. If your vendor calls back quickly but doesn't seem to understand your explanations, you may have the wrong person. The service provider is the expert and should be able to ask you specific questions that can help him or her develop a working diagnosis. Once the problem is diagnosed, this person should be able to explain it and suggest simple ways to solve it without using arcane jargon.

Before you hire from an outside source at the technician level, consider the manufacturer as a service provider. New equipment is often covered by a three-year onsite service contract. With a responsible attitude toward obsolescence (replacement at least every four years), you should be able to limit your hardware liability to a brief exposure.

Standards (see below) can also help in reducing the requirement for technicians. By making every workstation as much alike as possible, spares can be stored strategically for instant replacement as needs arise. Broken machines can be repaired while the spares serve in their place. On a permachine basis, this policy can save enormous sums when compared with on-site service contracts.

If you're going to hire a technician from the outside, do so strategically. Develop a relationship with a vendor on a per-call basis whenever possible. Computers are very reliable. The use of spares as replacements and a good obsolescence policy should mean that you will need to request few service calls. It's wise to pay only for the services you use. However, make sure that you develop a relationship with a vendor *before* you need help, and remember to negotiate a maximum response time in advance — not when faced with a crisis.

Outside vendors for staff development training can be a big cost saving, but don't underestimate the size of the task any staff developer will face. It can take as much as eight years to train a novice teacher to fully integrate computers into everyday practices. Outside trainers may make use of progressive techniques, which can be very effective for preliminary training, but insiders can be more responsive to individual nuances and local conditions. Insiders can also develop important relationships of confidence and trust and so make the learning experience more productive for the faculty. Finally, insiders can offer support on an ongoing basis, whereas an outside training session is usually limited to the training phase alone.

One rule for selecting outside vendors is that they must be sensitive to the unique characteristics of schools. An excellent corporate vendor may be useless to a K-12 district. Concepts like released time, the school day, and the school calendar are alien to the world outside of education. Often, outside vendors expect the individual to be available when they call. If their call isn't answered, they don't call back. Good outsource vendors are just as hard to find as good employees. And both are worth their weight in gold.

Standardization

In any system, there will be a tradeoff between flexibility and standards. Predictability and familiarity may breed contempt, but they are welcome components of computer systems on many levels. A standard system is designed to use similar components, and this limits the number of vendors and tends to make the system more dependable. However, too much consistency may stifle creativity and limit the options available to the professional staff. It's important for policy makers to strike a balance between the desire for a system to be stable, reliable, predictable, and familiar and the ability of the system to meet a wide range of differing requirements.

Still, a set of firm and well-chosen standards is the single most important contribution an administrator can make to limiting the costs of System 2000. In the absence of equipment standards, there is great freedom but little control. Many districts that have failed to put standards in place are already spending more than $300 per computer per year on system maintenance. And that cost is going to grow each year. For System 2000, with potentially many times the current number of computers and a far more complex configuration, expenditures in the range of $750 per computer are not impossible. However, a district that implements a strategy that strictly enforces hardware and software standards can expect to spend no more than $300 per computer per year on maintenance, regardless of the size or complexity of the system.

The past decade of corporate experience suggests that standards are critical to controlling the costs of network management, maintenance, and support. Common practice indicates that nonstandard networks that include many protocols, hardware types, and operational tools require one support person for every 50 to 70 computers. Highly standardized systems, on the other hand, require one support person for every 500 to 700 computers. Clearly, a highly standardized system is desirable from a staffing standpoint alone.

The single most significant standard in any computer system is agreement on a common hardware platform for use in every possible situation. Whether one chooses PCs or Apple Macintosh computers, the choice of a single platform is often the best way to limit other related expenses. Without a standard platform, the parallel infrastructures of support, staff development, technical staffing, maintenance, spare parts, network management, and policy will all have to be considerably larger and consequently more expensive than would otherwise be the case.

In a multi-platform plan, staff development will be required on both types of computers. So will help-desk support for hardware and software. Separate specialists trained on each type of machine will be necessary. Technicians will have to draw on considerably larger inventories of spare parts. Policy issues will become more complex. Given a free choice, building staff may wish to choose their standard platform. That decision might be permitted at the building level, the department level, the grade level, or the teacher level, but each such choice will present different challenges to technical administrators.

Another important step in controlling the overall cost of System 2000 is through the thorough implementation of *functional identity*, which means making every workstation or file server in a functional group identical to every other. The benefits of this kind of standardization are manifold. If every machine used for a similar purpose is identical (same keyboard, mouse, processor, monitor, manufacturer, model, and so on), then staff development can be collaborative. Every staff member will know how to use every computer everywhere in the district. Teachers can help one another with problems. An exact replacement computer can be kept in a central location to minimize downtime in the event of a breakdown. A much smaller inventory of spare parts will have to be maintained, and technical staff members will need to be proficient in servicing only a limited number of machines and models. Consequently, they can be better trained and more intimately familiar with those models.

Hardware standards should not be limited only to computers, of course. Peripheral devices, such as printers, digitizing tablets, scanners, and plotters, can be standardized as well. So too can be the infrastructure hardware of hubs, routers, bridges, transceivers, and the like. The many benefits of less training for staff, greater familiarity for technical staff, smaller inventories of spare parts, and more predictable behavior will surely result in a more stable system that will be easier and cheaper to maintain.

Even when restricted to a single hardware design, System 2000 will make use of more than a hundred different software programs across all levels from kindergarten to high school. Controlling the quantity of titles a district owns is absolutely fundamental to maintaining the budget at reasonable levels. This applies not only to the direct cost of licensing (which is often only a small contributor to the total price of ownership), but also to related expenses, such as technical staff training, instructional staff development (both teacher teaching and the development of training materials), installation, license monitoring, testing, support, and ongoing maintenance. These expenses will all be proportionally greater as the number of software titles increases.

Selecting a single hardware platform is one way in which the total number of software titles used in a district can be controlled. Choosing a single title for each of the five or six clearly defined functional areas already established by the software industry is another. Such functions as word processing, database management, collaborative e-mail, electronic spreadsheets, and presentation development software can be standardized for all students and faculty members at nearly all grade levels. (The earliest grades are an exception, because reading skills are necessary for many titles.) Software may also be purchased at lower cost when it is bought in greater quantities. Many publishers offer site licenses at a greatly reduced rate for institutions willing to commit to single titles systemwide.

In the PC world and to a lesser extent in the Macintosh world, several standard suites of tools are available to meet the large measure of general computing tasks. These suites, which integrate the various software programs into a cohesive unit, can provide benefits to a school district. One such benefit is the ability of the individual programs to function smoothly together — an outcome often wished for but seldom realized in the past. Another advantage is the similarity in "look and feel," menu design, and command structure of the individual modules. This allows for the ready transfer of users' knowledge from one program to another and thus enables users to learn faster and to remember more thoroughly than would be possible with separate programs. Selecting software suites is also the most economical way for school districts to purchase software titles and often permits them to obtain four or five strong applications for the price of one or two.

Software standards encourage thorough testing of programs before they are installed. A cogent set of rules can filter out poorly designed programs that require a great deal of maintenance in favor of more professional, smoothly operating products. In most cases, a district will find it profitable to set up a test environment with network capabilities where the staff can subject recommended titles to careful scrutiny in a safe and well-monitored laboratory. This will improve the reliability of a system because titles that are not acceptable can be identified before general distribution creates systemwide problems. If specific titles are deemed irreplaceable, installation can be isolated to the workstations where they are mandated, while the integrity of the overall system is protected.

An analysis of current practices in the software industry suggests that publishers are moving toward a model of license compliance in which fees are paid according to the number of simultaneous users. Central monitoring will become increasingly necessary for districts that wish to comply with the terms of their license agreements. Standards permit the choice of software that lends itself to just such central management.

An often neglected set of standards is that which defines the underlying design. Before equipment is chosen, its features should be evaluated in the context of the wide area network's communications solutions, expansion options and goals, internetworking schemes, backup strategies, anticipated compatibility with future technologies, and so on. Once selected, consistency should be established from wiring closet to wiring closet and from server to server — even if this means additional expense. Every upgrade should be systemwide, and the implementation should signal a change to corresponding processes, operating manuals, training materials, maintenance schedules, and so forth.

File servers should have standard configurations for all situations. This makes them interchangeable and thus more easily replaced in the event of a single machine's failure. Careful design may permit servers to have identical software configurations, volume sizes, volume names, and so on. Moreover, these advantages will echo throughout the useful life of the system.

Access to System 2000 should be controlled in the same way for all users. Whatever security scheme is implemented, it will become intolerably complex unless a formal set of rules is established. Designers should keep in mind the total number of users (students and faculty) who will have to be supported for the life of a system. Moreover, access should be controlled sensibly and without unnecessary restrictions.

School districts are increasingly building large and complex computer systems to meet changing requirements for technology-rich education. These systems will require a new kind of administrative organization: the Information Systems Department.

In order to limit the size of the ISD and control costs generally, districts can take several approaches. Two that are covered here are outsourcing and standardization. Outsourcing can affect management costs only marginally, but it does limit the number of in-house staffers. Standardization can significantly limit costs and reduce staffing needs. However, it should be implemented carefully, so as not to limit choice and flexibility and so stifle individual creativity.

The Modern Land of Laputa
Where Computers Are Used in Education

BY CHRIS MORTON

While the real world uses computers to move forward, schools often use them in a misguided effort to support 19th-century instructional practices, Mr. Morton charges.

I N THE 17th century, satirist Jonathan Swift described his hero, Gulliver, visiting a flying island where science and technology were primary functions. One would expect this land to be a very modern and progressive place. But Laputa turned out to be a limited place where nothing was ever accomplished, because its people, deaf to change, reveled in following the same ludicrous procedures over and over again. With minimal rewriting, this satire might well describe many schools today and their use of technology.

In the 1970s schools crippled the first stage in the educational use of computers by insisting that teachers learn BASIC as an introduction to technology use in classrooms. The teachers returned to their schools

CHRIS MORTON is president of the International Institute for Information Analysis, Yorktown Heights, N.Y., a think tank and research group focusing on online information use, technology-use planning, and network design. He is a founding member of the International Education and Resource Network, which serves international schools in 27 countries. He can be contacted at the following e-mail address: cmorton@igc.apc.org.

Illustration by Brenda Grannan

 From *Phi Delta Kappan*, February 1996, pp. 416-419. © 1996 by Phi Delta Kappa, Inc. Reprinted by permission.

The idea of "computer as tool" permits the ignorant to justify their decision to reject it.

to find that they had no use for their training and, as is almost always the case, no time for reflecting on or developing new directions for using technology. Disillusionment quickly set in.

In the 1980s and 1990s we continue to destroy the foundation that would allow the development of educational uses of computers by defining the technological infrastructure in ways that discredit it, that mislead planners, and that provide ready ammunition for those who oppose such uses of technology. The new rush to fund computer systems through bond issues does nothing to alleviate the situation. Indeed, it may soon exacerbate the problems. It is time to take stock of these expanding mistakes, which are being perpetrated primarily by poorly trained educational administrators, particularly school superintendents.

Computers as 'Tools'

The April 1987 issue of *School Administrator*, the official organ of the American Association of School Administrators, featured on its cover a computer and a pencil, as if the one were an extension of the other. Inside, the editorial confirmed this perception, and the "official" misconception of "computer as tool" was born, at least for administrators.

The concept of "computer as tool" misleads educational planners and relegates computer technology to the level of "supplies" — pencils, paper, pens, and paper clips. Because of this definition, school business managers and educational planners (particularly curriculum planners) conceptually align computers with traditional classroom "tools" that can be used as "alternatives." This view leads them to put computers on a cost continuum with pens and pencils and allows decision makers to reject computers as "expensive alternatives" to things we already use.

But that's not all. The concept of "computer as tool" allows the uninformed to make easy decisions about the use of computers in schools. It allows administrators and teachers to reject the computer as simply one "tool" among many, without having to understand what its capabilities for learning and productivity really are. The idea of "computer as tool" permits the ignorant to justify their decision to reject it.

Human beings were initially distinguished from other animals as "tool users." When anthropologists noted that many wild animals use tools, they changed the definition to "tool makers." However, once it was discovered that some wild animals make tools (e.g., chimpanzees strip twigs to dip insects out of their nests), humans became the "information gatherers and storers."

To suggest, therefore, that computers are simply tools entirely misses the point about their expanding capabilities and their interaction with humans. In the larger society, the computer is a symbol of the future and all that is good about it. We should not be surprised that educators would want to update their largely 19th-century practice by using computers as tools to support their efforts. But while the real world uses computers to move forward, educators too often look studiously backward, and Laputa is reborn.

Computer systems in schools should be viewed as structured learning environments with complex and comprehensive capabilities to access and manipulate information. They should be seen as interactive learning extensions of the children themselves.[1]

We live in a society in which the technological environment is an accepted part of our lives. It is only in schools that we consider the computer to be an add-on, a thing little related to skills development or communications.

Computers as Add-Ons

The stereotype of the "computer as tool" promotes the view of the "computer as add-on." But the "add-on" concept goes a lot deeper; it allows curriculum developers to continue implementing their traditionally fragmented, subject-based, single-discipline-focused instructional plans,[2] rather than regarding and using the computer as the driving force behind an integrated, cross-disciplinary learning environment that emulates the "real" world. Computer technology provides learning environments that promote individual attainment, group interaction and sharing, a choice of various approaches to a particular project, and access to current information.

Curriculum development and training are traditionally considered to be at the core of instructional development and the integration of learning models. This is a Laputian truism that is repeated again and again. What it leads to is a glacial system whose movement is frozen. Curriculum change takes most schools and education departments many years to implement and sometimes produces hilarious situations, such as a 10th-grade curriculum called "Global Studies" whose 10-year-old content and textbooks still refer to Russia as part of the U.S.S.R. The exclusion of computer technology from the processes of planning, managing, and implementing curriculum and instruction keeps change in education moving at a snail's pace and maintains the old instructional models.

Because the computer environment has the potential to stimulate learning, because it is pervasive in society, because computer-based skills must be taught to children, because of the speed at which the computer can support change, and because of the expanded vision that the computer gives to students and teachers, it is difficult to understand why curriculum planners exclude computer-based learning environments from curriculum development. Instead of being integral to curriculum development and completely integrated into it, the computer environment remains peripheral, an "add-on" in space and time that many teachers and administrators can reject.

This "add-on" is often provided in laboratory settings, where scheduled periods allow students to "do" computing. In such settings everything positive and creative about the computer environment is destroyed. Moreover, individual teachers who would like to embrace a computerized learning environment are forced by these arrangements to compete with other teachers for access to these sporadically used "tools."

The worst-case scenario (usually in late middle school or early high school) typically involves students' going through a process of acquiring "computer literacy" by sitting in rows and being exposed a couple of times a week to those "tool skills" — such as word processing, keyboarding, and spreadsheet use — which are thought to be important for them to master at some point in their school careers. In these settings students do not learn that the computer environment is all-embracing, that it provides enormous opportunities for learning, and that it can encourage student engagement and access to the "real world." In these settings teachers are not able to realize the instructional potential of the computer systems they control.

When the computer is viewed as "add-on," student learning is as regimented and boring as it has ever been in a one-desk-behind-another environment. The real discouragement of learning in these settings is that they pander to 19th-century didacticism and never come to grips with the genuine benefits of a future-directed computer-based environment with a new skills base.

Computers as Part
Of the Same Old Game

In 1989-90 a survey of superintendents in New York and Rhode Island, conducted by the Division of Information Research and Development of the Putnam/North Westchester Board of Cooperative Educational Services, showed that 85% of them knew nothing about computers, had never used a computer, and did not intend to use one. Ninety-five percent of the superintendents knew nothing about educational computing and were not prepared to do anything about this lack of knowledge. And yet these are the people who make decisions about student and teacher uses of computers in schools.[3] While times may have changed to some degree, it doesn't seem likely that all these folks have had significant changes of heart, and there is no reason to believe that the statistics would be any different had the survey been conducted nationally. As Jean Zlotkin, a school board member, says, "It is disastrous to empower unqualified people with critical decision-making power."[4]

In the same years a national survey of 500 universities was conducted to find out whether they included computer training of any sort in their courses for educational administrators. Just 2% of the colleges surveyed said that they provided regular courses for their trainees, 14% said that they offered training through another department, and the rest offered nothing. None of them provided computer-based curriculum training, and only 7% said that their professors used computers in their courses. Yet these institutions are supposed to train school administrators to develop schooling for our children — schooling that prepares them for the next century. Again, time has passed, and computers have proliferated, but 1989-90 was not exactly the Dark Ages.

It is not surprising, therefore, to find that school administrators balk at the development of computer use in their schools and misdirect planning for it.[5] It is not surprising that, when financial problems plague schools, computing is one of the first areas to suffer cuts. It is not surprising that, when new experimental computer-based programs are introduced into schools, they are treated in the same way as other pilot programs: three years to complete and integrate into the curriculum, with annually declining financing. Of course, we are told that in industry 18 months is the projected desk life of a computer. New computer-based programs require at least a four-year implementation period, with *increasing* funding, if they are to attain the planned goals and to be upgraded as necessary. Given all these facts, it is hardly surprising that, when schools begin to look at change and to focus on student-based outcomes, computer environments are not considered integral to this planning.

With regard to educational policy development, funding, and change, it is well to keep in mind that almost all of a state education department's staff is made up of educational administrators. Their lack of a clear focus on computer technology has been demonstrated on numerous occasions. A few examples suffice:

• California cut its most innovative intracurricular computer program five years ago. The program focused on technology integration into classrooms with trained support teams.

• New York has split up the responsibility for computer-use development so that nobody knows what to do. The state has spent millions of dollars on regional training centers that have been in place for 10 years and have produced no measurable change in instruction or computer skills development. Moreover, the state has augmented all of this effort with an out-of-date telecommunications system that nobody wants.

• Massachusetts has recently begun to develop a plan for its schools, after having left such planning to local authorities for the last 15 years.

• Utah has given the responsibility for K-12 computer technology planning to a university-based group; the same group is also responsible for training educational administrators.

Time and again, opportunities have been lost at the state level because of local squabbling, because of a lack of real educational leadership, and because of misleading direction from the federal government.[6]

Computer Environments
And Budgeting

It is always important to talk about school budgets.[7] School district budgets in most parts of the country are under fire. They suffered from the recession, and many continue to suffer. Computer environments change often and change comprehensively, but they change much more quickly than educational authorities and planners are accustomed to. School budgets do not adapt well to this rapid pace of change.

Superintendents and school business officials say that schools cannot hope to keep up with the changes in equipment that are taking place in industry. But this is another misconception. Schools *must* follow the changes in industry because these changes reflect changes in the skills required of students when they leave school.

The new rush to use bond issues to fund computer systems in schools will cause new problems because administrators and school boards refuse to accept the idea that funding for computer systems (including teacher training, software upgrades, video upgrades, satellite use, and system maintenance) must be part of the annual budget and must be looked on as a necessary expense. Bond issues fund hardware and cabling today, but nothing else. If continued funding is not provided, these new systems paid for with millions of taxpayer dollars will become obsolete within five years or less.

School budgets can accommodate technological change by using "technology-based budgeting." This is a simple concept: school budgets must have a minimum percentage of their total funds allocated to technology maintenance and change every year. This minimum is 3% of the total operating budget. Changes can then be gradual and carefully planned. Educational authorities must simply accept the fact that computer technology has a built-in obsolescence period and must be changed regularly.

Serious mistakes on the part of school administrators in budgeting for technology use in schools have left many districts in disastrous positions. Whole systems have become useless, and replacing them has meant the expenditure of huge amounts of money from single budgets. The process of annual "budget hopping" (leaving an item out one year and picking it up the next year or the year after) cannot continue, because the public will not accept the huge outlays or bond issues every three to five years to replace old equipment and planning structures en masse.

Computers, Research, And Skills Development

Many school district administrators (and school board members, who are usually slightly less knowledgeable than their superintendents about educational computing) are demanding research data that show that computer use enhances academic (or other) achievement. This perspective shows a distinct lack of understanding of the computer learning environment.

Special education has shown a better understanding of the potential of computers. The value of a computer environment is not so much the improvement of students' achievement through computer use as it is the improvement of students' ability to achieve. The difficulty of understanding this crucial difference is exacerbated by the focus on "tool use," which insists that the computer is there to enhance abilities already developed.

If the computer is not to be seen as the means of improving achievement in education, then perhaps it should be seen as an integral part of an environment that is structured to engage students in the learning process. Perhaps it should also be regarded as an essential element in an educational approach that focuses on gathering information (and on learning how to transform it into new knowledge), on the changing role of teacher-as-facilitator,[8] on the involvement of children in experiential learning, and on the expanded world of lifelong learning. Educational planners have overlooked these perspectives almost entirely.

In the development of standards and outcomes, nationally and regionally, there is almost no mention of a supporting environment of computer technology. But the skills that graduating students take with them into the world must be a major focus of any serious effort to reform schools, and such computer-based skills as the ability to access and manipulate current information, the ability to communicate globally, the ability to expand creativity, and the ability to test new knowledge through sharing and rebuilding can only be developed in a supportive computer-based environment.[9]

To look for research that shows that computers have improved student performance is misguided for two reasons: 1) schools are not teaching the skills that computer environments best support, and 2) schools have not recognized the skills that students will need in the future.

For the most part, computer environments will not drastically improve students' attainment in the traditional content that we adhere to in our current curricula and that we reinforce with our didactic methods. If teachers want students to be able to do repetitive tasks and to be able to use ditto masters, then they shouldn't spend thousands of dollars on systems that support computer-assisted instruction. If teachers want to reinforce their didactic role and their role as information providers, then they should also leave computers alone.

Educational administrators must understand that the promise of computer environments is that they support changes in the educational structure, in instructional processes, and in the development of lifelong learning within the whole population. We all pay lip service to the importance for everyone of changing these features of the American educational landscape. But it takes leaders with guts to pursue these future visions and to develop truly different and innovative learning environments that are integrated into technological environments that serve the whole community. From digital television to voice recognition systems, from personal information managers to the Internet, educational challenges and opportunities are here to stay.

If schools refuse to recognize and work with these challenges and opportunities, then they may well follow many of our outmoded industries into decline. Our schools will become ever more like the Laputian community with its repetitive procedures — but, while Laputa continued to exist in its repetitive ignorance, our schools, like some of our industries, will not.

1. Seymour Papert, *The Children's Machine: Rethinking School in the Age of the Computer* (New York: Basic Books, 1993).

2. Sylvia Farnham-Diggory, *Schooling* (Cambridge, Mass.: Harvard University Press, 1990); and Don Nix, ed., *Education, Cognition, and Multi-Media* (New York: Pergamon Press, 1989).

3. Louis Tornatzky and Mitchell Fleischer, *The Process of Technological Innovation* (Lexington, Mass.: Lexington Books, 1990).

4. Jean Zlotkin, "Rethinking the School Board's Role," *Educational Leadership*, October 1993, p. 23.

5. Papert, p. 39.

6. Lewis J. Perelman, *School's Out: Hyperlearning, the New Technology, and the End of Education* (New York: William Morrow, 1992), pp. 169 ff.

7. Ibid., pp. 251 ff.

8. Katy Smith, "Becoming the Guide on the Side," *Educational Leadership*, October 1993, pp. 35-37.

9. Mitchell Resnick, "New Paradigms for Computing, New Paradigms for Thinking," available online from The Media Laboratory, Massachusetts Institute of Technology, http://ics.www.media.mit.edu/groups/ed/projects.

The Battle over Information-Age Technology

New information technologies will transform education, but only after a battle royal with the education establishment.

By James H. Snider

Most people now recognize that new information technology is radically changing the economics of education. Many also believe that, if only the schools could get the best technology and train teachers how to use it, the wonders of the Information Age will come to K-12 education.

But this belief, held by such prominent individuals as the president of the United States and the U.S. secretary of education, is faulty.

In the shift from Industrial Age to Information Age education, most educators will lose money, status, and power. They cannot be expected to accept this change without a fight. Insofar as public education responds to political and not economic forces, educators have a good chance of preserving, or at least slowing the erosion of, their position.

Until the full dimensions of this problem are understood, the promise of technology in education will never be fulfilled.

The new economics of education include the following trends:

• **From labor intensive to capital intensive.** Industrial Age education uses little technology. It is low tech and labor intensive. According to the Educational Research Service, more than 95% of a typical public school's budget goes to teachers; less than 5% goes to instructional capital such as books, software, and computers. Since improved technology tends to drive up productivity, the high proportion of education dollars spent on labor is often used to explain why education has the worst productivity record of any major economic sector in the United States.

Information Age education, in contrast, is capital intensive. Education resources, including individualized instruction, are delivered via the information superhighway, high-definition television, multimedia PCs, and so on.

• **From local to national.** Industrial Age education is transportation intensive—the learner must physically travel to the key educational resources. As a result of the high cost of travel, education is geographically bound. Students attend the neighborhood school, not one that is thousands of miles away.

In contrast, Information Age education is communications intensive: The learner can access educational resources produced and distributed anywhere in the world. The traditional textbook with national reach is now joined by the "virtual course," the "virtual classroom," and the "virtual school."

THE TEACHING COMPANY

"Star teacher" Linwood C. Thompson dresses like a Viking for a history lesson offered on videotape. A national faculty of the best teachers could replace less-competent local educators, according to Snider.

How?

• **From small-scale to large-scale production.** Public schools (K-12 level) employ some 6 million individuals, about half of whom are teachers. Tens of thousands of teachers teach similar subjects such as Introductory Spanish, U.S. History, and Biology I. At least one highly skilled professional teacher per classroom is considered necessary for adequate instruction.

Information Age education requires far fewer teachers to achieve the same or better results. A few thousand of the best teachers in the United States could replace many of the other 3 million. For example, today's 40,000 Algebra I teachers could be largely displaced by a handful of star teachers working nationally.

• **From small-scale to large-scale evaluation.** Industrial Age education requires classroom-by-classroom evaluation. Since each classroom has relatively few students and is a largely private and inaccessible space, comparative course evaluation is an extraordinarily expensive and impractical undertaking.

Information Age education courses may be taken by thousands or even millions of students over many years. This creates a large market for course evaluations; there could be national evaluations for courses, just as there are for cars, mutual funds, and colleges.

• **From monopoly to competition.** Industrial Age education is a natural monopoly. Students find it impractical to travel long distances to different schools to take different courses, so students often have a choice of only one course and teacher for a given grade and subject matter.

By eliminating geographic barriers, Information Age education makes it possible for students to choose among many courses and classmates, thus creating natural competition.

In summary, the new education economics suggest a shift in power away from regional educators to national educators and to students. National educators gain power because the key education resources are increasingly being produced and distributed on a national basis. Students gain power because they now have choice; they are less dependent on what their regional (e.g., neighborhood) educator provides. Regional educators lose power because their monopoly over education resources is broken.

The vital question for the future, then, is the extent to which the politics and economics of education are coming into conflict. To the extent that regional educators are successful in using political influence to preserve their power, children and parents will have amateurish, expensive, and unnecessarily restricted education services to choose from.

The Politics of Educational Technology

One of the classic tales of capitalism is the propensity of new technologies to put people out of work. Witness the decline in the agricultural sector from more than 90% of the work force in 1800 to less than 3% today. Or consider the loss of tens of thousands of bank-teller jobs with the introduction of the automatic teller machine over the last few decades.

Public education differs from these other industries in that it primarily responds to political, not economic, forces. Laws, not supply and demand, dictate the working condi-

THE TEACHING COMPANY

Algebra I teacher Debra K. Pizzuto conducts class via videotape. Today's 40,000 algebra teachers could be replaced by a smaller group of star teachers working nationally, suggests author James Snider.

tions, pay, skills, and education requirements of educators. Just think of the many school districts with 500 to 1,000 applications for a teaching position that nevertheless are unable to fire an incompetent teacher. Previous economic conditions may have been embedded in law, but the political process, often most responsive to entrenched interests, may take decades to catch up with new economic conditions. Accordingly, an extraordinary web of laws has been designed to protect and enhance the monopoly power of regional educators. And these educators have a conflict of interest in implementing Information Age technology.

In the nineteenth century, the Luddites sought to prevent the introduction of new technologies by literally smashing the job-destroying machines. Today, educators can hinder the introduction of new technologies with far more subtle mechanisms, such as:

• **Public-school unions.** Public schools have about 6 million unionized employees, including teachers, administrators, and maintenance workers. These unions are extremely influential in setting local education policy and budgets. Since every dollar spent on capital is a dollar taken away from labor, unions favor more spending on labor. In New York City, out of a total spending of about $8,000 per pupil in 1994, only $44 was budgeted for classroom materials. Much of the money spent on technology in the classroom comes from the federal government, grants from companies in the information industry, PTA fund raising, and special technology bonds. Money subject to union wage demands rarely stays allocated to technology for long.

Unions also oppose efforts to introduce competition among educators by granting parents vouchers to choose their own educator. Unions oppose choice even when parents are restricted to choosing among public schools. The National Education Association has already launched a campaign to restrict technology-based choice in higher education. Across the United States, candidates for political office who support educational choice are consistently and vigorously opposed by the local unions.

• **Teachers in the classroom.** Technology can be a direct threat to the teacher's authority in a classroom. Students can already access long-distance and video-based foreign

> "An extraordinary web of laws has been designed to protect and enhance the monopoly power of regional educators."

language instruction superior to that in most U.S. secondary schools. When a mediocre teacher must compete with an outstanding teacher in the same classroom, the mediocre teacher feels threatened. The teacher has little incentive to beg the administration and school board for this type of instructional resource. And if the resource is nevertheless provided, the incentive to use it properly is weak.

An important exception to this argument is that certain applications of computers in the classroom are non-threatening. These include using technology to teach productivity skills such as keyboarding and using a computer, to mark grades and take attendance, to communicate with peers, and to access impersonal reference works.

• **Education schools.** Education schools in the United States employ close to 18,000 professors and annually enroll hun-dreds of thousands of students. Almost every professional position in a public school, including superintendent, principal, and classroom teacher, requires a special and expensive license only offered by these schools. Moreover, education schools and educator unions have formed a close alliance. The time-consuming licensing program keeps down the supply of educators and thus bolsters wages. Any time supply decreases, price increases. If education schools act in their self-interest, then they will be a formidable opponent of change.

• **Other laws and regulations.** Thousands of laws, regulations, and contractual agreements serve to preserve the monopoly power of regional educators, including: (1) state licensing laws that prevent people from teaching who haven't spent thousands of dollars and countless hours earning an obsolete education degree; (2) state licensing laws that prevent teachers from teaching across state lines (e.g., via telecommunications) where they don't hold licenses; (3) state licensing laws that prevent people with general management skills, but without extensive training in an education school,

FUTUREKIDS

Children learn to use a computer. Computer-related technology can offer students and parents alternatives to traditional schools.

from attaining positions such as school superintendent; (4) collective bargaining contracts that dictate working conditions, such as limits on virtual or real class sizes; (5) collective bargaining contracts that require all teachers to be paid the same amount, regardless of the demand and supply for their particular positions and level of job performance; and (6) labor laws that make it hard to replace employees ill-suited to using technology in education.

The Battle to Come

A policy battle between the advocates of Industrial Age and Information Age education is brewing. Here are some of the battle lines likely to arise:

• **History.** Advocates of Industrial Age education will point to the failed promises of educational technology enthusiasts; the well-documented discrepancies between technology hype and reality are an embarrassment.

Advocates of Information Age education will point to the printing press as a technology that fundamentally transformed and improved education. Many technologies (e.g., the airplane, telephone, and fax) take decades to mature and become widely available, but eventually have a major impact. Much of the new educational technology is now at that take-off point.

• **Equity and public schools.** Industrial Age advocates will point to the historic role of public schools in providing equal opportunity for all. They will see anything that weakens public schools as fostering inequality.

Information Age advocates see today's public schools as a great bastion of inequity and racism in American society, as a result of an education system that is too geographically based: As long as schools are so heavily based on geography, they will represent the geographic distribution of wealth in America.

• **Equity and technology.** Advocates of Industrial Age education will emphasize the tendency of technology to create information haves and have-nots. Technology, they will also claim, replaces labor to cut costs, and so results in impersonal and inferior instruction.

Advocates of Information Age education will again point to the precedent of the printing press and the great democratization of education that followed. Just as the printing press brought high quality and affordable education to the masses, new educational technologies should do the same. By reducing the cost of access to the best instruction in the world, these new technologies, if properly implemented, should decrease the discrepancy between the information haves and have-nots.

• **Choice and parental competence.** Industrial Age advocates will argue that education consumers are not competent enough to make decisions and therefore should not be given choice. They will point out how difficult it would be for the average parent to comparison shop for education. Choice will create a hucksterish and highly inefficient education market.

Information Age advocates have more faith in the responsibility and competence of parents. They will argue that new technologies will greatly facilitate comparison shopping for education. The emergence of reliable education assessment systems will mean that educational success will be more closely tied to a student's eventual economic success

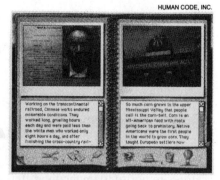

HUMAN CODE, INC.

Personalizing education via *SkyTrip America*. This multimedia program lets students record video clips and write their own stories, making them feel more connected to the learning process and minimizing the need for teachers to "teach to the middle."

and that this in turn will lead students and parents to take education more seriously than they do now.

• **Diversity.** Industrial Age advocates will compare public and private schools, suggesting that public schools offer more student and intellectual diversity. Information Age advocates will compare geographic to non-geographic schools, arguing that the latter offer far more intellectual and geographic diversity. Looking at the tiny course and teacher offerings of regional schools, as well as their narrow and homogeneous distribution of students, they cannot conceive of how any regional

HUMAN CODE, INC.

A scene from *The Cartoon History of the Universe*. Interactive, multimedia educational software allows students to peruse the past.

1. INTRODUCTION

school is intrinsically more diverse.

• **Educators' motives.** Advocates of Industrial Age education will argue the dangers of putting for-profit companies in control of education. Such companies will be out for the fast buck, hurting kids and wasting taxpayers' money in the process.

Information Age advocates will point out that schools are not currently run by altruists. Today's educators are not fundamentally different from other human beings. What counts is not the motives of educators, but whether those motives can be harnessed to serve the public interest. If parents are given multiple options and good information on those options, they will not choose exploitive and incompetent educators.

• **Individualized instruction.** Industrial Age advocates will argue that labor-intensive instruction is the same as individualized instruction. Technology in education fosters passive learning, much as television does.

Information Age advocates will counter that one-on-one instruction has been prohibitively expensive for traditional schools. Schools have had to put 20 or more students in a single classroom, often forcing teachers to "teach to the middle." Moreover, the limited choice of teachers, courses, and fellow students means that instruction may not be appropriate to the individual learner's needs. They see labor-intensive public schools as fostering a one-size-fits-all system regardless of a student's individual differences in motivation, knowledge, learning style, and ability.

• **Socialization.** Industrial Age advocates will argue that technology-intensive education is anathema to the development of social skills.

Information Age advocates will maintain that social relations can take place over an interactive, multimedia network just as they can take place in a classroom. Moreover, these are the type of social relations that people will likely have at work in the future. Today's concepts of socialization in the schools reflect an outmoded concept of the world and the workplace, for which schools have traditionally prepared children. Many athletic, cultural, and academic activities will continue to offer opportunities for traditional social-

ization. But the new balance of social relations, including different modes of interaction and increased contact with people of different ages and locales, will be more reflective of the real world that today's children will live and work in tomorrow.

The New Education Leaders

Although many regional educators are enthusiastic about new educational technology, they are unlikely to lead us into Information Age education because it is not in their self-interest to do so. It is telling that, when technology is introduced

> "[Home schoolers] are already the leading users of educational technology in the United States."

into schools, it comes in the guise of resources provided by some outside donor such as a Parent–Teacher Association, telephone company, supermarket coupon program, wealthy individual, or special tax increase.

The people who lead us into Information Age education are likely to be those who benefit from new technologies, not regional educators. These new leaders include parents. According to the Software Publishers Association, American families spent more than $500 million on educational software in 1994, almost double the $277 million spent the previous year. Leading this growth were parents buying computers to provide some degree of "home schooling."

Hard-core home schoolers, despite their reputation for anachronistic values, may be the only ones motivated enough to lead U.S. education into the Information Age. These home schoolers, who seek to completely bypass regional educators, have grown from 10,000 to over 500,000 in the last 20 years. They are already the leading users of educational technology in the United States.

Other parents do not take their children out of public schools but supplement the school curriculum with home education. These parents are also likely to be a constituency for meaningful change in education. In general, new technologies make it easier for ambitious and affluent parents to bypass the public schools. As public school budgets for extra-curricular and after-school activities shrink, parents turn to other providers to make up the difference. The dollars spent by these home schoolers on educational technology provide national educators with the research and development funds necessary to develop the next generation of educational technology.

Other advocates for the new technology will likely include such beneficiaries as star administrators and teachers who will have the potential to develop national followings, textbook and software publishers, computer and telecommunications companies, and rural and inner-city homeowners whose property values have been depressed by the comparatively inferior quality of local schools.

Industrial Age educators will fight Information Age education tooth and nail. This opposition will be hard to overcome. However, in the long run they will probably do no more than slow the implementation of an emerging and vastly improved educational system. Not only is the encroachment of information technology into children's lives inevitable, but it is critical to their future—and ours.

About the Author

James H. Snider, co-author of *Future Shop* (St. Martin's, 1992) and a former school board member, is a university fellow at Northwestern University. His address is Northwestern University, Department of Political Science, Scott Hall, 601 University Place, Evanston, Illinois 60208. Telephone 847/256-0884; e-mail jhs235@nwu.edu.

21st CENTURY CLASSROOM

by Vance Viscusi

Mr. Viscusi is an undergraduate student at Austin Peay State University in Texas.

The Virtual Classroom is virtual reality taken to its maximum potential. It can best be explained by taking you through the average day of a high school student. But first, a description of the equipment that makes the Virtual Classroom so unique is in order. The Introspection Machine (IM), is the answer to students' number one challenge to educators: How does what I am learning relate to me? The IM inspires students to answer this question by placing them in an environment in which the decisions they make result in immediate consequences. This introspective environment provides the students with the opportunity to learn about themselves while at the same time acquiring basic educational skills. The Introspection Machines have become so popular that they are affectionately called "I ams" (IMs),

referring to both the machine's name as well as its introspective capabilities. Each Virtual Classroom is equipped with approximately forty to fifty introspection booths, each one subject-specific . The IMs provide the Virtual Classroom with a peer-pressure-free environment in which the students feel free to explore their creativity and learn about themselves while acquiring a basic foundation of knowledge.

First-period English class is a creative writing class. The class begins with the teacher assigning a selection of topics, and then the students head to their booths. In the booths all decisions are made by the students; it is their world. In the virtual creative writing classroom students choose the environment that will make them most comfortable. They can control what they will hear, see, smell, feel, and taste, just as they can in all of the Virtual Classrooms. Upon entering the booth the student is greeted verbally by the Introspection Machine. The machine simply asks, "How

may I be of service today?" The student is not given an array of options. It is the student's responsibility to create the environment for interaction. For example, a student may choose the setting of a bright sunlit attic apartment, with little background noise, a hint of baked cookies in the air, and a cushy velvet seat at a hardwood desk. Near the end of every period the true value of the Introspection Machines is apparent. In this creative writing class, a student chooses to call on Maya Angelou to discuss the writing that he has worked on that day. The Introspection Machine's programming is advanced enough to allow for interactive discussion to take place so that the student may gain insight into his own work.

Second-period math class works in a similar manner, but third period American history is a little different. Although time marches on, the student hypothetically heads in the opposite direction, becoming an active participant in the historical event he or she is studying.

From *TechTrends*, April/May 1996, pp. 41-42. Reprinted with permission from the Association for Educational Communications and Technology, Washington, DC.

There are certain guidelines, however. In order to get a thorough understanding of a particular historical event, the student is required to assume the roles of a variety of people who perhaps view the same event from different perspectives. For example, while studying the Civil War the student may be required to assume the role of a Confederate infantry soldier, an African slave, a Southern widow, a Union spy, or perhaps see the war unfold through President Lincoln's eyes. You can fight at Gettysburg, be hunted down like an animal as you run for your freedom, receive the news that your husband has been killed in battle, and deliver the Emancipation Proclamation all in one week. The Virtual Classroom allows the student to experience history first hand.

On to fourth-period science: The Science Virtual Classroom provides the ultimate laboratory. With unlimited ability to arrange any type of experiment, the only limitations in the Science Virtual Classroom are those of student's imagination. A journey through blood vessels to study the circulation system is not unusual in a biology class; nor is a venture through our solar system an oddity in an astronomy class. The Science Virtual Classroom allows the student to use the entire universe as a laboratory.

A favorite among many students is the Music Virtual Classroom. Any amateur musician will tell you it is his or her dream to jam with a favorite artist. The Music Virtual Classroom makes it possible. Jam on the stage before a sold out Madison Square Garden with Aerosmith, swing with Count Basie and Duke Ellington, or sing a duet with Barbara Streisand.

Last period is foreign language class, the ultimate cultural experience. Where else can you better learn the foreign language you are studying than in the country of origin? One student spends an hour per day, five days per week in Tokyo, learning Japanese. Some days are spent strolling through the city learning to communicate and interact with sales people and other citizens, while other days are spent with a host family (which the student has created) to provide for a well-rounded cultural experience.

Virtual Classroom is the classroom of the twenty-first century. The high schools in the United States are the best in the world due to the technology of private industry. Learning is at its best in our Virtual Classrooms. The Introspection Machines have acquainted our students with the intrinsic value of education: insight. Our students have access to unlimited information, and have the freedom to be creative and innovative with this information. The only limitations students have are their own imaginations. Education is most valued when students have the opportunity to learn for themselves.

UNFILLED PROMISES

CAN TECHNOLOGY HELP CLOSE THE EQUITY GAP? MAYBE—BUT IT HASN'T HAPPENED YET

BY JANE McDONALD, WILLIAM LYNCH,
AND GREG KEARSLEY

When your school board considers plans for adopting new educational technology in your schools, how often are you told that it will bridge the learning gap between the "haves" and the "have-nots"? Since the early 1980s, the drive for educational equity has fueled school high-tech purchases—notably purchases of integrated learning systems, computer networks, satellite television, and "assistive" technology for students with disabilities.

The progress in these areas confirms that potential. But it has been our experience—confirmed by research and expert observation—that technology will not automatically satisfy equity concerns.

INTEGRATED LEARNING SYSTEMS

In the 1980s, many school districts installed integrated learning systems (ILS) in their schools. An ILS generally uses a local-area network to connect from 20 to 40 computers to

Jane McDonald is an associate professor of educational administration, William Lynch is an associate professor and director of educational technology leadership, and Greg Kearsley is a consultant and adjunct professor of educational technology leadership at the George Washington University, in Washington, D.C.

the same server, often all in the same computer lab. The server stores and distributes a set of instructional software that teaches the standard curriculum in comprehensive fashion. Entire classes of students generally go to the lab for a 40 or 50-minute period, two or three days a week.

For many school officials, the ILS has been a neat, simple solution to acquiring computers, because everything comes in one package from a single vendor. The software comes loaded on the computer, eliminating the need to buy individual software programs or deal with floppy disks. The system also features administrative software to track students' progress and generate detailed reports. Finally, the vendor installs everything and provides technical support and product updates.

In the 1980s—the heyday of the ILS—most of the systems' instructional software focused on basic arithmetic, reading, and language skills. That focus was no accident, as a great deal of federal and state money was available during that period for the education of disadvantaged, or at-risk, students, who tend to be weak in basic skills. The software approached those subjects through a series of routine drill-and-practice exercises, sometimes enlivened with graphics and audio.

The ILS drill approach does benefit some low-achieving students, according to such observers as technology writer Gerald Bailey and Kenneth Komoski of the Educational Products Information Exchange (EPIE) Institute. But the systems also are used by many students who aren't considered at-risk. Unfortunately, students of all ability levels are often bored by the repetitive and sometimes trivial nature of the programs—which some teachers refer to as "drill and kill." In addition, the design of the ILS does not involve teachers to a significant degree. In fact, teachers often use the time as a planning period, while a lab assistant supervises the students in the computer lab. When computer sessions are not integrated with the other classroom activities, teachers and students perceive them as supplemental; that's fine, except for the great amounts of money and time that schools have invested in these systems.

In the 1990s, many school administrators and teachers have turned away from the ILS approach and started using computer labs as resources for independent student work—using word-processing and other "tool" software. Many schools have distributed the computers among classrooms. In addition, grant agencies have grown leery of funding ILS acquisitions.

Students from families of limited income often have no access to computers at home

COMPUTER NETWORKS

Many school leaders today are betting on advanced telecommunications as the best way to give all students an equal educational opportunity. Powerful computer networks let students and teachers exchange e-mail or hold on-line conferences and allow them to collect information by searching through distant electronic databases. And if a school network is linked to the globe-circling Internet—or even better, the World Wide Web—the amount of available information increases immeasurably.

Suitably equipped, even the most impoverished school or school district can gain equal access to these informa-

tion troves and communication tools. Although efficient use of the Web calls for a fairly powerful computer and a speedy modem, older machines with slower and cheaper modems work fine for many network activities.

Large-scale use of the Internet does require multiple telephone lines, however, and these are scarce commodities in most schools. A school needs 20 phone lines, for example, to let 20 users access the Internet simultaneously. The calls themselves are usually at local rates, but school budgets may preclude providing service for more than a handful of networked computers. That could change in time: Already, large colleges and universities give nearly all their computer labs full Internet access. And the educational value of such access may increase as more homes acquire modems and accounts with network providers or on-line services. But remember: Although for many students, computers are a natural part of everyday life both at school and at home, students from families of limited income often have no access to computers at home. For them, school computing is their only experience with computing.

Even if students have easy access to networks, schools still face the difficulty of preparing teachers to use them effectively. Networks—and the information to which they provide access—will be used meaningfully only if they are a significant component of the curriculum. For that to happen, teachers must understand how to use networks in their classes and must have sufficient time to prepare suitable activities.

Use of computers by teachers and students to gain access to, manipulate, and generate their own information from the labyrinth of cyberspace breaks the traditional role of classroom instruction. Teachers who have solid technology training are more confident and more apt to use technology creatively as a tool to connect education to students' lives and aspirations. But unfortunately, most teachers today have neither the training nor the time to take advantage of these possibilities.

SATELLITE TELEVISION

In the 1990s, schools and corporations alike have greatly expanded their use of satellite television in formats referred to variously as teleconferences, teleclasses, and distance learning. In the K-12 world, this increase has been spurred by the U.S. Department of Education's Star Schools program, which has awarded millions of dollars to consortiums of school systems to buy equipment, develop curriculum, and train teachers. The corporate world has embraced satellite TV as a cost-effective way to train employees as well as customers.

For educators, the primary benefit of satellite television is that it allows an instructor to teach students at any location within range of the satellite signal. Each "remote" site needs a satellite dish and receiving equipment, which together cost approximately $1,000—a relatively minor expense, considering that the easy-to-use equipment can serve an entire school.

Although the interplay between students and the instructor (usually via two-way audio) falls well short of that in a standard classroom, it is sufficient for most kinds of courses. In fact, in our experience, most schools find satellite TV classes at least as effective as traditional lecture instruction in a single classroom.

Satellite technology can address the equity gap by allowing students in rural areas and inner cities to take specialized courses—such as a foreign language or advanced placement class—that their school systems cannot afford to provide. Similarly, corporations are using teleconferences to deliver employee training that normally would be uneconomical due to travel or instructional costs.

But satellite TV also has major limitations. Although the receiving equipment is inexpensive, the costs to produce and deliver the courses are enormous—running into the thousands of dollars per hour of instruction. Many of those costs are passed on to schools in programming charges. And school districts that want to become providers of satellite courses also must hire considerable technical expertise.

The potentially enormous audience that a satellite program can reach creates significant economies of scale. But most school systems (and many companies) would find it difficult to allocate the large budgets needed for TV production.

ASSISTIVE TECHNOLOGY

The educational equity gap also affects students who are disadvantaged by disabilities and handicaps. Fortunately, a broad range of "assistive" devices are available, ranging from special computer keyboards and mice to software designed to compensate for visual, hearing, physical, or mental disabilities. Such technology allows handicapped students to participate fully in class activities (or perform a job) and have learning opportunities similar to those enjoyed by their nondisabled peers.

So far, however, schools have been slow to adopt assistive technology, due to its high cost and the small numbers of students who may need it at a given school. What's more, teachers and other staff members (including those with special education backgrounds) who are trained in the use of assistive technology are even more scarce than teachers who are trained in other areas of educational technology.

In many communities, then, the burden of buying and using assistive technology falls on the families of students with disabilities. And that naturally leaves behind children who need this extra help but come from poor families. The current emphasis on "mainstreaming" or "inclusion" of special education students in regular classrooms and the influence of the Americans with Disabilities Act should increase the role of assistive technology in the years to come.

THE ROOT OF THE PROBLEM

As these examples illustrate, technology does have considerable potential to reduce the learning gap between the haves and have-nots. Indeed, hundreds of schools, along with other organizations, are exploring this potential. Yet those efforts, so far, are small compared to the need.

As the schools' experience with integrated learning systems shows, solutions that appear to help disadvantaged students may contain pitfalls. The ILS experience has proven false the notion that disadvantaged students need computing activities that are fundamentally different from those of other students. And the ILS experience demonstrates (once again) that technological reforms fail when teachers are not involved meaningfully.

As for computer networks, satellite television, and assistive technology, a common theme emerges: Schools need money to buy up-to-date equipment and software—and, just as important, to pay for teacher training and technical support. Poor choices in technology acquisition and teacher training drain scarce resources and put students in socioeconomically depressed areas at a further disadvantage compared to those in more affluent areas.

Solving the money problem is difficult but not a pie-in-the-sky proposition. Many communities—even cash-strapped cities—could reallocate a small share of the millions often spent on sport stadiums, convention centers, and other public works to invest in technology. Large technology corporations certainly could be more generous in donating equipment to schools and colleges and in subsidizing service and support. And as for society at large, the nation's current investment in educational technology for public schools— some $4 billion annually—could be measured against expenditures in other areas and adjusted accordingly.

These solutions are easier stated than accomplished, of course. Changing the public's priorities requires, among other things, better leadership from board members and school officials. Most school leaders—like their counterparts in other organizations—are unaware of how technology can reduce the gap between the haves and have-nots. Many senior-level school officials don't have firsthand experience with technology and are uncomfortable with the responsibility of acquiring and implementing it. (Schools of educational administration have contributed to this situation by failing to prepare administrators for these roles.)

School districts also need to revitalize their skills in planning for technological change. Many districts have technology plans, but often those plans are outdated and inflexible. In other districts, the use of educational technology remains almost completely ad hoc. Careful planning can ensure that educational technology is implemented in high-payoff areas, such as serving disadvantaged students, and that adequate attention is paid to using the technology, not just acquiring it. Flexible planning ensures that districts can adapt to new technological trends.

Backed by solid plans, school boards will more easily persuade their communities to increase their investments in technology. Revitalized district-level planning can also provide grist for national efforts to formulate technology policies. If district ideas can filter up to converge with federal and state grant programs and evolving legislation, technology may indeed begin to bridge the gap between the haves and the have-nots.

Curriculum and Instructional Design

A curriculum is a plan for action that includes strategies for achieving desired goals. Curriculum design is the organizational pattern or structure of a curriculum. There is a broad level that involves basic value choices and a specific level that involves the technical planning and implementation of curricular elements. The curricular elements are needs, problems, goals, objectives, content, learning activities, and evaluation procedures. These elements can be used as a blueprint for instructional strategies and human interfaces. For example, interactivity is a learning activity that can be used in various learning environments. Interface design provides learners with a comfortable way to manipulate data and other learning objects and in so doing increases learner interaction.

In addition, it is necessary to provide adaptive learning facilities that use graphic user interfaces to provide learning opportunities that meet the learner on the appropriate learning plane. In order to provide such a curriculum, teachers and designers must infuse technology-based learning tools into teacher-designed implemented lesson plans. If this can be done, each school could contribute to the creation of a technology-based interactive instructional curriculum library.

Articles in this unit provide specific strategies and tactics for designing, developing, integrating, and delivering curriculum-driven, technology-based learning and it begins with William Milheim's discussion of interactivity and its overall purpose in various learning environments. He describes its benefits and its specific use in computer-based education.

In "The Relevance of HCI Guidelines for Educational Interfaces," David Gilmore presents Human Computer Interface (HCI) guidelines for interface design. Gilmore lists the strengths of direct manipulation as an interaction technique. He demonstrates how good performance can be associated with low rates of transfer. Then, Akpinar and Hartley discuss the details of how interactive computer-assisted learning (CAL) environments are able to adapt to different styles of learning and teaching. They describe the design principles for interactive, adaptive learning environments using a module on the learning of fractions.

Finally, the article "Design and Application of Teaching Software" focuses on the graphical user interface (GUI) and the benefits of the common screen interface across all environments. Emphasis is on the advantage of navigation and interactive self-paced instruction made possible by the GUI.

Looking Ahead: Challenge Questions

Assume you are a mathematics teacher. How would you design a criteria sheet to aid in the selection of instructional technology components for infusion into the curriculum and your daily lesson plans? How would you justify such selections? How would you spread the use of such a strategy to other teachers?

UNIT 2

INTERACTIVITY AND COMPUTER-BASED INSTRUCTION

ABSTRACT

Interactivity is one of the most important factors in the design and development of effective computer-based instructional materials. The following article describes this instructional component, its overall purpose in various learning environments, benefits that can be gained from its utilization, and its specific use within computer-based instruction. A number of strategies are also provided to assist instructional designers in their utilization of this significant program element.

WILLIAM D. MILHEIM

Penn State Great Valley, Malvern

INTRODUCTION

Within computer-based instruction, there are a number of factors that contribute to the overall effectiveness of a specific instructional module including general screen design, the appropriate utilization of graphics and text, and effective testing strategies, among others. When combined appropriately, these factors provide computer-based materials that meet the requirements of the instructional content as well as the learning needs of a specific group of learners.

One of the most important of these instructional attributes is interactivity, or the two-way communication that can occur between the instructional medium (in this case, the computer) and the learner. While other factors obviously influence the overall effectiveness of an instructional program, interactivity may be one of the most important, since it directly impacts the overall communication between the educational materials and the intended learners.

The purpose of this article is to provide a detailed description of interactivity as a general instructional attribute as well as its specific use within computer-based materials. A number of instructional strategies for integrating this component within a computer-based lesson are also presented.

DEFINING INTERACTIVITY

As described above, interactivity can be defined simply as the two-way communication that occurs between learners and the educational materials that are presented during an instructional lesson. In this sense, material is provided through an instructional medium to an intended learner, who responds in some way to this mediated presentation, which then, in turn, adapts to the learner's responses.

Traditionally, this type of interaction has been provided through media such as programmed instruction, group discussion, role plays, and interactive video [1], although chalkboards, media kits, and overhead projectors may also be conducive to interactive strategies [2].

In terms of specific interactive components, Borsook and Higginbotham-Wheat list a number of key ingredients for effective interactivity, generally focused on their use within computer-based instruction [3]. These factors include:

- *Immediacy of response* so that learners can retrieve information when needed without delay;
- *Non-sequential access to information* where material is responsive to audience requirements as required;
- *Adaptability* where communication is based on audience needs or requests;
- *Bi-directional communication* where both the learner and the computer present information; and

"Interactivity and Computer-Based Instruction," William D. Milheim, *Journal of Educational Technology Systems*, Volume 24, No. 3, pp. 225-233, Baywood Publishing Company, Inc., 1995-96.

• *Grain size* (the length of time between user responses) where learners are able to frequently interrupt presentations or initiate specific actions.

The importance of feedback and a variety of user options are also listed by these authors as important components of interactivity.

In addition, interactivity can be viewed from both quantitative and qualitative perspectives [4]. From a quantitative viewpoint, this factor can be seen as a fixed number (or ratio) of questions included within a specific instructional module, with interactivity simply providing an increased opportunity for the learner to produce appropriate responses and receive feedback. On the other hand, the qualitative view of interaction includes a much stronger utilization of cognitive psychology and a greater emphasis on the learner's role in actually controlling the interactions within a given lesson. From this view, interactivity focuses on the cognitive engagement of the learner, including the intentional and purposeful processing of lesson information [4] as learned by the student through a true dialog with the computer [5].

BENEFITS OF INTERACTIVE LEARNING

Interactivity has been discussed by Baker-Albaugh as paramount to good instruction and a requirement for most current instructional computer applications [2]. A number of benefits from the use of interactive learning in a variety of instructional environments are also described by this author including:

• Increased student interest,
• Higher cognitive processing,
• Development of cooperative learning skills,
• Teacher involvement,
• Curriculum integration, and
• Teacher/student collaboration.

Traditional passive learning situations (books, videotapes, classroom lectures, etc.) often do not include significant interaction since the writer, actor, or instructor typically supplies the knowledge that the learner is expected to simply absorb [6]. Even with these media, however, interactivity can be included to some degree through increased instructor participation or the instructional manipulation of the media presentation (e.g., breaking an existing videotape into individual segments that can be used by individuals or utilized in group-led interaction) [7].

In addition to its educational potential, interactivity is also specifically appropriate in corporate training situations where this attribute is a key component for effective instructional design. In support of this view, Smith states that interactive systems in corporate settings allow trainees to control their own learning and free trainers to design new instructional programs or handle individual problems [7].

INTERACTIVITY IN COMPUTER-BASED INSTRUCTION

In the past, interactive programs were primarily developed and utilized with mechanical teaching machines or programmed texts [7] where the learner overtly responded to the presented material and was not merely a passive recipient of the instructional information. While earlier programmed instruction was generally linear, with learners simply using recall from short-term memory as the primary learning strategy [8], later programs utilized branching instruction and adaptive strategies as needed to increase the effectiveness of a given instructional module.

Hazen strongly supports the overall importance of interactivity within computer-based learning, describing interaction as the most important feature of instructional computing software [9]. Borsook and Higginbotham-Wheat agree with this position, stating that this potential for interactivity actually sets the computer apart from other types of instructional media [3]. Heines attaches even more importance to interactivity within computer-based instruction, stating that the medium is neither instructionally nor financially justifiable without meaningful interaction [10].

Based on the importance of interactivity within computer-based instruction, Hannafin provides a number of specific interactive characteristics that directly relate to this medium [4]. These functions include:

• *Confirmation* for verification that student learning has occurred or that specific branching has been executed;
• *Pacing control* for lesson speed or the execution of specific procedures;
• *Inquiry options* for student questions, help routines, or the verification of completed lesson sections;
• *Navigation control* through menus and/or allowing students access to various sections of the overall program; and
• *Elaboration* where students are able to interactively combine previous knowledge with new information from the instructional program.

Interactivity within computer-based instruction can also be defined as either reactive or proactive, based on the purpose of the interaction within a specific lesson [11]. Reactive strategies, for example, refer to relatively simple responses by learners such as pressing the space bar to advance the program or simple menu choices which generally do not require hypothesis generation or a deeper understanding of the material to be learned. Proactive strategies, on the other hand, are based on a constructivistic approach to teaching and learning and involve learners as significant decision makers in their own learning through self-initiated activities and self-monitoring. In addition, these two strategies can be combined into an interactive model where both strategies are incorporated into a single learning system that provides the learner with a personalized learning experience that includes beneficial aspects from both perspectives.

A similar continuum has also been discussed by Rhodes and Azbell who describe four similar forms of interactivity within computer-assisted interactive video [12]. These levels include:

- *Reactive* control where users have very limited control of program content and structure, with many of the interactions predetermined by an instructional designer;
- *Coactive* control where users have somewhat more control over lesson content and structure through learner choices concerning feedback and presentation style;
- *Proactive* control where learners can make decisions about what will be presented and how it will be presented within a given course; and
- *Transactive* control where users communicate through and interact with a wide range of media and develop their own problem definitions, analytic procedures, and potential solutions to various problems.

RESEARCH CONCERNING INTERACTIVITY AND COMPUTER-BASED INSTRUCTION

As shown earlier, interactivity is assumed to be an extremely important instructional variable that can be used to increase the effectiveness and affective appeal of computer-based instruction. However, there appear to be relatively few studies that specifically investigate the effectiveness or use of interactive strategies within individual instructional lessons.

One of the most comprehensive descriptions concerning the use of interactivity within computer-based instruction is provided by Pritchard, Micceri, and Barrett who evaluated 213 computer-based corporate training packages [13]. The topics for these instructional programs were quite diverse and included content areas such as computer literacy, applications training, accounting, marketing, and sales techniques, among others.

The results of this research concerning the interaction between the various computer programs and their intended learners showed that:

- Approximately 95 percent of the programs provided feedback to the learner in some manner;
- Nearly 50 percent of the courses utilized positive feedback to the learner during more than half of a given course;
- On-line help was available in approximately 40 percent of the programs, with only 15 percent providing context-sensitive help;
- Virtually all of the courses prompted the learner in some way when necessary to continue the lesson, although single keystrokes were the most common (82%) form of user interaction; and
- In general, the courses included only a very shallow level of interactivity which did not stimulate the learner to think deeply about the instructional material.

Although this study is somewhat dated, it does indicate the relatively high amount of interactivity within corporate computer-based instruction, although these interactions were generally lower level and did not require extensive learner engagement in the learning process.

A second study by Schaffer and Hannafin was designed to compare the effects of various types of interactivity on learning from an interactive video (multimedia-based) lesson covering the production of graphic effects for television [14]. The learners for this study were high school students divided into four treatment groups of gradually increasing interactivity including: 1) a video only group, 2) a treatment using video and embedded questions, 3) a group with video as well as questions with feedback for learner responses, and 4) a full treatment including all of the above interactions plus branching to previous video segments when learning was not demonstrated.

Results from this study indicated a number of important points concerning interactivity and computer-based interaction including:

- Significant effects based on the amount and type of interactivity;
- The highest level of recall associated with the fully interactive question;
- The longest time on task for the learners in the fully interactive group; and
- The shortest time on task associated with the simple video presentation (the least interactive).

While these results obviously demonstrate the instructional power of interactive materials, they also indicate the increased instructional time on task required for these treatments to be effective.

A later study using somewhat similar treatment groups with university students, compared the learning effectiveness of an interactive video (multimedia) sequence about pharmaceuticals to a linear videotape presentation utilizing limited interactivity (stop/start video options and a related test booklet) [15]. In comparison to the earlier research, this study showed no significant differences between groups for student achievement or time on task, although students did express a significant preference for the interactive videodisc.

INSTRUCTIONAL STRATEGIES FOR UTILIZING INTERACTIVITY IN COMPUTER-BASED INSTRUCTION

Based on the descriptive and empirical literature described above, the following strategies are suggested for use by instructional designers and developers to increase the effective utilization of interactivity within computer-based programs. While this list is certainly not exhaustive, it should provide general guidance for the use of this important instructional component within computer-based learning environments.

1. Design Interactive Programs with Comprehensive Navigation Options that are Easy to Use

While early programmed instruction was often quite linear in nature, current systems tend to be much more interactive, with complex menus, help systems, branching, and other navigation aids. Within this context, Smith suggests using menu titles that are descriptive and interesting, help functions that can be called up at any time, branching based on learner's responses, as well as program modules of appropriate length to reduce the boredom that may occur with extremely long instructional segments [7].

Newer technologies have also significantly improved the ability of students to move through and interact with computer-based instructional programs. Hardware devices such as light pens and mice allow students to point to items on the computer screen in any order [10], and remove a learner's dependence on typing skills for data input and manipulation. Other hardware options such as voice recognition using natural language [4] and virtual reality have the potential to more fully normalize the interaction between the learner and the computer and further increase a student's ability to effectively interact with a specific instructional lesson.

2. Utilize Questions that Require Students to Significantly Interact with Instructional Material

Simple "electronic page turning" is generally not sufficiently interactive to increase a learner's attention to the material within a computer-based program. Interactivity should instead require deeper cognitive processing and avoid less significant interactions, such as verbatim questions that merely require students to write down textual information that appears on the computer screen [9]. The learner should also be encouraged to relate new material to prior learning and construct elaborate mental representations [8] instead of simply responding to the information within the computer program.

Hannafin lists several strategies that may help promote cognitive engagement and deeper processing including [4]:

- *Queries* where learners can pose questions rather than simply provide answers to questions generated by the computer program;
- *Notetaking* which encourages students to elaborate based on notes they have taken during an instructional presentation;
- *Hypertext* which allows learners to access computer-based materials based on self-assigned pathways through the content; and
- *Cooperative dialogue* among groups of students using computers to elaborate basic instructional content and perhaps help overcome problems resulting from insufficient numbers of computers.

As an additional option, students may be permitted to manipulate existing information that has previously been entered into an instructional program rather than personally inputting all of the relevant data (a non-relevant interactive task). In addition to saving time, this option allows students to consider and respond to a large number of information parameters [10], which can be significantly more effective than simply manipulating relatively small test cases that must be input each time an instructional program is executed.

3. Evaluate Learner Responses in a Manner that is Personally Meaningful to the User

Simply stating that an answer is correct or incorrect is not sufficient for effective learning to occur. The feedback from the computer program to each student should be personally relevant and closely tied to the specific answer provided by the learner. Hazen, for example, suggests using a variety of feedback types including informative, confirmational (indicating whether performance was correct or not), motivational, and instructional (providing explanations, hints, or cues toward the correct response) [9]. Errors or variations in the format of the learner's response to a specific question may also be allowed when the answer format is not significant for the content being learned.

On the other hand, there may also be occasions where there is no need to evaluate a learner's response after each question [10], particularly when these answers are not specifically relevant to the mastery of particular program objectives. Care must be taken, however, to include evaluation as often as required (based on lesson content, audience characteristics, etc.) so that students consistently know how well they are performing as they move through a specific lesson.

CONCLUSION

Based on the idea that students want to be active rather than passive learners [2], this article has presented a number of factors related to interactivity in general as well as its specific utilization within computer-based instructional materials. When taken as a whole, these factors define interactivity as an instructional strategy that is extremely important for the delivery of effective instruction in a variety of corporate and educational settings.

According to Reimer, interaction translates into more effective education since its use allows students to learn faster, retain knowledge longer, and transfer and apply knowledge more readily in real situations [6]. It is hoped that the above discussion will assist instructional designers and developers in their use of this important instructional variable within computer-based instruction and training.

References

1. D. R. Hudspeth, Interactivity and Design of Case Materials, *Performance Improvement Quarterly*, 4:1, pp. 63–72, 1991.

2. P. R. Baker-Albaugh, Definitions of Interactive Learning: What We See Is Not What We Get, *Journal of Instruction Delivery Systems*, 7:3, pp. 36–39, 1993.

3. T. K. Borsook and N. Higginbotham-Wheat, Interactivity: What Is It and What Can It Do for Computer-Based Instruction? *Educational Technology*, 31:10, pp. 11–17, 1991.

4. M. J. Hannafin, Interaction Strategies and Emerging Instructional Technologies: Psychological Perspectives, *Canadian Journal of Educational Communication*, 18:3, pp. 167–179, 1989.

5. D. H. Jonassen, Introduction to Part II, Interactive Designs for Courseware, in *Instructional Designs for Microcomputer Courseware*, D. J. Jonassen (ed.), Lawrence Erlbaum Associates, Hillsdale, New Jersey, pp. 97–102, 1988.

6. K. Reimer, Taking the Active Route Means Better Results, *Computing Canada*, 18:19, p. 51, 1992.

7. J. Smith, How to Design Interactive Training Programs, *Training*, 20:12, pp. 30–45, 1983.

8. D. H. Jonassen, Interactive Lesson Designs: A Taxonomy, *Educational Technology*, 26:6, pp. 7–16, 1985.

9. M. Hazen, Instructional Software Design Principles, *Educational Technology*, 25:11, pp. 18–23, 1985.

10. J. M. Heines, Interactive Means Active: Learner Involvement in CBT, *Data Training*, 4:4, pp. 48–53, 1985.

11. J. O. Thompson and S. Jorgensen, How Interactive Is Instructional Technology? Alternative Models for Looking at Interactions between Learners and Media, *Educational Technology*, 29:2, pp. 24–26, 1989.

12. D. M. Rhodes and J. W. Azbell, Designing Interactive Video Instruction Professionally, *Training and Development Journal*, 39:12, pp. 31–33, 1985.

13. W. H. Pritchard, Jr., T. Micceri, and A. J. Barrett, A Review of Computer-Based Training Materials: Current State of the Art (Instruction and Interaction), *Educational Technology*, 29:7, pp. 16–22, 1989.

14. L. C. Schaffer and M. J. Hannafin, The Effects of Progressive Interactivity on Learning from Interactive Video, *Educational Communication and Technology Journal*, 34:2, pp. 89–96, 1986.

15. J. A. Summers, Effect of Interactivity upon Student Achievement, Completion Intervals, and Affective Perceptions, *Journal of Educational Technology Systems*, 19:1, pp. 53–57, 1990–91.

The Relevance of HCI Guidelines for Educational Interfaces

David J. Gilmore

ESRC Center for Research in Development, Instruction, and Training, Psychology Department, University of Nottingham

Human-computer interaction (HCI) has gathered many guidelines for interface design and has discovered the strengths of direct manipulation as an interaction technique. However, to date it has been generally assumed that these guidelines apply generically across all applications. This article challenges this assumption in relation to educational software. First, it is considered why educational software is different from other products, such as databases or word processors. Then, a variety of evidence is presented that suggests that designing for learning might be harder than designing for use. Current guidelines are good for optimizing current performance, not future performance.

The experiments presented show how good performance can be associated with low rates of transfer, how poor initial performance can give rise to more robust knowledge for harder problems, and how command giving rather than direct action, may produce better learning. A full psychological explanation is still awaited, but one can speculate that (a) interfaces that encourage planning, rather than situated action, may produce better learning; (b) learners need a "sense of engagement" (Hutchins, Hollan, & Norman, 1986) with the learning materials, not the interface; and (c) the interface, the learning context, or the tasks may individually or together cause changes in strategy from implicit to explicit or vice versa.

It is commonly believed that interface guidelines, principles, and recommendations are generic and application independent. To a certain degree this assumption must hold true, or else human-computer interaction (HCI) would not have succeeded to the extent that it has. My concern is that for

Requests for reprints should be sent to David J. Gilmore, ESRC Center for Research in Development, Instruction, and Training, Psychology Department, University of Nottingham, Nottingham, NG7 2RD, UK. E-mail: david.gilmore@nottingham.ac.uk.

systems where the user's goal is substantially different from performance of the task at hand, the guidelines and principles may be misleading.

TWO FOCI OF LEARNING

I should distinguish between two sorts of learning that one can refer to in relation to HCI. First, there is learning about the application being used, and second, there is the use of educational technology to support learning about some external domain; external, that is, to the computer interface and application.

In the first instance, the emphasis is on the transparency of the interface, because users want to focus on the goal of writing, say, rather than on the details of using the word processor. There is an implicit assumption in this model that improving the ease of use of the word processor will improve performance on the external goals. This can be expressed in terms of a reduction in the amount of cognitive effort being directed at the interface, making more attention available for the task goals.

In the second instance, the emphasis is not on how well the user achieves the current task goals, but on how well he or she learns about the nature of that task in some general, abstract way.

Another way of thinking of this difference is that in the first instance it can be assumed that the user knows how to write and simply has to learn how to use an interface, whereas in the second case the user has to learn to use the interface and also to discover the generalities and abstractions of the domain.

Laurillard (1993), writing about educational technology in a University setting, stated that

The student's reflection must be centered on the content of learning, on the meaning of their interaction, not on how to operate the program. *This means the interface must be operationally transparent* [italics added] . . . the introduction of icons and mouse clicks has brought operational transparency to many types of computer tool. (p. 204)

Although the first and last statements are acceptable, the connection between them (italicized) is not based on any scientific evidence. Rather it is based on the assumption (widely believed) that interface guidelines and principles apply uniformly to all kinds of information technology.

WHY ARE EDUCATIONAL SYSTEMS DIFFERENT?

The aforementioned distinction raises one difference between conventional systems and educational systems, in that the user has more to learn in the educational context.

Another dimension on which the systems vary is the focal goal of the user. There has been a tendency within HCI to imagine users as having a single main goal to be achieved (e.g., Card, Moran, & Newell, 1983), but once one accepts multiple goals, the question becomes, which of these many goals is the user focused on?

Taking systems as a whole, it is clear that there are multiple goals that a user may have, which are at such different levels that it does not make sense to think of them as subgoals of each other. Thus, although some argue that Goals, Operators, Methods, and Selection analyses (see Card et al., 1983) are flawed because we cannot be sure what the user's goal is, these criticisms are themselves flawed, because they still tend to assume a single goal.

In fact, users can have interface goals (e.g., trying out some new features), current task goals (getting this paper into American Psychological Association format), long-term task goals (e.g., making the argument in this paper broader and more accessible), and personal goals (e.g., to be perceived as demonstrating the value of a psychological perspective). Although one can think of some of these as subservient to others, it is hard to perceive them as subgoals in the conventional sense.

In educational situations, the focal goal ideally will be a long-term educational goal (e.g., "I want to learn about . . ." or "I want to pass the exam"), but it often will be a personal goal (e.g., maintaining peer respect). Interface goals and current task goals in an educational system are often subservient to personal and interface goals (peer respect is often related to appearing to be in control of the "interface"—whether a computer interface or not). The existence of "teacher driving" as a concept in education is an indication of the extent to which learners master the control of the system as easily as they master the material to be learned.

Although word processing, for example, contains long-term goals (e.g., rhetorical goals), few writers seem to be driven by them. However, it is worth pointing out that there are writers who have argued that direct manipulation word processors impair the quality of writing—precisely because they shift the focal goal from the communication of some argument to the production of a paper that looks good and uses the word processor's new features.

Of course, this argument may be rejected by claiming that it is too hard a problem to consider the richness of human goals and that science traditionally progresses by simplifying and reducing problems to a more manageable scale. However, although this may work for the gradual accretion of scientific knowledge, it always follows that any resulting conclusions should not be applied without careful consideration of which issues have been omitted. In many respects the argument advanced in this article is that the omitted issues have a serious impact on the applicability of our knowledge.

DOES THE DIFFERENCE IN GOAL FOCUS MATTER?

The implicit assumption behind most HCI research is that factors influencing current-task performance do not interact with performance of the other goals that an individual might have. As mentioned already, the psychological justification for this is probably based on the belief that cognitive effort saved by good interface design can be reallocated to other more important activities.

An alternative perspective would be that design for achievement of goals at these different levels does interact with performance. In other words, designing for performance at the current task may impair performance on personal or long-term goals.

Although the first perspective is most commonly held, the latter is equally plausible; this article will illustrate this by focusing on three assumptions made by the first perspective:

- Performance on a system should relate closely to learning of the system.
- Whatever is learned in using a system should transfer to new interfaces to the same system.
- Interfaces that are good for performance should be good for learning.

The following sections will illustrate how these assumptions are not necessarily true.

Performance and Learning

The assumption that performance should be closely related to learning can only hold where it is certain that performance is based on skills being taught.

In a study related to modeling of real-time performance, we found a good example of how apparent poor performance may be a good thing in learning. Using two different training regimes (varying in difficulty), we found the group that performed worst in training performed best on a final harder task.

The context for this study was an Air Traffic Control game in which players had to direct airplanes from a given entry point to an airport or exit point, in real time and avoiding collisions and near misses. The game operated in 15-sec cycles, with the planes moving in discrete steps; this required some practice to become familiar. Within these 15-sec cycles the user could give commands to as many planes as possible. Giving a command involves selecting a plane on either the "Record Strip" or on the radar screen and then indicating either (or both) the angle through which the plane should turn or the altitude to which it should ascend or descend. Within one 15-sec cycle, a good player might be able to command 3 or 4 different planes.

Our interest was in whether people learned better while controlling individual planes (becoming familiar with the movement patterns of single planes), or whether learning about configurational properties was more useful, even if this was at the cost of learning about individual patterns of movement.

All participants learned by controlling the same nine aircraft from the same entry point to the same exit point (no airports), either as nine individual trials (9 × 1), or as three trials with three planes to be controlled concurrently (3 × 3).

Following this learning phase, all participants were tested on the same scenario of eight planes to be controlled. These eight planes arrived on screen at regular intervals. Thus, although they did not appear simultaneously, they were on the radar screen at the same time (as shown in Figure 1).

Results

Learning phase. The easiest performance comparison is between the number of deviations between actual and ideal exit points (in altitude, bearing, and location). These results show that the participants controlling nine individual planes (9 × 1) performed significantly better than those controlling three groups of three planes (3 × 3). The mean discrepancies were 0.35 and 2.22, respectively.

Test phase. The reverse pattern revealed itself in the test phase—the 3 × 3 participants performed significantly better than the 9 × 1. For the number

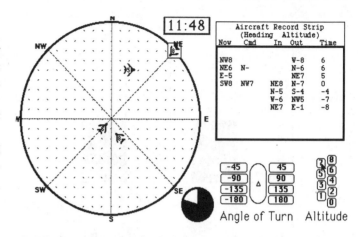

FIGURE 1 An example screen from the Air Traffic Control game with multiple aircraft to be controlled.

of discrepancies, the scores were 2.21 and 4.31, respectively.

Closer analysis of the protocols revealed that the primary source of this difference was a substantial difference in the speed at which a plane was instructed to turn (for planes not required to fly straight across the screen—means = 5.2 and 1.54 for the 9 × 1 and 3 × 3 groups, respectively—see Figure 2). The 3 × 3 group appeared to have learned the benefits of keeping planes away from the center of the radar screen where congestion occurs (turning a plane early does not automatically lead to higher score, but it makes the task easier to manage).

Summary

This study serves as a good illustration that performance-oriented computer-based learning can fail to provide good strategic learning for future performance.

It is important to remember that the two groups were not equal in their original performance, but that the 9 × 1 group were significantly better in the learning phase. The crux of the matter here is that the training received by the 9 × 1 group did not adequately prepare them for the realities of the test phase.

A clear requirement for systems design is that there is an unambiguous statement of the learning goals as well as the performance goals for a system. Although all good teachers know the importance of articulating educational goals, it is not clear that those building interfaces to educational systems address themselves to both educational and performance goals.

Transfer of Learning

In one of our first experiments that began to look at these issues, we examined a task that seems to give rise to implicit learning (automatic, uncon-

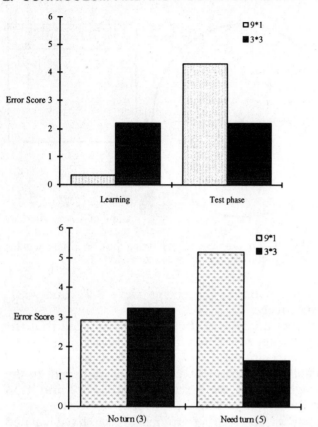

FIGURE 2 Results from the Air Traffic Control game for all planes (top) and comparing those flying straight across and those requiring a turn (bottom). The y axis indicates an error score based on deviations in altitude, bearing, and location from the desired position for each aircraft.

scious learning). One of our questions was whether this implicit learning would show genuine task-based abstractions about the task itself, or whether it was interface specific.

The task involved learning to control a city transport system—the participant enters a pair of input values (bus interval and parking fee), and these are used as input to a pair of simultaneous equations, to determine a pair of output values (bus load and parking availability).

These give rise to a system whose behavior is both complex enough that learning is hard, and sufficiently simple that people learn to control the system within 20–30 minutes (see, e.g., Sanderson, 1989). No participants ever learn the actual equations.[1]

In the experiment we gave people either a congruent or an incongruent interface (see Figure 3), and we gave a "mental model"-like description of the system and the essence of the equations un-

[1]The equations are $bl = 220bi + 80pf$, and $pa = 8pf - 2.5bi$, where bl = bus load, pa = parking availability, bi = bus interval, and pf = parking fee. Given that the input values for bi and pf were on similar scales, bl is primarily influenced by bi and pa by pf. It is this that gives rise to congruent and incongruent graphical interfaces.

derlying it (without the coefficients) to half of the participants. The nature of the congruence/incongruence manipulation was that the primary variable for the output on the x axis was represented on the input graph's x axis for the congruent interface and on the input graph's y axis for the incongruent interface.

The mental model, when provided, gave participants an indication of the role of the input variables in determining the output values, but without giving any indication that equations underlay the system. The model included statements such as

So, if the parking fee is increased, more people will travel by bus and there will be more available parking spaces, but if the bus interval is increased, then fewer people will travel by bus and there will be fewer available spaces.

According to the implicit learning literature, the mental model should be of no assistance in performance, and only the group given the mental model should show verbalizable knowledge about the task, which should be uncorrelated with performance.

Furthermore, HCI would suggest that the congruent interface should be easier for performance and, by assumption, for learning also. The learning was tested by getting participants to transfer to a textual input version of the task in which participants had to type in the input values as digits.

Results

The main dependent variables for this task were time taken and the number of moves necessary to reach the target values. The results for both of these variables are very similar (Figure 4). For the learning phase, they show an interaction between interface and model provision and improved performance with the congruent interface, whereas in the transfer phase there is no interaction and only a main effect of model provision.

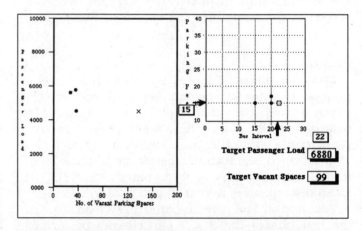

FIGURE 3 Incongruent interface for City Transport Task.

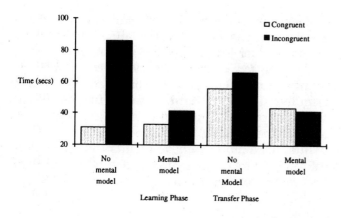

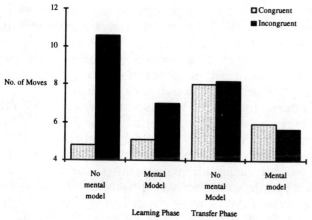

FIGURE 4 Results for time taken (top) and number of moves (bottom) for the City Transport Task.

During the learning phase, the provision of the mental model is of no benefit to those using the congruent interface, whereas it makes a substantial difference to those using the incongruent interface. Furthermore, the congruent interface is easier than the incongruent interface.

On transfer to the textual interface, the results show a quite different pattern: Possession of the mental model is critical to success, and it makes no difference which interface was used during learning. It should also be noted that none of the participants could answer the questionnaire of verbalizable knowledge particularly well, but as expected, the mental models group were better. Furthermore, their performance on the transfer interface makes it appear that transfer is a task requiring explicit knowledge, because it behaves very similarly to questionnaire performance.

Discussion

The critical point here is that initial performance was not correlated with useful learning. The two groups without the mental model performed very differently in the learning stage, but were indistinguishable in the test. Similarly, but less so, the two groups provided with the mental model performed differently in the learning stage, but were indistin-

guishable in the test phase. Conversely, the two groups of congruent interface users were indistinguishable during learning but were different at test.

One interpretation of these results is that the congruent interface supports performance through context-specific effects. Thus, when the context changes, performance is impaired. The fact that this was not so for the incongruent interface group (they got better when the context changes) suggests that the context specificity is related to the congruence of the interface. It is possible, therefore, that the very features that make it easy to use also make it poor for learning.

The fact that the mental model group with the congruent interface was not impaired by the transfer could have two interpretations—either they were learning about the task differently (even though achieving the same performance), or else they had a residual memory for the mental model instructions that they could apply on transfer (the experiment lasted about 30 min). Neither of these is entirely satisfactory—some combination may be better; further research is still needed.

We have conducted other studies that show that use of the graphical interface impairs transfer to the textual interface, but learning of the textual interface supports transfer of knowledge to the graphical. However, the latter group never performs as well on the graphical interface as those who have always used a graphical interface—suggesting that their original learning may have been different.

These studies demonstrate how interface decisions can affect performance and learning separately. There is, of course, an apparently trivial explanation—namely, that the congruent interface can be used without understanding, and therefore it is not surprising that there is little evidence of learning. However, proponents of this explanation must recognize that allowing the design of the interface to be driven by performance concerns will lead to systems that may be used easily without understanding.

Performance Impairing Learning

A more general issue is whether interfaces designed using principles such as direct manipulation (intended to improve performance) are good interfaces for learning. Svendsen (1991) provided a clear suggestion that direct manipulation may not be a good principle for interfaces for learning. Using the Tower of Hanoi as his task, he showed how participants performed better on a transfer task (a larger tower) when they had used a command language interface rather than a direct manipulation interface.

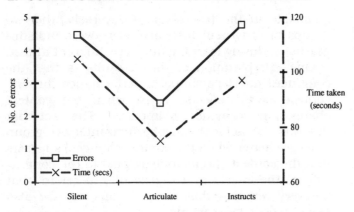

FIGURE 5 Performance on a four-ring Tower of Hanoi, with the number of errors on the right hand *y* axis and time taken (seconds) on the left-hand *y* axis.

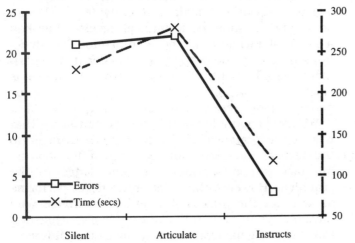

FIGURE 6 Subsequent performance on a five-ring Tower, with the number of errors on the right-hand *y* axis and time taken (seconds) on the left-hand *y* axis.

However, his results could be due to particular features of the interfaces he used, with the generality of his results open to doubt—especially given that direct manipulation is widely accepted as a good thing. For this reason, we replicated the study without using computer interfaces at all.

In our study, participants did the Tower of Hanoi themselves, either silently or while articulating their actions, or else they gave instructions to the experimenter about which disks to move. Thus, two groups of participants engaged in direct manipulation of the disks, and two groups were articulating equivalent information about disk movements.

The learning was performed with a four-ring tower, whereas the test required them to perform the task with a five-ring tower. Time taken and the number of erroneous moves were both measured.

Results

On the four-ring tower, we find that the group articulating their own actions made fewest errors and were faster than either of the other two groups

(see Figure 5). Only the time measure was significant. However, it appears that articulating your own actions is good for performance. However, on transfer to the five-ring tower, there was no difference between the two groups engaging in direct action—both of whom found the task hard. However, the instruction-giving group was significantly faster and less error-prone on the five-ring tower (see Figure 6).

Thus, once more we have results that show good performance in the learning phase being uncorrelated with transfer performance.

Summary

From this study, it is difficult to be certain what gave rise to the huge effect of giving instructions. However, now that we can be confident that it is not the artifact of a particular interface, we can repeat it with computer interfaces and store more complete protocols about performance.

Informally noticed in this study was a major difference between the articulators and instruction givers with regard to the time at which the move was described. For those articulating their own actions, the articulation came after the action had occurred (it was effectively a commentary), whereas instruction givers were obliged to give the instruction first, before seeing the effect of the action.

Thus, the articulators' behavior may be driven by the context and then commented on, whereas the instructors were required to think about good moves and evaluate different possibilities before giving an instruction. It could be argued that instruction giving leads to a strategy that involves more planning and forethought, and it may be this that is beneficial to learning.

Subsequent experiments in Norway (Heim & Svendsen, personal communication, January 1994) have shown that the effect diminishes if the direct manipulation interface is made to respond more slowly or if the command interface is made easier and quicker. Thus, the time-scale of actions and maybe the potential cost of a mistake may also influence the selection of a more reflective strategy. O'Hara and Payne (1994) found comparable effects in problem-solving performance when an interface enforces a delay between each of the user's actions.

It would seem that learning can result from an interface, or situation, in which the planning of actions rather than situated action is encouraged. These results seem to be in line with those obtained from peer interaction studies where peer interaction leads to benefits in performance and learning when the context of group activity encourages a planning or reflective strategy rather than a situated or reactive strategy.

For this reason, the benefits of direct manipulation for office users of technology may be a disadvantage to educational users. This gives rise to an interesting challenge, because educational interfaces still need to be easy and fun to use, but they need to provoke appropriate planning and reflective activity.

DISCUSSION

The argument presented is that:

- Learning can be interface specific—an issue often overlooked in evaluations of educational software.
- Computer-based learning can produce very good performance at the same time as not providing training in critical strategies for real performance.
- Learning may benefit from the prevention of direct actions on the objects of learning.

To develop educational technologies that provide real skills training we need to understand the role of the interface on the problem-solving or learning strategy. In so doing we need to remember that much of human skill development is not fully available to conscious attention, and there may be processes that are supported by our interfaces that are not available to introspection or verbalization.

Indeed, the psychological literature on implicit and explicit learning (Berry & Dienes, 1993) would claim that there are two different types of learning that have very different implications for knowledge transfer to new domains and new contexts. It is probable that implicit learning is based on surface features and is context specific, whereas explicit learning is semantically richer and is rule based. Across different educational contexts we may prefer interfaces that support either of these, but it is important to understand how interface design decisions can influence the use of the different learning processes.

There are a number of interesting connections between these results and those of John Sweller (e.g., Sweller, 1988), who argued that certain forms of problem-solving behavior (e.g., means-end analysis) are inconsistent with learning through schema acquisition. His results appear to show similar patterns of comparable performance in two different groups during learning, but differences in the transferability of the knowledge acquired. His explanation of the effects is based on the increased cognitive load imposed by these problem-solving processes. It is not immediately apparent that such an explanation can be used for the results described here, because the poorer interfaces could reasonably be expected to increase cognitive load, yet they also lead to improved learning.

An explanation of all these results together might include the effects of problem-solving strategy and cognitive load (among other factors) on attentional processes, with learning being dependent on the learner's attention being directed toward relevant domain features, rather than relevant task characteristics. This is a possibility that is currently under investigation in our department.

Converting these into guidelines is an important process that is only just beginning. Before it can be done authoritatively, some replications and new results are necessary. Nevertheless, for the time being it seems that we can speculate the following possibilities:

- interfaces that encourage the planning of actions, rather than situated action, may be better for learning. By their very nature, situated actions are context specific, whereas as the goal of learning is often context-independent abstraction.
- learners need a "sense of engagement" (Hutchins, Hollan, & Norman, 1986) with learning materials, not the interface. What is traditionally viewed as "good" interface design may fail to encourage the appreciation that the objects being manipulated have real-world equivalents or analogues.
- the interface, learning context, or tasks may individually or together cause changes in strategy from implicit to explicit or vice versa.

ACKNOWLEDGMENTS

Some of the research reported here was funded by a Nuffield Foundation Undergraduate Bursary to Megan Barker and by the UK Defence Research Agency. We are grateful to J. Bright, R. Wright, E. Churchill, R. Molland, R. Peters, K. Littardi, R. Ake, and J. Hunt for their contributions.

REFERENCES

Berry, D., & Dienes, Z. (1993). *Implicit learning: Theoretical and empirical issues.* Hove, UK: Lawrence Erlbaum Associates, Inc.

Card, S., Moran, T., & Newell, A. (1983). *The psychology of human-computer interaction.* Hillsdale, NJ: Lawrence Erlbaum Associates, Inc.

Hutchins, E. L., Hollan, J. D., & Norman, D. A. (1986). Direct manipulation interfaces. In D. A. D. Norman, S. (Ed.), *User-centered system design.* Hillsdale, NJ: Lawrence Erlbaum Associates, Inc.

Laurillard, D. (1993). *Rethinking university teaching: A framework for the effective use of educational technology.* London: Routledge.

O'Hara, K. P., & Payne, S. J. (1994). *Cost of operations affects planfulness of problem-solving.* Unpublished manuscript, University of Wales, Cardiff.

Sanderson, P. (1989). Verbalizable knowledge and skilled task performance: Associations, dissociations and mental models. *Journal of Experimental Psychology: Learning, Memory and Cognition, 15,* 729–747.

Svendsen, G. B. (1991). The influence of interface style on problem-solving. *International Journal of Man-Machine Studies, 35,* 379–397.

Sweller, J. (1988). Cognitive load during problem-solving: Effects on learning. *Cognitive Science, 12,* 257–285.

Designing interactive learning environments

Abstract As computers become more prominent in classroom instruction their modes of use are extending, for example as surrogate teachers in tutoring or as curriculum enrichment in simulation applications where students are more investigative in their learning methods. However, within the classroom such programs often have effects and are used in ways that were not always anticipated by their designers. This argues for computer assisted learning (CAL) environments in which the software is interactive but is able to adapt to different styles of learning and teaching. This paper argues for and describes the design principles of such environments, taking as illustration an application in the fraction domain. Following its implementation, initial evaluation data taken from schoolchildren showed marked performance improvements, and indicated how design features of the system *(FRACTIONLAB)* contributed to their understanding.

Keywords: Computer assisted learning; Fraction domain; Interaction languages; Interactive learning environments.

Y. Akpinar and J. R. Hartley

Computer Based Learning Unit, Leeds University

Introduction

The capabilities of the electronic computer have stimulated the design of a variety of instructional programs. Responding to behaviourist views of a feedback-controlled shaping of learning, tutorial packages have been developed and shown performance improvements particularly in achieving competence objectives through practice (e.g. Suppes *et al.*, 1968). However in these types of programs the initiatives given to the student are limited. The material, tasks and feedback comments are pre-stored, and the user has to operate under the control of the program, answering questions or undertaking tasks within highly directed formats. Spontaneous questions or suggestions from the student, or other requests for remedial help are not permitted unless they have been specifically anticipated by the teacher author, since the program has no conceptual knowledge of the domain but operates under pre-stored prescriptions. These programs are, nevertheless, conceived as surrogate teachers able to be assimilated within the conventional organisation of the classroom. But they need careful preparation so that error and diagnostic feedback will be understood and related to the underpinning concepts of the domain. Limited resources may also encourage teachers to have pairs of students working together with the advantage of increasing peer interaction (Carney, 1986; Hawkins *et al.*, 1982) and this can be an important influence on learning (Podmore, 1991). Hence the introduction of even such prescribed and directed programs can cause a shift towards greater learner and teacher involvement in instruction though the programs were not specifically designed to encourage this re-orientation.

Accepted: 9th May 1995
Correspondence: J. R. Hartley, Computer Based Learning Unit, Leeds University, Leeds, LS2 9JT, UK   Email: postmaster@cbl.leeds.ac.uk

So-called artificial intelligence techniques have led to the development of tutorial programs that contain domain knowledge in a form which allows them to generate task materials and answer types of students' questions (Anderson *et al.*, 1985; Anderson *et al.*, 1986; Burton & Brown, 1982; Brown, 1985). These systems can, therefore, give greater interactive support to students but they tend to be highly specialised and have been implemented as proof-of-concept rather than as institutional packages which are used in day-to-day teaching. Moreover, as Newman *et al.* (1989) point out, such systems though sophisticated, are far from taking adequate account of the social context of learning. Although relatively few evaluation studies of these types of programs in the context of classroom learning are in evidence, a two-year qualitative study of eight classrooms by Schofield *et al.* (1994) with Anderson's geometry tutor (Anderson, 1986) noted that rather than replacing teachers, the program became an additional enriching resource. Moreover, while recognising the greater skills of the human teacher, students very much welcomed the program since it placed the type and amount of support more clearly under the control of students, and to which the teacher could respond. But as Schofield *et al.* noted "none of these changes were envisioned by the system's developers".

Similar comments can be made about other forms of computer assisted learning. Simulation programs are designed to encourage investigation as students form and test hypothesis about the underlying model. However this again requires careful preparation so that learners have an adequate conceptual framework on which to base and modify their hypotheses (Bork, 1987) and simulation programs are not usually designed to deliver this support. In the classroom, the programs are often used by small groups of students and there is evidence (Van Lehn, 1988) that these student interactions and explanations result in clear learning benefits. However the Conceptual Change in Science Project (Hartley *et al.*, 1991) which used both simulation and qualitative modelling programs showed that unless such discourse reached the students' causal beliefs (in contrast to operational talk about the system and its displays) conceptual change could not be guaranteed. A teacher is required to engineer such interchanges, but the designers had not given detailed consideration to these wider modes of use and classroom support and the changing styles of teaching/learning that might ensue. To be fair, these consequences were illuminated by evaluation studies that focused not only on learning benefits but on the social context in which the learning took place.

A further example is that of *LOGO* (Papert 1980) which provides pupils with a computer language to reveal, exploit and extend their knowledge in a principled way, for example in Turtle geometry. A computational metaphor of variables, patterns, nested procedures and recursions acts as a framework for this development which links children's direct experience (e.g. in drawing shapes) to organised procedures expressed in the *LOGO* language. Papert's conception was that of individual learners building up their own 'libraries' of *LOGO* procedures that represented their extending knowledge. However in practice, and not entirely as a result of a shortage of computing resources, *LOGO* is seen as a collaborative activity for small groups of children, though the language was not designed from this viewpoint.

In summary we argue that computer assisted learning programs should be designed to take greater account of their possible and differing modes of use, and the varying requirements of direction, support and exploratory/investigatory methods that might be employed in the classroom. Hence the aim is to widen the design focus to develop what we consider to be interactive learning environments (ILEs). What is meant by the term and its functional components will be described briefly, and then illustrated by an example (*FRACTIONLAB*) taken from the fraction domain. Data from two initial validation studies with school children form a concluding discussion.

Interactive Learning Environments

ILEs should be designed to support a variety of teaching and learning styles, regulating the locus of control between student and system, and accommodating task-based methods that are feedback rich, illustrative mechanisms that support conceptual understanding, and learner-controlled investigations and problem solving. The functional components of such ILEs have been discussed in detail elsewhere (Akpinar, 1994) but in outline they consist of:

- an 'object world' representing the domain, together with:
- a student-system interaction language by which learners can operate on the object-world in ways which show the effects of their actions (thus providing immediate feedback) and which link to representations of the object world and its relations at higher levels of abstraction.

Thus learning is envisaged not only as an improvement in performance but as a development of understanding at a more abstract and general level. Further components are:

- a *Lesson Office* (Draper *et al.*, 1991) that is needed for specifying and managing the task curriculum, and providing student records;

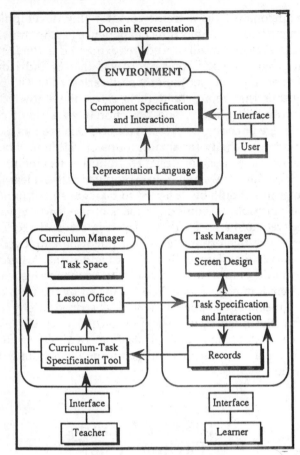

Fig. 1. The architecture of ILEs

termined sequence or adaptively by taking performance records into account) and manage the actual interactions with the learner. Typically a task specification includes instructions and/or material for the student, the domain objects and ILE facilities permitted to be used by the learner, and any additional feedback or concluding information that is to be displayed. The system-learner interface allows students to undertake the tasks (via the interaction 'language') and to see the consequences of their actions and decisions. Hence, via the *Lesson Office* task specifications, the teacher can follow a directed or an exploratory approach and also adjust the ILE for individual or small group working.

The *FRACTIONLAB* ILE

As proof of concept, and to test and illuminate the design principles, an ILE was designed for the fraction domain. This is a topic which, although its influence in the mathematics curriculum is declining, causes learning difficulties for school children (Hart, 1981; Behr *et al.*, 1992) in understanding concepts (e.g. equivalent fractions) and symbolic notation, in manipulating fractions and in solving problems (see Kerslake, 1986; Harel, 1990; Ohlsson, 1991; Streefland, 1991; and Dugdale, 1992). Further it is a domain where types of instruction are likely to be varied and include exposition and illustration, procedural explanation and practice, and problem solving. Hence the ILE, following the principles and components noted above (namely the 'object world', the student-system interaction language, the *Lesson Office* and the user-system interface) should include the following features to support the approaches to learning and instruction:

- user-system interfaces which are required for students to apply the interaction language and manipulate the object-world, and for teachers to specify and customise types of curriculum tasks for the *Lesson Office*.

A more detailed architecture of an ILE is shown in Fig. 1 and it is clear that a domain representation (i.e. the conceptual and procedural knowledge summarising the curriculum) is a crucial prerequisite for the ILE design since it determines the 'objects' (concepts or procedures) their attributes and inter-relationships and hence the operations users can perform on them. This is shown in the 'Component Specification and Interaction' box in the Environment panel which also has an interface to allow the teacher/designer to set out this analysis of the domain. The representation language (i.e. the student-system interaction language) should, as noted above, enable students to operate on the object-world and, ideally, allow them to develop their procedural or explanatory models of the 'world' at higher levels of abstraction.

The domain representation also guides the curriculum of tasks to be specified by the teacher. These are placed in the Lesson Office, from which the Task Manager is able to display the appropriate task (selected in prede-

- interactive 'fraction' objects and operators that are visual and can be directly manipulated by pupils;
- mechanisms to check the validity of students' methods, and to provide feedback on the appropriateness of their actions in relation to the task;
- supporting links between the concrete and symbolic representations of fractions, with the ILE able to display these forms so that the equivalence (and meaning) between them is apparent; the system should also be able to move its presentation modes to the symbolic (e.g. through a 'fading' of pictorial or graphical representation) as students gain in competence;
- allow experimentation with concepts and procedures in ways that relate to the pupil's experience; thus supporting guided discovery as well as more directed methods of instruction; allow the learning to be contextualised and procedural via the types of

task that are specified and managed through the Lesson *Office*.

Following discussions with teachers, who suggested fractions as a topic with which their students had difficulties, the fraction domain was represented as a semantic network showing the relations between fractions, their components, equivalent fractions, and procedures of addition, subtraction, multiplication and division of fractions. A fraction was conceived as a manipulable object (an equal division of a whole, or equivalently as a ratio) which could be segmented, measured, combined with other fractions, and represented in pictorial and symbolic forms.

Hence the metaphor of a *FRACTIONLAB* was developed with the learner being able to directly manipulate 'fractions' and 'wholes' through a set of operators that include a *Segmenter, Measurers, Sticker, Copier, Adder* and *Subtracter*. The working of these operators was under student control with each phase of the procedure shown visually, and linking to a symbolic representation. For example the *Segmenter* takes as input a circle, visually displays an 'equal partitioning' under instruction from the user, and generates a fraction placing it in a box and showing the graphical form of the fraction with the symbolic form available by pointing the mouse at the fraction object. The *Segmenter* can also rotate the fraction segment, but its main feature is that it links the operational stages to the symbolic representation. For example, *Segmenter* can have a whole circle object (1 as the numerator) dropped into it, which is divided into segments (e.g. 8 the denominator) producing (1/8). Thus all the symbols have an operational meaning related to the stages of processing and using the operator sequence as a 'language' which links the pictorial and symbolic representations.

A further requirement is for an operator *(Measurer)* that enables students to 'measure' fractions (shown in Fig. 2 as shaded segments of a circle). Students might also wish to compare or order fractions, to test their equivalence or to consider the various equivalent values that can label the same fraction. For those objectives *FRACTIONLAB* is able to provide more than one *Measurer* for pupils to use simultaneously. Similar to the *Segmenter*, the Measurer(s) was designed to have three display units corresponding to the phases of measurement. The input is a fraction segment, which is placed in a measuring 'circle' on being given the scale value (e.g. 8) and which the student employs as a measuring ring. When the segment to be measured corresponds exactly to a scale mark the student can request the segment to be labelled with its scale value and placed in a fraction box. If the scale doesn't fit (which can be perceived visually) the user is required to alter the scale measure. For example, if the fraction is a quarter segment, the user may scale the *Measurer*

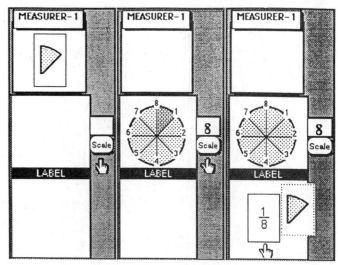

Fig. 2. The process of measuring

as 4, 8 or 12 and thus obtain 1/4, 2/8 or 3/12 as labels for the fractions. Also when the measured segment slides into the fraction box the shaded area clears (see Fig. 2). Note that in the figure the stages have been shown side by side, but in the program, the process is an animation (with each phase under user control) in a single column *Measurer*.

In performing tasks with *FRACTIONLAB* the student may wish to take copies of fractions either for experimentation or for combining them with the *Sticker* operator. Hence the operator, *Copier*, is a useful aid that functions as a type of duplicating machine.

A further procedure the student may wish to undertake is 'sticking' or 'adding' fraction segments. The combination could then be measured and so pupils could investigate the preliminaries of equivalence and addition. The teacher, for example, can set tasks which introduce the notion of common denominator and provide a useful preliminary to understanding the formal addition of fractions. [Note that *Sticker* accepts fraction boxes and their contents in pictorial and/or symbolic form, and its output is a combined fraction which may then be labelled using one of the *Measurers*.] Pupils will need to undertake more formal operations (such as addition and subtraction) of fractions. Therefore, *FRACTIONLAB*, as well as illustrating the procedure, has to assist children to understand the reasons for determining common denominators when adding and subtracting, and to reinforce the concept of equivalent fractions. The addition and subtraction operators have a structure similar to the *Measurer*, i.e. scaling the contents of the fraction box and helping students to determine an appropriate equivalence before completing the operation.

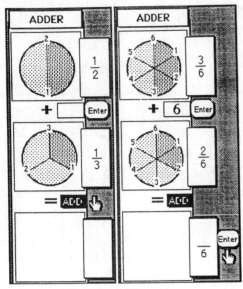

Fig. 3. The adding process

forms (pictorial and symbolic) and the use of direct manipulation principles that are alternatively discussed by Shneiderman(1992).

The *Lesson Office* and Task Management

The specification of tasks is achieved in the ILE through the *'Lesson Office'* which allows the task content, the specification of objects, fraction boxes (and their representations of fractions) and operators to be stored, and tasks to be placed in sequence to define a curriculum that is managed by the ILE.

Answers are also specified (as checks for the system) and the teacher can provide comments and overall task feedback. Cards are displayed by mouse pointing and the teacher uses them to store this information. [See Fig. 4 for an example of the interface].

The *Lesson Office* passes the sequence of curriculum tasks to the ILE Task Manager which controls the interactions with students and keep records or their progress. Note here that the Lesson *Office* can accommodate prescriptive tasks (such as practice examples), or closely defined problems (such as those used in the evaluation studies described in the next section), or more open ended exploratory assignments (in which only task goals are given—even allowing pupils to construct their own problems).

A principal design consideration was the user-system interface through which these interactions take place, and *FRACTIONLAB* uses graphical and symbolic object manipulation to a high degree. Through a mouse/icon interface pupils are able to directly manipulate the *FRACTIONLAB* objects for example by pointing to fraction boxes, dragging and moving them, switching representations of them, labelling, combining, storing,

For the system to evaluate/control these operations accurately, *FRACTIONLAB* carries out its own manipulations formally, and provides a mapping between the visual and symbolic representations so that the ILE can assist the more formal development of students' understanding in a seamless way. For example the pupils can place two fraction boxes and their contents in the relevant compartments of the *Adder* or *Subtracter,* but the pictorial shape of the fraction is seen when the mouse is moved out of the top compartment (see Fig. 3). The student must then manipulate the 'enter' box with its number (e.g. 6) thus determining the common measure scale which is to be applied to both the fraction segments to be added or subtracted. Since these segments are displayed in heavier shading the student can determine when the assigned measure scale (in effect, the common denominator) is suitable for both fraction segments. The pupil can then request the addition, but the system requires the numerator (of the result) to be entered by the pupil before the addition proceeds. Feedback comments are provided together with a dynamic picture showing the two segments oriented and coagulated within the same measure. [The two input values remain on display for comparison.] If an incorrect numerator is given the pupil is asked to try again, with the visual picture remaining as a hint. Fraction boxes produced by using the operators are likely to be required for further work or reference, and so *FRACTIONLAB* also provides a Working Store where pupils can place these components.

Note that the purpose in providing these details of *FRACTIONLAB* is to illustrate general design principles of the user-system interaction language and its interface, namely the linking of different representational

Fig. 4. An example card of the *Lesson Office*

Table 1. Relation between test questions and *FRACTIONLAB* tasks

Topic	Pre-test/post-test questions	*FRACTIONLAB* task
Fractions and their reprsentations	1, 2	1, 2, 4
Equivalent fractions	3	3, 5, 6
Additional fractions	4	7, 8, 10
Substitution of fractions	5	9

and using all the permitted range of *FRACTIONLAB* operators.

The design has established a clear functional role for each of its components (e.g. the *FRACTIONLAB* operators and the *Lesson Office*). The operators associated with the tasks are arranged sequentially on the display screen which shows the task objects and working store on the left, then the *Segmenter*, the *Measurers*, the *Copier*, and the *Sticker* in one window, with the *Adder* and *Subtracter* being placed in another window. These are easily accessed and brought to the fore by mouse clicking. The main point is that the interface, through its mouse-driven direct manipulation, provides the learner with close control of the operators and objects, and all these actions have clear visual effects.

Evaluation Studies

The ILE was implemented in HyperCard/HyperTalk on a Macintosh microcomputer, and the development was assisted by continual discussions with school-teachers. The initial system was demonstrated in two schools and groups of teachers commented on its ease of use, its potential value to their students, and the ways *FRACTIONLAB* could be employed in the classroom. Their observations were taken into account in the final version of the ILE and in the preparation of introductory material for pupils using the system.

Teachers themselves had no difficulty in specifying tasks to the *Lesson Office*, and of particular interest was their discussion on the possible modes of use of *FRACTIONLAB* in the classroom. They noted illustrative demonstrations to small student groups, prescriptive practice closely controlled by *(Lesson Office)* tasks and feedback, more open ended problem solving examples where the task instructions encourage investigatory use of *FRACTIONLAB*, and discovery methods where students set up their own tasks. In brief, while teachers had some reservations about pupils' ability to manage the interface (which the evaluation studies discounted) the ILE was considered to be a flexible and potentially useful educational tool.

A small evaluation study was then conducted in two local schools. Because of the constraints on learning time and computing resources, in discussion with teachers it was decided to base the studies on a sequence of problems (set in everyday contexts) designed to improve understanding of the fraction concept and its representation, equivalent fractions, comparison of fractions, and addition and subtraction of fractions. Accordingly a set of ten *Lesson Office* tasks were prepared with the teachers, and arrangements made for individual pupils (aged ten years) to leave their classes for one hour to work through them. The experiment took place in a side room and pupils were asked to think aloud as they attempted their solutions. The experimenter was prepared to act as a reluctant aid if anyone was unable to manage the *FRACTIONLAB* system. All sessions were video-recorded for detailed analysis.

In choosing the experimental sample it was decided to select pupils who were having difficulties with fractions. In collaboration with the teachers a five compound-question test (covering the topics noted above) was administered to the classes of twenty six and twenty eight pupils respectively in the schools and a sample of ten children chosen from each. When these students had completed their sessions with the *FRACTIONLAB* each pupil was then given, individually, a post-test, similar to the pre-test. Finally pupils' comments on using the system were noted.

Full details of the case study are available (Akpinar, 1994) but this paper summarises the results which are shown in Table 2 and Table 3. To aid interpretation the

Table 2. Performance records in Case Study 1

Tests		Pupils									
Item in	No	1	2	3	4	5	6	7	8	9	10
Pre-test	1	✓	✓	✓	✓	✓	✓	✓	✓	✓	✓
	2	✓	✓	✓	✓	✓	✓	✓	✓	✓	✓
	3	✓	✗	✗	✗	✓	✓	✓	✓	✗	✓
	4	✗	✗	✗	✗	✗	✗	✗	✓	✗	✓
	5	✗	✗	✗	✗	✗	✗	✓	✗	✓	✓
FractionLab	1	✓	T-✓	✓	T-✓	✓	T-✓	T-✓	✓	✓	✓
	2	T-✓	✓	✓	✓	✓	✓	✓	T-✓	✓	✓
	3	✓	✓	✓	✓	✓	✓	✓	✓	✓	✓
	4	✓	✓	✓	✓	✓	✓	✓	✓	✓	✓
	5	✓	†	✓	✓	✓	✓	✓	✓	✓	✓
	6	†	†	T-✓	✓	T-✓	✓	✓	T-✓	T-✓	✓
	7	†	†	✓	T-✓	✓	T-✓	✓	✓	✓	✓
	8	†	†	✓	T-✓	T-✓	T-✓	T-✓	†	T-✓	T-✓
	9	†	†	✓	✓	T-✓	T-✓	✓	✓	✓	✓
	10	†	†	✓	T-✓	✓	†	†	†	†	†
Post-test	1	✓	✓	✓	✓	✓	✓	✓	✓	✓	✓
	2	✓	✓	✗	✓	✓	✓	✓	✓	✗	✓
	3	✓	✗	✗	✗	✓	✓	✓	✓	✗	✓
	4	✱	†	✱-ℛ	✱	✱-ℛ	✱	✱	✓	✱	✓
	5	†	†	✱	✱-ℛ	✱	✱-ℛ	✓	✱	✓	✓

Key to symbols:
- ✓ correct answer
- ✗ incorrect answer
- T systematic trial and error for finding a (common) scale
- † the subject didn't study the task
- ✱ a pre- and post-test difference
- ℛ the subject was asked to refer to *FRACTIONLAB* and subsequently provided the correct response.

2. CURRICULUM AND INSTRUCTIONAL DESIGN

Table 3. Performance records in Case Study 2

Tests		Pupils									
Item in	No	1	2	3	4	5	6	7	8	9	10
Pre-test	1	✗	✓	✓	✓	✓	✓	✓	✓	✓	✗
	2	✓	✗	✓	✗	✓	✓	✓	✓	✗	✓
	3	✗	✗	✗	✓	✗	✗	✗	✗	✗	✓
	4	†	†	✗	✗	✗	✗	✗	✗	✗	†
	5	†	†	✗	✗	✗	✗	✗	†	†	†
FractionLab	1	T✓	T✓	T✓	T✓	T✓	T✓	T✓	T✓	✓	T✓
	2	T✓	✓	✓	✓	✓	✓	✓	✓	T✓	✓
	3	✓	✓	✓	✓	✓	✓	✓	✓	✓	✓
	4	✓	T✓	✓	T✓	✓	✓	✓	✓	✓	✓
	5	✓	T✓	T✓	T✓	✓	✓	✓	T✓	✓	✓
	6	†	T✓	T✓	T✓	✓	T✓	✓	T✓	T✓	†
	7	†	†	T✓	✓	✓	T✓	T✓	T✓	✓	†
	8	†	†	T✓	✓	T✓	T✓	✓	✓	†	†
	9	†	†	✓	✓	✓	T✓	✓	†	†	†
	10	†	†	✓	†	✓	†	✓	†	†	†
Post-test	1	*	✓	✓	✓	✓	✓	✓	✓	✓	*
	2	✓	*	✓	*	✓	✓	✓	✓	✓	✓
	3	*	*	*	✓	*	*	*	*	*	✓
	4	†	†	*	*R	*R	*R	*R	*R	*	†
	5	†	†	*	*R	*R	*R	*R	✓	†	†

Key to symbols:
✓ correct answer
✗ incorrect answer
T systematic trial and error for finding a (common) scale
† the subject didn't study the task
* a pre- and post-test difference
R the subject was asked to refer to FRACTIONLAB and subsequently provided the correct response.

topics referenced in the pre- and post-test and in the related *FRACTIONLAB* tasks are shown in Table 1. [All pupils completed the introductory materials on using the facilities of *FRACTIONLAB* before commencing the experiment].

While the constraints of the case studies must be borne in mind i.e. small numbers of pupils and limited time for testing and working at the *FRACTIONLAB* tasks, interesting data were collected. All the pupils were able to manage the *FRACTIONLAB* interface without assistance, but, as can be seen from the Tables 2 and 3, there were wide variations in the times pupils took to complete the tasks. As can be seen from the Tables, not all pupils were able to perform all the tasks. However in other aspects of performance, and for other pupils, there were noticeable improvements between pre- and post-tests (see Tables 2 and 3). In study 1, although pupils answered pre-test questions on the representation of fraction correctly, there were many errors on the other test items. After the *FRACTIONLAB* experience there were correct performances on all the post-test items attempted. Similar improvements in study 2 were even more pronounced.

There was some evidence that *FRACTIONLAB*, perhaps because it required the tactical choice of operators (as well as their management) to solve the problem tasks, assisted post-test performance by enabling pupils to run a mental (*FRACTIONLAB*) model. In some instances (shown in Tables 2 and 3) where pupils were having some difficulty with post-test items the investigator suggested they 'think what you would do in *FRACTION-LAB*'. In all cases a correct response was then given. As well as the tactical use of operators the investigatory features of *FRACTIONLAB* assisted learning. This was particularly true for the *Measurer*(s) and the *Adder/Subtracter* where the pupils had to decide an appropriate scale reading (i.e. a denominator) for fractions to be 'measured'. This type of activity was needed for fraction comparisons, fraction equivalence and addition/subtraction, and illustrated not only the meaning of a fraction denominator, but assisted the student to link and work with symbolic representations. The systematic investigatory use of these operators is shown in the Tables 2 and 3 (the tasks are marked with a q) and note that this approach was used even with some of the easier tasks (1, 2, 3 and 4) of *FRACTIONLAB*.

Overall these modest studies give some encouragement to the value of the ILE design for learning, and further work has utilised these methods in more abstract domains of graphical concepts and the physics of motion. For example, the Conceptual Change in Science Project (Hartley *et al.*, 1991) employed similar techniques to produce significant learning improvements in students' conceptual understanding of kinematics. This potential flexibility of the modes of use of ILEs in the classroom (Twigger *et al.*, 1991) should also encourage further research.

References

Akpinar, Y. (1994) *Computer Based Interactive Environments for Learning School Mathematics*, PhD Thesis, University of Leeds, Leeds, UK.

Anderson, J. R., Boyle, C. F. & Reiser, B. (1985) Intelligent Tutoring Systems, *Science*, **228**, 6, 456–462.

Anderson, J. R., Boyle, C. F. & Yost, G. (1986) The Geometry Tutor. *Journal of Mathematical Behavior*, **5**, 1, 5–19.

Behr, M. J., Harel, G., Post, T. & Lesh, R. (1992) Rational Number, Ratio and Proportion. In *Handbook of Research on Mathematics Teaching and Learning* (ed. D. A. Grows). Macmillan, New York.

Bork, A. (1987) *Learning with Personal Computers*. Harper & Row, London.

Brown, J. S. (1985) Process versus Product: A Perspective on Tools for Communal and Informal Electronic Learning. *Journal of Educational Computing Research*, **1**, 2, 179–201.

Burton, R. R. & Brown, J. S. (1982) An Investigation of Computer Coaching for Informal Learning Activities. In *Intelligent Tutoring Systems* (eds. D. Sleeman & J. S. Brown) pp. 79–98. Academic Press, London.

Carney, C. C. (1986) Teacher + Computer = More Learning. *The Computing Teacher*, **13**, 6, 12–15.

Draper, S. W., Driver, R., Hartley, J. R., Hennessey, S., Mallen, C., Mohamed, R. O'Malley, C., O'Shea, T., Scanlon, E. & Twigger, D. (1991) Design Considerations in a Project on Conceptual Change in Science. *Computers and Education*, **17** 1, 37–41.

Dugdale, S. (1992) The Design of Computer-Based Mathematics Instruction. In *Computer-Assisted Instruction and Intelligent Tutoring Systems* (eds. J. H. Larkin & R. W. Chabay). LEA, New Jersey.

Harel, I. (1990) Children as Software Designer. *The Journal of Mathematical Behaviour,* **9,** 1–10.

Hart, K. M. (1981) Fractions. In *Children's Understanding of Mathematics 11–16* (ed. K. M. Hart). John Murray, London.

Hartley, J. R., Byard, M. J. & Mallen, C. L. (1991) Qualitative Modelling and Conceptual Change in Science Students. In *Proceedings of the International Conference on the Learning Sciences* (ed. L. Birnbaum) pp. 222–230. Northwestern University, Chicago, USA.

Hawkins, J., Sheingold, K., Gearhart, M. & Berger, C. (1982) Microcomputers in Schools: Impact on the Social Life of Elementary Classrooms. *Journal of Applied Development Psychology,* **3, 4,** 361–373.

Kerslake, D. (1986) *Fractions: Children's Strategies and Errors.* NFER-NELSON, London.

Newman, D., Griffin, P. & Cole, M. (1989) *The Construction Zone: Working for Cognitive Change in School.* Cambridge University Press, Cambridge.

Ohlsson, S. (1991) Knowledge Requirements for Teaching: The Case of Fractions. In *Teaching Knowledge and Intelligent Tutoring* (ed. P. Goodyear). Ablex Publishing, New Jersey.

Papert, S. (1980) *Mindstorms: Children, Computers and Powerful Ideas.* Harvester Press, Sussex.

Podmore, V. N. (1991) 4-year-olds, 6-year-olds, and Microcomputers: A Study of Perceptions and Social Behaviours. *Journal of Applied Development Psychology,* **12,** 1, 87–101.

Shneiderman, B. (1992) *Defining the User Interface: Strategies for Effective Human Computer Interaction.* Addison Wesley Publishing, Massachusets, USA.

Schofield, J. W., Eurich-Fulcer, R. & Britt, C. L. (1994) Teachers, Computer Tutors and Teaching: The Artificially Intelligent Tutor as an Agent for Classroom Change. *American Educational Research Journal,* **31,** 3, 579–607.

Streefland, L. (1991) *Fractions in Realistic Mathematics Education.* Kluwer Academic Publishers, Amsterdam.

Suppes, P., Jerman, M. & Brian, D. (1968) *Computer-assisted Instruction: the 1965–66 Stanford Arithmetic Program.* Academic Press, New York.

Twigger, D., Byard, M. J., Draper, S., Driver, R., Hartley, J. R., Hennessy, S., Mallen, C. L., Mohamed, R., O'Malley, C., O'Shea, T. & Scanlon, E. (1991) The 'Conceptual Change in Science' Project. *Journal of Computer Assisted Learning,* **7,** 2, 144–155.

Van Lehn, K. (1988) Student Modelling. In *Foundations of Intelligent Tutoring Systems* (eds. M. Polson & R. R. Richardson). Lawrence Erlbaum Associates, New Jersey.

Design and Application of Teaching Software

Glenn G. Hammack, O.D.

Abstract

Software has been developed for interactive, self-paced instruction using commonly-used personal computers. HyperCard® stacks have been written, all using a common screen interface, and are being utilized in curriculum courses at the University of Alabama School of Optometry. The common interface has these features: forward navigation, reverse navigation, search navigation, awareness instructions, the information presentation area, and exit of the software. Instructional delivery of course material is done using text and graphics. Interactive questions are placed into the software at occasional points to allow students to self assess their retention of the material. Printouts of course material are easily produced for handouts, and contain all text and graphics from the screens. The software is being used by one instructor in a multi-instructor lecture/lab course, and in a semi-problem based learning course. A survey evaluation comparing this instructional modality to other methods was completed by students. The software-based instructional session scored better than a traditional handout-and-slide/overhead session to a statistically significant level. The software session scored comparably to a lecture session using slides, computer graphics, and video.

KEYWORDS: Computer-assisted education, teaching software, evaluation, Hyper-Card software, Macintosh Computers

Background

Applications of computers in education have held promise since the advent of the computer into common usage. Early applications used custom written software on mainframe computers at large institutions and met with limited success[1]. The personal microcomputer and its subsequent adoption into the educational setting for word processing, financial, and statistical applications set the stage for further development in the area of computer-based instruction. Early applications brought out several early promising features of computer-based education: interactivity, simulation, evaluation, and user tracking[2]. Their success, however, was limited due the difficult nature of authoring teaching materials (basically computer programming) and the scarcity of resources to make the materials widely available to students [3,4].

The development of the optical videodisc offered photorealistic still and motion images along with sound to computer-based education[5]. Videodiscs for teaching applications flourished, but successful use of these was limited due to costly and very specific hardware and software requirements for widespread implementation[6].

In both cases, implementation difficulties prevented the widespread use of very well developed instructional tools. In spite of these drawbacks, the efficacy of computer-based instruction continues to be documented [7,8,9,10,11]. A promise for future applications of computer-based education lies in the new generation of reasonably priced personal computers and software. Personal computers are now increasingly used by students through institutionally-maintained computer laboratories, and many students are acquiring their own to supplement their education.

This increasing availability of student personal computing can be used to improve the implementation of computer-based education, as long as computer-based instructional tools can be written with a commonality of computing performance in mind. Software for computer-based instruction is often written to showcase special features and hardware of new computers which are not available on more basic models. This limits usage as most computers available to students (or purchased by them) are not equipped with the special and costly features designed into the teaching software. This is the primary consideration in our design for software for interactive, self-paced instruction. The software is designed to run on limited specification machines which are more available to students.

The Software

Apple Macintosh HyperCard® software is a combination database, graphics, and programming tool designed as a general utility program for home and business use. A version of HyperCard® is provided with every Macintosh sold. Much in the same way that a word processing program such as WordPerfect 5.1® or Microsoft Word® uses computer files separate from themselves to store documents, HyperCard® stores program information in separate files called stacks. These stacks can be written by users, and distributed without licensing constraints. They can be used on any Apple Macintosh® which retains the HyperCard® software installed on it when manufactured.

Dr. Hammack is assistant dean for clinical affairs at the University of Alabama at Birmingham School of Optometry.

From *Optometric Education*, Winter 1996, pp. 44-49. © 1996 by the Association of Schools and Colleges of Optometry. Reprinted by permission.

Table 1 contains a listing of topics for which HyperCard® stacks have been written, all using a common screen interface, and all being utilized in curriculum courses at the University of Alabama School of Optometry.

Software Features -
Graphic User Interface

The HyperCard® program runs on the Apple Macintosh®, which inherently has a graphical user interface (sometimes referred to as a GUI), where computer programs and files are represented by named icons and graphics on the screen. The Apple Macintosh® environment, Microsoft Windows® , and IBM's OS/2® are all graphic user interfaces.

Navigation Controls and Basic Interface

Figure 1 shows the basic user interface for the HyperCard® stacks, which is common to each screen which the student uses. The screen has six features which are important: forward and reverse navigation, search navigation, awareness instructions, an information presentation area, and exiting the software.

Forward and Reverse Navigation

Forward and reverse navigation is the ability to move from one screen of information to the next, or prior. At the lower right and left corners of each screen are controls labeled above by the words "Go On" and "Go Back." These control "page turning" of the information.

Search Navigation

Search navigation is the ability to move from screen to screen of information which contains a typed-in keyword. When the "Find" button used, a box appears into which text is typed for a keyword search. Search navigation allows topic specific reviews of the instructional material.

Awareness Instructions

In the lower left central area of each screen is an area where general instructions appear. The purpose of this area is to advise and guide the novice user for successful use of the software.

The Information Presentation Area

The majority of the screen is occupied by the large information presentation area, where any combination of

TABLE 1.
Listing of UAB Authored Stacks, by course and title

Clinical Evaluation of the Visual System
1. Introduction to Teaching Software
2. Case History
3. Presbyopia 1 - Correction Basics
4. Presbyopia 2 - Clinical Methods
5. Biomicroscopy 1 - Basics of the Instrument
6. Biomicroscopy 2 - Clinical Methods
7. Autorefractors and Autokeratometers
8. Automated Perimetry

Environmental Vision
1. Week 2 - Obtaining Information, the Task Analysis Method
2. Week 3 - Focal Distance, Functional Field Issues
3. Week 4 - Functional Field, Illuminance and Contrast Issues 1
4. Week 5 - Contrast Issues 2
5. Week 6 - Task Analysis Wrapup: Binocularity, Efficiency, Hazards
6. Week 7 - Threats and Natural Protection
7. Week 8 - Protection Modalities and Recommendations
8. Week 9 - Special Tasks Prescribing

text, graphics, and questions can be organized. For large amounts of information, this area can be scrolled.

Software Instructional Delivery
Use of Text and Graphics

Instructional delivery is done using text and graphics, either drawn or scanned. Figure 2 shows an example of an instructional screen comprised of text only. This text is typed in by the software author. The software does automatic word wrap and the size and characteristics (normal, bolded, underlined, italicized, superscript, and subscript) of the text can be modified.

FIGURE 1:
New Stack Screen, Navigation Controls Only

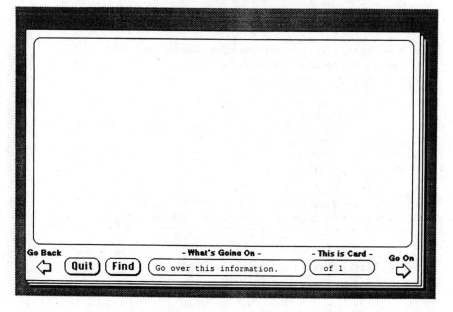

TABLE 2.
Results of Student Survey

Individual Ratings - (higher percentage indicates higher agreement)

Survey Question	Multi-mode	Software	Traditional
Handouts informative and valuable...	0.94	0.92	0.81
Classroom visuals clear and understandable...	0.90	0.90	0.85
Information organized and pertinent...	0.92	0.90	0.88
I was able to learn the information ...	0.92	0.90	0.83
I would like to see future lectures like this...	0.98	0.94	0.90
Overall (grouping of all areas)...	0.93	0.92	0.85

Summary - Student's T-statistic*:

Survey Question	Multi-mode vs. Software	Multi-mode vs. Traditional	Software vs. Traditional
Handouts informative and valuable...	0.292	0.034	0.088
Classroom visuals clear and understandable...	0.500	0.219	0.137
Information organized and pertinent...	0.292	0.169	0.336
I was able to learn the information ...	0.292	0.048	0.109
I would like to see future lectures like this...	0.218	0.083	0.083
Overall (grouping of all areas)...	0.114	0.001	0.004

Drawn graphics are created by the software author (or a computer illustrator) by the use of drawing tools. Figure 3 shows an instructional screen which uses drawn graphics. Graphics can also be scanned in using document scanners. Figure 4 shows an instructional screen which contains scanned graphics.

Use of Interactive Question Screens

Multiple choice, true-false, or similar response questions can be included in the programs. These screens allow students to self-assess their retention of the material. Figure 5 shows a sample interactive question screen, titled in most cases as a "Self-Assessment." These interactive question screens can provide feedback at various levels, ranging from simple correct-incorrect responses to automatically providing review of the screens which pertain to the question asked. Both figures 5 and 6 show sample self-assessment question screens.

Printouts of Instructional Materials

The HyperCard® software package has provision for providing laser printouts. Figure 6 shows a sample stack printout. The answers to the question screens are not provided on the printouts.

Application of the Software in UAB's Curriculum

Usage in a Multi-Instructor Lecture/Lab Course

Clinical Evaluation of the Visual System (a.k.a. CEVS) is a three academic quarter course track given in the first and second professional years at UAB which covers basic optometric clinical skills and procedures. This course is taught by four instructors, with each instructor responsible for different topics within the course track. One of the four instructors uses instructional software as the primary media for instruction; others use traditional lecture techniques. Printouts of the instructional software for a particular topic are provided to the students prior to the class meeting on

FIGURE 2:
Instructional Screen Of Text Only

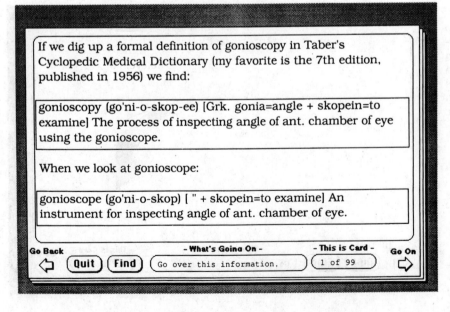

If we dig up a formal definition of gonioscopy in Taber's Cyclopedic Medical Dictionary (my favorite is the 7th edition, published in 1956) we find:

gonioscopy (go'ni-o-skop-ee) [Grk. gonia=angle + skopein=to examine] The process of inspecting angle of ant. chamber of eye using the gonioscope.

When we look at gonioscope:

gonioscope (go'ni-o-skop) [" + skopein=to examine] An instrument for inspecting angle of ant. chamber of eye.

Go Back   - What's Going On -   - This is Card -   Go On
(Quit) (Find)   (Go over this information.)   (1 of 99)

that topic. During the class meeting, the software is used as the primary lecture resource in a lecture room equipped with a computer and classroom projection equipment, and the software lesson is reviewed by the class guided by the instructor. The software is also available for additional review on student access computers located around the building, and is provided free for students to use on their own computers. In this class, software is used primarily by students as test preparation or by students who were absent on the class meeting day.

■

Each week's software program is designed to take approximately one hour for the student to review,

Usage in a Semi-Problem-Based Single Instructor Course

Environmental Vision is a single academic quarter course given in the spring of the third professional year which covers occupational task analysis, ocular hazards, protection methodologies, standards, and special task prescribing. This course is organized into weekly one-hour class sessions over ten weeks. The first class session is spent reviewing the syllabus of the course, which includes the class expectations: self-study, biweekly evaluation by short answer quiz, and attendance at class sessions. Also at the first class, the usage and availability of teaching software is reviewed. Software has been written containing the instructional materials for weeks 2 through 9. The material for each week is divided into distinct software assignments, labeled by the week. Each week's software program is designed to take approximately one hour for the student to review, either alone or in small groups. The software is available 24 hours a day on student access machines around the optome-

try building (5 machines) or can be used on computers in the adjacent health sciences library (5 machines). Students may also obtain copies of the software at no charge to run on machines they may have. This has proven adequate for our class size of 40 students.

Students are expected to review the instructional software before coming to class. In the class sessions, questions on the software contents are addressed, and then clinical cases applying the ideas presented in the software are reviewed. The short answer quizzes are based upon the clinical cases.

The course design is intended to offer the student the chance for application of the information covered in

FIGURE 3.
Instructional Screen Of Text And Drawn Graphics

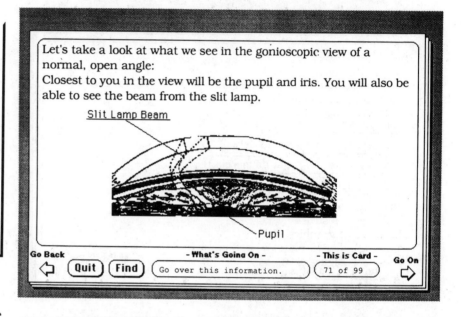

FIGURE 4.
Instructional Screen Of Text And Scanned Graphics

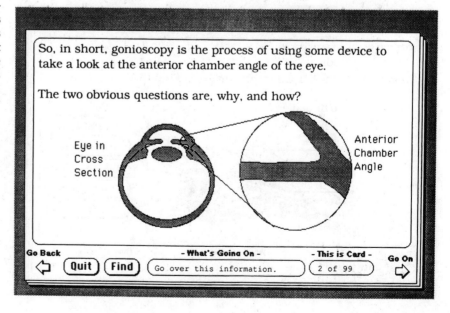

the instructional materials, rather than simple retention. Using class meeting times for case review allows this application as well as peer feedback as to the correctness of actions taken. This use of the teaching software for the delivery of the instructional material as self-study frees class time for higher levels of applying the material.

Evaluation of Student Impressions on Teaching Software Use

Multi-Instructor Lecture/Lab Course -Instructor Ratings

The use of teaching software in the multi-instructor lecture/lab course has been rated well by students. At the conclusion of each term, UAB students are asked to complete a course evaluation for each course taught. This evaluation is anonymous and surveys the student's ratings of course content, delivery and examinations, and also allows for commentary narrative on each form. The instructor using the teaching software has been comparatively rated equal or superior to other instructors (who use traditional methods) in content, clarity, and presentation indices tracked by these evaluations. Positive comments on the evaluation forms have included liking the completeness of the handouts, and the ability to review the complete contents of lectures at other times. Negative comments have not been encountered on the evaluations.

Multi-Instructor Lecture/Lab Course - Survey Evaluation
Survey Design

A survey was conducted which asked the students in the multi-instructor class to rate certain areas of three lectures, all delivered by the same instructor. First of the lectures was a well-developed, labor-intensive session using slides, overheads, computer graphics, handouts, videotape, and live demonstration. Second of the lectures was a session using the computer software as the classroom visuals with a software printout as the handout. Third was a lecture developed along the lines of traditional lectures in the course, using an outline-form handout and overhead projector diagram visuals. Handouts were similar in design in the traditional and multi-mode lectures, and were based on handouts developed by previous instructors. Students were asked to rate each lecture in five areas, stating their level of agreement or disagreement to five statements. The statements were:

1. The handouts were informative and valuable.
2. The classroom visuals were clear and understandable.
3. The information was well-organized and pertinent.
4. I was able to learn the information well from the presentation and the handout.
5. I would like to see future lectures done in this format.

Survey Results

The results of the survey are seen in Table 2. Grouping the five area questions all as positive indicators, the software session and the labor-

FIGURE 5.
Sample Self-assessment Screen

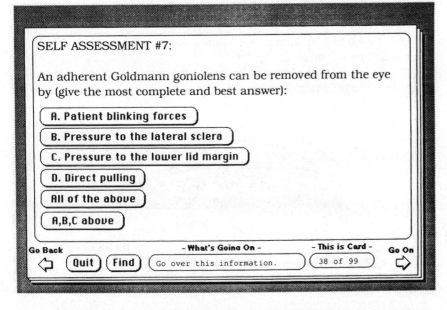

FIGURE 6.
Sample Self-assessment Screen

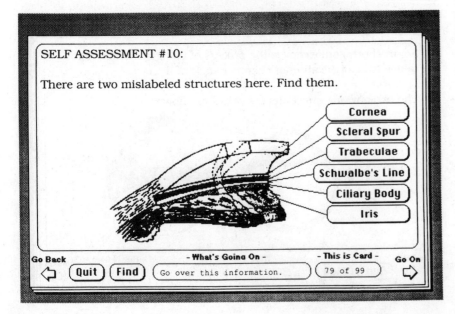

intensive multi-modality session both scored higher than the traditional lecture to a statistically significant level (Student's T-statistic, p<.005)

In the specific individual areas of (a) handouts being informative and valuable and (b) the student feeling they were able to learn the information, the labor-intensive multi-modality session scored higher than the traditional session to a statistically significant level (Student's T-statistic, p=.03 and p=.05, respectively). In all other specific areas, the software session and the labor-intensive multi-modality sessions scored higher than the traditional session, but not to a statistically significant level.

■

Instructional software continues to show promise as a powerful adjunct to the educational process.

Semi-Problem-Based Single Instructor Course - Instructor Ratings

The use of teaching software in the semi-problem-based single instructor course has been similar. Again, instructor evaluation by students has rated the instructor using teaching software equal or superior to prior instructors of the course who used traditional methods. Survey form comments again included a preference for reviewing the instructional material when convenient for them, as well as considering the self-assessment questions very useful.

Discussion

The use of computer software for instruction has been attempted at many levels using many models of implementation. Although not considered here, many factors stand against the use of computers in instruction, including (but not limited to) accessibility problems in large class size schools, inefficiency compared to traditional lecture methods in many applications, student and faculty computer unfamiliarity, and

perceptions of "replacing" the human instructor through automation.

As the computer becomes a more familiar instrument in the academic setting, creative developments are occurring where instructional software continues to show promise as a powerful adjunct to the educational process. As with the 35mm slide and the ½-inch VHS videotape, adoption of an instructional technology will occur as useful and convenient applications are developed. The design and implementations described here are not meant to be specific recommendations, but are instead offered as a description of what has worked in a contemporary optometric curriculum application.

Conclusion

Computer software for interactive, self-paced instruction has been developed that has been implemented into portions of the curriculum at the University of Alabama at Birmingham. Students being taught using this software score this learning experience as highly as being taught from a well-developed, labor-intensive multi-modality lecture, and score it higher than being taught by traditional handout/slide lecture methods.

References

1. Caldwell R. Computers and computer courseware: New directions for helping children learn. Journal of Children in Contemporary Society 1981; 14(1):55-71.1
2. Berman J. Feasability of incorporating alternative teaching methods into clinical clerkships. Teaching and Learning in Medicine 1990; 2(2):98-103.
3. Cohen P, Dacanay LS. Computer-based instruction on health professions education: A meta-analysis of outcomes. Evaluation and the Health Professions 1992; 15(3):259-81.
4. Gjerde CL, Xakellis GC, Schuldt SS. Medical student evaluation of self-selected learning modules. Family Medicine 1993; 25(7):452-5.
5. Hammack GG. The computer controlled videodisc: A new technology in optometric education. Journal of Optometric Education 1985; 10(4):8-11.
6. Xakellis GC, Gjerde C. Evaluation by second-year medical students of their computer-aided instruction. Academic Medicine 1990; 65(1):23-6.
7. Gathany NC. Putting life into computer-based training: The creation of an epidemiologic case study. Educational Technology 1994; 34(6):44-47.
8. Hooper JA, Bronzino JD, Noyes NT, Taylor D. EquipTeach: a computer-aided instruction to teach users how to operate specific medical equipment. Biomedical Instrumentation & Technology 1993; 27(5):394-9.
9. Macura RT, Macura KJ, Toro VE, Binet EF, Trueblood JH, Ji K. Computerized case-based instructional system for computed tomography and magnetic resonance imaging of brain tumors. Investigative Radiology 1994; 29(4):497-506.
10. Schwartz W. Using the computer-assisted medical problem solving (CAMPS) system to identify student's problem-solving difficulties. Academic Medicine 1992; 67(9):568-71.
11. Tunget CL. Evaluation of DILearn: An interactive computer-assisted learning program for drug information. American Journal of Pharmaceutical Education 1993; 57(4):340-3.

FIGURE 7.
Sample Stack (partial) Printout Page

Page 9 of Gonioscopy

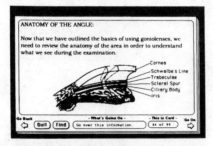

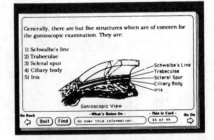

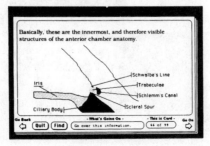

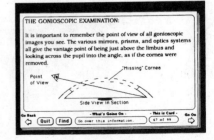

Classroom Applications and Software Evaluations

Software is the fuel that brings computers to life; it is also the magic that makes networked interactive multimedia happen. It contains the grain of creativity that causes us to wonder, "How did they do that?" Computer-based multimedia can capture the learner's imagination and help demonstrate ideas. However, it must be chosen with certain criteria in mind, such as the purpose for using it, who will be using it, and whether it will be effective in satisfying the learner's needs. We must guard against being persuaded by the combinations of immediate access, sound, graphics, video, and animation that stimulate our senses but fail to meet the objectives of our curriculum or the needs of our learners. Using systematic evaluation techniques such as those found in this unit can help us select networked- or CD-ROM-based interactive computer-based multimedia applications that meet our selection criteria.

In the first article, the focus is on early childhood software. The NAEYC position paper, "Technology and Young Children—Ages Three through Eight," states that proliferation of early childhood software is forcing early childhood educators to examine critically the impact of technology on children and to be prepared to use technology to benefit children. This position statement addresses several issues related to technology's use with young children.

Next, Anastasia Samaras provides us with a set of anecdotes that illustrate that teachers can use computers to accommodate children's learning styles and abilities. Without teacher support, however, children may revert to a trial and error process that is devoid of task conceptualization and minimal learning. The author believes it is critical for teachers to be part of the software evaluation and selection process in order for them to be committed to its use.

In the article "Software Evaluation," Daniel Shade discusses software evaluation in general terms and provides a checklist for teachers to use in evaluating software. He also provides a list of 10 resources that can be used to develop a knowledge base for software availability and review.

The following article provides six anecdotal accounts of how students are using computers to become better problem solvers and more computer capable. The authors provide readers with four rules to compute by.

Finally, Dempsey, Lucassen, Haynes, and Casey, in "Instructional Applications of Computer Games," discuss criteria for selecting an instructional game. They also describe a study in which 40 computer games were sampled by 40 adult participants. The authors supply results of the study, a list of games used, and a list of instructional benefits of various games.

Looking Ahead: Challenge Questions

Locating software that meets a particular set of objectives can be a challenge. Describe how you would search for specific applications packages. Discuss what criteria you would use to determine whether you should purchase the program or develop your own.

Develop an evaluation instrument specifically designed for your teaching area. Pilot test it with a software package in your subject area and share the results with colleagues. Does your instrument thoroughly evaluate the package? Were you able to communicate your findings in an understandable manner? Refine your instrument based on these results.

NAEYC Position Statement:
Technology and Young Children—
Ages Three through Eight

Adopted April 1996

In this position statement, we use the word technology to refer primarily to computer technology, but this can be extended to include related technologies, such as telecommunications and multimedia, which are becoming integrated with computer technology.

Technology plays a significant role in all aspects of American life today, and this role will only increase in the future. The potential benefits of technology for young children's learning and development are well documented (Wright & Shade 1994). As technology becomes easier to use and early childhood software proliferates, young children's use of technology becomes more widespread. Therefore, early childhood educators have a responsibility to critically examine the impact of technology on children and be prepared to use technology to benefit children.

Market researchers tracking software trends have identified that the largest software growth recently has been in new titles and companies serving the early childhood educational market. Of the people who own home computers and have young children, 70% have purchased educational software for their children to use (*SPA Consumer Market Report* 1996). While many new titles are good contributions to the field, an even larger number are not (Haugland & Shade 1994).

Early childhood educators must take responsibility to influence events that are transforming the daily lives of children and families. This statement addresses several issues related to technology's use with young children: (1) the essential role of the teacher in evaluating appropriate uses of technology; (2) the potential benefits of appropriate use of technology in early childhood programs; (3) the integration of technology into the typical learning environment; (4) equitable access to technology, including children with special needs; (5) stereotyping and violence in software; (6) the role of teachers and parents as advocates; and (7) the implications of technology for professional development.

NAEYC's position

Although now there is considerable research that points to the positive effects of technology on children's learning and development (Clements 1994), the research indicates that, in practice, computers supplement and do not replace highly valued early childhood activities and materials, such as art, blocks, sand, water, books, exploration with writing materials, and dramatic play. Research indicates that computers can be used in developmentally appropriate ways beneficial to children and also can be misused, just as any tool can (Shade & Watson 1990). Developmentally appropriate software offers opportunities for collaborative play, learning, and creation. Educators must use professional judgment in evaluating and using this learning tool appropriately, applying the same criteria they would to any other learning tool or experience. They must also weigh the costs of technology with the costs of other learning materials and program resources to arrive at an appropriate balance for their classrooms.

1. In evaluating the appropriate use of technology, NAEYC applies principles of developmentally appropriate practice (Bredekamp 1987) and appropriate curriculum and assessment (NAEYC & NAECS/SDE 1992.) In short, NAEYC believes that in any given situation, a professional judgment by the teacher is required to determine if a specific use of technology is age appropriate, individually appropriate, and culturally appropriate.

The teacher's role is critical in making certain that good decisions are made about which technology to use and in supporting children in their use of technology to ensure that potential benefits are achieved.

From *Young Children*, September 1996, pp. 11-16. © 1996 by the National Association for the Education of Young Children. Reprinted by permission.

Teachers must take time to evaluate and choose software in light of principles of development and learning and must carefully observe children using the software to identify both opportunities and problems and make appropriate adaptations. Choosing appropriate software is similar to choosing appropriate books for the classroom—teachers constantly make judgments about what is age appropriate, individually appropriate, and culturally appropriate. Teachers should look for ways to use computers to support the development and learning that occur in other parts of the classroom and the development and learning that happen with computers in complement with activities off the computer. Good teaching practices must always be the guiding goal when selecting and using new technologies.

2. Used appropriately, technology can enhance children's cognitive and social abilities.

Computers are intrinsically compelling for young children. The sounds and graphics gain children's attention. Increasingly, young children observe adults and older children working on computers, and they want to do it, too. Children get interested because they can make things happen with computers. Developmentally appropriate software engages children in creative play, mastery learning, problem solving, and conversation. The children control the pacing and the action. They can repeat a process or activity as often as they like and experiment with variations. They can collaborate in making decisions and share their discoveries and creations (Haugland & Shade 1990).

Well-designed early childhood software grows in dimension with the child, enabling her to find new challenges as she becomes more proficient. Appropriate visual and verbal prompts designed in the software expand play themes and opportunities while leaving the child in control. Vast collections of images, sounds, and information of all kinds are placed at the child's disposal. Software can be made age appropriate even for children as young as three or four.

When used appropriately, technology can support and extend traditional materials in valuable ways. Research points to the positive effects of technology in children's learning and development, both cognitive and social (Clements 1994; Haugland & Shade 1994). In addition to actually developing children's abilities, technology provides an opportunity for assessment. Observing the child at the computer offers teachers a "window" onto a child's thinking. Just as parents continue to read to children who can read themselves, parents and teachers should both participate with children in computer activities and encourage children to use computers on their own and with peers.

Research demonstrates that when working with a computer children prefer working with one or two partners over working alone (Lipinski et al. 1986; Rhee & Chavnagri 1991; Clements, Nastasi, & Swaminathan 1993). They seek help from one another and seem to prefer help from peers over help from the teacher (King & Alloway 1992; Nastasi & Clements 1993). Children engage in high levels of spoken communication and cooperation at the computer. They initiate interactions more frequently and in different ways than when engaged with traditional activities, such as puzzles or blocks. They engage in more turn taking at the computer and simultaneously show high levels of language and cooperative-play activity.

Technology extends benefits of collaboration beyond the immediate classroom environment for children in the primary grades who can already read and write. With the potential of access to the Internet or other on-line "user friendly" networks, young children can collaborate with children in other classrooms, cities, counties, states, and even countries. Through electronic field trips in real time or via diskette, children are able to share different cultural and environmental experiences. Electronic mail and telecommunications opportunities through the Internet facilitate direct communication and promote social interactions previously limited by the physical location of participating learners.

3. Appropriate technology is integrated into the regular learning environment and used as one of many options to support children's learning.

Every classroom has its own guiding philosophies, values, schedules, themes, and activities. As part of the teacher's overall classroom plan, computers should be used in ways that support these existing classroom educational directions rather than distort or replace them. Computers should be integrated into early childhood practice physically, functionally, and philosophically. Teachers can accommodate integration in at least five ways:

• Locate computers in the classroom, rather than in a separate computer lab (Davis & Shade 1994).

• Integrate technology into the daily routine of classroom activity. For example, a teacher might introduce musical rhythm with actions, recordings, and a computer used as an electronic rhythm-matching game. The children then would work in small groups with the computer program serving as one of several learning centers.

• Choose software to enrich curriculum content, other classroom activities, or concepts. For example, the program in the computer learning center might allow children to invent their own rhythms that they could simultaneously hear played back and see displayed graphically. They could edit these rhythms on the computer, hearing and seeing the changes.

• Use technology to integrate curriculum across subject-matter areas. For example, one group of children used the computer to make signs for a restaurant in their dramatic-play area (Apple Computer Inc. 1993). The rhythm program helps children connect mathematical patterns to musical patterns.

• Extend the curriculum, with technology offering new avenues and perspectives. For example, exploring shapes on the computer provides opportunities to stretch, shrink, bend, and combine shapes into new forms. Such activities enrich and extend children's activities with physical manipulatives.

4. **Early childhood educators should promote equitable access to technology for all children and their families. Children with special needs should have increased access when this is helpful.**

> *Educators using technology need to be especially sensitive to issues of equity.*

A decade of research on the educational use of computers in schools reveals that computers maintain and exaggerate inequalities (Sutton 1991). Sutton found gender, race, and social-class inequalities in the educational uses of computers, which Thouvenelle, Borunda, and McDowell summarize below.

• Girls used computers in and out of school less often than did boys.

• African American students had less access to computers than did White students.

• Presence of computers in a school did not ensure access.

• Teachers, while concerned about equity, held attitudes that hindered access—they believed that better behaved students deserved more computer time and that the primary benefit of computers for low-achieving students was mastery of basic skills (i.e., drill-and-practice software).

• Richer schools bought more equipment and more expensive equipment. (1994, 153–54)

These findings identify trends that, unchecked, will almost certainly lead to increased inequity in the future. Early childhood educators must find ways to incorporate technology into their classrooms that preserve equity of access and minimize or even reverse the current trends. For example, anecdotal reports indicate that preschool-age boys and girls show equal interest in computers, but as they grow older girls begin to spend less time with

computers than do boys. There are a number of ways educators can proactively work to maintain girls' interest in computers and technology: (1) consider girls' interests and interaction styles when selecting and evaluating software for classroom use; (2) model the use of the computer as a learning and productivity tool and invite children, especially girls, to observe and assist them in the work; and (3) promote equity by offering special times for "girls only" use of computers, which permits girls to explore the computer without having to directly compete with boys (Thouvenelle, Borunda, & McDowell 1994).

Considerations of equity in curriculum content require qualitative judgments. For example, research evidence indicates that children who are economically disadvantaged have less access to computers at home and at-home access is related to attitudes and competence (Martinez & Mead 1988). If schools wish to provide equity to children of low-income families, with respect to their confidence and competence concerning computer learning, these children need to be provided more in-school computer access (Sutton 1991). And that access must be meaningful, moving beyond rote drill-and-practice usage.

Preschool-age children spend time in a variety of diverse settings (e.g., homes, child care centers, family child care), which further complicates the issues of equity and access. Some of these settings have considerable access to technology while others lack the very basics. The more early childhood educators believe in the benefits of appropriate use of technology at the preschool age, the more responsibility we bear in ensuring equity and access to this important learning tool.

> *Efforts should be made to ensure access to appropriate technology for children with special needs, for whom assistive technologies may be essential for successful inclusion.*

For children with special needs, technology has many potential benefits. Technology can be a powerful compensatory tool—it can augment sensory input or reduce distractions; it can provide support for cognitive processing or enhance memory and recall; it can serve as a personal "on-demand" tutor and as an enabling device that supports independent functioning.

The variety of assistive-technology products ranges from low-tech toys with simple switches to expansive high-tech systems capable of managing complex environments. These technologies empower young children, increasing their independence and supporting their inclusion in classes with their peers. With adapted materials, young children with disabilities no longer have to be excluded from activities. Using appropriately designed and supported computer applications, the ability to learn, move, communicate, and recreate are within the reach of all learners.

Yet, with all these enhanced capabilities, this technology requires thoughtful integration into the early childhood curriculum, or it may fall far short of its promise. Educators must match the technology to each child's unique special needs, learning styles, and individual preferences.

5. The power of technology to influence children's learning and development requires that attention be paid to eliminating stereotyping of any group and eliminating exposure to violence, especially as a problem-solving strategy.

Technology can be used to affirm children's diversity.

Early childhood educators must devote extra effort to ensure that the software in classrooms reflects and affirms children's diverse cultures, languages, and ethnic heritages. Like all educational materials, software should reflect the world children live in: It should come in multiple languages, reflect gender equity, contain people of color and of differing ages and abilities, and portray diverse families and experiences (Derman-Sparks & A.B.C. Task Force 1989; Haugland & Shade 1994).

Teachers should actively select software that promotes positive social values.

Just like movies and television today, children's software is often violent and much of it explicit and brutally graphic, as in most of the best-selling titles for the popular game machines. But, often, violence is presented in ways that are less obvious. In all of its forms, violence in software threatens young children's development and challenges early childhood educators, who must take active steps to keep it out of their classrooms (see the *NAEYC Position Statement on Violence in the Lives of Children* 1994).

Some software programs offer children the opportunity to get rid of mistakes by "blowing up" their creations—complete with sound effects—instead of simply erasing or starting over. As a metaphor for solving problems or getting rid of mistakes, "blowing up" is problematic. In the context of a computer software experience, it is more troubling than in the context of television or video. Children control the computer software, and, instead of being passive viewers of what appears on the screen, with the computer they become active decisionmakers about what takes place on the screen. Software programs that empower children to freely blow up or destroy without thought of the actual consequences of their actions can further the disconnection between personal responsibility and violent outcomes.

Identifying and eliminating software containing violence is only one of the challenges facing early childhood educators. A related, opposite challenge is discovering software programs that promote positive social actions. For example, software has the potential to offer children opportunities to develop sensitivities to children from other cultures or to children with disabilities. Much could be done to help children develop positive responses to cultural and racial diversity by offering software programs that enable children to explore the richness within their own and different cultures.

6. Teachers, in collaboration with parents, should advocate for more appropriate technology applications for all children.

The appropriate and beneficial use of technology with young children is ultimately the responsibility of the early childhood educator, working in collaboration with parents. Parents and teachers together need to make better choices as consumers. As they become educated on the appropriate uses of technology, parents and teachers are more likely to make informed decisions and to make it known to developers of technology when they are unhappy with products. Working together, parents and teachers are a large consumer group wielding greater influence on the development of technology for young children. Following are specific recommendations for early childhood professionals as they advocate for more appropriate technology applications for all children.

• Provide information to parents on the benefits and use of appropriate software.

• Advocate for computer hardware that can be upgraded easily as new technology becomes available.

• Encourage software publishers to make previewing of software easier for parents and educators.

• Advocate for a system of software review by educators.

• Promote the development of software and technology applications that routinely incorporate features that cater to the needs of learners with different abilities.

• Advocate for software that promotes positive representation of gender, cultural and linguistic diversity, and abilities. Software publishers should create a balance of programs that appeal to both boys and girls.

• Encourage software publishers to create programs that support collaboration among learners rather than competition. Fostering cooperative learning enhances the acceptance of the abilities of all learners.

• Encourage software publishers to develop programs that reflect appropriate, nonviolent ways to solve problems and correct mistakes.

• Develop formal and informal information sharing and support for teachers, parents, and appropriate organizations and community-based programs. Encourage free community access to technology through libraries, schools, and so forth.

• Support policies on federal, state, and local levels that encourage funding that supports equity in access to technology for young children and their families.

7. **The appropriate use of technology has many implications for early childhood professional development.**

> *As early childhood educators become active participants in a technological world, they need in-depth training and ongoing support to be adequately prepared to make decisions about technology and to support its effective use in learning environments for children.*

To achieve the potential benefits of technology, both preservice and inservice training must provide early childhood educators with opportunities for basic information and awareness. These efforts must address the rapid proliferation and fast-paced change within the technology arena. Opportunities that emphasize evaluating the software in relation to children's development are essential.

Institutions of higher education and other organizations and groups that provide preservice and inservice education have a responsibility to

• incorporate experiences that permit educators to reflect on the principles of early childhood education and how technology can support and extend these principles;

• give teachers concentrated time to focus on how best to use educational technology and to develop a plan for the use of educational technology in a school or early childhood program;

• provide hands-on training with appropriate software programs to assist teachers in becoming familiar and comfortable with the operation and features of hardware and software; and

• provide on-site and school-based training on effectively integrating technology into the curriculum and assessment process.

At the classroom level, teachers need staff-development experiences (Kearsley & Lynch 1992) that permit them to

• use teaching techniques that fully use the technology;

• encourage parental involvement with technology;

• match technology applications to the learning needs of individual children;

• look for cross-curriculum/cross-cultural applications;

• facilitate cooperative interactions among children; and

• use technology to improve personal efficiency.

The potentials of technology are far-reaching and ever changing. The risk is for adults to become complacent, assuming that their current knowledge or experience is adequate. "Technology is an area of the curriculum, as well as a tool for learning, in which teachers must demonstrate their own capacity for learning" (Bredekamp & Rosegrant 1994, 61). As teachers try out their new knowledge in the classroom, there should be opportunities to share experiences and insights, problems and challenges with other educators. When teachers become comfortable and confident with the new technology, they can be offered additional challenges and stimulated to reach new levels of competence in using technology.

> *Early childhood educators should use technology as a tool for communication and collaboration among professionals as well as a tool for teaching children.*

Technology can be a powerful tool for professional development. Software can provide accessible information and tools for classroom management, planning, and creation of materials. Telecommunications and the Internet can enable teachers to obtain information and new ideas from around the world and to interact with distant experts and peers. Early childhood educators can incorporate principles of cooperative learning as they assist distant peers in acquiring new skills; share curriculum ideas, resources, and promising practices; exchange advice; and collaborate on classroom and professional development projects. Providing training and support for access to services available via on-line networks and the Internet has the potential of opening the doors to worlds of additional classroom resources. With a responsive on-line system, mentors can assist novices in becoming more technology literate and more involved in actively using technology for professional benefits. As educators become competent users of technology for personal and professional growth, they can model appropriate use for young children.

References

Apple Computer Inc. 1993. *The adventure begins: Preschool and technology.* Videocassette. (Available from NAEYC.)

Bredekamp, S., ed. 1987. *Developmentally appropriate practice in early childhood programs serving children from birth through age 8.* Exp. ed. Washington, DC: NAEYC.

Bredekamp, S., & T. Rosegrant. 1994. Learning and teaching with technology. In *Young children: Active learners in a technological age*, eds. J.L. Wright & D.D. Shade, 53–61. Washington, DC: NAEYC.

Clements, D.H. 1994. The uniqueness of the computer as a learning tool: Insights from research and practice. In *Young children: Active learners in a technological age*, eds. J.L. Wright & D.D. Shade, 31–50. Washington, DC: NAEYC.

Clements, D.H., B.K. Nastasi, & S. Swaminathan. 1993. Young children and computers: Crossroads and directions from research. *Young Children* 48 (2): 56–64.

Davis, B.C., & D.D. Shade. 1994. Integrate, don't isolate!—Computers in the early childhood curriculum. *ERIC Digest* (December). No. EDO-PS-94-17.

Derman-Sparks, L., & the A.B.C. Task Force. 1989. *Anti-bias curriculum: Tools for empowering young children.* Washington, DC: NAEYC.

Haugland, S.W., & D.D. Shade. 1990. *Developmental evaluations of software for young children: 1990 edition.* New York: Delmar.

Haugland, S.W., & D.D. Shade. 1994. Software evaluation for young children. In *Young children: Active learners in a technological age*, eds. J.L. Wright & D.D. Shade, 63–76. Washington, DC: NAEYC.

Kearsley, G., & W. Lynch. 1992. Educational leadership in the age of technology: The new skills. *Journal of Research on Computing in Education* 25 (1): 50–60.

King, J.A., & N. Alloway. 1992. Preschooler's use of microcomputers and input devices. *Journal of Educational Computing Research* 8: 451–68.

Lipinski, J.A., R.E. Nida, D.D. Shade, & J.A. Watson. 1986. The effect of microcomputers on young children: An examination of free-play choices, sex differences, and social interactions. *Journal of Educational Computing Research* 2 (2): 147–68.

Martinez, M.E., & N.A. Mead. 1988. *Computer competence: The first national assessment.* Tech report no. 17-CC-01. Princeton, NJ: National Educational Progress and Educational Testing Service.

NAEYC position statement on violence in the lives of children. 1994. Washington, DC: NAEYC.

NAEYC, & NAECS/SDE (National Association of Early Childhood Specialists in State Departments of Education). 1992. Guidelines for appropriate curriculum content and assessment in programs serving children ages 3 through 8. In *Reaching potentials: Appropriate curriculum and assessment for young children, volume 1*, eds. S. Bredekamp & T. Rosegrant, 9–27. Washington, DC: NAEYC.

Nastasi, B.K., & D.H. Clements. 1993. Motivational and social outcomes of cooperative education environments. *Journal of Computing in Childhood Education* 4 (1): 15–43.

Rhee, M.C., & N. Chavnagri. 1991. *4 year old children's peer interactions when playing with a computer.* ERIC, ED 342466.

Shade, D.D., & J.A. Watson. 1990. Computers in early education: Issues put to rest, theoretical links to sound practice, and the potential contribution of microworlds. *Journal of Educational Computing Research* 6 (4): 375–92.

SPA consumer market report. 1996. Washington, DC: Software Publishers Association (SPA).

Sutton, R.E. 1991. Equity and computers in the schools: A decade of research. *Review of Educational Research* 61 (4): 475–503.

Thouvenelle, S., M. Borunda, & C. McDowell. 1994. Replicating inequities: Are we doing it again? In *Young children: Active learners in a technological age*, eds. J.L. Wright & D.D. Shade, 151–66. Washington, DC: NAEYC.

Wright, J.L., & D.D. Shade, eds. 1994. *Young children: Active learners in a technological age.* Washington, DC: NAEYC.

Children's Computers

Anastasia P. Samaras

Anastasia P. Samaras is Assistant Professor, Curriculum and Instruction, and Director of Teacher Education, Catholic University of America, Washington, DC.

*I*n an early childhood classroom, a young boy sits at the computer, which faces the wall. His fingers fly over the control keys. He is quiet, content and occupied. His teacher occasionally looks over at him with a peaceful smile as she cuts out colored circles for the next day's classification lesson. Why is this scene dismaying?

◆

A decade of studies have questioned whether computers would change early childhood education. Those studies addressed such major issues as children's development (Barns & Hill, 1983; Cuffaro, 1984; Ziajka, 1983), cognitive gains (Papert, 1980; Piestrup, 1981) and social interactions with peers (Borgh & Dickson, 1986; Natasi, Clements & Battista, 1987). While more recent studies examine the appropriateness of specific software (Haugland & Shade, 1994; Henniger, 1994; Isenberg & Rosegrant, 1995), the teacher's contribution to children's learning during computer instruction remains unexamined.

To a large degree, teachers and the social context determine what children acquire from computer experiences. Computers should support and extend children's learning, not just entertain or occupy them. They have the potential to reveal children's understanding and development of problem-solving strategies (Samaras, 1991) and to provide for individualized private assistance (Schofield, Eurich-Fulcer & Britt, 1994). Using software programs or having a brief introduction does not guarantee children's strategy acquisition.

Structuring Children's Learning

Studies of play training (Smilansky & Shefatya, 1990) and computer play (Wright & Samaras, 1986) reveal that teachers can interpret, remark upon and extend children's abstract thinking and help them develop problem-solving strategies. Teachers need to be sensitive observers, master questioners and scaffolders of children's development and learning (National Association for the Education of Young Children and the National Association of Early Childhood Specialists in State Departments of Education, 1991).

Vygotskian theory (1987) asserts that while it is only possible to teach children what they are able to learn, instruction should be tailored to what children can achieve *with assistance*. Research findings indicate that adult involvement enhances children's attention span, memory and thinking (Berk & Winsler, 1995; Rogoff, 1990).

Effective adult scaffolders tailor their instruction according to the perceived skills and needs of the child and offer gradations of support through general and specific statements. They offer both verbal and nonverbal assistance by organizing the environment and materials, demonstrating the task when necessary and providing contingent-on-error assistance (Wood, Bruner & Ross, 1976). Building upon a subset of skills, adults can tap children's ability to learn new skills that extends slightly beyond their unassisted or developmental capabilities. Interactive language allows children to test their constructed notions against the thinking of others. Gradually, the responsibility shifts from joint to independent problem solving.

Adults offer children a repertoire of problem-solving strategies. Self-regulation, or children's capacity to plan, guide and monitor their own psychological processes, is possible when children replace their inadequate strategies with those mediated by a more experienced problem-solver (Diaz, Neal & Amaya-Williams, 1989). One strategy adults use when constructing a puzzle, for example, is to refer to a pictorial representation.

The Puzzle Paradigm

Puzzles of varying degrees of difficulty call upon

different child competencies for their solutions. Simple puzzles require matching and hand-eye coordination skills; their cues (such as shape, color, pattern and location) are coordinated to facilitate correct placement. More difficult puzzles, which eliminate shape cues entirely, consist of individual pieces that are color-patterned parts of a larger picture. Solving those puzzles requires children to consult the intact picture or model as a guide.

When putting puzzles together, children under age 5 do not typically use or understand a model-consultation strategy (Wertsch, McNamee, McLane & Budwig, 1980). A model must be studied. Young children, however, have difficulty scanning and extracting relevant information from a picture (Vurpillot, 1968). Often, they do not know what attributes to look for, or how to pay attention to certain objects in a picture. Olson (1970) suggests that young children's perceptual world is enhanced by others who model an awareness of a model's critical features.

Such is the case in the computer program *Peanuts Picture Puzzlers* (Pelczarski & Lubar, 1984). Sixteen pieces represent a picture of two Peanuts characters. Players choose one piece at a time and "insert" them into the puzzle by using the space bar. A completed puzzle can be consulted at any time, as often and as long as necessary. Tutorial interactions highlight differences in teachers' instructional roles and children's subsequent use of problem-solving strategies. A teacher providing optimal assistance helps children to consult a puzzle model, termed "access," and strategically examine a puzzle picture, termed "analysis."

Computer Alone

One child who did not receive the access and analysis mediation completed the puzzle using a trial-and-error approach. He was brimming with self-confidence because he accomplished the task all by himself:

Sampson: Oops *(incorrect piece).* No *(incorrect piece).* This is what I regular do so I know what, where it goes. *(Using one hand, he presses the piece selection key without looking through the selection and then immediately presses the space bar to insert the piece.)* Some of them won't go in at all. *(Now using two hands, the child rocks his upper body synchronically with the key presses. He moves more quickly as the probability of choosing the wrong piece lessens. Choosing an incorrect piece, he shouts out:)* No way, José!

In this situation, the teacher told the child that the escape key could be used to access the puzzle model, but did not offer any suggestions for its use during the activity even when the child experienced difficulty finding a correct puzzle piece. Neither was the child offered any perceptual or spatial cues of puzzle piece location. The teacher did not point to the puzzle or talk about one piece's location in relation to others. When the child chose the correct piece, the teacher offered a general statement of praise, but did not ask the child to reflect on why the piece seemed to belong.

Teacher Mediation of the Access and Analysis Strategies

A teacher offering optimal assistance demonstrates and talks about her puzzle-solving strategies while encouraging the child to solve a puzzle. She reminds the child to look back at the model. Pointing to puzzle areas that are causing the child difficulty, the teacher encourages the child to make a strategic visual scan of the picture. The teacher can check and monitor the child's actions using two computer screens that display the dissected puzzle and the puzzle model. The teacher offers reflective assessments of the child's performance, constantly redirecting the child's attention back to the model. It is important to avoid en-

Student and teacher explore a Peanuts puzzle.

couraging a sense of dependency, as the following example illustrates:

Jody: *(The child moves through the piece selection by holding down the cursor key.)* I think that one will be fine.

Teacher: O.K. You can try it. *(The child tries.)* That one doesn't belong so let's look back at the whole picture. We're looking for this piece. *(The teacher points to the area on the puzzle model and describes the picture segment.)* We have Charlie Brown's hat, and now we're looking for a little piece of Snoopy's nose.

Jody: *(The child returns to the divided puzzle and then quickly scans the piece selection.)* O.K. Did I pass it?

Teacher: You can look at the pieces as you go through. Don't go too fast.

Jody: How about Snoopy's eyes?

Teacher: Maybe we should go back and look at the puzzle.

Jody: *(The child points to the puzzle model.)* Snoopy's eyelash. Now what are we looking for? So how about Snoopy's ears?

Teacher: We have to look at where the small white box is and that's right here. *(Teacher points to the computer cursor.)*

Jody: What are we looking for?

Teacher: You can go back and look at the whole picture.

Jody: O.K. Is that it?

Teacher: Remember what key to use. You do it, you try it. *(With a reminder from the teacher, child presses escape key then finds the correct piece and inserts it.)*

Jody: I think that's it!

Teacher: Good, and you're right. That's great. All right, good.

Jody: It worked.

Teacher: Yes. It belonged. Snoopy is beginning to look like the whole picture. O.K. Good.

The following conversation illustrates that children do not always understand computer program demands. By listening carefully to the child's statements, the teacher in this episode identifies the child's perceptual and spatial understanding, and adjusts her questioning accordingly:

Vickie: Now what are we doing?

Teacher: Remember where you are now. See Snoopy sitting right here on the red dog house?

Vickie: You mean he's sitting on the dog house and we're supposed to do that piece?

Teacher: Yes.

Vickie: Now where are we looking or what piece are we looking for? *(Murmurs.)* I'm looking for her hair.

Teacher: Oh, we're down here. *(Teacher points to the segment of the divided puzzle that is not a piece of a character's hair.)*

Vickie: Let me see something. *(Child now looks back at the model independently.)*

In the following example, the child grasps the access strategy but does not realize the strategic significance of consulting the model. The child holds one finger on the cursor while pressing the escape key to look at the model. Note the use of the word *we* in this joint problem-solving episode as the child talks aloud:

Frosina: We want that part. *(Looks back at the model.)* All right, we want that part *(incorrect piece)*. O.K., we want that part. No, not yet. *(Looks back at the model.)* We want a part of the tree. There it goes. No, it doesn't. Hmm. Back to the puzzle. We want that part, O.K.? *(Gets correct piece.)*

Teacher: Good job! *(Child laughs.)*

Frosina: I knew how to do this puzzle. I need to do another.

The social context for instruction is quite different in these episodes than in the first one described. Here, the teacher's role is to observe and evaluate the child's understanding of the task. Guided feedback that is contingent on the child's errors should be offered during the activity. Praise should be truthful and specific to the child's actions. The child and teacher work together to solve the problem with the adult sharing, but not reciting, sophisticated strategies. Joint reference during the activity enables the child to hear and see the teacher's thinking while providing a gentle support for the child's developing competencies.

Transitions to Competence

Two days later, while working on a different puzzle, the child uses both the access and analysis strategies:

Frosina: Hmm, the part. I guess I'm going to look at the picture. *(Returns to the model.)* All right, we're looking for the tree branch. Oh, yeah, that's it.

Teacher: Terrific, Frosina!

Frosina: There it goes. *(Selects incorrect piece.)*

Teacher: That's all right. Try another piece.

Frosina: *(Looking slowly through the piece selection.)* No, that, that, there it goes *(laughs)*.

Teacher: Great job!

Frosina: *(Looking at the picture.)* Let's see. All right, we want the sky. All right, there it goes.

Teacher: Terrific. You are doing such a good job.

Frosina: We want that one.

Conclusion

Without teacher support, children in computer contexts may experience an unsustained locus of control through a trial-and-error process that is devoid of task conceptualization. The anecdotes collected in this article illustrate that teachers can adapt and extend children's learning within the computer context. In these cases, the computer allowed teachers to make a uniform problem presentation while witnessing children's cognitive capabilities, listening to their metacognitive thoughts and offering alternative problem-solving approaches. The computer context extended the teachers' power as adaptive tutors, allowing them to mediate between the child and the computer. Computers enable teachers to accommodate children's different learning styles and abilities.

Not every computer encounter entails this type of instruction, nor should it. Computers can be superb teaching tools for a variety of learning tasks. Recent innovations that combine the use of computers and digital video allow teachers to help young children capture and talk about their performances while developing portfolios (Forman, 1995). As teachers seek mechanisms to support and extend children's learning, they should ask themselves how the computer can help.

After a decade of studies, researchers are still asking if computers will change early childhood education (Haugland, 1995). I agree with Papert (1993) that computers cannot revolutionize the way children are taught unless teachers examine how they teach without computers. Educators must address the purpose, quality and social context of computer-instructional experiences for children.

◆

References

Barns, B., & Hill, S. (1983). Should young children work with microcomputer-Logo before Lego? *Computing Teacher, 10*(9), 11-14.

Berk, L., & Winsler, A. (1995). *Scaffolding children's learning: Vygotsky and early childhood education.* Vol. 7 of the NAEYC Research into Practice Series. Washington, DC: National Association for the Education of Young Children.

Borgh, K., & Dickson, W. P. (1986). Two preschoolers sharing one microcomputer: Creating prosocial behavior with hardware and software. In P. F. Campbell & G. G. Fein (Eds.), *Young children and microcomputers* (pp. 37-44). Englewood Cliffs, NJ: Prentice Hall.

Cuffaro, N. K. (1984). Microcomputers in education: Why is earlier better? *Teachers College Record, 85*(4), 561-568.

Diaz, R. M., Neal, C. J., & Amaya-Williams, M. (1989). The social origins of self-regulation. In L. Moll (Ed.), *Vygotsky and education: Instructional implications and applications of sociohistorical psychology* (pp. 127-154). New York, NY: Cambridge University Press.

Forman, G. (1995). *Building a sense of belonging using technology for young children.* Keynote address. Summer Conference on Educational Technology. Bridging the Gap: Children, Teachers, and Media. Sponsored by the National Learning Center, Washington, DC.

Haugland, S. (1995). Will technology change early childhood education? *Day Care and Early Education, 22*(4), 45-46.

Haugland, S., & Shade, D. (1994). Software evaluation for young children. In J. Wright & D. Shade (Eds.), *Young children: Active learners in a technological age.* Washington, DC: National Association for the Education of Young Children.

Henniger, M. L. (1994). Software for the early childhood classroom: What should it look like? *Journal of Computing in Childhood Education, 5*(2), 167-175.

Isenberg, J. P., & Rosegrant, T. (1995). Children and technology. In J. Moyer (Ed.), *Selecting educational equipment and materials for school and home* (pp. 25-29). Wheaton, MD: Association for Childhood Education International.

Natasi, B. K., Clements, D. H., & Battista, M. T. (1987). *Effects of Logo programming and CAI problem solving on social and social-cognitive behaviors.* Paper presented at the Annual Meeting of the American Educational Research Association, Washington, DC.

National Association for the Education of Young Children and the National Association of Early Childhood Specialists in State Departments of Education. (1991). Guidelines for appropriate curriculum content and assessment in programs serving children ages 3 through 8. *Young Children, 46*(3), 21-39.

Olson, D. R. (1970). *Cognitive development: The child's acquisition of diagonality.* New York: Academic Press.

Papert, S. (1980). *Mindstorms.* New York: Basic Books.

Papert, S. (1993). *The children's machine: Rethinking school in the age of the computer.* New York: Basic Books.

Pelczarski, M., & Lubar, D. (1984). (Graphics). Peanuts trademark, Schulz, C. M. *Peanuts Picture Puzzlers* [Computer program]. New York: Random House Electronic Publishing/McGraw Hill.

Piestrup, A. M. (1981). *Preschool children use Apple II to test reading skills program.* Portola Valley, CA: Advanced Learning Technology. (ERIC Document Reproduction Service No. ED 202476)

Rogoff, B. (1990). *Apprenticeship in thinking: Cognitive development in social context.* New York: Oxford University Press.

Samaras, A. P. (1991). Transitions to competence: An investigation of adult mediation in preschoolers self-regulation with a microcomputer-based problem-solving task. *Early Education and Development, 2*(3), 181-196.

Schofield, J. W., Eurich-Fulcer, R., & Britt, C. L. (1994). Teachers, computer tutors, and teaching: The artificially intelligent tutor as an agent for classroom change. *American Educational Research Journal, 31*(3), 579-607.

Smilansky, S., & Shefatya, L. (1990). *Facilitating play: A medium for promoting cognitive, socio-emotional and academic development in young children.* Gaithersburg, MD: Psychosocial & Educational Publications.

Vurpillot, E. (1968). The development of scanning strategies and their relation to visual differentiation. *Journal of Experimental Child Psychology, 6*, 632-650.

Vygotsky, L. S. (1987). The development of scientific concepts in childhood. In R. W. Rieber & A. S. Carton (Eds.), *The collected works of L. S. Vygotsky. Vol. 1.* (pp. 167-241). New York: Plenum.

Wertsch, J. V., McNamee, G. D., McLane, J. B., & Budwig, N. A. (1980). The adult-child dyad as a problem-solving system. *Child Development, 51*, 1215-1221.

Wood, D., Bruner, J. S., & Ross, G. (1976). The role of tutoring in problem-solving. *Journal of Child Psychology and Psychiatry, 17*, 89-100.

Wright, J., & Samaras, A. (1986). Play worlds and microworlds. In P. F. Campbell & G. G. Fein (Eds.), *Young children and microcomputers* (pp. 74-86). Englewood Cliffs, NJ: Prentice Hall.

Ziajka, A. (1983). Microcomputers in early childhood education? A first look. *Young Children, 38*(5), 61-67.

Software Evaluation

Daniel D. Shade

© BmPorter/Don Franklin

The "NAEYC Position Statement on Technology and Young Children—Ages Three through Eight" emphasizes the central role teachers must take to ensure that the potential benefits of technology for young children are realized (see Wright & Shade 1994 for further discussion). Decisions such as what software to use or whether to use the computer as an add-on or integrate it across the curriculum are just a few of the critical decisions teachers must make as computers become part of their early childhood curriculum.

The most critical decision a teacher can make is that of software selection. After all, a computer is little more than plastic and electronic circuitry until software is loaded. Just as how crayons are used depends on whether children are given blank paper or coloring books (Elkind 1987), the use of a computer is determined by the developmental appropriateness of the software selected.

Ten years of amazing, light-speed hardware and software development

Much has occurred in the past 10 years that has had an impact on the evaluation of software di-

Daniel D. Shade, *Ph.D., directs the Technology in Early Childhood (TECH) program at the University of Delaware in Newark. He has been studying the effects of computers on young children and developing teacher education methodology in the same area for more than 13 years.*

rectly and indirectly. The following are examples.

• Computing power has grown at an exponential rate, bringing us more computer power at lower costs and therefore making computers available to a larger proportion of the population. (Computers have yet to fall to a price where every family could afford one.)

• More computing power has made computer technology more accessible to young children (i.e., computer speech capabilities allow young, nonreading children to use the machine independently).

• The advent and mass acceptance of CD-ROM (compact disk read-only memory) technology has allowed software companies to make vast improvements in the quality of software for young children. These include but are not limited to smoother animation,

the inclusion of video clips, true life sounds and music, improved computer verbalizations for children, and astounding graphics.

• Software companies have recognized children and their homes and schools as a vast, potential market. Approximately 300 (Buckleitner 1994) software titles are released each year, forming what many feel has become a software glut, with which it is difficult to maintain stride.

All of the above advances have contributed to the length of time it takes and the difficulty involved in software evaluation. In 1983 when most educational software was designed to run on as little as 16K (kilo) bytes of RAM (random access memory) and the entire software program could be stored on one floppy disk, the predominant drill-and-practice

From *Young Children*, September 1996, pp. 17-21. © 1996 by Daniel D. Shade. Reprinted by permission of the author.

Avoid drill-and-practice software. Look for software that allows the child to make decisions about what she wants to do and which she can operate with little help.

software of that day took about 15 minutes to evaluate. In 1996 when software can have from 4 to 32 to 64 megabytes (thousands of K-bytes) of RAM to run with and large, hard-disk drives on which programs often larger than 10K can be stored, software can be quite elaborate and present a "microworld" (Papert 1980) that children can explore for hours. For such software, evaluation can take as long as two hours. (See "Resources" to help teachers locate software that has already been evaluated by competent sources.)

Ten years of "two-steps-forward and one-step-back" software development

Some things have remained fairly steady through the past decade in spite of all the software evaluation that has occurred.

• Drill-and-practice software (requiring children to respond with one right answer to closed-ended questions) still dominates the marketplace. Haugland and Shade (1994) estimated that approximately 25 to 30% of the software available for young children is developmentally appropriate. However, hidden in that small percentage are found approximately 160 developmentally appropriate software programs for both platforms (PC-compatible and Macintosh).

• Software companies are still trying to market large, integrated learning systems or solutions. Touted as all you need for your language arts or math curriculum, software applications like these have the least success in helping children read or do math, as research has clearly shown (Clements & Nastasi 1993).

• Schools continue to place computers in isolated labs where children are taught "computer literacy skills," which Papert (1993) states is the most useless thing we could teach children as the technology skills they learn today will not be the same skills needed in the future.

All three of these trends continue to make finding appropriate software very difficult. What is the teacher to do who finds himself or herself drowning in a sea of software purchased by school administrators? There appears to be a high correlation between computer labs and drill software. Someone continues to buy large, integrated learning solutions, which automatically narrows a teacher's software choice to zero. And software companies continue to produce drill software because the overhead is low (requiring little programming time compared to open-ended software) and profits are high. Fortunately, some more recent, open-ended, creative software has been well received, and, perhaps, software companies will follow the trend.

Evaluating software: What to consider

The box on the next page provides a checklist of features to look for when evaluating software. The checklist represents an overview of eight early childhood software evaluators summarized in Haugland and Shade (1994). Three main areas to consider in evaluating software are child features, teacher features, and technical features.

Child features

The primary question to ask in evaluating the child features of a piece of software is this: Can the child make decisions about what he wants to do and operate the software to accomplish that task, with minor help from adults?

Such checklist terms as *active learning, child controlled interaction, possible experimentation, children set the pace and stop anytime, operate from picture menu,* and *child uses independently* all connote children using software in a manner that cannot be associated with drill and rote responses but more likely with open-ended, discovery-oriented software. Furthermore, software with these characteristics will produce independent computer users. Young children must be independent users if computers are to function in such settings as public schools, child care centers, and private schools, where not enough people are available for there to be someone beside the computer at all times to help the children. Fortunately, software having the features described above will promote independence.

Teachers be warned, however! Just as any new material brought into a classroom full of young children causes excitement (Davidson 1989), the first few weeks the computer is in the classroom even more excitement should be expected. Maintaining control over this enthusiastic response from the children may require the teacher to remain in close proximity of the computer area until the novelty effect wears off (Lipinski et al. 1986).

A few child features need more explanation, perhaps, such as *concrete representations, child is agent of change,* and *low entry, high ceiling.*

> **Avoid large, integrated learning systems. Look for software that allows the child to set the pace and stop anytime, experiment, operate from a picture menu, and control the interaction.**

Concrete representations refers to the graphics the child is manipulating on the screen. Screen graphics should be manipulable and should function accurately (i.e., a representation of an airplane flies but does not talk). What about spacecraft and aliens? Can children successfully manipulate representations of objects with which they have had no experience?

Perhaps too many of us have been stranded in Piaget's stage of concrete operations for so long that we have begun to take the word *concrete* literally, as Clements and Nastasi state, "what is concrete to the child may have more to do with what is meaningful and manipulable than with its physical characteristics" (1993, 259). In other words, since young children are very familiar with fictional aliens (E.T., Alf, and others in both books and visual media) and spacecraft (the Space Shuttle, the U.S.S. Enterprise, and others in both books and visual media), then concrete representations on a screen can be manipulated. It is a misnomer to conclude that Piaget meant only three-dimensional, solid forms when he used the word *concrete* (Shade & Watson 1990). How long have we been using flat, two-dimensional picture books in early childhood education (Piestrup 1985)?

Child is agent of change is another important Piagetian principle (Haugland & Shade 1990). If young children can manipulate graphics on the screen, then the children should be the agent of cause and effect within the software, not some far-distant programmer.

In drill software, although a child is given a choice (pick the triangle out of three shapes), the computer often performs the operation for the child if he happens to get it wrong or waits too long. In developmentally appropriate software, children should have the power to move graphics on the screen and then observe the results or consequences of their actions. This corresponds very closely with the principle suggested by Chaillé and Littman (1985) that software should highlight cause-and-effect processes for young children. Such a feature as *process highlighter* can be activated by the child by pressing particular keys. For example, the child might be able to watch her last action (instant replay) or slow down the growth of foliage in a ecology program (special effects) or view the horizon and zoom in for a closer look (pan and

Figure 1. A Checklist for Evaluating Software for Young Children

CHILD FEATURES		TEACHER FEATURES		TECHNICAL FEATURES	
Active Learning Emphasized	__	Can be Customized	__	Animation Other than Reward	__
Age Appropriate Concepts	__	Childproof	__	Aesthetically Pleasing	__
Child Controlled Interaction	__	Curriculum Congruence	__	Available on Mac & IBM	__
Child is Agent of Change	__	Delivers on Ad Promises	__	Corresponding Sound Effects	__
Children Can Stop Anytime	__	High Educational Value	__	Corresponding Music	__
Children Set the Pace	__	High Value per Dollar	__	Designed with Children in Mind	__
Child Uses Independently	__	Mixed Gender/Role Equity	__	Digitized Human Speech Used	__
Concrete Representations	__	Mult. Languages Available	__	Easy Installation on Hard Drive	__
Concrete Reps. Function	__	Represents Differing Ability	__	Fast Installation and Set Up	__
Creativity (Divergent Thinking)	__	Represents Differing Ages	__	Max Use of Computer's Power	__
Discovery Learning	__	Represents Alt. Family Styles	__	No Gratuitous Music & Sounds	__
Engages Student Interest	__	Represents People of Color	__	Realistic Sound Effects/Music	__
Experimentation Is Possible	__	Supplemental to Curriculum	__	Realistic, High-Res Graphics	__
Intrinsically Motivating	__	Understandable Users Manual	__	Runs Quickly--Min. Waiting	__
Logical Learning Sequence	__	Universal Focus (all children)	__	Speech is Clear and Distinct	__
Low Entry, High Ceiling	__				
Not Skill Drilling	__				
Makes Learning Fun	__				
Models World Accurately	__				
Open-Ended	__				
Operate From Picture Menu	__				
Process Highlighter	__				
Process not Product Oriented	__				
Simple & Precise Directions	__				
Speech Used When Helpful	__				
Teaches Powerful Ideas	__				
Verbal Instructions & Help	__				

Name of the Program: _____

Publisher: _____

Special Skills or Scaffolding Required by Children: _____

Content Appropriate for Integration into My Curriculum: _____

Age Range Indiated on Box: _____ Child-Tested (yes/no): _____

This Program is Appropriate for My Students (yes/no): _____

This Program Contains Valuable Educational Concepts (yes/no): _____

This Program Contains Powerful Ideas and Concepts (yes/no): _____

NOTES:

The above checklist has been developed from the overviews of the various software evaluation methods reviewed in this chapter. No effort has been made to compute a score based upon this checklist. Rather it is intended that as a teacher fills out the checklist, s/he will come to a general decision about the appropriateness of the program. This form may be duplicated for personal and classroom use.

Source: Reprinted by permission, from S.W. Haughland and D.D. Shade, "Software Evaluation for Young Children," in *Young Children: Active Learners in a Technological Age*, eds. J.L. Wright and D.D. Shade (Washington, DC: NAEYC, 1994), 74. Copyright © by the authors.

zoom). Young children interacting with computers should have this much control and more.

Low entry, high ceiling describes software that has expanding complexity and can be used by children at various developmental levels. A three-year-old would be able to use a specific piece of software because of its easy access, while a seven-year-old would benefit from the more complex knowledge and skills the same software teaches.

Teacher features

[handwritten: broader outlook in my software reviews]

Has the teacher purchased a powerful tool program that can be integrated across the curriculum (suitability), a program that will empower the children to learn through self-directed exploration rather than through rote memorization or drill—the *educational value*? Also, a teacher should be concerned that the software is representative of the diverse composition of the classroom. Software should reflect our diverse society by representing people of color, people with differing ages and abilities, and people from a variety of family styles (Haugland & Shade 1994). There should be something familiar about the software for all children—*universal focus* (Haugland & Wright in press). As our society becomes ever more diverse, we must be careful that educational materials fairly represent all ethnic groups.

One critical feature that teachers and educators have been asking for quite some time is having control over software to customize it for the children or a particular child in a class. We already have excellent software utilities for *child proofing* the computer and keeping active minds and hands away from the hard-disk drive, but teachers need more control than just file protection. Some open-ended, creativity programs begin with hundreds of tools with

which the child can create. Many teachers and children are overwhelmed by so many choices. Imagine how it would be for teachers to be able to shut off some of the options or tools and scale down the software to fit particular circumstances (first introduction to computers), to fit a particular group of children (special needs or younger age), or even to reduce the amount of time the teacher needs to spend in the computer areas until the novelty effect wears off.

Technical features

Does the software maximize the potential of the hardware? In other words, does your $45 software look and run well on your computer? One safeguard is to check the minimum requirements of a software package to see if the capabilities of your computer are powerful enough to run the software well. Software manufacturers list the minimum requirements (for example, processor speed, RAM, hard-disk storage, color-monitor requirements, etc.) on the outside of each software package. If your classroom computer does not meet minimum requirements of a piece of software, then purchasing the program would be a mistake and a disappointment to teachers and children alike.

Technical features are, perhaps, the area in which we have witnessed the greatest change in software. Vast improvements in hardware have allowed software to become more friendly, more complex, and more aesthetically pleasing. These changes have nothing to do with the content of

the software. The worst drill program can be just as glitzy as the most developmentally appropriate piece. Research has shown (Shade 1992) that little correlation exists between winning an editors' or parents' award and being developmentally appropriate. It is this author's belief that most software wins industry awards (those not given out by educators) because of slick technical features. Therefore, although improved technical features have made things possible for children's software, one still needs to look carefully beyond the bright packaging and wonderful graphics to see what the software is really doing.

Conclusion

[handwritten: classroom mgt. issue]

This article discusses software evaluation in generalities only. The next step is for teachers or other adults to use the checklist on page 19 to evaluate a few pieces of software. I remain open to your inquiries—after you have evaluated two or three pieces of software, you may reach me on e-mail at Comps4Kids@Aol.Com with specific comments or questions.

Resources

II Alive: Celebrating the Apple II—For Apple II users (especially teachers) this is a good way to keep your Apple II system current. Contact: Quality Computers at 800-777-3642.

Children's Software Revue—If you want timely, up-to-the-minute reviews and information, subscribe to this newsletter. It includes detailed reviews on the latest resources and contains an "All-Star Software" list of the magazine's top-rated programs. Contact: Warren Buckleitner, Editor, *Children's Software Revue,* 44 Main

---

Look for software that three-year-olds can access, yet seven-year-olds can benefit from because of the more complex knowledge and skills the same software teaches.

St., Flemington, NJ 08822; 908-284-0404, fax 908-284-0405.

***Child's* Best Software Awards**—Watch for the December issue of *Child* magazine, which presents the best children's software of the year. Software is judged by Warren Buckleitner, Susan W. Haugland, and Daniel D. Shade. Available at $2.95, on most newsstands.

Computers and Young Children: A World of Discovery—Susan W. Haugland and June L. Wright have a forthcoming book from Allyn & Bacon, which will contain numerous software evaluations.

Early Childhood Education Journal—Susan W. Haugland has a quarterly software review column in this journal. Contact: Human Sciences Press, Inc., 233 Spring St., NY 10013-1578.

Education Resources Catalog—A good mail-order source for buying discounted software, many with 30-day trial periods. Contact: 800-624-2926.

Family PC—for Multimedia, PC, and Mac. This magazine is directed at families but is certainly appropriate for educators. Software reviews cover latest releases and both platforms. Included also are lots of tips and trade secrets. Contact: *Family PC*, Box 400454, Des Moines, IA 50340-0454.

Peak Learning, Inc.—A catalog of evaluated software published by Jay Turley. Contact: Peak Learning, Inc., 4252 S.W. Luana Beach, Vashon Island, WA 98070; 206-463-6787, fax 206-463-5658.

Software Publishers' Annual Codie Awards—A broad range of awards for all age groups and most subject areas. Contact: Loni Singer, Software Publishers Association, 1730 M St., NW, Suite 700, Washington, DC 20036-4510; 202-452-1600, fax 202-223-8756.

Young Children: Active Learners in a Technological Age. NAEYC book edited by June L. Wright and Daniel D. Shade. If you a have a question, this book has a chapter about it.

References

Buckleitner, W. December 1994/January 1995. Hardware news: 1994 in review. *Children's Software Revue* 2 (6): 12.

Chaillé, C., & B. Littman. 1985. Computers in early education: The child as theory builder. In *New directions for child development—Children and computers,* no. 28, ed. E. Klein, 5–18. New York: Jossey-Bass.

Clements, D.H., & B.K. Nastasi. 1993. Electronic media and early childhood education. In *Handbook of research on the education of young children* 1st ed., ed. B. Spodek, 251–75. New York: Macmillan.

Davidson, J.I. 1989. Supporting early childhood education with computers. Paper presented at the National Association for the Education of Young Children Annual Conference, 2–5 November, Atlanta, Georgia.

Elkind, D. 1987. *Miseducation: Preschoolers at risk.* New York: Knopf.

Haugland, S.W., & D.D. Shade. 1990. *Developmental evaluations of software for young children.* Albany, NY: Delmar.

Haugland, S.W., & D.D. Shade. 1994. Software evaluation for young children. In *Young children: Active learners in a technological age,* eds. J.L. Wright & D.D. Shade, 63–76. Washington, DC: NAEYC.

Haugland, S.W., & J.L. Wright. In press. *Computers and young children: A world of discovery.* New York: Allyn & Bacon.

Lipinski, J.M., R.E. Nida, D.D. Shade, & J.A. Watson 1986. The effect of microcomputers on young children: An examination of free play choices, sex differences, and social interactions. *Journal of Educational Computing Research* 2 (2): 147–68.

Papert, S. 1980. *Mindstorms—children, computers, and powerful ideas.* New York: Basic.

Papert, S. 1993. *The children's machine: Rethinking school in the age of the computer.* New York: Basic.

Piestrup, A.M. 1985. Silicon chips and playdough. In *Beginnings and beyond: Foundations in early childhood education,* eds. M.G.A Browne & K.W. Browne, 399–402.

Shade, D.D., & J.A. Watson. 1990. Computers in early education: Issues put to rest, theoretical links to sound practice, and the potential contribution of microworlds. *Journal of Educational Computing Research* 6 (4): 375–92.

Shade, D.D. 1992. A developmental look at award winning software. *Day Care and Early Education* 20 (1): 34–36.

Wright, J.L., & D.D. Shade, eds. 1994. *Young children: Active learners in a technological age.* Washington, DC: NAEYC.

WHERE COMPUTERS DO WORK

In these six classrooms, PCs promote learning, excite students and free up teachers to teach

Ever since Thomas Edison declared that his motion picture camera would revolutionize education, Americans have hoped the latest gizmo would inspire students to soar. Radio. Filmstrips. Television.

And, for more than a dozen years, computers. High-tech businesses will rake in some $4 billion this year from elementary, middle and high schools on instructional technology, twice as much as five years ago. President Clinton has proposed an additional $2 billion in federal money so that "every 12-year-old can log on to the Internet." Countless parents and private groups pour sweat equity and millions of dollars into bringing wires and computer wares into schools.

So where's the payoff? Few teachers are trained to use computers or to navigate the Internet. School boards don't know what to look for. Good software is rare. And nobody seems to have enough time to think up the best ways to harness the undeniable potential of these powerful machines.

Make that *almost* nobody. *U.S. News* has found six schools with lessons to teach all of us about computer technology. The most important is that technology is not magic. Money matters far less than the dedication and innovative spirit of the teachers in these classrooms.

LESSON 1: IT'S NOT THE PCs THAT MATTER. IT'S HOW THEY'RE USED

THURGOOD MARSHALL HIGH SCHOOL
SAN FRANCISCO

As computers go, the PCs in Dennis Frezzo's classroom in San Francisco Thurgood Marshall Academic High

School are Paleolithic. Some are '286 machines nearly as old as the 50 or so sophomores and juniors in Frezzo's robotics class. The creaky Compaq, Wyse and IBM systems, many of them well-intentioned castoffs from local banking and accounting firms, help teach the students how to program robots that are assembled from Lego blocks. And they do just fine.

"They let me pose very real electrical and mechanical problems," says Frezzo, who keeps track of time with a stopwatch slung round his neck. "If the students type in the wrong computer code, their robot does some stupid thing and they begin to see the logic in programming."

Getting with the program. Students first learn the rudiments of Lego Logo, a robotics language that orders robots to perform such functions as rotating and positioning a mechanical arm and picking up and dropping objects. Then Frezzo unleashes his charges to devise, assemble and program their creations. The students start out on paper, then hunker down in front of a computer to see if their laborious programming works.

Sometimes it doesn't, as 15-year-old Omar Khaliq discovers when his group's robot arm, instead of stopping as it was supposed to do to pick up a Lego block, overshoots it by several inches. As his group's code writer, Omar has to go back into the program so that the arm, tethered to the computer through a cable, will move for precisely 3.5 seconds. It takes him 30 minutes of trial and error, but Omar doesn't mind. "It was interesting to figure out," says the young engineer, whose test scores were mediocre at the beginning of the year. Now Omar is among the top programmers in his class.

Raphael Crawford-Marks, 16, finds Frezzo's class far more engaging than the basic programming course in Pascal he took last year. "We get to figure out

how to use the computer to run something that affects the real world," says the sophomore, whose short blond locks sport a healthy splash of green. "It's a lot more satisfying to get a robot to work than to make the computer spit back pictures of little spaceships blowing up space aliens."

Marshall opened only three years ago, the result of a 1983 federal court consent decree requiring San Francisco schools to offer minority students greater educational opportunities. The student body is 21 percent Hispanic, 25 percent black and 38 percent Asian, none with significant prior exposure to math or science.

To Omar, the school's emphasis on computer-aided education is a boon to his personal future. "This world is going to be high tech, so it's better we know [computers] now," says the lanky teen as he rummages through a box of wires and robot parts.

Frezzo thinks too many educators are overly eager to use computers. "Computers have to be critically applied," he says. "We can't just put students in front of computers and say, 'OK, learn.' "

LESSON 2: LET STUDENTS LEARN AT THEIR OWN PACE

LANGLEY HIGH SCHOOL
PITTSBURGH

Ninth grader William Kirchner regards the algebra problem on the glowing screen, punches in numbers and hesitates when they turn to italics—the signal that he did something wrong. The software posts a suggestion, and William glides toward the solution. "I like the computer," he says, calling up the next problem. "You don't always have to have a teacher."

But teacher Maura Moran is there if

needed. A girl across the room is stumped. If she makes 50 cents for each snow cone she sells but has to pay a friend $50 to use his snow-cone machine, how does she calculate the profit on 200 snow cones? After two suggestions and a pat on the back from Moran, the student makes x the number of snow cones sold and figures out that her profit is equal to .50x-50. Moran walks away, and the now smiling student resumes her work.

The air fairly hums with high-intensity concentration. Some of the students mutter to themselves as they work; others talk at the screen, which offers neither color nor sound. All 22 students are doing algebra at their own speed, moving to more advanced problems as they master the skills. They can always call on Moran, who wanders from student to student.

Here math is no abstraction. Teachers instruct all ninth and 10th graders three days a week in such real-world problems as calculating wages, evaluating car-rental rates and comparing cellular phone plans. The other two days they do similar work on computers that track individual progress. The key is Intelligent Computer Tutor, software developed at Carnegie Mellon University that blends research into the psychology of learning with programming that lets the computer correct and coach at any point during the problem-solving process.

Clear thinkers. First tried in 1992, the program now is standard for all Langley first-year algebra and geometry classes and has spread to seven other Pittsburgh-area schools. In a Carnegie Mellon study covering school years 1993-94 and 1994-95, Langley algebra students scored about twice as high in problem-solving skills and ability to work with graphs, charts and equations as their traditionally taught schoolmates did. They also did 15 percent better on math questions from the Scholastic Assessment Test. The suburban students did just as well.

Teachers credit the independence fostered by the software, which doesn't penalize students for taking risks. Rather, it guides them, picks up weaknesses and helps students overcome them by posing new problems. "It knows what I have to work harder on," says Diane Schwenninger, a ninth grader at Hampton High School in Pittsburgh's suburbs.

Students say they'd much rather calculate the life span of a threatened rain forest or how many trips a medevac helicopter can make on a set budget than slog through the contrived problems that haunt traditional textbooks. Hampton teacher Kathy Dickensheets rolls her eyes: "Those two trains that were always headed toward each other: Did we ever just let them crash?"

LESSON 3: E-MAIL CAN BE MORE THAN CHATTER

WINDSOR HIGH SCHOOL
WINDSOR, CONN.

Arms control diplomats from Russia generally don't wear flannel shirts, baseball hats and sneakers during work hours. They probably don't bring Ring Dings and pretzels to international summits. But these six "Russian" weapons experts are role-playing students in a Global Education class at Windsor High. Since they conduct negotiations via modem, appearance and eating habits hardly matter.

On this rainy autumn afternoon, the six seniors huddle near their classroom windows in front of one of four PCs their teacher has begged from the school or snared through a grant. The students and their classmates are taking part in the University of Connecticut Project in International Negotiation.

CPIN is a high-tech version of the Model United Nations programs, which bring high school students to spots all over the country to form mock committees and debate global issues. Each CPIN class adopts the identity of a different country. Over a six-week span, the teams discuss international arms control, the environment, drug trafficking and human rights by exchanging thousands of E-mail messages posted each day and in eight online chats that take place in real time after school. Before the students even sit down at the keyboards, they scour newspapers, magazines, encyclopedias—and, of course, the Internet—for data that support their country's position and undermine their opponent's.

As the students try to figure out the best way to get what they want, they begin to think the way diplomats do, sorting through the issues and reducing them to a manageable few. "I get the feeling we'll be doing a lot of damage control," says 17-year-old Jamie Durning as he burrows into a heap of background material about nuclear weapons, the specific topic of today's after-school summit on the broad question of arms control. Before they log on, the "Russians" settle on two main goals for today's agenda: to tell the world their country supports the principle of disarmament and to sweet-talk the United States into an alliance. They hope that an agreement will enhance both their stability and their global profile.

Keeping cool. Things don't go according to plan. Within the first 20 minutes, America proposes to tie each country's arms expenditures to a percentage of its gross national product. Such a limit, argue the U.S. delegates, would help nations conserve funds for "fundamental social needs." Among themselves, the Russians explode. The system unfairly favors America, they complain. But like good ambassadors, they hide their anger behind a dispassionate reply: "If cooperation is to be accomplished," reads their reply on the screen, "such self-interest must be avoided."

Making dry subjects absorbing and letting students learn by doing help ensure the lessons stick. With Windsor High School's Global Education class a year behind him, University of Connecticut freshman Matt Wininger readily recalls the simulation in which he and his French arms control team united with China, figuring that "with 1.2 billion people on our side, we'd be stronger." The move brought condemnation from France's own human-rights team—and sanctions from CPIN's director, a University of Connecticut associate professor who broke up the union because he believed France would never actually pursue such a tactic. "We learned the phrase 'cause and effect,'" says Matt. "We didn't think the whole world would turn against us just because we allied ourselves with China. It was a gamble and we lost."

As they learn the unruly ways of the real world, Windsor students also get a hefty lesson in computers, which they rarely see in other classes. By the end of the six weeks, they know how to log on to the simulation server, send text files and conduct E-mail dialogues. Some even master the elusive art of finding useful information on the Internet. "At first computers feel intimidating," says senior Chris Ferrero. "But part of me realizes that this is the wave of the future. So latch on to it now or get left behind."

LESSON 4: TECHNOLOGY CAN HELP SPECIAL KIDS, TOO

HARVARD KENT SCHOOL
CHARLESTOWN, MASS.

Classmates Matthew Leung, 9, and Guerson Vincent, 11, have a tough time holding a No. 2 pencil or writing a legible sentence and get frustrated when they try to read their own writing or a book. It's understandable, since these are boys with Down's syndrome.

But settled in front of a Macintosh in Room 201 of the Harvard Kent School, a mouse at hand and teacher Jack McCauley, 33, hovering nearby, they happily take turns "reading" a CD-ROM version of Mercer Mayer's book *Just Grandma and Me.* They look at the pages on the screen while an animated female voice narrates, and turn to the next page by using the mouse to click on an arrow. With a program called My Words, they can retrieve familiar words from a vocabulary list and print out sentences using them—in large, easy-to-read type. Or they can draw and paint on-screen with Kid Pix software.

This classroom is filled with children who have two or more disabilities—cerebral palsy, Down's syndrome, autism and severely impaired vision are just a few of them—and who generally cannot keep up with their peers. The computer helps them pick up academic skills—reading, writing, counting.

But just as important, says McCauley, it functions as "a vehicle for inclusion." Because his students use *WiggleWorks,* the same book on CD-ROM from Scholastic Inc. as Harvard Kent's regular classes use, the technology stamps them "as kids who can learn, as part of the community," says McCauley.

Children with multiple disabilities learn better, says McCauley, if each one gets a personally tailored education plan that appeals to as many senses as possible. Computer programs offer visual and sound cues and can be customized almost infinitely, from expanding the on-screen type to inserting photos of the children into a story. From the pace of voiceovers and spoken directions to the mouse clicks required to execute a command, timing, volume, speech and speed all can be varied. The computer, says McCauley, "has galvanized this population. It encourages exploration, because you can't make a mistake."

His students' growing self-confidence underscores his claim. When Matt clicks on the mouse and greets the image that appears on the screen with a triumphant thumbs up, it's as though he has just walked through a door he has learned to open. This year Guerson's social skills are strong enough to enable him to navigate the building on his own with a hall pass just like any other kid, and, according to McCauley, technology is the catalyst. "It promotes independence," he says, "so when Guerson can work confidently by himself at the computer, then I can say, 'Let's try this, too.' "

The entire neighborhood becomes a classroom. When McCauley's students go on a "community experience" outing to a nearby store, they use Apple's Quicktake camera to snap pictures of themselves and the people they meet, upload the digitized images and print them out on the classroom's one Macintosh. "It helps me bring the world to them," says McCauley. Technology means immediacy, and for these students, "immediacy is vital. This is real-time teaching; the learning experience becomes specifically about *them* and what *they* are doing, not Dick and Jane."

LESSON 5: UNLEASH TEACHERS TO BE CREATIVE

NORTH EAST HIGH SCHOOL
NORTH EAST, MD.

It's a warm October afternoon in this sleepy river town at the northern tip of the Chesapeake Bay. On the second floor of the local high school, girls in Don Shaffer's sophomore biology class shed their white cheerleader jackets and boys roll up their shirt sleeves. They have exactly seven minutes to feed and water the classroom plants, insects and rodents. As soon as the last mouse is secured in its tiny cage, the students scurry to form groups around seven computers to work with digital oysters.

Most of the school's students make little use of computers. Shaffer's class is at them almost daily, creating complex models of global warming, poring over spreadsheets, entering data from field trips to a local stream. Last year, the students worked on eight-year-old Apple IIGS machines and four-year-old Macintosh LC II's in the computer lab next door. Now they use new Power Macs, thanks to two recent grants.

The students fire up the Chesapeake Bay Oyster, a CD-ROM program Shaffer wrote because his school couldn't afford to buy software. The students become scientists analyzing the decline in the bay's adult oysters. It is no hypothetical problem. While the bay is full of young oysters, it has yielded fewer and fewer adults. Some 200,000 bushels of oysters were harvested from the bay last year, compared with 1 million in 1987. Scientists are monitoring the oyster population closely, searching for ways to boost the falling numbers.

A map of the Chesapeake pops up on the screen, with a dozen real oyster beds labeled. A digitized voice (Shaffer's wife's) instructs students to select a bed for study. A four-girl group chooses the Swans Point bed, near the bay's eastern shore. A click of a mouse button sends an animated boat churning across the green water and reaching down with a dredge to bring up oysters. The catch mimics what scientists snagged there four years ago: 337 live adults, 279 "smalls"—oysters below the minimum market size of 3 inches across—and 13 dead. The students take a break for a narrated on-screen video of an actual oyster harvest, a slide of two oyster parasites and a close-up of an open oyster that inspires disgusted shrieks.

It's time to get serious. Armed with data about the water's oxygen levels, pollution, contamination by heavy metals and other variables, the students conduct experiments in four on-screen labs

to elicit reasons for the oyster decline. They check their hypotheses with a click of the mouse. "This kind of data would be impossible for students to get themselves," says Shaffer, who spent the last two summers gathering statistics and building the program around them.

"I like this better than listening to Mr. Shaffer lecture," says 15-year-old Jessica Simmons. "It's more interesting." And it's far more challenging than note taking, since the real-life statistics are full of complications and contradictions. "When you look at real data, the numbers are 'dirty,' " Shaffer explains. "That's the way the scientific world is. It gives students a taste of reality."

After an hour at "their" bed, the girls turn to the other 11 for clues. Oxygen levels look normal, they conclude. So do figures for phosphates, a measure of fertilizer runoff and use of detergents. "Between all of us, we can figure out what's going on," insists Jessica. After some debate, they blame Dermo and MSX, parasitic diseases that have devastated several other oyster beds and infected 23 percent of the Swans Point oysters. To test the hypothesis, the girls recommend infecting healthy oysters and seeing what happens. As the bell rings signaling the end of the 90-minute class, Jessica lets out a sigh. "This really makes you think," she says.

LESSON 6: USE THE INTERNET THE RIGHT WAY

DALTON SCHOOL
NEW YORK CITY

Malcolm Thompson teaches astronomy at this Upper East Side private school solely with seven Mac clones, $100 astronomy software and the World Wide Web. His students learn about eclipses with Voyager II, a program from Carina Software that can plot the movements of the heavens 5,000 years into the past—or the future. Students study the evolution of galactic clusters by downloading Hubble Space Telescope images from a National Aeronautics and Space Administration Web site (*http://cossc.gsfc.nasa.gov/apod /lib/galaxy_clusters.html*).

"Most of the explanations in astronomy emerge from observations done over long periods," says Thompson, 58. "Now you can compress the motions during those periods into a few seconds so you can conceptualize them." Says senior Jon Rameau: "You see how it works rather than the idea being told to you."

Using hand-held calculators, students previously had time to test theories such

RULES TO COMPUTE BY

Before committing to computers in their schools, educators and parents might take these guidelines to heart.

■ **Beware of flash.** Much educational software is slick but flawed. "It's not enough just to have software that *looks* good," says Linda Roberts, director of the U.S. Department of Education's Office of Educational Technology. Avoid drill- or game-oriented programs. Spreadsheet programs are a better choice. Inherently flexible, they can help teach biology, chemistry and algebra concepts. For English and history teachers, basic word-processing programs can help students edit and improve their writing.

■ **Use computers only where they make sense.** Good teachers boot up a computer only to help students in a way that otherwise would be difficult.

■ **Train teachers.** A principal would never stick a science teacher at a piano and expect Mozart to emerge—but he just might put her at a computer and demand that she be the next Bill Gates. Educator after educator says training is the most crucial ingredient of an effective computer program and the one that is underfunded the most often. "I would rather not afford the technology than not afford the training," says Jeri Hodges, executive director of instructional technology applications for the Dallas public schools.

■ **Don't expect miracles.** Computers don't always result in higher test scores, and they certainly can't turn a flailing school system around by themselves. Before investing, ask yourself what you expect computers to do for your school. If the answer is simply to teach keyboarding skills, a roomful of refurbished machines may be adequate. If you hope to weave software into the general curriculum, computers in each classroom work best. And if you want computers to overcome poor teaching, overcrowded classrooms or unmotivated students, forget the whole thing.—B.W.

---

as Hubble's Law only on a few examples. The law holds that because the universe is constantly expanding, the distance between an observer on Earth and a far-off galaxy can be determined from the rate of expansion. Computers let the students quickly verify the law on a dozen galaxies. "One of the things about kids is that they won't ask a question if it will take them a long time to answer it," says Thompson.

The students download Milky Way photos from another NASA site (*http://cossc.gsfc.nasa.gov/apod/lib/aptree.html*), check sunspots at a site maintained by the National Oceanic and Atmospheric Administration (*http://www.sel.noaa.gov:80/images*) and browse astronomy libraries from Australia to Japan. Naturally, the course outline, assignments and student work are on the Web (*http://www.dalton.org/groups/astro*).

Some 10 to 20 students got better jobs or internships partly because of their newfound Web skills, says Thompson. "Before this year, I didn't exactly consider myself a Web crawler," says senior Wei-San Tjong. "But if you want to find something out and [Thompson] doesn't want to help you and gets moody, you have to find it yourself."

And the results? A group of Thompson students did 33 percent better than a group of their classmates on a 1993 test of their skill at analyzing and interpreting data. "In educational research, that's a big difference," says John Black, a professor at Columbia University's Teachers College who administered the test as part of an overall assessment of Dalton's technology program.

The night sky is still part of Thompson's course. Early in the course, the students prepare for an evening on a New York City rooftop by setting the Voyager II program to the date and time and predict the positions of various planets, stars and constellations. When they conduct their nighttime observations, they check their findings against the program's predictions. "If you just had [Voyager II] and you never told the kids they were looking at the sky, it would be a video game," Thompson says. "This experience takes the kid from where he is in his experience of the world and says: 'Here is how this connects to the formal systems of science.'"

BY BETSY WAGNER IN WINDSOR AND NORTH EAST, STEPHEN GREGORY IN SAN FRANCISCO, RICHARD BIERCK IN PITTSBURGH, MISSY DANIEL IN CHARLESTOWN AND JONATHAN SAPERS IN NEW YORK CITY

Instructional Applications of Computer Games

Paper presented at the 1996 annual meeting of the American Educational Research Association, New York City.

**John V. Dempsey, Barbara A. Lucassen,
Linda L. Haynes, & Maryann S. Casey**

University of South Alabama

Background

The use of games as instructional tools is well established. There is evidence that games were used in China as early as 3000 B.C. Since the early 1960's there has been a rapid growth in the use of gaming and simulation in all areas of teaching. Children in elementary schools play word games. The military uses games and simulations in training. Medicine uses games to practice skills needed when assessing patient conditions. Business uses management games and simulations to create experiential environments for learning managerial behavior. For example, Faria (1987) has reported that 4,600 of the larger U.S. firms he surveyed used business or experiential games in training or development. Some wide ranges of benefits for which educational researchers and theorists ascribe to games include improved practical reasoning skills (Wood & Stewart, 1987), higher levels of continuing motivation (Malouf, 1988), and reduced training time and instructor load (Allen, Chatelier, Clark, & Sorenson, 1982). Diverse training applications, such as attention reduction or automaticity training (Jacobs, Dempsey, & Salisbury, 1990) and complex problem solving (Hayes, 1981), are hypothesized to be prime candidates for game strategies.

The actual research in the use of gaming for educational or instructional purposes is sparse. A review of some 100 instructional gaming articles (Dempsey, Lucassen, & Rasmussen, 1996) revealed little substantive research concerning ways that computer games could be used for educational purposes. The limited amount of study in this area has led some researchers (e.g., Bredemeier & Greenblat, 1981) to question many claims made on behalf of educational games because of lack of sufficient empirical support. Even so, games, particularly computer games, are considered by many to be powerful tools to increase learning. It seems almost self-evident that educational computer gaming is a growth area and one worthy of exploration by applied researchers. Despite findings that, for example, arcade-style gaming is a social and not an achievement oriented activity (McClure & Mears, 1986), gaming activity is increasing greatly because of more sophisticated and lower priced hardware and software in personal computers.

Educational researchers will be more frequently asked how to incorporate games into learning environments and will continue to be perplexed about how [to] arrange studies that respond to this summons. Much of what occurs in a gaming environment may not be easily measurable or, at least easily reduced to a few variables. The validity of the assessment of an instructional game is quite different from with other learning environments and, according to Reuben & Lederman (1982) is dependent on rules, interactions, roles, goals, and criteria.

Therefore, although experimental studies have an important place in the instructional gaming literature, there is a budding movement to recognize the limitations of objective-oriented research for assessment and [to] look at the effects of incidental learning as well as intentional learning (Barnett, 1984; Remus, 1981).

From *American Educational Research Association*, 1996. Reprinted from ERIC ED 394 500.

3. CLASSROOM APPLICATIONS AND SOFTWARE EVALUATIONS

Purpose

The purpose of this paper, as the title suggests, is to discuss some instructional applications of computer games, particularly as they apply to adults. We will first offer a definition of games and propose a selection criteria for adapting existing computer games for education or training. Next, we will describe our study, over a two-year period, of adults playing relatively unsophisticated computer games. Based on preliminary analyses of the 160 observations in this study, we will discuss aspects of computer gaming particularly as they apply to gender and motivational influences, learning styles, game features, strategies used by adults to play, and applications of computer games to education. An enormous amount of qualitative and quantitative data was collected during the course of these observations. Parts of the data [are] still under study to uncover trends and patterns detected by multiple instruments across several of the 40 games observed in this study. Our focus therefore is *not* to present the study in all its particulars. Rather, we are here recording some of our perspective on instructional computer gaming and reporting aspects of our observations in particular areas.

What is a game?

Our experiences in playing, reviewing, and designing computer games; our prior reviews of the gaming literature; and discussions among ourselves and those in electronic research forums (e.g., PSYGAME) have led us to our present definition of a game.

A *game* is a set of activities involving one or more players. It has goals, constraints, payoffs, and consequences. A game is rule-guided and artificial in some respects. Finally, a game involves some aspect of competition, even if that competition is with oneself.

Most games are intended to be entertaining, not instructional. Often, the reason a person chooses to play a game is to experience the fun of engaging in the gaming activity. Learning is usually incidental, or intentional only for the purposes of one becoming a better gamer. The challenge for educators, therefore, is to take the learning that does take place in a game from activities, such as exploring a route through a maze or improving a motor skill on a keyboard, and apply that incidental knowledge or ability to an intentional learning task.

Educators have long advised that instructional designers look for existing gaming strategies when developing or adapting games for instructional purposes (See Driskell & Dwyer, 1984). The focus of our study, hence, was to probe for components or structures of existing computer games that would lend themselves for use in an educational or instructional setting. Concurrently, we wished to identify, primarily through observations and questionnaires, those attributes that were either motivating or distracting to adult players and to deter-

mine if these attributes tended to vary because of the gender of the player.

Game Selection Criteria

Our first task was to decide what criteria were most likely to make a game a good candidate for study. We selected five criteria.

To be more synchronous for intentional instructional purposes, a game:

(1) *must be relatively simple to play:*

This criterion arises from our belief that gaming used for instructional purposes should not be overly complex. Complex rules and scoring require the learner to use limited learning time to understand the game (Jacobs, & Dempsey, 1993). An exception, would be a game that is intrinsically motivating and directly related to the intended learning outcome. We define an *intrinsically motivating instructional game* as one in which game structure itself helps to teach the instructional content.

(2) *Can be adapted and reprogrammed cheaply:*

To maintain a reasonable cost-benefit, the value of resources that must be sacrificed to gain benefits or effects must be comparatively less than the value of the benefits or effects themselves (see Levin, 1983).

(3) *must have some identifiable potential for educational use, if adapted:*

Here we liberally interpreted "potential" to be any reasonable possibility of applying the game to education or training. For example, card games such as "Acey Ducey" require some arithmetic skills and therefore have some potential for intentional educational use and application to specific learning outcomes.

In addition, for the purposes of our study, we decided that a game:

(4) *must be different from the other games in its category:*

In order to study as many kinds of games as possible.

(5) *must be able to be played by a single player:*

This was an arbitrary decision. One person is the lowest common denominator in computer game playing and we felt that it would be less confounding to restrict our study, at this point, to a single player. Many of the games we reviewed could be played by either one or more than one player. One of the frequent comments made by players during game play is the wish to collaborate or, more frequently, to compete with another human player.

Subjects

Forty adults, 20 females and 20 males, participated in the study. Ages of participants ranged from 18 to 52. All volunteered to participate. Educational achievement was rather evenly divided among high school, college, masters, and doctoral degreed individuals. Most were moderately to very experienced using computers.[1] A majority [of] subjects reported that they enjoyed playing games. Slightly fewer adults reported that they enjoyed games which use computer technology.[2] Although the numbers of games (of any kind) played per month was relatively balanced between males and females, males played technology games more often and in greater frequency than did females.[3]

Only a small percentage of participants reported that they played no games at all per month.[4] The number of adults playing no technology-based games, however, was double that amount. Slightly over half of the participants reported that they were competitive or very competitive when they did play games. Respectively, subjects were most experienced playing card games, board games, puzzles, and word games.[5]

Figure 1.

Games Used in Study

Eight categories with five games per category (total 40 games) were chosen for the study. The games chosen were originally designed to be entertaining, not instructional.

Card Games
Vagas Poker
Pyramid
Mac Jack
Red Dog
Acey-Ducey

Puzzles
Mazer 3D
Color Rhodes
ICON Quest
Faculty Towers of Hanoi
Number Fubar

Arcade Games
Save the Farm
Bloodsuckers
Maelstrom
Glidor
Gang War

Adventures
Scarab of RA
Camel
Quest of a Quert (Red Readers)
Murder in the Stacks
Save Princeton

Word Games
Lembracs
Hyper Jotto
Cryptogram
Flash IQ
Mac Triv 3.0

Board Games
Think Ahead
Influence
Five Stones
Susan
Battle Cruiser

Miscellaneous
Test of Minds (color)
Bird Race
Concentration
Flec Family
RePete

Simulations
MacNasty
Assault II
Cannon Fodder
Rescue
Wall Street 2.0

Materials

Forty computer games were used in this study (see Figure 1). The largest selection of games came from a collection of games entitled MACnificent 7.1—Education & Games CD-ROM (1993). By preference, we adopted the eight divisions the producers of that CD-ROM used to categorize games. These categories consisted of puzzles, adventure games, board games, simulations, card games, arcade games, word games and miscellaneous games. Some of the games used color and others were black and white. Each category was comprised of five games serving as a sampling of the variety of games found in each area. Each game was played by two females and two males. Ten packets containing four games each [were] randomly assigned to the 40 volunteers (160 observations).

Instruments

A Demographic and Gaming Experience Questionnaire was used to gather information about the subjects' age, gender, and educational experience. It includes a scale related to the subjects' predisposition toward game playing, technology-based game playing, frequency of game playing, and frequency of technology-based game playing. Kolb's Learning-Style Inventory was implemented to look for patterns in participants' experiential styles and game preferences. The CAS-Q questionnaire (Seligman) was administered in this study to measure subjects' degree of optimism and [to] compare that to observations of their game playing behavior. Experimenter observations were recorded for each gaming experience on a two-page observation protocol. Finally, two gaming scales were specifically developed for this study and were administered after each game. The first was a modification of Keller's Instructional Motivational Scale. The scale includes statements related to attention, relevance, confidence, and satisfaction specifically oriented toward computer gaming. The second gaming scale was derived from articles from the gaming literature review. The areas analyzed from this scale included: challenge, fantasy, curiosity (Malone, 1981); fidelity, artificiality, interactivity (Duchastel, 1991); Complexity (Jacobs & Dempsey, 1993); and control (Westrom & Shaban, 1992).

Procedure

Subjects received information concerning the purpose of the study. They were asked to complete a demographic and gaming experience questionnaire, as well as the Kolb and Seligman scales mentioned above. Following the surveys the subjects were given verbal instructions on how to play the game selected and to comment freely during the game play about feelings and strategies. An evaluator was present as the games [were] played. The evaluator assumed a participant-observer role recording observations and comments during the play. Specific areas of interest and concerns were defined prior to the actual commencement of the game playing segment of this study. After each game observation, follow-up sessions were conducted as a means of stimulating discussion about the game play. In addition to the follow-up interview, the subjects completed ARCS Gaming Scale and the second scale derived from articles from the gaming literature review. Most of the observations took place on a computer with a color monitor in an isolated university office.

Gender and Motivation

The most diverse patterns between males and females occurred in simulation gaming. Females in this study may have been less motivated to engage in the simulation games because the games did not capture their interest or attention. For example, females stated that the screen designs were boring and there was not enough screen variety in the simulation games[6,7].

Challenge is usually considered to be an important component of motivating game play for engaging in game play. More females than males felt it was not important to complete simulations successfully[8]. It may be that males were more challenged by simulation games than females.

Subjects did not have a high level of confidence for success in any of the game categories. Again, there were some differing trends for males and females observed for simulation games. Females were much more likely than males to say that they were not confident that they could succeed during simulation games[9]. Subjects of both sexes felt that they were not in control of simulation games[10]. On the other hand, both females and males did not indicate that they found simulation games to be too difficult.[11]

A much larger percentage of females than males expressed a dislike of violent or aggressive games.[12] A sizable percentage of men felt that the more active categories of games were "male" games.[13]

Learning Styles

Subjects in this study covered all four quadrants of the Kolb's learning styles. A larger percentage of females, were accommodators and divergers. Males comprised a larger percentage of convergers and assimilators.[14]

Many of the learning style patterns that were observed or reported by the subjects may have been due in part to gender differences. For example, accommodators, with a larger percentage of females were less competitive[15] and less likely to be experienced using simulations[16], and were generally more pessimistic on Seligman's CAS-Q Scale than were the other learning groups[17]. Although we have some initial results regarding the way different learning styles play games, we have decided to reanalyze the data, controlling (where possible) for the effects of gender.

Features

Qualitative data, especially, show many key features that subjects regard as essential for a good gaming environment. Three main concerns were, first, the need for clear, concise instructions describing how to play the game. Secondly, the game should be challenging. Third, the player should have control over many gaming options such as speed, degree of difficulty, timing, sound effects and feedback. Each of these concerns was listed in all eight of the gaming categories.

Aesthetic issues, such as screen design, color, text, action, animation and graphics quality were considered important as well.[18] The need for opportunities for success was isolated as an area of concern in all gaming categories except adventure, arcade and board games. Subjects felt that clear goals and objectives were needed in adventure, board, card games and simulations.

An overview of player position was considered an important feature in adventure games. A desire for variety was expressed in arcade games. Players reported that help functions, hints and examples were necessary in adventure, miscellaneous and word games. Some games contained an element of mystery, intrigue and suspense. These characteristics were pleasing to some players. Many liked the idea of games with familiar scenarios or stories.

Subjects did find certain features to be distracting. Violence was seen as distracting in arcade games and simulations. Lack of goals, instructions, control and interactivity across all game types were a main source of frustration for many of the players. Many of the games used in this study were typical shareware games lacking in three dimensional color graphics. The subjects found the screen designs to be boring. They remarked about the lack of color in some of the games and the lower sophistication of some of the screen designs.

Strategies

In this study, strategies in playing computer games included trial and error, reading instructions, reliance on prior knowledge or experiences, and development of a personal game playing strateg[y] by the subject. Trial and error was, by far, the predominant strategy used[19] even in cases where subjects reported that they know a more efficient strategy.

Trial and error in computer gaming is defined as the absence of a systematic strategy in playing a game. This particular strategy involves actions and reactions to circumstances, consequences and feedback within the game framework. Knowledge of how to play the game is accumulated through observation and active participation in the gaming process, not by reading rules and instructions. Trial and error was the dominant strategy used across all game types[20].

People playing puzzles read instructions more than those playing other games.[21] Subjects were also observed using visual imagery techniques when playing the puzzle games.

Personal strategy development included visual imagery (puzzles), note taking (simulation), memorization and pattern matching (miscellaneous games involving sound), use of help, hint and game tools (adventure, board, puzzle, simulations) and systematic use of alphabet characters (word). The amount of experience a subject had in playing a particular game did

Figure 2.

Suggested Use of Computer Games in an Educational Setting

Adventure Games
Survival Skills
Inventory
Supply & Demand
Probability
Consequences
Problem-Solving
Navigating
History
Purchasing
Budgeting
High-order thinking skills
Learning verbs/nouns
Spelling/writing

Arcade Games
Hand-eye Coordination
Reflexive Action
Motor Skills
Speed Simulations
Multiple problems/priorities
Timing
Angles, Trajectories
Air current
Planning
Decision making

Board Games
Budget
Logic Strategy
Counting
Planning
Problem-solving
Deductive reasoning
Critical Thinking
Coordination
Navigation

Card Games
Probabilities
Calculate Risk
Develop Strategies
Addition
Pattern Recognition

Miscellaneous Games
Logic
Pattern Recognition
Short-term Memory
Learning Alphabet
Probabilities
Pattern Matching
Audio/visual discrimination

Puzzles
Planning Strategies
Thinking Ahead
Spatial Orienation
Map reading
Architectural Design
Problem-solving
Hand-eye coordination
Pattern recognition
Matching
Assembly/disassembly

Simulations
Writing Fiction
Teaching Framing
Tactical & Strategic Planning
Coordinates
Velocity, speed, wind, angles
Decision Making
Consequences

Word Games
Vocabulary
Spelling
Problem-solving
Remediation
Verbal Information
Drill & Practice
Reinforcement

not appear to influence the amount of time spent in game play.[22]

Applications

Subjects were asked how they thought particular computer game formats might be used in an educational/instructional setting. Their suggestions for use for each of the eight game categories is summarized in Figure 2. Although many of the responses were specific for the topic of the game for which they had most recently engaged, some subjects offered suggestions which were more general in nature. It was felt that adventure, arcade, board, simulations, puzzles and word games could be used for teaching problem solving and decision making. Many of the computer games could be constructed in a manner to address particular topics. Depending on the learning outcome desired, one type of game may be more suited than another.

There were specific games that subjects felt did not have a place in an educational setting. Most players, male and female, felt that games containing violence had no place in education. Several card games depicted a gambling scenario. Several players felt this was inappropriate, especially for children. Because the highest suggested use of card games involved instruction in probability and risk calculation, perhaps this type of game should be limited to an adult population.

Discussion

Computer games can be very complex, particularly simulation and adventure games. Arcade, card and word games are based on a more simple structure. Each of these eight categories of games has potential for educational or instructional use.

3. CLASSROOM APPLICATIONS AND SOFTWARE EVALUATIONS

Whether verbal information, motor skills or intellectual skills are the object of the instruction, computer games can be designed to address specific learning outcomes.

Based on the data collected from this study, it appears that specific features a game displays are of the some importance. Players want clear and concise instructions, challenging games, control over gaming options such as speed, difficulty, timing and help functions. Screen design, color action and appropriate use of sound and feedback are also desired. Because of the availability of fast action, multifaceted computer games on the market today, games lacking the features listed above may not keep a player engaged a significant amount of time for learning to occur.

Over 79% of the subjects in this study used trial and error as their game playing strategy. We feel that this choice of strategy was due to several reasons related to what the subjects themselves expressed as being important: lack of clear instructions, goals of the game not being defined and the desire on the part of the subject to discover the object of the game while playing the game. Oftentimes, the subjects would begin playing the game using trial and error and then would look for guidance by reading instructions or hint screens. As a result, computer games in an instructional setting should be constructed to allow for discovery learning, but clear and concise instructions and goals should be available for the player to access if needed.

It also appears that clear and precise instructions are required to encourage game players to proceed with a game. Likewise, a statement of goals and objectives [is] important to encourage engagement in a game. Often, game players were frustrated when they were unsure of the game's objective.

Providing examples of how to play the game, *winning prototypes,* can facilitate engagement in a game as well as incidental learning. Similarly, game players could acquire winning prototype learning strategies which would transfer to other learning tasks. In a "dog eat dog" economic simulation game used in this study (MacNasty), a framing strategy could clearly organize the details of the game action and maximize the players' opportunities for success. Once learned this strategy could transfer to intentional academic goals requiring problem organization or establishing relationships through logical inference.

Aesthetic issues, such as screen design, color, text, action, animation, and graphics quality were considered important by the adult players. For example, color, screen design, appropriate use of sound and feedback were listed as very important to sustain interest in the game in 87.5% of the games studied.

Increased confidence encouraged adults to continue a game of skill. Where confidence was low persistence was short-lived. Aspects of confidence, personal control and self-attribution [were] perceived as highly lacking especially by females[23] for certain types of games. Consequently, success, particularly positive consequences, was frequently observed as an indicator of satisfaction with the game.[24]

Notes

1. Eighty-eight percent of all participants reported that they were moderately to very experienced using computers.
2. Sixty-seven percent enjoyed playing games (30% neutral). Adding technology (e.g., computer games) to the game-playing experience, changed these percentages only slightly (63% like to play; 30% neutral). Only about 4% of the participants disliked game-playing in any form.
3. The numbers of individuals playing occasionally (1 to 3 games per month) was evenly matched (33 each). Males in this study, however, played technology-based games more frequently. Of those reporting that they played 10 or more games per month, 28 were males versus only 8 females.
4. Forty-seven percent of the subjects reported playing 1 to 3 games per month. 17% reported playing 4 to 6 games, 6% played 7 to 9 games, and 8% played 10 to 12 games. Only, 11 percent played no games at all.
5. Of the eight game categories considered in this study, participants reported being experienced or very experienced to the following extent: card games (78%), board games (56%), puzzles (52%), word games (48%), miscellaneous games (28%), simulation games (22%), adventure games (19%), and arcade games (8%).
6. 60% of females stated "mostly true" and 60% of males stated "not true" for boring screen designs.
7. 60% of females stated "not true" and 40% of males stated "mostly true" for screen variety to keep their attention.
8. 50% of females states "mostly true" and 50% of males stated "not true" in response to the statement, "Completing the game successfully was not important to me."
9. 60% of females and 20% of males stated "not true" that they were confident they could succeed.
10. 65% of all subjects felt that they were not in control of simulation games.
11. 40% of females and 50% of males stated "not true" that the game was always too difficult. 10% of females and 20% of males stated "mostly true."
12. 67% of females did not like warlike aggressive games.
13. Over 40% of the males felt that the adventure, arcade, board and simulation games were male-oriented games.
14. Accommodators 23% (78% female, 22% male); Divergers 23% (67% female, 33% male); Convergers 23% (33% female, 67% male); Assimilators 33% (31% female, 69% male).
15. Assimilators appeared to be most competitive (77%), while Divergers tended to be least competitive (78%). Less competitive divergers tended to be female. There appeared to be no set difference for assimilators.
16. Accommodators and Divergers were least likely to be experienced with simulations and tended to be female. One-third of Convergers and Assimilators indicated being experienced to very experienced and these respondents tended to be male.
17. Divergers scored equally as "average" or "very pessimistic" (33% respectively). 38% of Assimilators scored "very pessimistic" while 31% were "moderately optimistic." 55% of Convergers tended to be "very pessimistic." 67% of Accommodators were more likely to be "very pessimistic."
18. Color, screen design, appropriate use of sound and feedback were listed in 87.5% of the gaming categories.
19. The breakdown of strategies used was:
    126 of 160 games played used trial and error (79%)
    12 of 160 games played read instructions (8%)
    6 of 160 games played used prior knowledge (4%)
    13 of 160 games played using personal strategies developed by subject (8%)
20. Trial and error was used 100% of the time in arcade games. It was used least in puzzle games—being used only 55% of the time. All of the remaining games fell within the 55 to 100% range.
21. 30% (6 of 20) of the subjects playing puzzle games took time to read the instructions. Simulation and board games had 10% of its players reading instructions.
22. Arcade games had the least amount of time engaged in game play. (11 min) Simulations had the highest amount of time engaged in game play. (22 min)
23. Overall, 46% of females and 22% of males felt that when they succeeded, they were lucky.

24. Again, females were noticeably less satisfied with the computer games. Overall, 50% of females versus 32% of males did not feel they got much out of playing the game.

References

Allen, J. P., Chantelier, P., Clark, H. J., and Sorenson, R. (1982). Behavioral science in the military: Research trends for the eighties. *Professional Psychology,* **13.,** 918–929.

Braun, C. M., Goupil, G., & Giroux, J. (1986). Adolescents and microcomputers: Sex differences, proxemics, task and stimulus variables. *Journal of Psychology,* **120**(6), 529–542.

Bredemeier, M. E. & Greenblat, C. E. (1981). The educational effectiveness of games: A synthesis of findings. *Simulation and Games,* **12**(3), 307–332.

Dempsey, J. V., Lucassen, B., Gilley, W., & Rasmussen, K. (1993–1994). Since Malone's theory on intrinsically motivating instruction: What's the score in the gaming literature? *Journal of Educational Technology Systems,* **22**(2), 173–183.

Dempsey, J. V., Lucassen, B., & Rasmussen, K., (1996). *The Instructional Gaming Literature: Implications and 99 Sources.* Manuscript submitted for publication.

Driskell, J. E. and Dwyer, D. J. (1984). Microcomputer videogame based training. *Educational Technology,* **24,** 11–17.

Duchastel, P. (1991). Instructional strategies for simulation-based learning. *Journal of Educational Technology Systems,* **19**(3), 265–276.

Faria, A. J. (1987). A survey of the use of business games in academia and business. *Simulations and Games,* **18**(2), 207–224.

Jacobs, J. W., & Dempsey, J. V. (1993). Simulation and gaming: Fidelity, feedback and motivation. In J. V. Dempsey & G. C. Sales, *Interactive Instruction and Feedback.* Englewood Cliffs, NJ: Educational Technology Publications.

Jacobs, J. W., Dempsey, J. V., & Salisbury, D. F. (1990). An attention reduction training model: Educational and technological implications. *Journal of Artificial Intelligence in Education,* **1**(4), 41–50.

Levin, H. M. (1983). *Cost-Effectiveness: A Primer.* Newbury Park, CA: Sage Publications

MACnificent 7.1—Education & Games CD-ROM [Computer Software]. (1993). Grand Rapids, MN: Wayzata Technology, Inc.

Malone, T. W. (1981). Toward a theory of intrinsic motivating instruction. *Cognitive Science,* **4,** 333–369.

Malone, T. W. (1981b). What makes computer games fun? *Byte,* **6,** 258–277.

Malouf, D. B. (1988). The effect of instructional computer games on continuing student motivation. *The Journal of Special Education.* **21**(4), 27–38.

Remus, W. E. (1981). Experimental designs for analyzing data on games: On even the best statistical methods do not replace good experimental control. *Simulation and Games,* **12**(1), 3–14.

Westrom, M., & Shaban, A. (1992). Intrinsic motivation in microcomputer games. *Journal of Research on Computing,* **24**(4), 433–445.

Wood, L. E. and Stewart, R. W. (1987). Improvement of practical reasoning skills with computer skills. *Journal of Computer-Based Instruction,* 14(2), 49–53.

Teacher Training

The goal of teacher education should be to advance all aspects of education, including fundamental research, technology, curriculum, and professional development. However, the most important product derived from teacher education over the past two decades has been the emergence of a vision of what technology has to offer education. Earlier thinking focused on technology as supporting the rote and mechanical aspects of learning (drill and practice). The new vision focuses on using technology to support excellence in learning (searching, inferencing, deciding). In this vision, students tackle much harder problems, work on larger-scale and more meaningful projects, have a greater and more reflective responsibility for their own learning, and are able to work in a variety of styles that reflect differences in gender, ethnicity, or simply individual personality. This new vision shows that creative use of technology by skilled teachers offers a promise quickly and effectively to restructure education as we know it. The new vision will ensure that students are afforded classroom or at-a-distance instruction at a pace that suits their learning styles and in a way that gives them a more active role in the learning process. Schools must provide adequate teacher training, at both the preservice and inservice levels, that enables teachers to become fully aware of and skilled in using the vast resources that today's technology offers.

Today, teacher education programs are using structured e-mail to create productive discourse among student teachers with their university-based professors. During inservice training teachers are creating e-mail diaries in order to learn how to use e-mail. Teacher education today uses the computer as a communication device as well as a teaching tool. Teacher education programs are beginning to fully utilize the power of the computer to empower teachers in their important role of shaping future generations.

The articles presented in this unit provide evidence that action is being taken to bring the benefits of technology to teachers as well as children. In the first report, Schlagal, Trathen, and Blanton report that a structured electronic mail environment is a key element in providing a model for assisting novice teachers to apply, critique, and think critically about the knowledge they bring with them into teaching. In addition this communication is connecting student teachers with their methods courses, other classrooms, and their peers, and is enabling them to discuss their experiences with their cooperating teachers.

Next, Ann Russell identifies six stages that 30 in-service teachers go through as they learn to use technology to communicate electronically through e-mail. The following article, by Mazur and Bliss, describes a project that centered on the development of a series of five secondary and five elementary cases that capture the dilemmas and accomplishments of teachers involved in reform. The cases were used to train teachers in the use of telecommunications for ongoing professional development and collaboration.

Abell, Cennamo, and Cambell, in "Interactive Video Cases Developed for Elementary Methods Courses," report on a project that developed interactive videodisc materials about teaching elementary school science. The goal of the project was to use the interactive video cases to facilitate the development of teachers who taught science to elementary students.

Finally, Miguel Guhlin describes a technology training program to address teachers' issues during weekends, after school, and in the summer. The program taught teachers how to integrate technology into their everyday classroom activities.

Looking Ahead: Challenge Questions

Will communication technology such as listserv and e-mail become a major part of teacher education? Why or why not?

Will schools of education focus on structuring telecommunications to create a distributed learning environment for student teachers?

What will the classroom of the twenty-first century look like? How will it be equipped? What are the benefits of such a classroom to teachers and students?

What effect does the implementation of instructional design and the use of application software have on teacher education programs?

Structuring Telecommunications to Create Instructional Conversations About Student Teaching

Bob Schlagal, *Appalachian State University*
Woodrow Trathen, *Appalachian State University*
William Blanton, *Appalachian State University*

Preservice and inservice teachers view student teaching as an essential component in teacher preparation (Clift, Meng, & Eggerding, 1994), but some researchers question the efficacy of traditional student teaching models (Feiman-Nemser & Buchmann, 1987; Goodlad, 1990; Guyton & McIntyre, 1990; Zeichner, 1990) and document shortcomings in the structure of traditional student teaching (Griffith et al., 1983). They contend that these shortcomings hinder students from bridging the gap between university and school in effective and coherent ways. Some research on student teaching suggests that interns abandon what they have learned in teacher education courses in as little as 2 weeks (Richardson-Koehler, 1988). Rather than working to apply what they have learned, they adapt and replicate the practices of their cooperating teachers.

Disconnection

Traditional student teaching often occurs in disconnection. Placed in a school, student teachers are largely isolated from university faculty and coursework. Their connections with university supervisors are limited by the demands on supervisors' time. Supervising faculty are seldom those who taught earlier methods courses, so connections that might be made among ideas, methods, or practices learned on campus occur haphazardly, if at all. When clinical supervisors and interns talk, their conversations usually focus on immediate classroom practices and routines (Horisego & Boldt, 1985; Tabachnick, Popkewitz, & Zeichner, 1979-1980; Zeichner, Liston, Mahlios, & Gomez, 1988). Although this practice helps students adapt to the demands of their particular classroom and cooperating teacher, it more deeply embeds them in the singularity of their experience. Realities and complexities of real classrooms often vary from those envisioned during methods courses (Clift et al., 1994). As a result, students often dismiss as irrelevant what they learned in teacher education courses (Richardson-Koehler, 1988). Site visits from university personnel and student-teaching seminars seem insufficient to bridge the gulf between the islands of university training and public school teaching.

Student teachers are disconnected from other classrooms. Once in a classroom, students find that the room becomes a world unto itself. They seldom visit other grades, other schools, or other teachers; they seldom reflect on and discuss their experience with their cooperating teachers (Feiman-Nemser & Buchmann, 1987). The students' images of classroom instruction, a particular grade level, the grade's curriculum, and the school environment are filtered through the lens of single class experiences. Confined to the isolated placement and interacting only intermittently with university personnel, apprentice teachers rely almost exclusively on cooperating teachers for guidance, information, and support. Because the smooth functioning of the classroom is ultimately the cooperating teacher's responsibility, discussions between teacher and student teacher focus on what will maintain the flow of events in the classroom (Richardson-Koehler, 1988). Thus powerful elements in the structure of traditional student teaching lead the intern to an uncritical replication of the cooperating teacher's attitudes and practices.

Student teachers are disconnected from their peers. Scattered in their placements, student interns are effectively cut off from those with whom they might share, compare, and

From *Journal of Teacher Education*, Vol. 47, No. 3, May/June 1996, pp. 175-183. © 1996 by Corwin Press, Inc., a Sage Publications Company. Reprinted by permission.

discuss their experiences, and from whom they might find support.

These varieties of disconnection in the internship leave student teachers to make do with whatever resources they find at hand. Disconnection prevents the kind of discourse between professors, teachers, and students that Blanton, Thompson, and Zimmerman (1994) argue is necessary to facilitate the development of reflective, inquiry-oriented teachers.

Isolated Construction of Meaning

Many researchers believe that student teachers are not critical and reflective enough about issues of knowledge and practice. Part of this problem relates to the separation between methods courses and the student-teaching experience. Often, prospective teachers are expected to transfer textbook learning to teaching during internships occurring two to three semesters after coursework. In conventional student teaching, students have little opportunity to develop *conditional knowledge* (Paris, Lipson, & Wixson, 1983), that is, knowing when and why to use specific techniques and strategies or when to advance particular information. Conditional knowledge is necessary for appropriate teaching in complex, dynamic settings like classrooms. Without it, students may view their university learning as static, as something that either works or does not, regardless of context. Because student teachers are typically *dropped into* classrooms, they are left to conditionalize knowledge as best they can. They frequently use trial and error approaches with little opportunity to reflect on their experiences. They often try out techniques learned in their methods courses. Unfortunately, they may not recognize the conditions for applying that knowledge. If their attempts are unsuccessful, they may lack the perspective or guidance to understand why the effort was unproductive and how they might improve it. Frustrated, student teachers may then reject the technique and turn to the cooperating teachers for *what really works.* Thus an uncritical dependency on cooperating teacher routines and practices grows.

Means and opportunity for students to develop as thoughtful professionals are missing from the structure of traditional student teaching (Feiman-Nemser & Buchmann, 1987; Wildman, Magliaro, Niles, & McLaughlin, 1990). Student

teachers lack opportunities to engage in joint construction of knowledge and reflective processes (see Mehan, 1981). In the disconnection of conventional student teaching, students are closed off from context-rich discourse wherein they might develop more subtle, refined, and meaningful command of their growing knowledge, roles, and consciousness. Isolated from the *instructional conversation* of teacher preparation (Goldenberg, 1993; Tharp & Gallimore, 1988), they develop meanings for their experience in idiosyncratic and uncritical ways.

A way to address this deficiency is to make students full participants with teachers, university personnel, and peers in critical conversation about the internship experience (Blanton et al., 1994). In this view, teacher, student, and professor are one, and communication is multi-sided, ongoing, and genuine. Joined in this community of discourse, students co-construct their professional selves through interactions with informed and involved partner/mentors invested in their development. The potential of this teaching triad, however, often remains unrealized. Research documents that poor communication among supervisors, interns, and cooperating teachers is commonplace, resulting in mutual misunderstanding and blame (Tittle, 1974). How can this conversation be initiated and sustained? New telecommunications technology may help resolve some of the problems of disconnection and limited meaning making. By enabling reflective conversations to occur, telecomunications technology may lead to more inquiry-oriented teacher education.

Telecommunications

Telecommunications can overcome limitations of time and distance and create active social contexts for goal-directed activity (Murray, 1991). Telecommunications can link members of the student-teaching triad, enabling participants to clarify and negotiate complex professional meanings through public discourse. Released from the isolation of the placement classroom, students can use e-mail to discuss their classrooms with the group and peer into others' classrooms, grades, curricula, and schools. As issues of knowledge, instruction, and behavior emerge among participants, students can learn to distinguish between common and unique issues in classroom teaching.

Researchers have examined the effects of telecommunications use by student teachers, particularly as a link between students and university supervisors (Merseth, 1991). Most researchers of e-mail correspondence among apprentice teachers have looked at the types of messages they created in relatively unstructured conditions (see Anderson & Lee,1995). In these circumstances, student teachers generated socioemotional correspondence rather than informational, professionally oriented correspondence. They used technology more for exchange of social and emotional support than exchange of ideas. In contrast, Thomas, Clift, and Sugimoto (1996 [this issue]) examined the kinds of communication prospective teachers generated in relation to course assignments and classroom observations and found that they used electronic mail successfully and conveniently to meet course requirements. Their study documented the usefulness of e-mail interactions for influencing the shape of ongoing coursework. Interns communicated in predominantly task-oriented ways, but they did not use E-mail as a forum for an exchange of ideas. They note that very little spontaneous discussion occurred between the student teachers.

In our view, the structure of their e-mail assignments might account for the paucity of student discussion. To avoid the socioemotional character of student-teacher messages found in earlier research, Thomas et al. (1996 [this issue]) may have overstructured the e-mail environment. Their students' electronic mail use seems, from our point of view, heavily assignment oriented. The direction of students' messages also may have contributed to the lack of spontaneity. Students sent only summaries of readings to the entire class, whereas they sent reflective journal entries and personal statements about literacy—items more likely to generate questions and reactions—to the instructors. Summaries of readings are somewhat self-enclosed utterances and do not invite discussion or exchange in and of themselves. Although the professors asked students to raise questions about assigned readings in the context of the e-mail summaries, they used the questions to feed subsequent classroom discussion rather than to stimulate e-mail exchange among students and faculty.

In this article, we describe an attempt to create a structure for electronic mail use by student teachers promoting exchanges of ideas, both deliberate and spontaneous.

Context of Study

Sixteen students and five professors participated in this yearlong project. All students understood that their coursework and student teaching experience would require them to use e-mail regularly. They had training in telecommunications. Faculty taught courses as part of the elementary education block (reading, math, social studies, and media methods, language arts/ children's literature) and a general methods course. During the first semester, the courses met intensively for approximately 10 weeks, after which students were assigned to classrooms in four participating schools. During this phase of the program, students returned to campus in the afternoons to continue methods seminars. For the second semester, the student-teaching phase of the program, students spent full days in the schools, returning periodically for day-long seminars and problem-solving sessions. Each school had a computer lab connected to the university's local area networks. For the internship and student-teaching phases of the program, students used these on-site labs for most of their communication. Students had 1-hour reflection periods as part of their day; many used portions of this time to write their messages.

After students began their field experiences, they were required to send at least two messages a week on electronic mail. They sent most messages to the entire cadre of professors, students, and teachers. Thomas et al. (1996 [this issue]) found that students in their study often read messages selectively. Many checked to see who sent the message and scanned the content for issues of interest, disregarding or skimming others. In our study, we asked students to sort their messages by content, directing them to particular lists. They created separate lists for separate concerns, addressed general issues in one list, and specific issues on classroom management or language arts, reading, or children's literature in others. The students and faculty each had separate lists for private group discussions. We thought that choosing a list for a message would help writers think about their content and focus their communication and would help readers, who would receive more focused, predictable messages.

Our e-mail assignments were open but linked to general observations and themes such as describing the reading and language arts program in a class (three of the four schools had separate reading/language arts programs), observing and assisting the Title I reading teacher, and describing how (or if) spelling was being taught. We encouraged students to be inquisitive, to look for connections between what they had learned in their courses and what they were seeing in their classes, and to raise questions about things that puzzled them or with which they disagreed.

Results

Data for this study consisted of electronic mail collected over time and archived for analysis. We divided the data into four categories: responses to class assignments; socioemotional exchanges; housekeeping queries and bulletins; and spontaneous, sustained exchanges of ideas. Because the focus of the research question is the emergence of instructional dialogue, we report descriptive analyses of the final category. We examined these e-mail messages for evidence of reflection, sustained dialogue, and exchange of ideas. We applied the following criteria: messages had to be focused on a specific topic, with five or more episodes extended across 2 or more weeks, and the discussion had to involve two or more professors and three or more students.

Several substantive strands of reflective dialogue emerged during the school year. We found detailed exchanges embodying the themes of invented spelling, dialect, classroom management, use of Ritalin to control behavior, formal spelling instruction, and process writing. The longest exchange occurred between September and February. We found inquiry into issues of classroom application (*How do I?* or *Why should I?*), observed practice (*Why does she?*), and model building (*Shouldn't we think about things this way?*). Each strand began as a question raised about complex issues in student teaching (*If I accept student errors won't students be permanently misled?*) or as a question raised in response to the classroom experience (*Several of my students cannot read the textbook; what can I do to help them?*) Most of the exchanges were between students and professors, although occasionally students jumped in, volunteering responses to one another's problems.

A Peek Inside a Conversation

We now describe an example of the developing themes to give a clearer picture of these exchanges. After students entered their placement classrooms in the fall, questions soon arose about elements of process writing and how it was being implemented. Helen, placed in a second-grade classroom, begins the exchange. (Process writing and all of its familiar elements had been covered early in the language arts coursework. Much of the inquiry generated here re-covers ground covered at the university, but questions are now raised in the context of application.)

Helen: *This morning we wrote for THREE HOURS!! It was not intended to last this long, I don't think, but we corrected students' spelling and grammar as they wrote. It was horrible!!! I was so tired of doing writing, so were my kids. While I still feel that teachers should write things correctly on the board, correcting papers as students write only puts everyone in a foul mood. I had kids asking if we could Please Stop Writing! I will never make kids write for this long without at least some sort of break.*

In this telegraphic message, Helen shares the children's and her visceral response to a painful exercise in writing. She asserts her own instructional countermeasures: *I won't correct children's papers while they are writing, I'll put errors on the board instead, and I won't allow a lesson to persist to the point of painfulness.*

Following this message, one of us responds to Helen's observations and complaints, requesting more information and discussing other ways such a session could be conducted. She writes back with more detailed information and a more precise formulation of the problem: Correcting grammar, punctuation, and spelling all at once during composition is too much for children to handle, mentally and emotionally. She concludes her second message by rearticulating this dilemma and describing (despairingly) how she is trying to cope with it:

Helen: *They were writing letters to the parents for open house that same night. The letters were to be left on the children's desks at the end of the day. As the kids wrote, if there was a word they could not spell, they were to raise their hands and have one of the three of us (teacher, assistant, and myself) spell the word. We also checked grammar and punctuation and monitored the room as they wrote. There were MANY mistakes, but all writing was legible and understandable. Their inventive spellings were superb!*

After this writing lesson, I have officially changed my view on correcting children as they speak and write. (NO gloating, please, Dr. S and Dr. T!) I feel that if the children misspell something that they have learned [been taught], it should be corrected (gently). For example, their spelling words (pot, hot, dog, etc.). But to correct a second grader's spelling of "marvelous" made me feel like an ogre!! I was thrilled that the little fellow used such a word! I am so afraid I am going to discourage their use of words they can't spell, while at the same time making them hate writing. What can I do when the teacher wants everything to be correct? I hate how this makes me feel, because it is not just one or two items per paper, their papers are full of mistakes! But they are still understandable and full of good ideas. I stress to the children that their ideas and meanings of stories are wonderful, but I know that can't be enough with someone always over their shoulders.

In Helen's second message, she cites the tension she and a number of her peers experienced between the poles of expression and correctness in process writing. Many believed that no error should go uncorrected at any point, whether in speech or in writing. Here we see her reexamine the issue based on direct observation. She now rejects her earlier opinion about correctness, having seen the value of invention. But she has not gone to the other extreme, rejecting the idea of correctness as an appropriate issue for second graders. Instead she qualifies the issue. She advocates applying a reasonable standard of correctness, one that will encourage free expression while gently holding children accountable for what they have been taught.

Eye-opening experiences like Helen's may be commonplace in traditional student teaching, but without an immediate connection, are unlikely to be discussed in a timely and useful fashion, if at all. Amid the press of student teaching responsibilities, issues of this kind can soon be shuffled aside, unresolved, while others take their place. Our students' ongoing e-mail duties enhanced the likelihood that experiences of this kind undergo public discussion, evaluation, and response.

The public nature of the exchange between Helen and her professors is as important as the exchange itself. Not only was the entire group included in Helen's experience, the issues raised in this discussion triggered parallel questions from other classrooms. (Inventive spelling, how to handle it, and when to expect students to make a transition to correct forms first arose in this context.)

Another student, Linda, raises a question about editing in her third-grade class. Dr. T congratulates her on what she is trying to do and helps her shape her understanding of it by expanding her ideas and intuitions and placing them in a larger context of developed strategies with strong theoretical underpinnings. He coaches her through what she herself is trying to do. At the same time, he gives her emotional, procedural, and intellectual support. Rather than giving her the advice she asks for, he extends a range of possibilities for her to consider.

Linda: *What do I correct and what do I let slide for my grade level, do [I] tell them directly what is wrong or do I have them proofread [on] their own and go with that. I have been having them come up to my desk and letting them read their stories to me and we discuss their mistakes when either they notice them or I direct them toward a mistake. My teacher has me doing a lot of editing with their writing. Please give me some instruction and direction in this area.*

Dr. T: *First, I am very pleased with the way you have set up the editing structure. Children write and then come to work with you one-on-one for editing. Together you read through the stories and DISCUSS the mistakes. You sequence the procedure form the 'inside out'—by that I mean you first give the children a chance to find [a] mistake and correct it on her own; next you direct (by asking guiding questions and giving hints) the child to the mistake so that it can be discovered and corrected. Finally, what you could do as a last step if the child doesn't find the mistake is to point it out and give her a chance to correct it at that point or you could simply correct it for her. This is a great sequence which gives children a chance to do what they are capable of doing—too often we as teachers are willing to jump right in and solve problems for children that they could solve for themselves.*

Second, I like that you are DISCUSSING the mistakes with the children. This to me means that you are tackling the concepts behind the mistakes—the rules or issues about conventions, etc.

Third, I am pleased that you recognize that

there are some things that you let slide—can't do everything in one lesson. The difficult question is how do you know what to focus on and what not to. One source of information in this matter is the curriculum. Certainly concepts that have been previously taught (spelling, punctuation, rhetorical form, etc.) are fair game at editing time—[you] can use [the] checklist idea that was touched on in [an] earlier message.

Here is an example of joint meaning making that could only be accomplished with great difficulty in ordinary student teaching. By helping her clarify and extend her understanding of her work, Dr. T supports her fledgling efforts and assists her toward independence. Without this kind of support, interns are dependent upon the busy cooperating teacher to help them make what sense they can of their efforts.

Another student, Sheena, asks about still another facet of the writing process from the perspective of her second grade class's experience.

Sheena: *My question is about writing drafts. Ms. K. is trying to get the children to write two drafts and then publish the third. Unfortunately they really are having a difficult time understanding what "draft one" is. Many of them have gone back and written a second story with a completely different topic and called it a first draft. We went over an example today so hopefully they will understand better. Is there a creative, interesting way to explain what a draft is that second graders can really understand? This program emphasizes story maps. I suggested today that the children can first write a first draft (and explain that they are putting their ideas down) and then have them put their ideas from their draft into the map worksheet and then write a second draft. Does that sound like a logical sequence or would it be more confusing for them? How do you talk about editing and when should you discuss their grammar and spelling? This writing process is very tricky!*

Sheena raises a number of challenging questions here that do not yield easy answers. Yet we see her working through a possible solution and asking for a professional opinion, further advice, and moral support. She is asking for help in formulating the conditional knowledge necessary to make a complex procedure work with younger children. By coaching over e-mail and through subsequent face-to-face conversation, Dr. T was able to encourage Sheena's resourcefulness and help her develop a more flexible and dynamic sense of the writing process. As a conse-

quence of these exchanges that began with e-mail conversation, Sheena requested and read a book by a prominent authority on process writing.

As her knowledge of the writing process grew, Sheena's questions became more sophisticated and focussed. The next exchange with Dr. S gives him the occasion to refine further her understanding of how process writing procedures work in second grade. Through such conversations, students' conditional knowledge of classroom methods are enhanced:

Sheena: *Another difficult question from me again. I have been noticing that some children are still writing stories such as 'I like it. I love it. You will like it. You will love it.' I thought that we could set up a standard for publishing stories. Or do you think we should start getting them to ask each other questions? Another question: Is there a second grade guide to teaching writing? I thought about making posters of Draft 1, Draft 2, and Publishing. Do you think this a good idea?*

Dr. S: *There is a kind of art to asking questions to help children unfold as writers. This is especially true at the lower grades. I like... and I love... are nice safe sentence frames, but need to be left behind. One way to help children do this is bring up specific questions during a revision session. Such questions should probably be for brief oral discussion. For instance, I might ask, 'You wrote that you love your dog, Zippo. What do you like about him? Tell me what's so neat about him?'*

Sheena's messages reveal strong curiosity and commitment. Her cooperating teacher, somewhat disorganized and passive, was teaching at the second grade level for the first time. Struggling herself with a curriculum new to her and a newly adopted literature- and writing-based language arts program, she was not able or willing to share much with her intern. The connections we were able to keep with Sheena and others in difficult placements through e-mail proved critical in her development. The occasional visits of a traditional supervisor are unlikely to have helped Sheena work through the many problems she confronted in process writing. Nor would they have revealed the degree of support that she really needed for a productive experience.

Beyond facilitating Sheena's growth as a professional, these public conversations provided a means for other student teachers in third, fourth, and fifth grade placements and in classrooms where process writing was evident to varying degrees to consider the conditional issues critical to the implementation of process writing in lower grades.

Discussion

Using telecommunications, we maintained vital links with students and their classrooms and engaged in a public dialogue that we believe critical to their development as professionals. The exchanges illustrated here reveal the joint construction of meaning as students and professors engage in public discussion over issues of teaching, application, and knowledge. Although some student electronic mail was merely a response to assigned tasks or school business, some did not rise above the level of routine, uninspired summations of experience, and some veered into purely socioemotional, a significant strand of professional conversations occurred spontaneously on important themes. These exchanges illustrate the capacity of electronic mail to create a community of discourse with the potential to strengthen and vitalize teacher preparation. Opening paths of communication among professors and interns adds to the quality and quantity of contacts with students and their classrooms. Without the connections e-mail made possible, we could not have responded to issues as they arose or helped students to conditionalize their course knowledge in field placements.

Students showed interest in what was happening in their peers' classes. Having access through e-mail to the problems, questions, and themes in other classrooms broadened students' sense of schools, grades, and curricula. The connections that electronic mail created among student-teaching peers also helped forge communities that have persisted beyond the year's experience: Several students from this group—now first-year teachers—continue to communicate with each other through e-mail.

Our results point to the structure of e-mail use as an important factor in eliciting spontaneous exchanges of ideas. Too controlled a structure seems to inhibit free exchange. In contrast, too free a structure (Merseth, 1991) appears to result in free-flowing, socioemotional rather than professional, task-oriented exchanges. Three factors in our structure promote reflective dialogue: open, thematic prompts; the direction and focus of messages; and time to write. Open, thematic prompts (*How should I deal with errors in children's writing?*) gave students focus for their observations and the opportunity to react to or question anything they saw. The direction and the focus of messages gave further structure for the writer and reader. Time budgeted into the student teaching day for e-mail communication enabled students to continue to communicate even as their responsibilities in the classroom grew.

Although we believe that using the electronic mail in a public forum with open, theme-oriented prompts led to some very spontaneous exchanges of ideas, not all parts of the triad were involved. Like Thomas et al. (1996 [this issue]), we had difficulty eliciting teacher interest in using the telecommunications at their disposal. We made training available to teachers, but they did not utilize it. Teachers cited lack of time as the reason for their lack of participation and expressed the opinion that this would be just one more thing added to an overly full day. We could budget time for e-mail into our students' schedules, but we could not do that in the teachers' case. Teachers' reluctance may have also been connected to the newness of this yearlong program and their general inexperience with telecommunications. The group of participating teachers for the following school year has expressed more interest in electronic mail than their predecessors.

The volume of e-mail exchanges was another challenge for the professors. The sheer number of messages generated and the time it took to read and respond to them was at times daunting. We found we could respond only selectively to the messages we received, pulling out those most in need of a response, those that articulated an issue we wanted to highlight through discussion, and those that posed problems with good generalizability. The intensity of this demand must be addressed if telecommunications is to be used to create apprenticeships in teaching. We found that the time investments in electronic mail transformed a 3-hour course into something like a 4- or even 5-hour course. Despite these challenges, however, we believe e-mail can powerfully deepen and enrich student teaching experiences.

E-mail promises to facilitate the creation of active social contexts in which professional conversation leads to professional growth. We experienced this to some degree but believe that fuller participation by teachers and other relevant personnel is critical to realizing its full success.

Certainly time is a factor for teachers. If full teacher participation in these professional and public dialogues about teacher preparation is important, finding time for them to take on this additional responsibility will be critical.

Because structuring the electronic mail environment is a key element in creating productive public discourse among prospective teachers, we may want to consider telecommunications use in the light of Goldenberg's (1993) concept of *instructional conversation*. Designed to help students think critically and variously about complex issues, we believe that the instructional conversation provides an apt model for assisting novice teachers to apply, critique, and think flexibly about the knowledge they bring with them into teaching. In particular, the instructional conversation's elements of structure (thematic focus, direct teaching, eliciting bases for statements, and so on) and openness (general participation, responsiveness to student contributions, focus on complex issues) may provide a systematic way of thinking about e-mail dialogue and its use to create ongoing communities of discourse in teacher education.

References

Anderson, J., & Lee, A. (1995). Literacy teachers learning a new literacy: A study of the use of electronic mail in a reading education class. *Reading Research and Instruction, 34*(3), 222-238.

Blanton, W. E., Thompson, M. S., & Zimmerman, S. O. (1994). Applications of technologies to student teaching. *Electronic Journal of Virtual Culture.*

Clift, R. T., Meng, L., & Eggerding, S. (1994). Mixed messages in learning to teach English. *Teaching and Teacher Education, 10*(3), 265-279.

Feiman-Nemser, S., & Buchmann, M. (1987). When is student teaching teacher education? *Teaching and Teacher Education, 3,* 255-273.

Goldenberg, C. (1993). Instructional conversations: Promoting comprehension through discussion. *Reading Teacher, 46*(4), 316-326.

Goodlad, J. (1990). *Teachers for our nation's schools.* San Francisco: Jossey-Boss.

Griffith, G. A., Barnes, S., Hughes, R., O'Neal, S., Defino, M., Edwards, S., & Hukill, H. (1983). *Clinical preservice teacher education: Final report of a descriptive study.* Austin, TX: Research & Development Center for Teacher Education.

Guyton, E., & McIntyre, D. J. (1990). Student teaching and school. In W. R. Houston, & M. C. Pugach (Eds.), *The handbook of research in teacher education* (pp. 450-465). New York: Macmillan.

Horisego, B., & Boldt, W. (1985). Critical incidents in the supervision of student teaching. *Alberta Journal of Educational Research, 31,* 113-124.

Mehan, H. (1981). Social constructivism in psychology and sociology. *The Quarterly Newsletter of the Laboratory of Comparative Human Cognition, 3,* 71-77.

Merseth, K. K., (1991). Supporting beginning teachers with computer networks. *Journal of Teacher Education, 42,* 140-147.

Murray, D. I. (1991). *Conversation for action: The computer terminal as a medium of communication.* Philadelphia: John Benjamin.

Paris, S., Lipson, M., & Wixson, K. (1983). Becoming a strategic reader. *Contemporary Educational Psychology, 8,* 293-316.

Richardson-Koehler, V. (1988). Barriers to effective supervision of student teaching. *Journal of Teacher Education, 39,* 28-34.

Tabachnick, B. R., Popkewitz, T. S., & Zeichner, K. M. (1979-1980). Teacher education and the professional perspectives of student teachers. *Interchange, 10,* 12-29.

Tharp, R., & Gallimore, R. (1988). *Rousing minds to life: Teaching, learning and schooling in social context.* Cambridge, England: Cambridge University Press.

Thomas, L., Clift, R. T., & Sugimoto, T. (1996). Telecommunication, student teaching, and methods instruction: An exploratory investigation. *Journal of Teacher Education, 47,* 165-174.

Tittle, C. K. (1974). *Student teaching: Attitude and research bases for change in school and university.* Metuchen, NJ: Scarecrow.

Wildman, T., Magliaro, S., Niles, J., & McLaughlin, R. (1990). *Promoting reflective practice among beginning and experienced teachers: Encouraging reflective practice in education.* New York: Teachers College Press.

Zeichner, K. M. (1990). Changing directions in the practicum: Looking ahead to the 1990s. *Journal of Education for Teaching, 16,* 105-132.

Zeichner, K. M., Liston, D. P., Mahlios, M., & Gomez, M. (1988). The structure and goals of a student teaching program and the character and quality of supervisory discourse. *Teaching and Teacher Education, 4,* 349-362.

Six stages for learning to use technology

Anne L. Russell

Queensland University of Technology

ABSTRACT

Learning to use technology for adults can be traumatic. This paper describes six stages adults may go through as they learn to use technology to communicate electronically.

An action research model has been used to develop a strategy for adult learners to understand the stages they will go through as they learn to use electronic mail as a communication tool. There are two cycles in the study reported in this paper. First, is the identification and description of six stages learners go through as the technology moves from being intrusive to becoming invisible. And secondly, is the application of metacognitive understanding of these stages by new naive adult learners as they use the technology.

When new technology learners apply the knowledge of these six stages to their learning, they appreciate they are not unique and inadequate in their ability to come to terms with the technology. In addition, teachers of technology who have knowledge of the six stages can identify the key times when they need to provide intensive support with the knowledge that the learner will require less support during the later stages.

INTRODUCTION

Access to technology can "allow people separated by distance and time to occupy a shared synthetic world, where they can collaborate to evolved common virtual experiences" (Dede in O'Neil, 1995, p. 11). In order for educators to keep up with, and to be actively involved in, national and international trends, it is an advantage to have the ability to communicate with colleagues across the globe. However, in the information age where the Internet may be a way of life for the young child, many adults find learning to use computer technology is very daunting. Adults who are not familiar with technology can feel left behind. Special attention needs to be given to ensure they learn without losing self-esteem and without dropping out all together. Simonson, Maurer, Montag-Rorardi, & Whitaker, (1987) identified 'that a positive, anxiety free attitude toward computing was a necessary prerequisite of computer literacy' (p. 233).

Researchers (Rosen, Sears, & Weil, 1993; McInerney, McInerney, & Sinclair, 1994) studied university students' levels of computer anxiety before and after taking computer courses. The type of computer course has been an important factor in reducing anxiety (Leslo & Peck, 1992). However, reducing anxiety through learning computer applications using a relevant activity combined with an understanding of stages a learner typically goes through during the learning process has not been considered. Learning in this context represents the new understanding and skills which occur when technology hardware and the software processes move from being intrusive and frustrating to being invisible. This allows an individual to develop confidence and consider creative uses of the technology.

The study reported in this paper is qualitative and based on personal e-mail diaries written by adult learners. It focuses on the identification of learning stages in these students' self-reports as they use e-mail for the first time. The second phase of the study involved introducing the identified stages to a new group of students also learning to use e-mail.

Computer Anxiety

In the information age adults believe they should be computer literate. Many feel inadequate about their abilities to develop computer skills and actively avoid using computers. Evans-Andris (1995) observed elementary teachers and found:

Approximately, 62% of the teachers tended to engage primarily in distancing routines, limiting their involvement with computers, whereas approximately 38% of the teachers engaged primarily in embracing routines, increasing their opportunities to use the equipment. (p. 20)

From *National Convention of the Association for Educational Communications and Technology*, 1996. Reprinted from ERIC ED 397 832.

Kolehmainen (1992) suggested computer anxiety will have negative effects when learning new technology because of a resistance to change. If this is so, it may be important to identify for learners a relevant purpose for learning which reflects and reinforces their current values. Involving students in a relevant task where the technological processes are merely a means to an end, may lead to overcoming computer anxiety earlier.

Rosen et al. (1993) and McInerney et al. (1994) found first-year university students in the 1990s to be computer anxious as they commence their compulsory computer studies. Both these studies reported many of the students still remained anxious at the completion of their computer course.

A computer literacy and computer anxiety test has been devised by Simonson et al. (1987) and has been used to measure the level of computer anxiety in university students before and after completing a computer course.

The type of computer course can have some influence on the level of anxiety of graduating students. Leso and Peck (1992) found students taking a software tool course (included word processing, spreadsheets, etc.) were more likely to come out with reduced anxiety than those students doing a programming course. However, the study did not explore the reason for this outcome. In fact, many students did not reduce their level of anxiety by the end of either course.

"Increased computer experience does not necessarily alleviate anxiety" is also reported by McInerney et al. (1994, p. 47). These authors suggested researchers focus "on building confidence and a sense of personal control in a non-threatening learning environment, individualized if necessary" (1994, p. 47). It appears the processes of learning to use computers can cause a decrease in self-esteem.

Becoming Computer Literate

Being computer literate implies being able to use a computer and to apply current understanding to new situations. In relation to this paper, computer literacy refers to common hardware and software 'tools' programs and, in particular, using e-mail. In early computer experiences the hardware and software are intrusive. As the learner understands how to manipulate the computer, more control over the technology enables the focus to shift to tasks to be completed.

Valdez (1989) suggested that "technology should be the means by which teachers and students are able to feel more empowered and in control of their lives" (p. 38). He identified awareness, adoption and refinement/adaptation as "three stages that most people experience when learning to use technology" (p. 37). The present study reports finding six stages which learners go through as the hardware and software processes move from intrusive to invisible.

Learning to use technology in this paper is presented from a constructivist perspective where learning occurs through immersing the learner in a real and relevant experience with collaborative faculty and peer support. The learner brings metacognitive understanding to the learning situation to help overcome some of the frustrations of learning and bring understanding to the task.

The learner constructs personal meaning through immersion in the situation and develops strategies for building an understanding of the practicalities of the technological processes. Apart from the physical presence of the technology there are other sources for help which range from printed manuals to faculty and peer support. The learner develops an understanding of how the technology operates and identifies the steps required to make it work in order to achieve success in the processes. The understanding will be such that the learner can accommodate flexibly when varied processes are required.

In the study reported here the students were given operation manuals, personal instruction, provided with faculty and peer support, but were encouraged to create their own mental scheme and processes to understand the technology. This is carried out through the immersion in a real and relevant task which involves children from schools across Australia.

THE STUDY

Initially thirty teachers studying in a post-graduate university course were involved in a compulsory assignment which required them to learn to use e-mail. The vehicle for their learning was to take the role of a character from a children's fiction book and respond to letters from school children. This Characters-on Line Project during a three week period provided a service to Australian schools (Russell, in press). All communications took place using e-mail. In addition to e-mailing to the children, each student was required to send three e-mail messages to their professor explaining how they were learning to use the technology. These messages, or metacognitive learning diaries, were sent at intervals throughout the learning experience.

Students came into the course with varying technological knowledge. While some had actively avoided using computers, others had practical experience in word-processing and school library automation activities. No student had previously accessed electronic mail.

Initially all students were on-campus attending university full-time. Over the following years the nature of the course changed and the majority of the post-graduate students became part-time external or open learning students, many of whom live in remote locations. They accessed e-mail and completed the project assignment with a borrowed modem from their home or at their local school.

Since the initial thirty teachers completed their e-mail assignment, some 400 students have repeated the process and e-mailed metacognitive reflections on their learning experiences. The e-mailed metacognitive reflections from students formed a pool of data which was analyzed using grounded theory (Lincoln & Guba, 1985). Categories of metacognitive reflections on the experience of learning technological skills related to using electronic mail were identified. Six categories emerged from the diary reports and these formed stages which learners typically go through as they learn to use technology:

Stage 1: Awareness
Stage 2: Learning the process
Stage 3: Understanding and application of the process
Stage 4: Familiarity and confidence
Stage 5: Adaptation to other contexts
Stage 6: Creative application to new contexts.

In the second stage of the study these six stages were presented to new students as they commenced their e-mail experience and learned to use the technology. These students were asked to reflect on their personal learning in relation to the identified six stages. This second aspect of the action research cycle validates the six stages as students reported similar feelings of frustration and success. This aspect will be explored after describing in more detail the six stages for learning to use technology.

PHASE ONE: STAGES FOR LEARNING TO USE TECHNOLOGY

The six stages learners usually pass through as e-mail technology moves from the intrusive to the invisible are described and supported by illustrations from metacognitive reports of the students.

Stage 1: Awareness
Here students are aware that electronic mail exists. Many students have actively avoided using computers and no student reported using e-mail prior to this compulsory activity. A sense of nervousness and fear was in the minds of some students while others were looking forward to having the opportunity to do something they had heard about.

I had no idea what was actually going to occur. I had heard of electronic mail, but had never seen it in operation. Because of this, I felt rather bewildered and to a certain extent concerned.

The very thought of such technology—computers, satellites, etc., was extremely daunting. I was also excited by the idea that I would have to be involved and get to know all about it.

Stage 2: Learning the Process
Reports of time-consuming assimilation of new information as new skills are mastered epitomizes this stage. Instructions are often misleading for the novice who does not understand the processes. Frustrations with complex technology render the equipment intrusive in the eyes of the user. The technology can overpower and intimidate the learner.

Some students without extensive computer experiences, are afraid of damaging equipment. Others, in hindsight enjoy this challenge and persevere to ably move beyond this stage. Most students find working within a group extremely valuable for providing moral support. Apart from peer support, this stage

requires extensive technical and positive encouragement from the teacher.

We experienced a variety of emotions: extreme frustration often when there appeared to be no logical explanation for things going wrong; annoyance about the amount of time wasted.

The handbooks were meaningless, until I had some "hands-on" experience.

Stage 3: Understanding and Application of the Process
As the learner begins to understand the logic behind the technological processes, the need to cling to step-by-step instructions can be relaxed. Where early instructions had no meaning and were therefore forgotten, now the learners have "hands-on" experience and they can accommodate new instructions within their basic understanding. The relevance of the task gives added incentive with a purpose to continue learning the processes. A sense of community is felt with the presence of peers who are also learning the processes and providing moral support.

After plodding through a couple of weeks, our knowledge of [e-mail] had increased and so, this time, some of the things began to make sense, and suddenly we could see where we had gone wrong. The next attempt brought success!

Stage 4: Familiarity and Confidence
With confidence the technological processes are applied to the task at hand as the learner can visualize the processes and anticipate logical outcomes for certain software commands or apparent inconsistencies. The technology is starting to become transparent when problems become 'hiccups' rather than major distracters. *only small problems!*

Sometimes there is a reversion to earlier stages, but confidence is more quickly regained. Self-esteem is increased as the learner is able to solve the problems through familiarity or logical analysis of the situation. Working things out alone gives a sense of knowing, understanding and confidence.

By the beginning of the second week I could successfully work on [e-mail] without the use of the much valued manual—something I was quite proud of.

Having overcome the problems of operating the system efficiently, I could then concentrate on the process of the task: assuming the role of the character of Wilbur. This was one of the highlights. Being able to communicate with children and sharing with them their thoughts and feelings on the book "Charlotte's Web".

Stage 5: Adaptation to Other Contexts
Now the technology and software are invisible and the learner can see the potential for use of e-mail in other curriculum situations. New understandings and experiences are transferred to other contexts. For example, one student reports a new sense of confidence when she assists school children as they learn a word processing package she has not previously seen.

Now that I know how to operate the system, I hope that I will have the opportunity to work on future [e-mail] projects. As well, this time has also made it evident to me that I will need to become more familiar with computers and associated pieces of equipment, if I am going to incorporate them successfully into my resource centre.

Stage 6: Creative Application to New Contexts.
This stage is reached by students for whom the technological processes become invisible and who naturally use electronic mail to extend their educational environment when this is appropriate.

Several years after this initial contact with e-mail, some students have reported that the experience led them to become the computer coordinator in their school. Other students have sent future assignments via e-mail when this was not an expectation. Recognizing implications and possibilities for other uses of e-mail was also evident.

Electronic mail could provide deaf children with the facility to participate in the visual form of natural language with their peers. It would also widen the audience for outback students.

PHASE TWO: METACOGNITIVE APPLICATION OF THE STAGES

Once the six stages most students go through as they learn to use the technology were identified, new students were introduced to the stages at the beginning of their on-line assignment. The diary reports they send reflected their personal learning in relation to the six stages. The intention was to provide the opportunity for the students to articulate their personal learning strategies and also to validate the six stages as being applicable for learners of new technology.

My reflection on their metacognitive insights helped me to identify how better to assist these and future students as they learn new technological processes.

The following discussion epitomizes e-mail diaries of sixty students doing the Characters-on-Line Project in 1995. It should be acknowledged that some students may not like to admit their feelings of inadequacy. However there are sufficient positive reflections to indicate students' computer anxiety is overcome at the completion of the task and confirmation of the six stages for learning to use new technology.

A case study of Pat will be presented here with her references to the six stages as she was learning to use e-mail. Her insights were typical of the other students. The following message was sent to me six weeks after a five hour introduction and hands on training session during an on-campus session at the university. Pat is a full-time teacher-librarian (media specialist) living in a country town too far to return to the university for assistance in using e-mail. She was a member of the team who took on the character of eight year old Jason from a picture book called Our Excursion by Kate Walker & David Cox (Omnibus Books). As "Jason", Pat replied to letters from school children across Australia.

Stage 1: Awareness
All my initial fears, phobias and woes seem long forgotten and I'm a bit sad to be saying good-bye to Jason and the [e-mail] kids. I jotted down a few notes regarding the six stages you propose. In Stage 1 I certainly had mixed feelings about what was going to occur. The best way to describe it I guess is that it was a strange mix of excitement and terror—do you know that feeling?

As I read the comments from students, I am conscious of their anxiety at the beginning of the project. Many have avoided using computers and others are afraid of the technology and the damage they will do to the hardware. These students need to have useful instructions, equipment that works and access to someone who knows the particulars of their computer setup. At the same time there are students who are confident and keen to extend their experiences with the technology.

Stage 2: Learning the Process
I felt fairly confident when I left uni (how those other students managed with a phone workshop I'll never know—I guess I'm a hands on learner), but when I got home I had trouble setting up the system and our shared phone line crashed for a few days. It threw me and I lost confidence. In Stage 2 I was pretty much frustrated and impatient. I felt uncertain and suddenly all the instructions that had seemed clear at uni didn't seem to make sense.

Stage Two requires direct non-threatening assistance from someone who has knowledge of the student's individual computer setup. Preferably this is someone who is readily available on site or via telephone. It is this stage where I receive many phone calls for assistance. Observation of two naive learners sitting together at one keyboard is fascinating. The person at the keyboard seems to have an empty mind and the observer knows all the answers and steps in the process. They then exchange positions and the empty minded person has all the answers as the former expert sits at the keyboard with an empty mind!

This stage requires confidence building. It is essential students do not feel or be made to feel stupid. A phrase I use often during this stage is, "The more mistakes you make the more you will learn." Permission and even encouragement to make mistakes is essential and acknowledges that others are equally unaware.

Stage 3: Understanding and Application of the Process
Stage 3 was reassuring because gradually things started to fall into place. Although I felt that I didn't know where my information was at any one time (cyberspace???? what is that???) I gradually was coming to grips with the [e-mail] concept. I learned the hard way to be accurate.

Less help is required from experts at this stage. Often students turn to each other via e-mail or telephone for assistance. They build confidence as they help each other overcome problems. My presence is seldom sought.

Stage 4: Familiarity and Confidence

Stage 4 was great. I was up and rolling and really having fun. I was in character with Jason and starting to develop a fondness for him. I enjoyed getting the kids' letters and even wrote to a couple and asked them to write back to me and tell me their dog's name etc. One letter was quite sad, about a recently deceased pet dog, and I felt Jason could identify with how he would feel if his dog died and maybe in some small way help the grieving of that child—Who knows? I enjoyed the freedom of the character and talking in an eight year-old way to the kids—don't show this to any psychiatry colleagues!

Even the way this is written reflects the freedom experienced when the technology begins to turn invisible and the task becomes the focus of attention. Letters I receive at this stage are longer and the students talk about their family and leisure time pursuits in addition to their involvement in the task.

Stage 5: Adaptation to Other Contexts

Stage 5: I started to think about how I could use [e-mail] in my job—perhaps to contact authors etc. I can see that it will be possible to use [e-mail] to communicate with other teacher-librarians etc. Is there a directory of users available?

Here Pat is moving beyond the immediate task and exploring the potential for relevant use of e-mail in other aspects of her job as a media specialist in a school. By now the technology is invisible and only a vehicle through which the wider world can be reached for personal professional development and for the benefit of student learning.

Stage 6: Creative Application to New Contexts

(Stage 6).

Thanks for the opportunity to [e-mail]. I have enjoyed it and it has given me a common experience to share with my student colleagues in the oft lonely land of external study. Cheers, Pat.

Being a member of an e-mail team has had a side benefit where colleagues have been brought together and shared problems and so come to know each other. In the future they may continue to be in touch through e-mail and so a network of professional communication has commenced.

Pat cannot reflect on Stage Six yet as, by its very nature, it will not be evident until some time after this project is ended. Then Pat may find she wants to achieve a particular vision and e-mail will be the most obvious way to achieve it. During the semester I have received requests for extensions and clarification related to assignments for other courses from students who were originally introduced to e-mail as a Character-on-Line.

While many students reported concluding the project with positive computer learning and less anxiety, no formal measure of computer anxiety either pre or post project was administered. Some students chose not to write about their learning in relation to the six stages. No close record was kept of students who claimed to be anxious at the beginning and their outcome comments at the end. As with many e-mail messages, the request for information is often not responded to. It could be possible that students not reporting their computer experi-

ences were either still anxious or the technology was so invisible they did not consider reporting to be of any consequence.

CONCLUSION

The six stages of learning to use a new technology has been validated through this study. The students seem to jump the hurdle of the computer anxiety in order to put their minds to the authentic task of being a character in a book and writing letters to real students in schools across Australia.

This empirical study is as applicable for teachers of computer anxious learners as it is for the learners themselves. Four recommendations are suggested for instructional designers of courses for naive computer users:

1. Use a novel relevant real-life task to encourage the student to jump the hurdle of the processes in order to become involved in the task. Leso and Peck (1992) found students learning word-processing and other tool skills likely to be less computer anxious at the end of the course. However, they still found a third of these students measured high on the computer anxiety scale. Perhaps a pre and post computer anxiety measurement where the course included a novel and relevant or authentic task as an outcome would find a lower number of computer anxious students at the completion of the task.

2. Introduce the six stages for learning a new technology to students before they commence a computer course. Frequently students report feeling inadequate and stupid and expect to be experts with their first computer experiences. Through knowing the stages they may relate to the frustrations of previous students and remove some of the pressure to be perfect at the first attempt. Knowledge that they will eventually succeed as other students have done can remove some of the stress.

3. Provide a non-threatening environment with extensive technical and moral support during Stages Two and Three when self-esteem can be low and problems are not easily solved by a naive learner. McInerney et al. (1994) suggested students develop confidence if the learning environment is non-threatening. At this time there is a need for mediation and coaching. It is preferable for a non-threatening expert to be readily available on site, but, if this is not possible, telephone contact with the teacher or another expert is appropriate. However, when students are unable to contact an expert they find solace and problems are solved through talking or e-mailing with a student colleague who is learning the same processes. It seems a learning community can be developed which builds confidence and understanding in all members of that group. This idea parallels Dede's suggestion (in O'Neil, 1995) of students sharing a 'synthetic world'.

4. Encourage students to articulate their metacognitive experiences in relation to the six stages. When students ver-

balize their learning, they can identify where they have come from, where they are now and the vision of success. The act of interacting with the six stages in order to clarify their own learning situation objectifies their learning and may remove negative subjective thoughts.

In the future the technological processes may not be electronic mail, but another technological innovation which needs learning through coaching and support with frustrating and time consuming focus on the processes before the technology invisibly becomes incorporated within an environment. Only then can creative and worthwhile uses be applied in a variety of contexts.

REFERENCES

Evans-Andris, M. (1995). An examination of computing styles among teachers in elementary schools. Educational technology research and development, 43(2), 15–31.

Kolehmainen, P. (1992). The changes in computer anxiety in a required computer course. A paper presented at the European Conference on Educational Research, University of Twente, Enschede, The Netherlands (ERIC document ED 350 975).

Leso, T., & Peck, K. (1992). Computer anxiety and different styles of computer courses. Journal of Educational Computing Research, 8(4), 469–478.

Lincoln, Y. S. & Guba, E. G. (1985) Naturalistic inquiry. Beverly Hills, Calif. Sage.

McInerney, V., McInerney, D. M., & Sinclair, K. (1994). Student teachers, computer anxiety and computer experience. Journal of Educational Computing Research, 11(1), 27–50.

O'Neil, J. (1995) On technology & schools: a conversation with Chris Dede. Educational Leadership, v.53(2), 6–12.

Rosen, L. D., Sears, D. C., & Weil, M. M. (1993). Treating technophobia: a longitudinal evaluation of the computerphobia reduction program. Computers in Human Behavior, 9, 27–50.

Russell, A. (In press) Teaching electronic mail using a real experience with 2000 children, in Berne, Z. and Collins, M. (eds) The Online Classroom in K–12—Volume 2: Teacher Education and Instructional Design.

Simonson, M. R., Maurer, M., Montag-Rorardi, M., & Whitaker, M. (1987). Development of a standardized test of computer literacy and a computer anxiety index. Journal of Educational Computing Research, 3, 231–246.

Valdez, G. (1989). Mind over machine: lessons learned from staff development efforts. Educational Technology, 29, 36–38.

Dimensions of a Knowledge Support System: Multimedia Cases and High Bandwidth Telecommunications for Teacher Professional Development

By Joan Mazur, University of Kentucky, and Traci Bliss, Idaho State University

The Common Thread Case Project is a multi-year project that uses multimedia compact disc technology and high-bandwidth telecommunications to provide a unique, case-based professional development network for teachers in the midst of reform.

Each case in the series, called The Common Thread Cases, is a true story which captures the dilemmas and accomplishments of teachers involved in reform. The Common Thread Cases (CTC) have been fully described elsewhere (Bliss & Mazur, 1995a). However, the case criteria are salient to the present discussion and are reiterated in Appendix A. The cases are designed for in-depth discussions that critically analyze pedagogy and promote reflection. The intent of the project is to provide teachers with case facilitation skills and technology to develop and support a professional community of teachers. In addition to case facilitation training, the project also is working with participants to explore telecommunications for networking. Currently, we are examining two questions potentially crucial to the project's long-term success.

(1) To what extent can the cases, along with accompanying study tools, resources, and telecommunications technology, become the nexus of a larger system of knowledge support that is essential for teacher professionalism?

(2) What are the dimensions of such a knowledge support system?

Background and Need for Knowledge Support

Teachers involved in systemic reform face unique challenges. We are focusing on Kentucky teachers because of the technological emphasis in the Kentucky reform effort. Now in its seventh year of implementation, the Kentucky Education Reform Act of 1990 (KERA) requires comprehensive reform in governance, finance, and curriculum. The reform also includes an extensive technology initiative and statewide network that comprise the Kentucky Educational Technology System. The purpose of the statewide network is to improve instruction and support teacher professional development (Kentucky Master Plan for Technology, 1992). Schools are now required to provide high-end desktop computing in classrooms. An integrated wide-area network connects all the states' school districts, colleges and universities, and governmental agencies. Such an extensive network in a largely rural state is intended, in part, to support the professional needs of teachers—teachers who are expected to engage in new types of teaching (e.g., portfolio assessment) and problem-solving activities. For novice teachers, performance is now assessed through portfolios in which they demonstrate what they know and are able to do consistent with state adopted performance standards.

Several recent studies of the KERA implementation have stressed the need for more strategic professional development approaches (Robertson Associates, 1995). Teachers want more examples of new practices and ongoing support for incorporating new approaches (Mathews, 1995; Daniels & Stallion, 1995). Moreover, to be more effective in meeting the needs of teachers, technology should be integrated into flexible professional development (Mazur, 1995).

Cases and Teacher Professional Development

Cases have been used for teacher professional development for some time and for a variety of purposes (Wasserman, 1993; Kagan, 1993; Kleinfeld, 1989). Among the most prominent uses of the case approach in a technology context are (1) to support collaborative work between experts and novices and to compare differences in novice and expert approaches (Borko et al., 1992; Borko & Livingston, 1989), (2) to frame situational learning (Koschman et al., 1990), and (3) to examine expert decision making in complex, ill-structured domains (Spiro et al., 1988). In addition, cases contextualize problem solving (Cognition and Technology Group, 1991, 1993; Risko, 1992b; Risko, Vount & Towell, 1991). However, electronic cases for educators (Fishman & Duffy, 1992, 1993; Desberg, Colbert & Trimble, 1995) have been developed only recently.

Each Common Thread Case CD-ROM contains the entire discursive text of the hard copy case transformed into a multimedia "animated narrative." That is, the text is augmented with accompanying non-discursive descriptive material consisting of high quality graphics, video clips and audio narration. These enhancements are intended to provide teachers with multiple ways of knowing the subject (Eisner, 1993). Strategic case content locators and graphical overviews provide several

From *National Convention of the Association for Educational Communications and Technology*, 1996. Reprinted from ERIC ED 397 821.

ways to navigate through the case content. A variety of resources designed to supplement study and discussion of the case are also provided: Case discussion questions, exhibits, case commentaries, a case bibliography, and relevant articles. Each CD contains telecommunications shareware that facilitates the use of on-line networks to discuss questions or issues related to the case. A World Wide Web homepage is also available (http://www.uky.edu/~casenet/ cases/index.html).

Knowledge Support and Performance Outcomes for Teacher Professionalism

The Common Thread Cases are consistent with a proposed approach to upgrade teachers' skills through integrating powerful new technologies with teacher professional development (Barron and Goldman, 1994). However, many of the problems related to technology and productivity identified by business and industry have resurfaced in professional development for teachers (Lieberman & McLaughlin, 1992). For example, educators, like their counterparts involved in training for business and industry, have seen the poor results of one-shot, one-size-fits-all training that does not provide opportunities for ongoing practice and feedback on performance (Savage, 1994). To combat this problem new systems, termed on-line performance support systems, have been designed to link innovative applications to new learning and collaborative paradigms (Schoenmaker, 1993). These systems have been described as *continuous learning environments* (Forman & Kaplan, 1994). That is, the system provides an array of integrated resources such as references, guidance, or tools on the desktop that are under the users' control. Delivered via computer, this new generation of electronic performance support systems (Stevens and Stevens, 1995) provides needed task- and situation-specific information accessible from electronic networks and/or multimedia databases. The strength of these new interactive and networked technologies lies in their potential to deal with complexity and sort out multiple factors involved in a problem (Savage, 1994).

What is the potential of these continuous learning environments for professional development in education? Despite some congruence with approaches generally termed constructivist (Duffy & Jonassen, 1993; Wilson, 1995), there remain significant conceptual differences between programs designed to support educational endeavors and the continuous learning environments used to support productivity in business and industry. One difference is the nature of the cognitive tasks involved in productive work. Teaching requires professional judgments that may vary widely in specific circumstances. Teachers' judgments require what has been termed narrative, rather than paradigmatic, knowing (Bruner, 1991). There is no one set of prescribed rules or procedures that will work in any given set of circumstances.

Another aspect of the educational situation that is significantly different from business environments is that both novices and veterans are assigned similar tasks regardless of experience. That is, a first year teacher and a twenty-year veteran may both be teaching a class of mixed ability second graders in an urban school. While each can learn from the other, the time and opportunity are usually lacking to capitalize on the possibilities for mentoring or peer assistance (Little, 1991; Raney and Robbins, 1989).

In addition, the traditional isolation of teachers has inhibited the sharing of pedagogical insights gained from experience.

The strategic role of dialogic conversation in enabling participants to create commonly shared meaning and to "transform their mindsets and think about change and education" has been recently conceptualized by Jenlink and Carr (1996, p. 34). Furthermore, Brown & Campione (1990) have described how essential a community of learners is to supporting critical thinking, reflection, and change. Specifically, networks of engaged participants can become the much-needed contexts for transforming practice (McLaughlin & Talbert, 1993).

Currently, there are a plethora of on-line services for teacher networking. But many users complain that electronic information is overwhelming, unfocused, or difficult to access (Harasim, 1990) and this perception has seriously limited the use of on-line resources for professional development. In their efforts to change practice, teachers need to engage in intensive, more structured professional communities and intellectual teamwork (Gallegher & Kraut 1991). The Common Thread Case Project addresses these issues through the integration of multimedia cases and telecommunications in an open, yet highly focused knowledge support system.

Dimensions of an Open Knowledge Support System

The knowledge support environment has to be robust enough to encourage thought and promote insight, open enough to allow users to raise topics that are personally relevant, and yet sufficiently focused to emphasize teacher performance standards. Thus, the design of the knowledge support system must include the following three dimensions:

(1) An *Instrumental Dimension*. The core content (the cases) and information contained in the resources must be rich enough to accommodate novice and experienced educators and appeal to a wide variety of experiences. Simultaneously, the performance standards must play a prominent role. In addition, the design and presentation of information should provide opportunities for studying complex pedagogy and offer multiple ways to access that information. Furthermore, the system's design should incorporate aesthetics (Saito et al. 1995) that capitalize on the expressive potential (Dewey, 1934) of multimedia technology to engage the educational imagination described by Eisner (1986). The system also needs to be flexible and accessible to accommodate teachers' scheduling demands.

(2) A *Relational Dimension*. To enable the teacher to thoroughly analyze various aspects of a case as it relates to teaching standards as well as to theory and practice, the knowledge support system should make available integrative tools and resources. Questioning or clarifying the case situation may involve examining, gathering, and linking information. Tools to help teachers elaborate on issues raised and to double check information embody a relational dimension that is structured not by the program's sequence but by the questions, interests, or concerns of the user.

(3) A *Communication Dimension*. This system must incorporate tools that encourage and enable teachers to communicate their analysis of the case issues to others who also use the case. Teachers can revise ideas, capitalize on the experiences of others and engage in the critical discourse essential to the development of professional communities.

4. TEACHER TRAINING

The chart below shows samples of knowledge support dimensions as related to prominent Common Thread case features and telecommunications tools (see Appendix B).

Samples:

Instrumental	Relational	Communication
Case content and accompanying visuals	Discussion Questions	Notebook
Exhibits	Explore Issues and Standards	E-mail Tools
Case Commentary	Case Content Locator	Web Site
State & National Performance Standards	Where Am I? Navigator	Desktop Video Conference
Bibliography/Articles		

Future Directions

The program has been field tested with approximately 200 new and experienced Kentucky teachers. The most obvious issues emanating from the field tests concern the communications dimension of the knowledge support system. Not surprisingly, users were uncomfortable with initiating on-line video conferences with strangers. Also, the notion of on-going professional development carried out via electronic mail was, in fact, so foreign to most teachers that they had difficulty incorporating contacts with other teachers into their regular routines. In order to truly utilize the highly accessible resources in continuous learning environments, teachers apparently need encouragement and follow-up on the use of on-line forums and databases to support their work and professional development activities. Most importantly, the issue of sustainability was raised. For example, many of those in our field test, once the initial contact was made, were quite enthusiastic about meeting a new "colleague." What is necessary to maintain professional conversation and community once it has been initiated?

At this point in the implementation of the Common Thread Case Project, the communications dimension needs careful investigation. As our research proceeds we will be examining which resources are most suited to supporting various aspects of professional discourse. For example, will features of teleconferencing be more valuable for certain types of discussions, or only as the initial contacts for collaboration? What kinds of discussion will be best suited for e-mail? Will the World Wide Web forum or two-way video conferencing be the most effective model for study group discussion? Perhaps, most importantly, will we discover that like networks in business and industry the key to sustainability is having a task orientation or work groups goal? As refinements to the development of the communications dimension of the knowledge support system proceed, we hope to develop the refinements necessary to the models for open, flexible communities that can be sustained over time.

Perhaps most importantly, we will discover that like business and industry, the key to sustainability is having a task orientation or workgroup goal.

References

Barron, L., & Goldman, E. S. (1994). Integrating technology with teacher preparation. In B. Means (Ed.), *Technology and education reform.* San Francisco, CA: Jossey Bass.

Bliss, T., & Mazur, J. (1995a). Making standards come alive. *Proceedings of the International Conference on Standards and Assessment* (ICSA). Chapel Hill: University of North Carolina, March 1995.

Bliss, T., & Mazur, J. (1998). *Secondary and middle school teachers in the midst of reform: Common thread cases.* Upper Saddle River, N.J.: Prentice-Hall/Simon & Schuster.

Borko, H., et al. (1992). Learning to teach hard mathematics: Do novice teachers and their instructors give up too easily? *Journal for Research in Mathematics Education, 23*(3), 194–222.

Borko, H., & Livingston, C. (1989). Cognition and improvisation: Differences in mathematics instruction by expert and novice teachers. *American Educational Research Journal, 26*(4), 473–398.

Bruner, J. (1991). Narrative and paradigmatic ways of knowing. In E. Eisner (Ed.), *Teaching and learning ways of knowing.*

Chrisco, I. (1989). Peer assistance works. *Educational Leadership, 44*(3), 31–35.

Christensen, C. R., Garvin, D., & Sweet, A. (1990). *Education for judgement.* Boston: Harvard University Graduate School of Business.

Cognition and Technology Group at Vanderbilt. (1991). Anchored instruction and its relationship to situated cognition. *Educational Researcher, 19*(6), 2–10.

Cognition and Technology Group at Vanderbilt. (1993). The Jasper experiment: Using video to furnish real-world problem-solving contexts. *Arithmetic Teacher, 40*(8), 474–478.

Connelly, F. M., & Clandinin, J. (1990). Stories of experience and narrative inquiry. *Educational Researcher, 37,* 2–14.

Daniel, B., & Stallion, B. (1995, August). *The implementation of Kentucky's school-based professional development.* Frankfort, KY: Kentucky Institute for Education Research.

Desberg, P. L., Colbert, J., & Trimble, K. (1995). Classroom Management: CD-ROM Cases. Computer Software and Compact disc. Boston: Allyn Bacon.

Dewey, J. (1934). *Art as experience.* New York: Perigee Books.

Duffy, T., & Jonassen, D. (1993). *Constructivism and Instructional Design.* Hillside: NJ: Erlbaum.

Eisner, E. W. (1993). Forms of understanding and the future of educational research. *Educational Researcher, 22*(7), 5–11.

Eisner, E. W. (1986). *The educational imagination: On the design and evaluation of school programs.* New York: MacMillan.

Fishman, B. J., & Duffy, T. M. (1993). Technology and Reform—What do teachers really need? *Educational Technology Research & Development, 26*(1), 34–46.

Forman, D., & Kaplan, S. (1994). Continuous learning environments: Online Performance Support Systems. *Instructional Delivery Systems, 8*(2), 6–12.

Galegher, J., & Kraut, C. (1990). *Intellectual teamwork: Social and technological foundations of cooperative work.* Hillsdale, NJ: Erlbaum.

Harasim, L. M. (Ed.). (1991). *Online education: Perspectives on a new environment.* New York: Praeger.

Kagan, D. (1993). Contexts for the use of classroom cases. *American Educational Research Journal, 30*(4) 703–723.

Kentucky Department of Education. (1992). *The Master Plan for Education Technology.* Frankfort, KY: Author Kentucky Office of Educational Accountability. Annual Report, 1993. Frankfort, KY.

Kleinfeld, J. (1989). *Teaching cases in cross-cultural education.* Fairbanks: University of Alaska.

Koschmann, T. D., Meyers, A. C., Feltovich, P. J., & Barrows, H. S. (1992). Using technology to assist in realizing effective learning and instruction. *Journal of the Learning Sciences, 3*(2), 35–68.

Little, J. W. (1982). Norms of collegiality and experimentation? Workplace conditions of school success. *American Education Research Journal, 19*(3), 325–340.

Mathews, B. (1995, August). *The Implementation of Performance Assessment in Kentucky Classrooms.* Frankfort, KY: The Kentucky Institute for Education Reform.

Mazur, J. *Researching KERA technological reform: Baseline data for implementation, planning, and assessment.* Paper presented at the Conference for International Standards and Assessment. University of North Carolina, Chapel Hill, October 1995.

Mazur, J. (1995b, October). *The implementation of the Kentucky Education Technology System (KETS).* Frankfort, KY: Kentucky Institute for Education Reform.

Means, B. (1994). *Technology and education reform.* San Francisco, CA: Jossey Bass.

McLaughlin, M., & Talbert, J. (1993). *Contexts that matter for teaching and learning: Strategic opportunities for meeting the nation's educational goal?* (CRC Publication R93-6). Stanford University, Center for Research on the Context of Secondary School Teaching.

Mullins, M. (1989). Embedded training: A bibliography. *Technical Communication, 36*(1), 19–25.

Phillips, D. C. (1994). Telling it straight: Issues in assessing narrative research. *Educational Psychologist, 29*(1), 13–21.

Raney, P., & Robbins, P. (1989). Professional growth and support through peer coaching. *Educational Leadership, 44*(3), 35–38.

Risko, V. J. (1992b). Developing problem solving environments to prepare teachers for diverse learners. In B. Hayes & K. Camperell (Eds.), *Yearbook of the American Reading Forum* (Vol. 12, pp. 1–13). Logan: Utah State University.

Risko, V., Yount, D., & Towell, J. (1991, April). *The effect of video-based case methodology on preservice teachers' problem solving and critical thinking.* Paper presented at the annual meeting of the American Educational Research Association, Chicago, IL.

Robertson Associates. (1995). *A survey of teachers, parents and administrators on the Kentucky Education Reform Act (KERa).* Frankfort, KY: Kentucky Institute on Education Reform.

Savage, C. (1994). *Fifth generation management.* Boston, MA: Digital Press.

Schoenmaker, J. (1993). Linking new applications to new design paradigms. *Computers in Education, 21*(1/2), 181–192.

Sykes, G., & Bird, R. (1992). Teacher education and the case idea. In G. Grant (Ed.), *Review of research in education, 18*(1), 457–521.

Wasserman, S. (1993). *Getting down to cases: Learning to teach with cases.* New York: Teachers College Press.

Wilson, B. (1996). *Constructivist learning environments.* Hillside, NJ: Erlbaum.

Appendix A

The Common Thread Case Criteria

Each Common Thread Case contains four elements:

1. A well-formulated narrative structure (Connelly & Clandinin, 1990).
2. A true, factually correct, compelling account. The authenticity of the case is essential and strategic, as suggested by Phillips (1994), who notes that one is more likely to accept what is true and more likely to be successful when what one acts upon is correct.
3. Tangible episodes of good teaching. Teaching episodes must include the particulars that become tangible to the reader. The importance of rich contextual details has been thoughtfully described elsewhere (Eisner, 1990).
4. Consequential Aspects of Standards-Based Practice. Each case includes events that are relevant to teacher performance standards. These standards are not models, but frames of reference. The holistic nature of teaching implies that various standards will often apply and even overlap in the same case.

Appendix B

Tools and Resources Available in the Common Thread Case CD-ROM Program

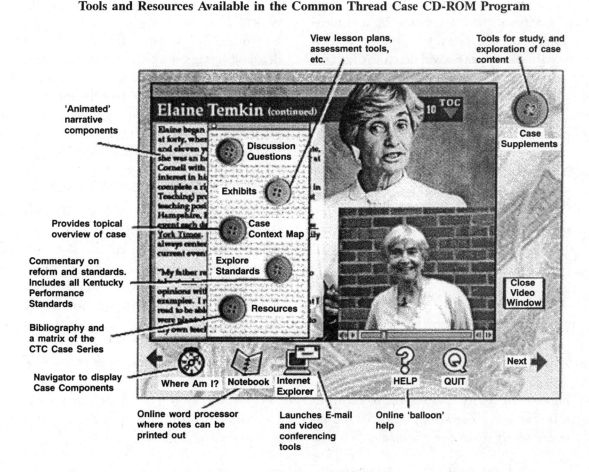

Interactive Video Cases Developed
for Elementary Science Methods Courses

by Sandra K. Abell, Katherine S. Cennamo, and Lois M. Campbell

Researchers in the U.S. and Europe are beginning to explore uses of integrated media in teacher education. Much of this work is occurs within the mathematics education community (Ball, Lampert, & Rosenberg, 1991; Dolk, van Galen, & Feijs, 1992; Frederick & Hatfield, 1991; Goldman & Barron, 1990), although researchers at Vanderbilt (Hoftwolt & Johnston, 1992) have begun using integrated media in science methods courses. However, a paucity of case materials, both written and video, presently exists (Merseth, 1991), especially in the context of elementary science education.

The purpose of our project was to develop interactive videodisc case materials about teaching elementary school science. The materials are being used in preservice elementary science methods courses to develop reflective thinking about teaching science. In this paper we will describe the various phases of materials development and discuss other project components. We believe that the development process we have invented will be instructive to others embarking on similar projects.

Stages of Development

1. Collaborating with classroom teachers.

In order to take the preservice teacher into a virtual classroom on videodisc, it was necessary to enlist the collaboration of elementary teachers in

Sandra Abell and Katherine Cennamo are professors in the Department of Curriculum and Instruction at Purdue University in West Lafayette, Indiana.
Lois Campbell is with the Department of Curriculum and Instruction at The Pennsylvania State University in University Park, Pennsylvania.

developing the classroom cases. We decided to focus on two teachers, one first grade and one fifth grade, one rural and one suburban. The teachers had worked with the senior author in a teacher enhancement project involving conceptual change science teaching (Osborne & Freyberg, 1985). They had demonstrated a clear understanding of this type of science teaching, were enthusiastic about using it in their classrooms, and willing to have their classrooms intruded upon by professors and film crew from the nearby university.

The senior author and each teacher met over a two month period to develop the curriculum that would be the focus of the science instruction. Together we selected topics in life science for the first grade and physical science for the fifth grade. As we had done in the teacher enhancement project, we worked together to define the conceptual understandings upon which the instruction would be based, and to develop a series of conceptual change activities. The first grade lessons revolved around the concepts of seeds and eggs. We built the fifth grade lessons upon the concepts of work, force, and load within the topic of simple machines.

2. Videotaping classroom lessons.

We hired a technical crew from the university's video production center to help us with the videotaping. We used two cameras (³/₄-inch CCD). Camera A, which moved, took the primary shots from the teacher viewpoint. Camera B, which was stationary, took supplementary shots from the student viewpoint. Portable lighting supplemented the available classroom light. To achieve quality audio for both teacher and student talk, we used two types of microphones: a wireless remote mike attached to the teacher's lapel, and a shotgun mike attached to a movable boom that followed student conversations in large and small groups.

From *TechTrends*, April/May 1996, pp. 20-23. Reprinted with permission from the Association for Educational Communications and Technology, Washington, DC.

Although we tried to be as non-invasive as possible, the presence of three crew members, the project director, and all the equipment was obvious to the students and teachers. To acclimatize them, we built one week of filming into the production schedule before the conceptual change science lessons began. This proved to be sufficient time for students and teacher to get used to their new classroom, to move beyond the "Hi, Mom" syndrome, and to feel somewhat natural interacting in the presence of the camera.

Each day we set up the equipment while students were out of the room or in quiet study. This took about one half hour. We filmed the entire lesson as naturally occurring events (without stopping the action or replaying shots). After each lesson, while the children left the classroom for lunch or recess, we conducted an interview with the teacher. In the interview, which lasted about 15 minutes, the project director asked the teacher to reflect upon the lesson, discussing its strengths and weaknesses, focusing on student understanding, and noting how the next lesson would proceed. We shot approximately 30 hours of tape in each of the classrooms over a three-week period. All tapes were then logged by time code and content in preparation for editing (see Figure 1).

Figure 1. Original videotape log.

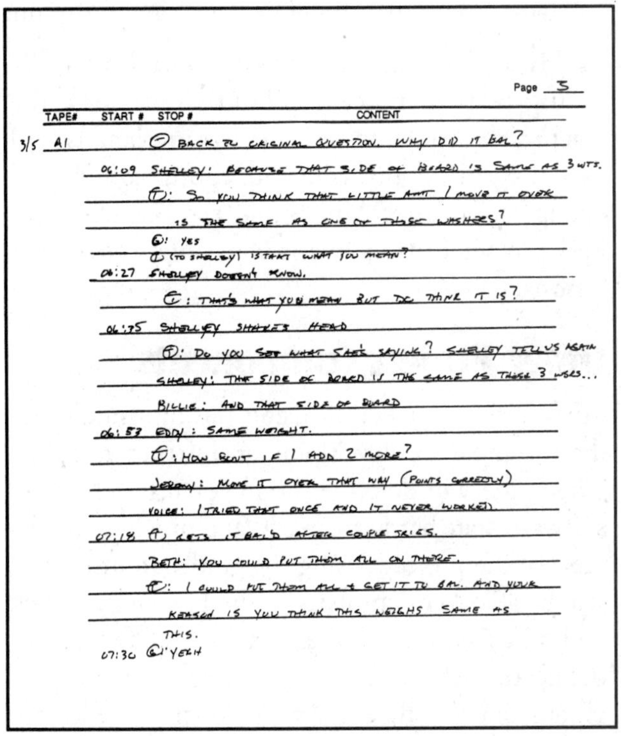
Page 3

TAPE# START # STOP # CONTENT

3/5 A1 (T) BACK TO ORIGINAL QUESTION. WHY DID IT BAL?
06:09 SHELLEY: BECAUSE THAT SIDE OF BOARD IS SAME AS 3 WTS.
(T): SO YOU THINK THAT LITTLE AMT I MOVE IT OVER IS THE SAME AS ONE OF THOSE WASHERS?
(S): YES
(T) (TO SHELLEY) IS THAT WHAT YOU MEAN?
06:27 SHELLEY DOESN'T KNOW.
(T): THAT'S WHAT YOU MEAN BUT DO THINK IT IS?
06:35 SHELLEY SHAKES HEAD
(T): DO YOU SEE WHAT SHE'S SAYING? SHELLEY TELL US AGAIN
SHELLEY: THE SIDE OF BOARD IS THE SAME AS THOSE 3 WSRS...
BILLIE: AND THAT SIDE OF BOARD
06:53 EDDY: SAME WEIGHT.
(T): HOW BOUT IF I ADD 2 MORE?
JEREMY: MOVE IT OVER THAT WAY (POINTS CORRECTLY)
VOICE: I TRIED THAT ONCE AND IT NEVER WORKED.
07:18 (T) GETS IT BAL'D AFTER COUPLE TRIES.
BETH: YOU COULD PUT THEM ALL ON THERE.
(T): I COULD PUT THEM ALL & GET IT TO BAL. AND YOUR REASON IS YOU THINK THIS WEIGHS SAME AS THIS.
07:30 (S): YEAH

3. Editing the videotape.

The task of editing was immense. We had to cut approximately 60 hours of classroom footage down to four 30-minute disc sides, two from each classroom. We made two rough edits and a final cut before tape was transferred to laser disc.

In order to make editing decisions, the development team had to agree upon what could constitute a classroom case. According to Carter (1992), "it is difficult to locate a literature that provides guidelines... to teacher educators who hope to generate and teach with case" (p. 113). Furthermore, since our cases were different from most in that they were videotaped, not written, the guidelines that do exist (Carter, 1992; Shulman, 1992) were insufficient. Examining Vanderbilt University mathematics teacher education videodiscs (see Goldman & Barron, 1990) provided some clues. However, the nature of teaching science compared to math presented some unique needs. We knew that our lessons extended over several days and that it would be necessary to capture the instruction over this extended time period for novices to understand about teaching science for conceptual change.

Thus our first editing challenge was to maintain a narrative structure that would include the chronology of the lessons within one class period and over several days of instruction, while providing information about the teacher, the students, and their interactions. Second, we wanted to represent two kinds of teacher tasks: "establishing and maintaining social order, and representing and enacting the curriculum" (Carter, 1992, p. 116). Also we attempted to reveal the problematic nature of science classrooms so that the preservice teacher, while interacting with the cases, would become engaged in reflection and problem solving. Finally, we had to decide how to use the teacher interview segments as a way of accessing teacher knowledge and beliefs about science teaching and learning.

The first edit. After reading the video log and highlighting sections that fit these guidelines, the project team met. We watched all sections of tape from Camera A that had been highlighted in any of our logs and made decisions about what to include and what to cut. From this decision list, we made a rough edit tape of about two hours per class site, accompanied by a new log. We distributed the tape to all team members and to the classroom teachers for comment.

The second edit. Individually, team members and teachers indicated which sections could be cut and which were critical to keep. The goal was to cut tape length in half. At this point we decided that the teacher interview tape would be used as a voice- over dub. In that way we could use more of the classroom footage yet retain the teacher reflection in some form. The project director collected and synthesized all suggestions into a second edit list. From this list a second tape was cut and sent to team members.

The final edit. On the basis of this second edit, we created new logs that included suggestions for correspondence with teacher interview segments and with Camera B (see Figure 2). During the final edit we added bridging shots from the stationary camera and stills of overhead transparencies and student products, making sure to stay within the 30- minute per disc side limit. This final edit was first sent to a company to boost the tape to one-inch and then to another company to master the laser discs.

4. Developing the hypermedia.

Simultaneously with the videotape editing, we created a HyperCard stack that allows flexible entry into the case and provides supporting text and visual materials. We began by creating a screen metaphor that would be inviting for preservice elementary teachers. On the screen we designed a classroom with a blackboard that presents menu items for user selection (see Figure 3). Subsequent screens provide access to the videodisc and to accompanying text materials in a consistent format.

The hypermedia allows access to the videodisc via stages of the lesson, various teaching strategies, and individual student interactions. Furthermore,

levers

classroom segments			teacher interview segments			camera 2 segments	
code	time	description	code	time	description	code	description
2.50-3.15	25	Josh, Ray, Jeremy--weight explanations					
3.32-3.37	5						
4.47-5.03	16						
5.40-7.01	81	more weight explanations--Shelly					
7.15-7.48	33	T pushing their explanation					
8..05-8.22	17	T balancing broom on fingers					
11.16-12.05	49	broom demo and discussion					
12.18-13.08	50						
13.19-13.22	3						
13.42-14.50	68						
15.00-15.21	21						
15.43-16.42	59						
23.12-23.23+	11	NOTE: add T, "so we have a tradeoff. greater distance, less load."					
25.50-26.33	43	T intro to seesaw activity; "fulcrum"					
34.33-35.21	48	Ray and Ahsley--group predictions					
35.45-38.10	145						
44.26-44.44	18	Ray and Ashley--lift instead of balance					
45.57-47.26	89						
49.32-50.47	75	Summary--term intro: lever					

Figure 2. Second edit log.

Figure 3. HyperCard home screen.

the HyperCard stack supports the videodisc by providing textual materials about the school, the teacher, the students, and the lesson plan, as well as background information about conceptual change science teaching, children's science ideas, and the scientific explanations involved in the lessons.

Other Project Components

To facilitate instruction using the integrated media cases, we are developing an instructors guide. The guide will describe the major features of the software, state hardware needs, and provide an overview of the project. Using the guide, an instructor will be able to orient users to the HyperCard stack and how to navigate within it. The guide will also delineate each of the three classroom cases, providing an event by event breakdown of the lesson.

Bar codes will provide direct access to specific video segments. Since we have designed the materials to be flexible in a number of different classroom formats — large group, small group, and individual — the guide must be instructive about these various uses. Thus, the guide will highlight instructional use options by providing vignettes of classroom discussions, small group interactions, and written assignments done in conjunction with the materials. Our purpose is to develop a guide that will not only orient an instructor to the hardware and software, but also provide windows into how the integrated media materials have been used in our courses.

Currently we are using the integrated media materials in the elementary science methods courses at our respective universities. Both courses devote a major portion of the syllabus to examining student ideas in science and developing curriculum based on a conceptual change model of science teaching. The integrated media materials enhance our instruction by allowing preservice teachers to see and react to conceptual change teaching in actual classrooms, not merely read about it or experience it as we role play a fifth grade science class. As we teach, we are developing case-based pedagogies for use with integrated media materials.

A final component of the project involves assessing the effectiveness of the case materials in promoting reflection among preservice elementary education students. We have invented a series of reflection tasks for use in the methods course in conjunction with the integrated media. We hope to develop a deep understanding of elementary science teachers' reflective thinking as mediated by the interactive video materials. Our ultimate goal is to use the interactive video cases to facilitate the professional development of a cadre of teachers who are able to reflect upon and thereby enhance their science teaching and, consequently, the science learning of their students. ∎

References

Ball, D. L., Lampert, M., & Rosenberg, M. L. (1991, April). Using hypermedia to investigate and construct knowledge about mathematics teaching and learning. Paper presented at the Annual Meeting of the American Educational Research Association, Chicago.

Carter, K. (1992). Creating cases for the development of teacher knowledge. In T. Russell and H. Munby (Eds.), Teachers and teaching: From classroom to reflection (pp. 109-123). New York: The Falmer Press.

Dolk, M., van Galen, F., & Feijs, E. (1992, April). Using interactive videodisc in teacher education. Paper presented at the Annual Meeting of the American Educational Research Association, San Francisco.

Frederick, H. R., & Hatfield, M. M. (1991, April). Interactive videodiscs, vignettes, and manipulatives: A mix that enhances the mathematics methods class. Paper presented at the Annual Meeting of the American Educational Research Association, Chicago.

Goldman, E., & Barron, L. (1990). Using hypermedia to improve the preparation of elementary teachers. *Journal of Teacher Education, 41*(3), 21-31.

Hoftwolt, C. A., & Johnston, J. (1992, November). Approaches to teaching science: An integrated media approach. Paper presented at the Annual Meeting of the Mid-South Educational Research Association, Knoxville, TN.

Merseth, K. K. (1991). The cases for cases in teacher education. Washington, DC: American Association of Colleges for Teacher Education.

Osborne, R., & Freyberg, P. (Eds.). (1992). Learning in science: The implications of children's science. Portsmouth, NH: Heinemann.

Shulman, J. (Ed.). (1992). Case methods in teacher education. New York: Teachers College Press.

Stage a Well-Designed Saturday Session and They Will Come!

By Miguel Guhlin

Teachers may grumble about Saturday morning or after-school sessions, but they are so hungry for technology training they will come.

"What? Come on a Saturday? Are you out of your mind?" said one elementary teacher when I suggested that instructional technology-training sessions be held on Saturday mornings.

Several years ago that response would have discouraged me. But experience has taught me that although most teachers will claim that they will not attend technology training, the fact is, they will come on Saturdays and to after-school training sessions as well.

According to the United States Office of Technology Assessment, the role of the classroom teacher is critical to the full development and use of technology in schools. If teachers are not the focus of the technology training, then technology will fail. Happily, more teachers are recognizing the necessity of integrating technology into the curriculum.

Effective technology training begins with careful design of a staff development program. The following points must be considered in design and implementation.

1. Technology's potential is underutilized. Over the years, various technologies have found their way into education. Most failed because administrators purchased them without involving teachers in the decision-making process or providing training in their use.

Although media specialists may write the proposal and technology plan, classroom teachers must be involved from the beginning because they will be the ones responsible for the actual integration. It is important to reassure them that extensive staff development will be provided.

2. Most teachers want to learn technology but lack time, access, and on-site support. In addressing this, it is wise to develop a campus technology plan that allows time for teachers to explore and learn to use a computer. Emphasize that while they may not become expert users, they will be able to use the computer and additional technology instructionally. Consider this staff development pattern:

a) Introduce ways to use technology for specific instructional tasks. Provide lots of hands-on time.

b) Provide individual follow-up modelling in the classroom.

c) Allow time for whole-class follow-up and sharing.

Training necessarily must take place before or after school, during the school day, and during the summer or on weekends. However, if a computer or the technology is not available in the classroom, teachers are seriously hobbled.

Research suggests that a classroom with one to four computers is a comfortable setting for teachers to begin using technology. Both students and teachers are more likely to use it when they need to, not when the computer lab is ready for them. Therefore, effective technology plans must allow teachers to earn hours towards obtaining computers for the classroom, and for weekend and summer use. This is a powerful incentive. Other incentives include providing copies of the software and manual that teachers are trained on, instituting educator computer purchase programs and providing summer and weekend loan programs.

On-site support is critical. Unfortunately, many technology coordinators are overburdened with classrooms and instructional technology duties. Site administrators must decide how to balance their load. Often, providing an extra planning period specifically for technology training works well. Coordinators can log their activities during that time and share them with the site administrator.

3. Lesson plans, related materials and curriculum guides must have clear and relevant objectives.

While hands-on training addresses a fundamental need to integrate technology, it has to be woven into the curriculum. In the beginning, teachers often take existing lesson plans and add technology. This approach works with some success, and it is a necessary developmental step for teachers. However, integrating technology will not be effective until it is used to do things that previously could not be accomplished without it.

Integrating technology involves redesigning lesson plans, a problem for the few teachers who use lesson plans from year to year without adjusting them to particular class needs. For the most part, however, teachers do change how they teach because they are genuinely concerned about their students' learning. The questions these teachers ask are: "How do we work technology into our already packed curriculum?" and "What do we do with the students once we start?"

The answer to the first question is not an easy one. Curriculum change is driven by what students need to know. In the past, math curriculums were driven by arithmetic and computation. Now, they are beginning to incorporate arithmetic and computation within the grander scope of creative problem-solving, decision-making strategies and cooperative learning. Technology is best suited to curriculum that involves discovery learning, developing higher-order thinking skills, and the comprehension and communication of ideas and information. If curriculum focuses only on lower-order thinking skills (basic skills) as a prerequisite to higher-order thinking skills (metacognition, problem solving and decision making), the computer will remain a drill-and-practice tutor.

The answer to the second question is much easier. After higher-order thinking skills are addressed, technology can become a tool for comprehending and communicating, serving both students and teachers. Nevertheless, writing lesson plans can be a difficult process. Developing databases that address these needs and assist in the development of lesson plans that incorporate technology is useful, but the job of integrating will fall on the classroom teacher and the curriculum writers.

As stated early in this article, the keys to integrating technology are the classroom teachers. Supporting them must be the first step in any technology training program. To quote the voice in the movie *Field of Dreams*, "Build it and they will come." Build a technology teacher training program addressing teachers' issues and they will come—after school, on weekends, during the summer, and in their free time. **Tc**

REFERENCES

Finkel, L. (1990). Moving your district toward technology. The School Administrator Special Issue: Computer Technology Report, pp.35-38.

Office of Technology Assessment Report. Power On! New tools for teaching and learning. U.S. Government Printing Office, Washington, D.C. Stock #052-003-01125-5.

Snyder, T. (January, 1995). Technology is cool, teachers are cooler. Teaching with Technology NewsFlash; #33.

Solomon, G. (October, 1990). Share the Spirit: 15 Ways to generate excitement and support for classroom technology. Instructor.

Miguel Guhlin is District Instructional Technology Specialist for the Mt. Pleasant (Texas) Independent School District.

Multimedia

Multimedia is important to education because of its potential to improve the quality of classroom and at-a-distance learning. It can pull together text and pictures, as well as audio and moving video in any combination, to provide a richer environment that will engage all of the senses. It provides a new means of communicating, an easier way to illustrate difficult concepts, and a way to entice the learner into becoming actively involved in controlling and manipulating information, anytime and anywhere.

Because of the nature of multimedia systems, it is easy to provide a variety of choices to the learner. This capability enables designers and developers to build systems that fit the requirements of interactive problem-solving instructional systems. Such systems are called multimedia inference engines. The engines provide learners with three types of buttons that include the following functions: navigation, access, and manipulation. The inference engines are used in conjunction with a knowledge base that is related to a subject matter area. The learner can access information in a variety of media forms in order to build inference models to solve problems based on inferences assembled from the knowledge base. The computer can then assess the learner's data and decide whether the learner has collected an adequate sample and if the conclusion reached is justified. Such systems will allow learners to develop their problem-solving skills. Without multimedia, instructional problem-solving systems would not be feasible, nor would we be able to enrich the problem-solving facilities within schools at a fraction of the cost of physical laboratories. Such applications of multimedia provide a cost-benefit ratio that is quite favorable, and return-on-investment analysis is one of the side benefits provided by this powerful technology.

The articles in this unit review some of the issues emerging from the widespread interest in designing, developing, implementing, and publishing multimedia titles. In the lead article, "Interactive Multimedia: Cost Benefit Analysis Issues," John Hirschbuhl addresses the opportunities provided by student-generated data for assessing return on investment. Hirschbuhl outlines the process for assessing the data and cites several case studies that illustrate the process. In addition, a multimedia inference engine is described along with its impact on student problem-solving ability.

The next essay describes the conversion of videotaped instructional programs to interactive CD-ROM-based desktop learning systems. The authors describe the use of various compression and decompression technology that provides full screen video capability.

"The 21st Century Classroom-Scholarship Environment: What Will It Be Like?" describes the development of a teaching-learning module in biology which makes creative use of the Internet and other communications and computing media. This is followed by Ali Jafari's report on the technical requirements for delivering multimedia capability to every desktop computer on the IUPUI campus. This system delivers interactivity, random access, random search, multimedia authoring, cross-platform Web environment, media digitizing, and more.

In "Multimedia and Cultural Diversity," Pacino and Pacino describe the development and implementation of a CD-ROM project. The project helps students react openly to dramatized issues and then express personal views.

Finally, R. Dwight Wilhelm clinically describes the process of optimizing each element in audio-visual material. The author takes the reader through the storyboard/scriptwriting process.

Looking Ahead: Challenge Questions

What is ROI? How would you perform a return-on-investment analysis? How would you determine what is a cost and what is a benefit?

Can we create virtual classrooms with interactive networked multimedia? What are the problems involved in implementing such technology? Can such classrooms provide instruction that is as good as the best of today's classroom instruction?

Interactive Multimedia: Cost Benefit Analysis Issues

BY JOHN J. HIRSCHBUHL

Today we are in a transition from a performance society to an information based learning society. There is a continual need to learn new skills before we have totally polished previously learned skills. We are caught up with the information age and the technologies that have generated it. (Hirschbuhl, 1992)

Multimedia Metaphors

We are now using multimedia as a tool to develop thinking skills needed to assimilate massive quantities of information needed to transform information into solutions in today's fast paced changing society. In order to optimize today's technology, multimedia can be used as an engine to enable learners to transform information into knowledge and problem solving skills by means of inquiry that is based on higher-level thinking.

In order to achieve this goal we can use a computer driven interactive communication system which creates, stores, retrieves and transmits audio, video, graphic, and textual clusters of information. These powerful systems can have a powerful impact on the learner's problem solving abilities which can generate a positive impact on an organization's bottom line.

A Multimedia Example

Perhaps you know this quotation from Robert F. Kennedy, Jr.: *If you live on a resource, if you hike on it, if you fish in it, if you walk by it occasionally, and it does something for you spiritually or aesthetically, then you have standing to sue a polluter who is going to defile it.*

This article is print, and I can't create multimedia in print, but look at the photo [on the next page]. Note the increase in impact of the message when I add an image. Now imagine what it would be like if I could add audio to this page so you could hear Robert F. Kennedy, Jr. saying it, or if I could add video so you could see him saying it as well. This is the essence of multimedia: providing a rich environment that engages all of the senses.

With the facilities of multimedia it is easier to provide a variety of choices to the entry level professional. This capability enables designers and developers to build systems that fit the needs of our former computer game players through interactive multimedia problem solving training systems. Such systems are called multimedia inference engines, which provide the user with a rich problem solving system. Multimedia engines entice the young professionals to become actively involved by:

- Navigation
- Accessing
- Manipulating

In the exercise pictured on the next page the users choose data collection sites, collect samples using simulated sampling instruments, conduct record searches for data recorded by previous studies, and keep a modeling book of their findings. These hands-on field experiments are made possible through the use of text, audio, photographs, video, animation, and maps. The program evaluates the user's methods of investigation and conclusions, and provides a mastery test. The user also writes an on-line final report of the findings, which can be evaluated by the instructor. The management system keeps records for each user, including sampling activity and performance on post test scores and final essay reports. The management system is the key to determining the effectiveness of the hands-on field experiments. The program's topics include:

- Introduction to Environmental Studies
- Legal Control of the Environment
- Geology of Homesite Selection
- Minerals for Society
- Radiation in the Environment
- Energy from Coal
- Streams and Floods
- Stream Pollution

The program is driven by multimedia inference engines. The engines are used in conjunction with a knowledge base that is related to a content area. Users can access a variety of media forms in order to build inference models for problem solving based on references assembled from the knowledge base. Then each user's inference sampling can be assessed to determine if the user has collected an adequate sample and if the conclusion reached is justified. In addition, inferential problem solving applications provide a favorable cost-benefit ratio.

This is the ideal higher level learning activity. Fortunately, it provides a perfect match with the type of computer learning experience today's entry level professionals are familiar with due to their experience with computer gaming and messaging activities on the Internet.

Return on Investment

What follows is a case study which illustrates surprising results that can be produced in a corporate environment when using well-managed networked multimedia. It includes a description of the requirements for designing, developing, and delivering networked multimedia CBT. The methods for assessing and reporting the return on investment are highlighted.

If training is the solution to a business problem, then the results of the training can be used to determine the return on investment provided by the training activity. The return on investment can be determined by:

- relating dollars spent to dollars returned.
- building the assessment on cost and return data.
- providing projections of how change will impact outcomes.
- determining if returned dollars are greater than invested dollars.

Training that pays back more dollars than are spent in funding the training is said to have a positive return on investment (ROI). An effective ROI is built on accurate information determined by

Cost of:
- Design
- Development
- Implementation
- Maintenance

Training returns of:
- Time to mastery
- Retention
- Morale
- Productivity
- Profits

Our case study begins with a Business Problem.

Business Problem:

200 Total Units Produced Daily. 32 Defective Units Produced Daily.

Table 1.

Personnel	Cost	Time to Correct Each Unit
Supervisor	$20/hour	10 min.
Auditor	$20/hour	15 min.
Employee	$16/hour	10 min.

Impact:

Table 2.

Personnel	Daily Loss	Weekly Loss	Yearly Loss
Supervisor	107	535	27,820
Auditor	160	800	41,600
Employee	85	425	22,100
Total	352	1,760	91,520

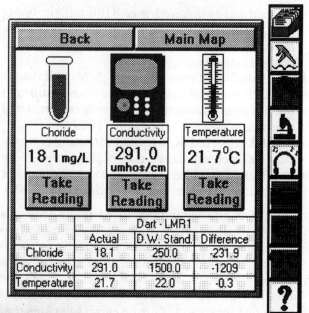

If no training is implemented, the company continues to lose $91,520 per year. Over five years, this would be $457,600.

Question. How much can be spent on training to correct the problem if the training is 95% effective? 80% effective? 70% effective?

- 95% = $86,944/yr. $354,720/5yr.
- 80% = $73,216/yr. $286,080/5yr.
- 70% = $64,064/yr. $240,320/5yr.

Notice that we could reduce the defects by as little as 70% and still produce a $160,320 positive ROI over 5 years on an investment of $80,000. In the case of a 95% reduction the ROI is $354,720 over 5 years, a 15.2% increase in each employee's productivity.

Solution. A 95% decrease in the number of defective units would result in an $86,944 savings in one year. The ROI on a training investment of $80,000 would be $354,720 over 5 years.

ROI. It seems reasonable to spend $80,000 on training to correct the problem because it could result in a net savings of $354,720 over 5 year, a substantial ROI.

Decision:

- Time to mastery — Reduced by 33%
- Retention — Increased by 100%
- Morale — Increased by 30%
- Productivity — Increased by 15.2%
- Profits — Increased by $354,720 over 5 years

Companies that have shown positive ROI using managed networked multimedia training:

- Federal Express saved over $100 million using multimedia CBT by cutting in travel expenses, reducing errors, and decreasing training time. (Wright, 1992)
- Institute for Defense Analysis, IBM, and American Airlines indicate computer based multimedia produced a savings of 68% over conventional classroom training. (Training, 1992)
- NYNEX reported 50% gains in training completion by tracking course usage. (Training, 1994)
- Steelcase saved 28% of training costs or over $1 million over five years. (Authorware, 1992)

Several of the companies cited make use of a networked management system. The use of managed networked multimedia CBT has several advantages. A major reason for implementing this managed approach is to show whether or not the company will realize financial benefit as a result of its training investment. Our research indicates that substantial gains often result from training, but they are seldom recorded or published. Part of this problem is due to the lack of an effective management system. Without such a system, data collection is cumbersome, time consuming, and incomplete. Hence, a management system should be a primary consideration when selecting or building networked multimedia CBT. Another consideration is how well this technology fits today's entry level computer generation. With their computer game, user experience, and development background, this technology is the paper and pencil of their time. Finally, it is our challenge as trainers to convince management that these managed, networked, multimedia systems are more effective, efficient, and productive than alternative conventional training.

References

Wright, E.E. (1994, September). "Making the multimedia decision: strategies for success." *Multimedia*, pp. 5-9.

IBM Corporation.(1992) *Instructional Technology Reports and Studies* (by the University of Oklahoma, University of Missouri-Rolla, Indiana University) Thornwood, NY.

Filipczak, B. (1994, December) "Tracking Training On The Network." *Training*, p 14.

Authorware, Inc. (1992). *Interactive Multimedia Analysis: Return on Investment*. Redwood City, CA.

Hirschbuhl, J. (1992). "Multimedia: Why Invest?" *Interactive Learning International*, Vol. 8, pp. 321-323.

About the Author

John J. Hirschbuhl Ph.D. holds degrees in Mathematics, Computer Science, and Education. He is currently Special Advisor for Academic Computing, Multimedia and Distance Learning and Professor of Education at the University of Akron, Akron, Ohio. In addition Dr. Hirschbuhl is currently Senior Vice President of Development and Operations for Computer Knowledge International. His work focuses on instructional technology: design, development and support as well as cost effective strategies for technology solutions for business and education problems. Dr. Hirschbuhl has served as an IBM Consulting Scholar and consulted with several Fortune 500 companies in matters concerning interactive training. During his career, he has given hundreds of presentations all over the world and published over 100 articles. His book, Computers in Education, is in its eighth edition. John can be reached at The University of Akron, Computer Center, Akron, OH 44325-3501, Phone (330) 972-6507, Fax: (330) 972-5238, email: hirschbuhl@uakron.edu

CONVERTING A TRADITIONAL MULTIMEDIA KIT INTO AN INTERACTIVE VIDEO CD-ROM

ABSTRACT

For twenty-five years, Educational Television (ETV) programs have been available to schools in Hong Kong through broadcasting and video tapes. Supporting materials including booklets of *Teachers' Notes* and *Pupils' Notes* are also produced and used together with the programs. The emergence of *desktop video* means that an ETV program together with the supporting teaching and learning materials can be converted into digital data, integrated into a courseware, and stored in a CD-ROM for easy retrieval. In addition, the advantages of interactivity, where a structure of linked elements through which the user can navigate, can also be of use. This article reports the development of a courseware with full motion and full screen video stored in a CD-ROM by making use of the latest compression and decompression (CODEC) technology.

**ANNIE Y. W. NICHOLSON AND
JOHNSON Y. K. NGAI**

Curriculum Development Institute, Hong Kong

INTRODUCTION

Educational video programs are useful resource materials to complement and enrich teaching. To provide such support for schools in Hong Kong, Educational Television (ETV) programs have jointly been produced by the Hong Kong Education Department (ED) and Radio Television Hong Kong (RTHK) since 1969. They have mainly been used in the local senior primary and junior secondary classrooms. Programs on six subject areas (including English language, Chinese language, mathematics, science, social studies and health education) for seven levels (from primary 3 to secondary 3) are available. Apart from these syllabus-based programs, special programs are also produced to meet specific educational needs. Cantonese is the medium of instruction used in all programs, except English language programs. Supporting materials including *Teachers' Notes* and *Pupils' Notes* are also prepared to provide information on the programs and suggestions for lesson preparation, follow-up activities, and consolidation exercises [1]. ETV programs are broadcast to schools via two local commercial television channels. Programs can be watched either through television broadcasting or video tapes.

Viewing ETV programs through direct broadcasting or through video tapes is linear and passive, as video images are stored sequentially and random access is not supported. However, by using the *desktop video* technology, ETV programs, together with the supporting materials, can be stored as digital video data and can be displayed in a computer system. This can provide users with greater flexibility and convenience as it supports random access, multimedia (integration of text, graphic, audio, and video data), and interactivity.

"Converting a Traditional Multimedia Kit into an Interactive Video CD-ROM," Annie Y. W. Nicholason and Johnson Y. K. Ngai, *Journal of Educational Technology Systems*, Volume 24, No. 3, pp. 235-248, Baywood Publishing Company, Inc., 1995-96.

123

This article reports the development of an interactive multimedia project in using an existing ETV English language program with the *Teachers' Notes* and *Pupils' Notes* to develop an interactive courseware to be stored on a CD-ROM. The ETV program was first converted into digital data by making use of the latest MPEG (Moving Picture Experts Group) compression technology. This project[1] also aimed to find out the benefits and problems associated with using multimedia technology in the local educational setting based on these first hand experiences.

DESKTOP VIDEO

Computers have different applications in education. They can be used to assist daily school administration, to provide an environment to train students' problem-solving abilities or to deliver instruction. When using computers to deliver programs to students, the support of full color, full motion, and full screen video playback on computer is desirable as video images are realistic and lifelike.

The display of video images on computers can be achieved in various ways. A common method to use video with the computer is using interactive video systems in which analogue signal of the video segment played back by the video cassette or laser disc player is connected to the computer system. Analogue video segment, handled by the video cassette or laser disc player, is fed through the display card to be viewed on the computer monitor. The computer then regulates the flow of the courseware, makes responses on users' input, and controls the video cassette or laser disc player. The set-up of an interactive video system is bulky and inconvenient as it involves the link-up of a number of hardware equipment. It also has to get access to both analogue and digital data sources, as analogue video segments are stored in magnetic tapes or laser discs, while digital data is stored in the computer.

Another way to display video images on computers is to make use of *desktop video*, which incorporates high resolution and full motion video of thirty frames per second onto a desktop computer. *Desktop video* enables the use of digital video with a desktop computer. It is an important step in turning a desktop computer into a true multimedia platform. Developing *desktop video* involves the following processes: 1) converting analogue video signals to digital ones, 2) compressing digital sound and video images to optimal file sizes, 3) storing large files of data, and 4) displaying digital video images in live motion.

To get full color, full motion, and full screen video into the computer involves very complex processes, as

video is extremely data-intensive. One uncompressed full-screen image, or one frame of video, with a resolution of 640 × 480 and 24-bit color, multiplied by 30 for full motion (video is 30 frames per second), equals approximately 27 MB of data for one second in real time. Thus, one minute of video segment comes to over 1.6 GB of storage. Apart from the storage problem, the system buses on most personal computers are not really fast enough to handle the amount of data to be transferred in real time and it also demands a high-speed computer system with a very large storage capacity.

To overcome the problem of large file size of digital video, the compression and decompression (CODEC) technologies can be used. Once the file size is reduced, the fast data transfer rate requirement will also be lessened. Different digital video vendors have proposed various video CODEC schemes based on different algorithms. Video for Windows, Quicktime, Captain, Crunch, Cinepake, Indeo, JPEG, and MPEG are some examples [2].

The digital video CODEC system supported by most manufacturers is MPEG l, which is now an ISO standard. ISO MPEG 1 is an open standard on the compression and decompression of video and audio data. Based on MPEG 1, video data can be encoded and compressed achieving a maximum compression ratio of 200. These video data can be stored either in the hard disk of a computer, a magnetic optical disk, or a CD-ROM. With MPEG 1, it is now possible to store seventy-four minutes VHS quality video on a CD-ROM. Random access is also one of the features available.

MPEG 1 has also overcome the problems of small screen size and slow playback rate of previous digital video based on other CODEC systems. Using an MPEG 1 decompression card, digital video data can be played back on computer desktop in real time. With CODEC technology, *desktop video* has become a reality. As a result, the computer has now turned into a true multimedia platform.

CONVERTING A TRADITIONAL MULTIMEDIA KIT INTO AN INTERACTIVE VIDEO CD-ROM

The Project reported in this article was to convert a traditional multimedia kit/package, which included an ETV program with supporting materials in printed format, into an interactive video CD-ROM by making use of the latest development in the MPEG technology. The video CD-ROM produced in this project was not just a kit, which combined the different components together. Instead, it was a multimedia courseware, as the materials were organized in a structured and systematic manner. Moreover, it had been adapted for interactive teaching and learning.

---

[1] The Project was developed by the authors between June and October 1994.

Multimedia can be defined as sequential or simultaneous use of a variety of media formats in a given presentation or a self-study program. However, the multimedia concept involves more than using multiple media for a given instructional purpose. It integrates each medium into a structured systematic presentation. Each medium is designed to complement the others so that the whole system becomes greater than the sum of parts [3, 4].

A *multimedia kit/package* is simply a collection of teaching/learning materials involving more than one type of medium and organized around a single topic; but a *multimedia system* is a combination of text, graphic art, sound, animation, and video integrated into a structured systematic presentation delivered by computer.

Multimedia becomes *interactive* when users, apart from viewing the presentation, are allowed to participate, such as controlling and making responses to the presentation. Viewer participation or involvement may take different forms, such as: answering questions, manipulating a control during simulation, or simply choosing which segment of material to view from a menu.

The degree of users' control over the pace and sequence of the presentation or instruction varies according to design. There are several levels of interactivity [5–7]. Level *one* interactivity can be direct or responsive. Direct interactivity means activating by user choice, while responsive interactivity occurs when the user is asked to select, recall, or in some way perform for the program, according to the materials he or she has been exposed to. Level *two* interactivity is exploratory. In this way, whole subject areas can be "explored" on the video segments and not on a user-selecting basis. When users explore a subject, they tend to learn and experience in more personal ways. Level *three* interactivity is creativity. The program here is flexible enough to allow a design the programmer has not yet thought of. In addition, the computer can evaluate and compliment the user if the sequence or construction is new and workable. Interactive courseware can also be classified into the following categories: drill-and-practice, tutorials, problem solving, simulations, and games.

The video CD-ROM produced in the project described was an interactive multimedia courseware, as it involved both level one and level two interactivity. It mainly used drill-and-practice and tutorials; and three types of exercises including: 1) yes/no answers, 2) multiple choice questions, and 3) fill in the blanks were incorporated.

THE DESIGN, DEVELOPMENT, AND PRODUCTION OF THE COURSEWARE

In this study, an existing curriculum resource kit/package was converted into an interactive multimedia courseware and was stored in a video CD-ROM, which was used as a delivery medium. The original kit included: a)

an ETV English language program for primary six pupils, titled "Nicki's Adventure," b) *Teachers' Notes,* and c) a set of the pupils' worksheets. The language focus of this program was giving simple instructions, warnings, and prohibitions. Examples of some of the instructions used in the program are as follows:

Use the door on your right.
Turn back. You're heading for danger.
Don't Touch. It's dangerous.

The program was about Nicki's tour in a computer maze. Through Nicki's adventure in the fantasy land, the language functions were introduced.

The following were the processes involved in developing the Courseware:

1. design of the courseware structure,
2. design of the user interface,
3. preparation of the raw data,
4. writing the courseware,
5. evaluation and revision, and
6. recording data onto a CD-ROM.

The structure of the Courseware was developed (see Figure 1). It included Teachers' Notes, Sound Play, the Programme "Nicki's Adventure," and Pupils' Activity. *Teachers' Notes* were mainly text files, introducing the Purple Series of ETV English language programs for primary six pupils, and the program "Nicki's Adventure." Print option was provided here to facilitate users to print hard copies of the text when required.

The second component was *Sound Play,* which aimed to show that practicing speaking English could be fun. Here the full advantages of graphic art, animation, and CD-quality audio capabilities were utilized. Since the aim here was to increase users' interest and sensitivity toward pronunciation, CD-quality audio was of great importance.

Part three was the video segment of *the Programme "Nicki's Adventure"* (approximately 13 minutes in length).

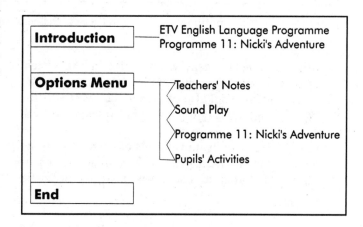

Figure 1. The structure of the courseware.

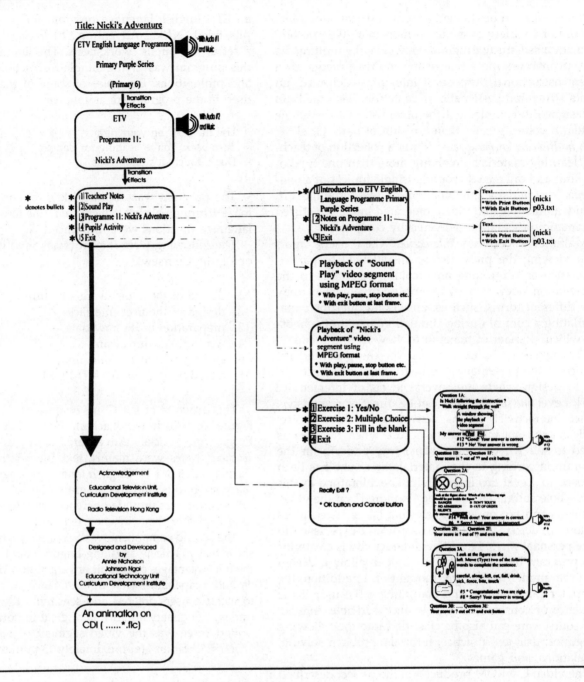

Figure 2. Outline of the user interface.

The original video segment was recorded in PAL system in Betacam format. By using MPEG technology, it had been converted to digital data (about 122 MB) and the playback of high-quality full color, full motion, and full screen video was supported.

In the *Pupil's Activity,* three kinds of exercise were included. They were interactive and encouraged user participation. The program had been designed to assess

pupils' responses. Verbal comment was given for each answer given. For example, *"Congratulations! You are right." "Well done! Your answer is correct."* or *"Sorry! Your answer is wrong."* were used to provide immediate feedback. Accumulated scores were also given at the end of each exercise. The outline of the user interface was further developed (see Figure 2). Based on this outline, more detailed storyboarding was prepared.

Each frame of the exercises was carefully designed to convey information clearly without being cluttered. Any single frame either served a single purpose or multiple purposes. It might also contain text, graphic, animation,

² All costing quoted in this article was based on market price in Hong Kong during the period when the project was developed. The exchange rate was approximately US$ 1.00 to HK$ 7.70.

digital audio, and digital video data. Samples of captured frames are provided in Figure 3.

In this project, teachers' notes and pupils' activity worksheets were entered as text data. The pictures of the pupils' worksheets were either drawn or scanned, and stored as graphic files. Audio segments were recorded in WAVE file format. Analogue video segments can be converted to MPEG digital video by specialized MPEG encoding boards, which were expensive. It costs around US$ 21,000.[2] Encoding high quality digital video can be time consuming and thus expensive. In this Project, the analogue video segments were sent to MPEG encoding

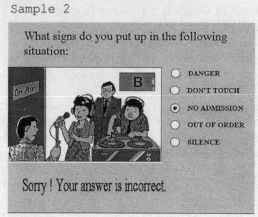

Sample 1

A. Is Nicki following the instruction?

ETOA.AVI

Stop running, or you'll fall down.

replay
next

My Answer is ☐ Yes ☐ No

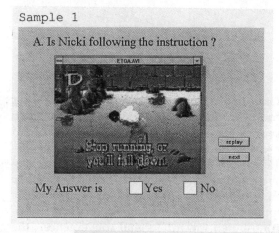

Sample 2

What signs do you put up in the following situation:

On Air

B

○ DANGER
○ DON'T TOUCH
◉ NO ADMISSION
○ OUT OF ORDER
○ SILENCE

Sorry! Your answer is incorrect.

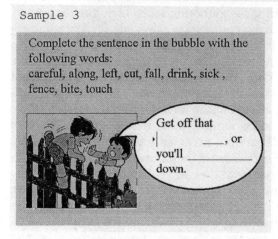

Sample 3

Complete the sentence in the bubble with the following words:
careful, along, left, cut, fall, drink, sick, fence, bite, touch

Get off that
▸| _____, or
you'll _____
down.

Figure 3. Samples of captured frames.

service bureau for encoding. This was more economical and saved production time for this particular project. The total file size of all the data of this Courseware came to approximately 144 MB after digital video compression based on MPEG 1.

In creating this Courseware, *Authorware Professional for Windows, version 2.0.1* was used. *Authorware Professional for Windows, version 2.0.1* is a powerful and commonly used authoring package in MS Windows environment [8]. By using an authoring package, tedious programming work was minimized. The *Authorware Professional* can support MPEG 1 digital video through MS Windows MCI commands.

Four criteria in evaluating this Courseware were considered: structural evaluation, functional evaluation, users opinions, and cost-effectiveness [9]. *Structural evaluation* refers to an assessment of the structure and appearance of the courseware. Assessment and revision in this aspect were carried out at different stages during the course of writing. A *functional evaluation* tests how well the courseware taught. In this case, since the learning materials used in this Courseware were adapted from existing resources, the learning effectiveness of the ETV program, the part on Sound Play and the exercises had not been tested. Instead, *opinions of users* on the exercises, especially on the users' interest and improvement after repeated drill, were gathered and considered. Finally, overall *cost* in developing this Courseware was analyzed. The following list of items involved either cost or man-days:

Design of courseware and storyboarding
Production of audio segment
Production of video segment
Scanning of pictures
Computer graphic work including menu screen
Animation production
Encoding of video segments to MPEG 1 format
Encoding of audio segments to MPEG 1 format
Authoring of courseware and computer programming
Technical testing
Evaluation
Recording of courseware onto CD-ROM

The actual expenditure on the Project was not high, but the time investment of individual officers was considerable. Since this was a developmental project, all the previous evaluation was formative. Summative evaluation could be carried out with the users once the Courseware was final. Data collected could then be used to guide users in selection and utilization.

Since the file size of the Courseware was about 145 MB (including 122 MB of 13 minutes video data), it was considered appropriate to store the data on a CD-ROM, as it could store a very large amount of data (up to 650 MB of data or 74 minutes of digital video data).

Moreover, a CD-ROM is inherently multimedia. Because of the nature of digital encoding, a CD-ROM can contain computer code and data, digitized audio, and digitized

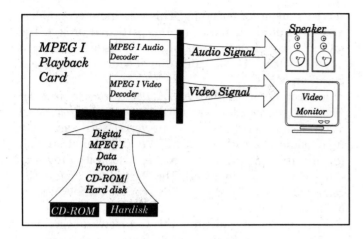

Figure 4. Data flow in the playback of the video CD-ROM.

- VGA display card, support at least 640 × 480 sixteen colors
- MPEG 1 playback card, compatible with ReelMagic, supporting full motion, full screen and full color
- CDF-ROM drive
- speakers

Software Tools:

- MS DOS 5.0
- MS Windows with Multimedia Extension
- MPEG 1 driver

video. Thus it is a suitable delivery medium for this interactive multimedia Courseware. This attribute helps to minimize the number of hardware and software required for use in instruction. Using CD-ROMs is particularly appropriate in this Project as they are portable, both in terms of size and weight, and of compatibility across all brands of CD-ROM drives. Since ISO 9660 has already become a standard, CD-ROMs provide a standardized format which ensures multi-platform compatibility.

There are also a number of other advantages. CD-ROMs can be produced at a relatively low unit cost. They can provide a long-lasting stable medium for storage. Since they cannot be overwritten, they will not deteriorate significantly with age and frequent use. They can also provide random access to information stored on them. Although the search times on a CD-ROM are not as fast as those on a hard disk, they are faster than those on a floppy disk.

HARDWARE AND SOFTWARE REQUIREMENT FOR USER PLAYBACK

Figure 4 shows the data flow in the playback of the video CD-ROM. The hardware and software requirement in using this interactive multimedia Courseware is not complicated. In addition to a standard 80386 or 80486 microcomputer (approximately US$ 1,400) and a CD-ROM drive (approximately US$ 240), an MPEG 1 playback card (approximately US$ 390) was required. The *minimum* requirement can be referred to the following lists.

Hardware Requirement:

- 80386/25 SX IBM-compatible microcomputer
- 2 MB *free* hard disk space
- 2 MB RAM
- VGA monitor

DISCUSSION

Instruction can be delivered by a variety of media, for example, books/worksheets, audio cassette tapes, video cassette tapes, compact discs, laser discs, computer hard disks, floppy discs, and CD-ROM. The experiences discussed in this article made use of CD-ROM as the medium to store a courseware containing interactive *desktop video* to deliver instruction. This was made possible by the development of CODEC technology. Such development has contributed toward "digital convergence," the result of which is a convenient multimedia platform for teaching and learning. This multimedia platform has considerable advantages over traditional multimedia kits and interactive video. It is more compact, flexible, and convenient to use. Individualized and group learning can also be catered for.

In developing the project, experience in applying the latest MPEG compression technology to develop *desktop video* is valuable. The quality of the digital video segments is reasonably good and the audio segments have a CD-quality which is particularly suitable for language learning. However, quality can be improved with more experience in the encoding process.

Authoring tools have become more powerful and easy to use. With these authoring tools, high quality interactive multimedia courseware providing feedback and remediation to learners can be designed and produced. In this study, no major difficulties were encountered in the authoring. With *Authorware Professional*, the development and production of this Courseware was rather easy. Although the design of the interface and the design of the exercises can be refined, these require greater input of time, which may not necessarily be cost effective. However, the effectiveness of the Courseware greatly depends on the instructional design.

Recording the Courseware containing digital video and audio data is technically viable. This program has taken up less than a quarter of the capacity of a CD-ROM. Courseware with more complicated design and longer video or audio segments can easily be supported.

CD-ROM is used in this project because of its advantages (as discussed earlier in this article), but it also has its limitation. Since CD-ROM is read-only, there is the problem of updating.

Playback of the Courseware requires hardware support. It needs the MPEG 1 playback card, on top of a standard 80386 or 80486 microcomputer system. Although the MPEG playback card, such as the ReelMagic, only costs approximately US\$ 240, this requirement makes the use of the Courseware less attractive. Moreover, like other computer-related software, users are required to have some training or experience in using computers. There are some areas in the playback that need improvement. For example, fast forward in the video playback is not yet incorporated. The scroll bar to provide random access has still to be added.

This project has demonstrated how existing resource materials can be adapted to make use of the advantages of an improved media format. However, authors have to be aware of the issue of copyright.

Desktop video, being interactive and economical, is suitable to deliver information and instruction. But it will be a long time before the application becomes commonly used in Hong Kong classrooms. The hardware and software tools required to use the *desktop video* are not standard equipment in the schools in Hong Kong. Moreover, the success of using a medium depends not only on its attributes but also on the attitude of the users. Training in the use of the medium for teachers and pupils would therefore be necessary.

References

1. Education Department, *Information Sheet: Educational Television Service*, Education Department, Hong Kong, pp. 1–3, 1993.
2. D. Coco, Squeezing Video onto the Desktop, *Computer Graphics World*, p. 51, March 1994.
3. R. Henich, M. Molenda, and J. D. Russell, *Instructional Media and the New Technologies of Instruction* (3rd Edition), Macmillan, New York, 1989.
4. T. Vaughan, *Multimedia: Making It Work*, Osbourne McGraw-Hill, New York, pp. 3–10, 1993.
5. S. Floyd, Thinking Interactively, in *Handbook of Interactive Video*, S. Floyd and B. Floyd (eds.), Knowledge Industry Publications, New York, pp. 3–8, 1982.
6. D. Hon, Future Directions: The Curtain Rises on Interactive Video, in *Handbook of Interactive Video*, S. Floyd and B. Floyd (eds.), Knowledge Industry Publications, New York, pp. 125–130, 1982.
7. J. E. Kemp and D. C. Smellie, *Planning, Producing, and Using Instructional Media* (6th Edition), Harper & Row, New York, pp. 283–285, 1989.
8. R. Raskin, Creating Multimedia to Die For, *PC Magazine*, pp. 209–251, February 1994.
9. E. L. Criswell, *The Design of Computer-Based Instruction*, Macmillan, New York, pp. 182–212, 1989.

REFERENCES NOT CITED IN TEXT

Debloois, M. L., *Videodisc/Microcomputer Courseware Design*, Educational Technology, Englewood Cliffs, New Jersey, 1982.

Gayeski, D. M. (ed.), *Multimedia for Learning: Development, Application, Evaluation*, Educational Technology Publications, Englewood Cliffs, New Jersey, 1993.

Iuppa, N. V., *A Practical Guide to Interactive Video Design*, Knowledge Industry Publications, Inc., New York, 1984.

Nicholson, R. I., Syder, D., and Freeman, M., Construction of a Visual (Video-Supported Active Learning) Resource, *Computers Education*, 22:½, pp. 91–97, 1994.

Schwier, R. A. and Misanchuk, E. R., *Interactive Multimedia Instruction*, Educational Technology, Englewood Cliffs, New Jersey, 1993.

Schwier, R. A., *Interactive Video*, Educational Technology, Englewood Cliffs, New Jersey, 1987.

THE 21st CENTURY CLASSROOM-SCHOLARSHIP ENVIRONMENT: WHAT WILL IT BE LIKE?

ABSTRACT

The convergence of computing, communications, and traditional educational technologies enables us to discuss, plan, create, and implement fundamentally unique strategies for providing access to people and information. The scientific process is used as an approach to teaching-learning through discovery. Over the last several years, SUNY Plattsburgh, like many universities across the world, has created a technology environment on campus which provides ubiquitous access to both on- and off-campus information resources for faculty and students. The article describes the development of a teaching-learning module in biology which makes creative use of the Internet and other communications and computing media. This example is placed in the context of strategies which must be employed—both locally and globally—in order to realize the authors' vision of the 21st century classroom-scholarship environment.

WILLIAM D. GRAZIADEI

SUNY at Plattsburgh, New York

GILLIAN M. McCOMBS

SUNY at Albany, New York

There will be a road
It will not connect two points
It will connect all points
Its speed limit will be the speed of light
It will not go from here to there
There will be no more there
We will all only be here [1]

INTRODUCTION

In order to implement the vision captured above in a recent MCI commercial, teaching faculty, students, and information specialists/librarians need to work together to realize the Internet's potential for curriculum and research support. The convergence of computing, communications, and traditional educational technologies through the Internet enables us to discuss, plan, create, and implement fundamentally unique strategies for providing access to people and information, thus using the scientific process as an approach to teaching-learning through discovery. In the industrial age we went to schools; today, schools can come to us with living color, sound, and motion. The convergence of technologies connects teacher and teacher, teacher and student, student and student, with library, dormitory, classroom, other universities, home, school and business in ways not previously possible. The teaching-learning module developed at SUNY Plattsburgh is just one example of the ongoing initiatives which provide a glimpse of what the 21st century classroom will look like.

INTERACTIVE LEARNING MODULE IN CANCER TREATMENT

Over the last several years, SUNY Plattsburgh, like many colleges and universities, has created a technology envi-

"The 21st Century Classroom-Scholarship Environment: What Will It Be Like?" William D. Graziadei and Gillian M. McCombs, *Journal of Educational Technology Systems*, Volume 24, No. 2, pp. 97-112, Baywood Publishing Company, Inc., 1995-96.

ronment which provides ubiquitous access to both on- and off-campus information resources for faculty and students. Technology-enriched (smart) classrooms and laboratories as well as presentation lecterns in small-, medium-, and large-sized lecture halls with a strong emphasis on multi-media capabilities have been set up. The latter include various devices such as computers (IBM compatible and Macintosh), a document camera and computer-controlled CD-ROM drives, laserdisc and VCR players as well as a slide-to-video projector, video camera, a computer and video overhead projection system, and telecommunication connections to local, Bitnet, and Internet services. Applications available include electronic mail (e-mail), Lotus Notes, electronic conferences, telnet, ftp, Gopher, Lynx, Mosaic, and WAIS utilities. These facilities have been created to take advantage of both present and future campus technologies.

The interactive learning module described here was developed for B10380 (Tele)Communicating Biology—Advanced Writing Course. It uses telephone, e-mail, Timbuktu, CUSeeMe, on-line library catalogs, FirstSearch, Gopher, and Mosaic to demonstrate a "real-time" need of a student in developing an undergraduate research paper on "Cancer, Chemotherapy, and Bone Marrow Transplant (BMT)." The entire BMT module can be accessed at URL:http://137.142.42.95/bmtCancer/bmt.html. (The Table of Contents is shown in Appendix I.)

In this module, text and graphics are pulled together to provide an overview of the topic. Hooks to video clips are provided on topics varying from a personal soliloquy by the student compiling this module to a clip of the actual BMT transplant procedure. Hooks are also provided along the way for more information as needed—particularly on the terms used—with a link made to a dictionary of cell biology. An online search request form is available for students to request database searches from the library, especially useful for databases that have controlled access (see Appendix II). An online examination is part of the package, complete with extensive instructions on the client/browser needed and other configuration requirements. The student is able to complete the form, click on the "Submit Examination" button to send the exam to the instructor, as well as add freeform feedback or questions. This allows the instructor to reply in real time, thus providing timely feedback to the student, and allowing for a more even workload redistribution. If students can take the exam at any time of day or night, again, this provides for flexible study and work schedules. The module also includes information on the Internet in general as well as links to other essential but more general reference tools such as THOMAS Legislative Information and EPA Resources. (A list of the equipment used in this teaching module can be found in Appendix III.)

VISION OF THE 21st CENTURY CLASSROOM-SCHOLARSHIP ENVIRONMENT

The vignette just described serves to illustrate what the 21st century collaborative classroom environment will be like, a space without floors or walls and hence no ceiling to learning. It will be a place where a faculty member sits down at a computer in an office on campus and connects to several students in the dormitory and/or at home via desktop video-conferencing and computer screen sharing. They will engage in a conference planning session to develop a strategy for a document they wish to collaborate on which they will subsequently develop and publish on the network. After they agree upon their approach and assign various tasks, they will search the network of databases on campus (and the links through the Internet to databases worldwide for text, image, video, and sound information). Several individuals in the "team" will search for information to incorporate into their document while others will create and search for multimedia files related to the topic. Each member of the group will create, as well as look for various types of text documents from independent sources, for video documentaries, and still photographs. They will explore an unfamiliar database on music and discover some classical songs whose lyrics and harmonies become an organized focus for a hypermedia presentation and lesson.

Downloading the information they need, the teacher and students will call up hypermedia word processor, authoring, and delivery programs such as Word and Mosaic/MacHTTP client/server software and various multimedia utility programs; they will select video clips, photos, music, and type and cite textual material. They will use the network desktop videoconferencing and screen sharing connections to train each other in the use of the various tools. Together they will synthesize the information and write an analysis and critique of the subject, cross reference it with hypermedia tags which can also lead to source citations, and provide several alternative pathways through the emerging work. They will animate the title and visual map guide to the hyperstructure of the work and log the presentation and lesson into the university database server. They will send an e-mail message to colleagues and other students asking them to examine and evaluate the module's effectiveness. Shortly, they will receive comments and suggestions for revision which they incorporate. Finally, they will notify the class that the *Presentation and Lesson* on the selected topic is ready for use. Other faculty and students may add to the module and incorporate portions of it into works of their own. A copy of each version can be logged into a public database and during the next year will be accessed by thousands of people worldwide.

THE USE OF MULTIMEDIA

The use of more than one type of media for communication in presentations, lessons, and assessments—or multimedia—is multi-disciplinary. A variety of multimedia-based technologies—video, videodisc, and CD-ROM combined with a variety of TCP/IP/client/server and screen sharing programs as well as desktop videoconferencing—are at the heart of interactive multimedia. The use of computer-controlled media is referred to as interactive because it enables a whole new level of user interaction with, and control over, materials in a number of forms, such as text, audio, graphics, animation, and video as well as utilities such as telecommunications. The computer's power to search for and retrieve information can be used to interlink and annotate related topics to create a "web of information." The teacher-learner follows a "uniquely" personal trail through the information, becoming an interactive participant in the flow of information to learning. Users can navigate through a multimedia presentation at their own speed, reviewing, assessing, and getting feedback where necessary and following up in more detail on items of remedial necessity or personal interest. There is also the opportunity for the instructor to tailor materials to individual students' needs. At the same time, students are more likely to understand the complex interplay of historical events such as art, history, music, science, and theater, when the material is presented in multimedia formats rather than through lectures and readings alone.

By providing telecommunications and multimedia capabilities in lecture halls as well as in specialized classrooms and public access facilities, the presentation of lectures, lessons, and assessments can be developed, discovered, enriched, and made more memorable. They can be broadened to include resources not available in the classroom, and made accessible WHERE, WHEN, and HOW learners need them. Not too long ago, producing interactive courseware packages would have required the work of several expert programmers and sophisticated, special-purpose hardware. But now, almost any subject matter expert, with appropriate in-service education and training, has the potential to create—and present—an exciting interactive learning experience. These tools have the potential for providing "real-time" training and assistance to all campus constituents using a SUNY Networked Electronic Teaching/Training Help Desk Centers concept, or ETs for short.

No two learners learn from the same presentation in the same way with the same results. No two instructors use the same medium in the same way or with equal effectiveness. No two lessons are appropriate for delivery in the same style or through the same medium. The task an instructor faces when considering what pedagogy to use in instruction should include a process that is diagnostic in nature. We must ask ourselves which channels are appropriate for which communication and teaching-learning style.

OTHER INITIATIVES

Other noteworthy examples of the 21st century classroom in action include a university-wide initiative which took place at the University of Stirling in Scotland [2]. Project VARSETILE, meant to imply a Versatile Varsity, a university flexible in its approach and receptive to change, is an acronym which stands for Value Added Re-use at Stirling of Existing Technology to support the Learning Experience. VARSETILE brings together and reinforces hypermedia teaching projects already under way on campus. The problem, as the University saw it, was how to preserve the distinctive quality of the learning experience with its accent on flexibility and high staff/student contact, at a time of expanding enrollment and shrinking resources. The University decided to increase its reliance on the support that could be provided by technology. This involved releasing academic staff from teaching duties so that they could be trained to use multimedia systems or to adopt and adapt material sources from elsewhere into their courses. Some individual projects at Stirling included a Cervical Cytology course with full text/image journals, and a course on Collaborative Molecular Modeling. The stated aim of the whole initiative was to "build an environment where the use of teaching and learning technology is as natural and as well supported as the use of textbooks" [2].

A recent issue of *BYTE* has a cover story on the use of educational technology and details a number of projects both on college campuses and in the K–12 system [3]. These include the FAST (Financial Analysis and Security Trading) Program in the Graduate School of Industrial Administration at Carnegie Mellon University, and the multi-disciplinary Principio Project initiated at the Peddie School in Hightstown, New Jersey. On a more personal note, the BMT Table of Contents shows an entry for an Equilibrium Dialysis Experiment. An e-mail received from a professor at the University of Toledo, asking permission to access the BMT module for 'classroom sharing,' generated this reciprocal link.

CRITICAL AREAS

The use of computer and telecommunication technologies connects and empowers librarians, faculty, and students to work together in unique and collaborative ways in the practice of teaching, learning, and scholarship. However, in order to design and plan for the 21st century classroom, three critical areas need to be addressed: a) **Content** (how to put together search strategies, look for information, process it, sift it, organize it); b) **Process** (how to use technology to maximum benefit); and c) **Policy** (lobbying for increased resources for technology, and creating the necessary infrastructure to support it).

a. Content

Interfacing technology with education creates a web of people, places, and information that allows for discovery, development, and training. With technology-based presentation lecterns, libraries, and classrooms, and personal computers in the home, office, and dormitory, the pedagogical and learning potential for both instructor and student becomes virtually limitless. The BMT module illustrates this. The computer's power to search for and retrieve information which can be used to link and annotate related topics to create a "web of information" is maximized by using hypertext, a technique for the handling of machine-readable files of full text [4]. There are many different types of hypertext systems, but they all provide facilities for the creation and searching of linkages (i.e., pointers that allow non-linear access to a series of texts). Although hypertext has been discussed for over two decades, it has only been taken up commercially with the advent of low-cost, high-resolution graphics facilities that are now widely available as Windows or Macintosh Graphic User Interface (GUI) applications. The linkages provide a simple and seemingly effective way of moving through a text from one part to other related parts. Thus the user is provided with a simple browsing tool that is far easier to use than the command-oriented searching facilities of conventional retrieval systems. The teacher-learner follows a uniquely personal trail through the information, becoming an interactive participant in the flow of information and the learning process.

However, it should be emphasized that the use of the pointer structure implies that the searcher can retrieve information only if the appropriate linkages have been set up when the hypertext document was created. Hypertext is based on the understanding that human idea processing occurs through association, which is considered to be the framework for effective communication of knowledge. Hypertext uses electronic capabilities to overcome the limitations of the linear nature of printed text, and allows for three-dimensional navigation through a body of data. There are design issues to be concerned with when creating hypertext teaching/learning modules, such as nonlinearity, presentation of information, the problem of losing the reader in hyperspace, consistent structure and organization, and the need to compensate for the lack of preconceptions that accompany hypertext.

The obvious advantages to hypertext are the graphics capabilities and the ability to take advantage of associative thought processes, but there are also some obvious disadvantages in that the hypertext links need to be humanly inserted. There is currently little ability to both "get off the beaten track" or to control one's entrances and exits to the world of information. Several of the browsers (a "browser" is a particular software package that facilitates easy access to WWW) that have been developed attempt to compensate for some of these problems by adding new ways to navigate, as well as tracking mechanisms that automatically log search strategy (history, as it is called in either Mosaic or Netscape). Future browsers are expected to become more "intelligent." They will allow the user to import "raw data" and then present it in a manner uniquely tailored to the user's needs.

b. Process

Peter Drucker has pointed out that "in order for a new technology to be successful, it must do the old job ten times better" [5]. Examples of this in higher education are word processing, e-mail, course registration, and library catalogs (OPACs). Currently, however, little instructional software application on the market at the collegiate level comes close to meeting Drucker's requirement [5]. A national learning infrastructure requires the creation and widespread availability of high-quality, self-paced learning materials. These materials must both be modularized and contain feedback mechanisms for student assessment. Modularization is necessary in order to respond to individual learning needs and preferences. The learning modules must be available in a variety of formats that correspond to the differences in individual learning styles. The learning assessment component accomplishes two objectives: determining student learning styles and what students already know. This component must also include a monitoring capability to assess how much the students learn during the process, and at the end of the learning experience in order to certify that learning has happened. The immediacy with which the instructor is able to grade the students' work and give feedback contrasts very favorably with the current paper-based environment.

One reason for teachers to utilize technology in their instruction is that unlike paper documents, which are bound forever in fixed form, electronic publishing and telecommunications can easily provide information for multimedia documents which can conveniently be updated to reflect new knowledge and to incorporate new graphics, video, audio material, or text. Telecommunications and multimedia can make course materials more readily available (without the barriers of time and space) at the convenience of the learner. There is also the opportunity for the instructor to tailor materials to individual students' needs. Not too long ago, producing interactive courseware packages would have required the work of several expert programmers and sophisticated, special-purpose hardware. The judicious use of both telecommunications and multimedia can make course materials more engaging. Through the provision of high-quality images and sound, multiple senses in the learner are engaged (i.e., seeing, hearing) in the learning process. When course materials are more engaging, they tend to be more "memorable." Almost any subject matter expert has the potential to create—and present—an exciting interactive learning experience. Using computers, telecommunications, and multimedia can invigorate the way we teach and the way students learn. If we integrate them well into a course, then these technologies can make a significant contribution to a better, more student-centered learning climate.

As a result of the use of technology in education, the traditional roles of teacher and librarian are being questioned. Students are exerting much more of an influence on the direction a class or a search strategy can take. It is a challenge to become more of an observer studying the learning processes of students. E-mail, conferencing, gopher, World Wide Web, and multimedia bring learners closer to teachers, learners closer to each other, as well as creating new contacts among colleagues.

It should be noted that in the model shown earlier, the computer network is primarily a mediator for communication rather than a processor of information. Computer-Mediated Communications (CMC) [6] signifies the ways in which telecommunications technologies have merged with computers and computer networks to transfer, store, and retrieve information, but the emphasis is always on communication. CMC, for instructional purposes, provides e-mail and real-time chat capabilities, delivers instructions, and facilitates student to student and student to teacher interactions across a desk or across the world. Thus we have a dialogic (or multilogic) virtual university. This provides for the accommodation of different learning styles and the empowerment of learners regardless of physical challenges or social/cultural differences. The changing educational paradigms and their implications for technology are nicely documented in a schematic by Andy Reinhardt which contrasts the old model of classroom lectures and passive absorptions with the new model of individual exploration and apprenticeship [3].

c. Lobbying

Why do we need to lobby? The chief reason for lobbying generally is to influence the passage of legislation. Without a federal mandate, it is unlikely that the National Information Infrastructure (NII)—as we envision it—will come to pass. The private sector is lobbying extremely hard to get all responsibility for and access to the NII moved into private hands. In order to keep the NII both free and available to the public, we have to lobby, to increase legislators' awareness of why this is so crucial.

Educators are part of a group of stakeholders which includes authors, publishers, librarians, and information technology providers. These stakeholders need to discuss the meaning of publication in the networked information environment, the integrity of such electronic works, the role of organizations like the Coalition for Networked Information. We need to have a greater understanding of and appreciation for the increasing diversity of publication or information distribution paths available to authors, and the implications of these choices for research and education. This process also needs to include some reassessment of the valuation currently placed on electronic channels and outputs in such areas as university tenure and promotion decisions, at the same time looking at new ways to validate research and insert the peer review process without losing professional credibility.

Important problems, however, have yet to be addressed if telecommunications and multimedia are to reach their full pedagogical potential. Besides issues of access and ease of use of the technology, the traditional structures of university teaching and learning create the biggest hurdles. Instructors need to rethink their assumptions about teaching, and students need to confront their entrenched expectations about classroom learning. One of the most promising aspects of technology-based teaching-learning is that it can help us rethink the current teaching-learning paradigm.

We must also turn our lobbying efforts to the provision of infrastructure. Why is infrastructure or a strong networking capability so important? After all, we can point to many examples of stand-alone, self-paced immersion learning applications that improve educational quality. The problem is that they are stand-alone—in one class, in one room, at one institution. They are neither replicable nor scalable. As long as students have to go to a lab, or faculty have to move equipment to a space separate from where they work and from where students learn, logistical problems will continue to dominate. In a non-networked environment, the need for staff to manage the process creates further obstacles. Either there are not enough support staff to do the job or the costs of providing sufficient staff are prohibitive. By contrast, Internet-based applications such as e-mail, gopher, WWW servers, TCP/IP screen sharing, and desktop video-conferencing are becoming more widely diffused in higher education.

The Internet represents new possibilities in communication, collaboration, and information delivery. However, it should be noted that until today's limited bandwidth Internet expands to a widely accessible broadband network, and the infrastructure is both robust and ubiquitous, and accompanied by a different level of support staff with strong networking, communications, and information management skills, stand-alone approaches will continue to predominate. Our lobbying efforts must target both the national and the local arenas in order to ensure that we are in a position both to influence policy and to be involved in strategic decision-making in the area of infrastructure.

CONCLUSION

What can faculty do to bring about the vision described here? First, lead by personal example, as all the people involved in the above-cited examples are doing. Celebrate the successes and showcase accomplishments, both in local and national arenas. At the same time, it is essential to work to empower the rest of the faculty with computers, to invest in professional development.

The change agents in any department must be rewarded, both for innovative use of technology as well as for the ability to take risks. Efforts must be made to change the current faculty reward system. We need to build alliances with computing professionals, librarians, and teaching faculty in other subject areas. Reaching out to software/hardware vendors can only benefit our efforts. In order to develop the permanent funding stream which can support these efforts, which will wire our campuses, we must get involved in committees that will implement policy. Above all, we must think strategically and plan for the future.

The above examples clearly illustrate the familiar principles of scholarship and research. This is what we do as scientists—DISCOVER, DEVELOP, SHARE, and EDUCATE. Hence, the take-home lesson is to teach what and how we DO what we do and not merely what we know! Telecommunications and multimedia provide us with a window to accomplish such a change in the teaching-learning practice. This is our vision of the 21st century classroom/scholarship environment.

APPENDIX I
Table of Contents—Bone Marrow Transplant Module

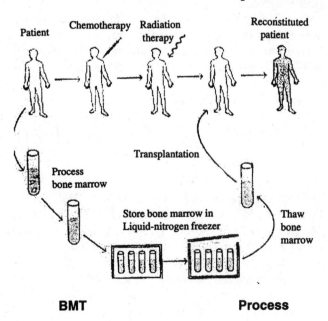

BMT   **Process**

Welcome to BMT & Cancer Treatment from Stephen Mahlstedt:

Click on Stephen to hear what he has to say about his project.

Bone Marrow Transplantation & Cancer Treatment

Author: Stephen Mahlstedt—**Advisor:** William D. Graziadei

Biological Sciences, SUNY Plattsburgh, Plattsburgh, New York 12901

BMT & Cancer Table of Contents

Introduction
Cancer Treatments
Human Immune System
Bone Marrow Transplant (BMT) Procedure
Bone Marrow Transplantation
Conclusion
Resources
On-line BMT & Cancer Examination
Frequently Asked Questions
On-line Resources Used. . . .

Why is the Internet useful?
W3 Search Engines
SUNY Plattsburgh FLAIR—login PLA_OPACX
SUNY Plattsburgh SPLAVA Go to PLAID, FLAIR
  & FirstSearch
  On-Line Literature Search Request Form
  Interlibrary Loan Form
  On-line Search Results
  Biological Sciences Gopher
  Veronica
  OncoLink
  WWW Libraries
  Library WWW Internet Applications
  WWWebCrawler Search Form
  WWW Spider Search Form

ENY ACRL Abstract—"Wiring the Trenches: Teaching Faculty & Librarians Working Together on the Internet" by William D. Graziadei & Gillian McCombs, Rensselaer Polytechnic Institute, Troy, New York
March 17, 1995
21st Century Classroom—Scholarship Environment by William D. Graziadei

5. MULTIMEDIA

FACT CIT'95 SUNY Institute of Technology May 30–June 2, 1995
Bio380 (tele)Communicating Biology—Advanced Writing Course

Other lectures/courses using the Internet & WWW:
Equilibrium Dialysis Interactive Simulation
World Lecture Hall
Virtual Classroom

APPENDIX II

Online Search Request Form—Bone Marrow Transplant Module

Welcome to Bio380 (Tele)Communicating Biology & Benjamin Feinberg Library

On-Line Library Database Search Form

This is a fill-out form, with multiple text entry fields, for requesting a library on-line database literature search.

IMPORTANT! Your WWW browser MUST support forms and the "mailto" URL type in order to correctly submit this request. Please use Netscape client since it is much more stable with forms and the mailto: function.

You can also click on **MUIRGD@splava.cc.plattsburgh. edu** or *GRAZIAWD@splava.cc.plattsburgh.edu* here or at the end of the form to send any feedback or questions.

The following information is needed to locate information regarding your status as well as to provide contact information for class activities that may require feedback or trouble-shooting as well.

Enter your first and last name here:

[Administration] [Faculty] [Staff] [Student] [Status Other]

Enter other status here:

Enter your EMail user id here:

Enter the course number and name here:

1. Enter the search topic here:

2. Enter the keyword(s)/descriptor(s) here (please put synonyms together):

3. Enter the known relevant citation here:

4. Enter the language limitations here:

5. Enter the range of years limitation here:

6. What type of references would you like?

7. How do you want to receive the search results?

8. What is your faculty/student status?
    1. Full-Time.
    2. Part-Time.

9. Would you like to be present when the search is done?
    Yes.
    No.

Type in your phone number:

Comments & Feedback Welcome

Please enter any other comments below:

To submit the query, press this button.

To Reset the query, press this button.

Things you may want to note:

The completed form will be sent to Dr. Graziadei at GRAZIAWD@baryon.hawk.plattsburgh.edu who will then forward it to Gordon Muir at muirgd@splava.cc.plattsburgh.edu.
It will give Gordon all the information needed for doing the database searches for you.
You can always send Gordon an EMAIL message (MUIRGD) as well if you have any questions.

Go to Bio380 Syllabus.

Go to Bone Marrow Transplant & Cancer Therapy.

Go to ILLForm.

Send comments and/or feedback to William D. Graziadei, PhD, Instructor at *GRAZIAWD@splava.cc. plattsburgh.edu* or Gordon D. Muir, Reference Librarian at *MUIRGD@splava.cc.plattsburgh.edu*

Go to Biological Sciences Home Page.

Go to SUNY WWW *PLAID* CWIS.

Go to SUNY Plattsburgh WWW HomePage.

APPENDIX III

Equipment Used

Mac PPC 6100/66
At least 33-66 mHz
16 MB RAM or greater
300 MB hard disk
MacTCP/IP 2.0.6 & IP Address for machine
System Software 7.0 or greater and Close View
Communication Program and/or NCSA Telnet for
 access to the Internet

Electronic Mail, Conferences, and Gopher

Electronic mail, conferences, and Gopher are relatively simple, yet fundamental technologies in supporting teaching-learning/service. Because they provide us with low-cost, relatively instantaneous communications, individuals and groups are able to maintain frequent contact with each other—setting up presentations, lectures, scheduling conference sessions, and preparing documents such as this one.

World Wide Web (WWW) Server/Client

The World Wide Web employs the popular client-server model of computing. A WWW, or Web server is a program running on a computer whose purpose is to serve documents to other computers. A Web client (often referred to as a Web browser) is a program that interfaces with the server and requests documents on behalf of the user. The World Wide Web is composed of thousands of these virtual transactions taking place per hour throughout the world, creating a web of information that will be used by all our stack holders, e.g. our preparation for this conference. It is our intention to coordinate and develop our Web efforts so that we can easily share information, documentation, course/library resources, and HELPDESK-related material.

Timbuktu

Timbuktu Pro, Farallon Computing, Inc., (800.344.7489), for Macintosh and Windows, is used for remote control and file transfer between two or more desktop computers on AppleTalk and/or TCP/IP networks (including the Internet). It allows one to share a common document, graphic, spreadsheet, or any application for teaching, learning, or training when used as a separate electronic "whiteboard" or "smartboard." When a session is finished, any document created can be saved and kept by anyone who wants it or wants to print it (no need to FAX or incur other costs). It can be used as a powerful just-in-time teaching-learning or training-support tool on a campus and just between campuses.

CUSeeMe (fttp: gated.cornell.edu)

CUSeeMe is a free Macintosh and PC desktop video/audio conferencing program that provides a one-to-one connection, or through the use of a "reflector," a one-to-many, a several-to-several, or a several-to-many conference depending on user needs and hardware capabilities. As such, it provides useful conferencing at minimal cost. One can simply use a standard camcorder to conduct desktop videoconferencing with other CUSeeMe users anywhere on the global Internet. We have found the audio component to be the most vulnerable to heavy traffic on the Internet and rely upon the telephone when it becomes problematic and difficult to hear.

Flexcam and Connectix Quickcam camera

Telephone

The telephone is one of the most overlooked, taken-for-granted forms of technology there is. Yet it is often one of the most dependable forms of communication. It can be used stand-alone or in conjunction with other technologies (often as a backup in case of failure). Many of our CUSeeMe conferences simply would not have been possible without the audio conferencing feature of the telephone (audio seems to suffer the most when conferencing over the Internet). Furthermore, without the communications infrastructure provided by "telephone lines" most of the communication and information technologies we have employed in our alliance simply would not have been possible.

REFERENCES

1. MCI commercial, as quoted by T. Peters, A Paean to Self-Organization, *Forbes ASAP*, 154:8, pp. 154–156, October 1994.
2. B. Ryan, The Multimedia Campus, *ITS News*, 30, pp. 30–32, 1994.
3. A. Reinhardt, New Ways to Learn, *BYTE*, 20:3, pp. 50–71, March 1985.
4. S. Al-Hawamdeh, R. de-Vere, G. Smith, and P. Willett, Using Nearest-Neighbor Searching Techniques to Access Full-Text Documents, *Online Review*, 15:3/4, pp. 173–192, June/August 1991.
5. C. A. Twigg, Navigating the Transition, *Educom Review*, 29:6, pp. 21–24, November/December 1994.
6. Z. Berge and M. Collins, *Computer-Mediated Communication and the Online Classroom: Overview and Perspectives*, Hampton Press, New Jersey, 1995. Also available electronically as *Computer-Mediated Communication Magazine*, 2:2, p. 6, February 1, 1995, URL:http://sunsite.unc.edu/cmc/mag/1995/feb/toc.html.

Video to the Desktop and Classrooms: The IUPUI IMDS Project

DR. ALI JAFARI, Director
Information Technologies Laboratory
Indiana University Purdue University Indianapolis, IUPUI
Indianapolis, Ind.

At first, the concept was very simple. The new IUPUI library information system should have "multimedia capability." More specifically, the new information system should be capable of receiving video on every Macintosh and PC computer in the building.

The concept and system design got more complex after additional functional and technical requirements were envisioned: including campus-wide access, interactivity, random access, random search, multimedia authoring, cross platform, Web environment, media digitizing and more.

A system with all the envisioned requirements could not be found on the market; therefore, it was quickly concluded that the "multimedia system" must be totally invented, developed and designed in-house. This is how the Interactive Multimedia Distribution System (IMDS) project started at Indiana University Purdue University Indianapolis (IUPUI).

■ Network to Spur Multimedia Use

In spring of 1994, the Information Technologies Laboratory at IUPUI teamed up a group of computer engineers, computer programmers and multimedia experts to research, develop and design the IMDS system. In the summer of 1995, the project was completed — after more than a year of intensive work by over seven full-time multimedia experts and completion of about 100,000 lines of original computer codes.

The IMDS hardware included an integration of state-of-the-art video storage systems, a fiber optics network, a distributed multimedia controller system and a variety of client workstation platforms. Since August 22, 1995, the IMDS has been in operation on all Macintosh and PC scholar workstations in the new IUPUI library and most classrooms across the IUPUI campus.

The IMDS project holds a record of being

> **It takes about 30 seconds before a student is able to view and control the media.**

the first interactive multimedia distribution system ever designed and deployed to fully support the university-wide interactive delivery, retrievals and authoring of multimedia resources for teaching and learning.

The educational applications of the IMDS system may be divided into four major types: video-on-demand, multimedia papers, advanced multimedia and classroom teaching applications.

■ Application: Video on Demand

The concept behind the video-on-demand capability is very simple. Students are able to select any archived video materials or television broadcast channel to view on their computer monitor. All videos are stored in a central location on campus, from which they are electronically distributed across the campus.

This concept provides similar functional capabilities as those of word processing provides in terms of display, search and navigation through a file. For instance, if a student would like to view a tape as part of his/her class assignment, he/she first clicks on the IMDS icon on the library information system's home page (http://www-lib.iupui.edu/). Second, he/she narrows down the selection to the archive video home page by clicking on the video tape and videodisc category. This selection links to the IMDS' videotape and videodisc holdings home page where the student finds his/her final selection (http://www-lib.iupui.edu/cgi-bin/mmIMDS4.pl).

Currently about 400 full-length video titles are available online. Once a title is selected by a mouse click, the IMDS launches the player program that automatically loads and links the video to the workstation. It takes about 30 seconds before a student is able to view and control the media by clicking on control icons (displayed in Figure 1).

Special attention has been given to the

human-computer interface design to simplify system operation. Besides basic control functions, a user can search any given location on the tape/videodisc; for instance, 1:20:05, or one hour, twenty minutes and five seconds into the videotape. Upon dragging the slider bar to this location, the IMDS automatically searches and starts video viewing at this exact location.

Every operation is transparent without human operator involvement behind the scene. The IMDS uses two robotics videotape management systems (see Figure 2) and a videodisc juke box to archive and retrieve video materials. Digital video servers will be used in the next phase of the project.

Besides providing the capability to interactively view archived video materials, the IMDS system can make available several live broadcast television channels. Students may view a distance learning channel originating live from other educational institutions in Indiana or down-linked via satellite.

The chancellor's State of the Campus address, for instance, was broadcast live on the IMDS network on December 7, 1995. Students, while surfing the Web, could watch the chancellor speak, live, in a window on their computer monitor.

Selected commercial educational channels are also available online including CNN, CSPAN, SCOLA, CBNC, PBS and the like (http://www-lib.iupui.edu/cgi-bin/mmCTV.pl).

■ Application: The Multimedia Paper

The second, and most interesting application of the IMDS is multimedia authoring — the multimedia "paper."

IMDS provides a very simple-to-use environment to write papers and reports in multimedia format: a paper that includes sound

Figure 1: IMDS Provides Access to Full-Motion Video Resources on Macs and PCs

and motion picture. This could be accomplished by running a word processor while a video or television channel is being viewed on the same computer monitor using the IMDS.

For instance, if a student would like to write a term paper, he/she may run a word processor of choice such as Microsoft Word or WordPerfect by clicking on the application's icon shown on the IMDS Control Panel. This places on his/her computer screen both the IMDS player software's window and the word processor window (as shown in Figure 3). Then one simply copies and pastes the movie clips or pictures being viewed in the IMDS window into the word processor window. This is accomplished by clicking on the multimedia Authoring icons in the IMDS Control Panel before clicking on the Paste icon or using the Insert option of the word processor program.

Shown back in Figure 1, the camera and camcorder icons in the VCR Control Panel digitize and copy images and video clips respectively. Each time the user attempts to copy an image or video clip, a copyright warning message pops up on the screen alerting them to possible copyright infringement.

Figure 2: Robotic Videotape Mgt. System Offers Fast, Automated Access to Hundreds of Titles

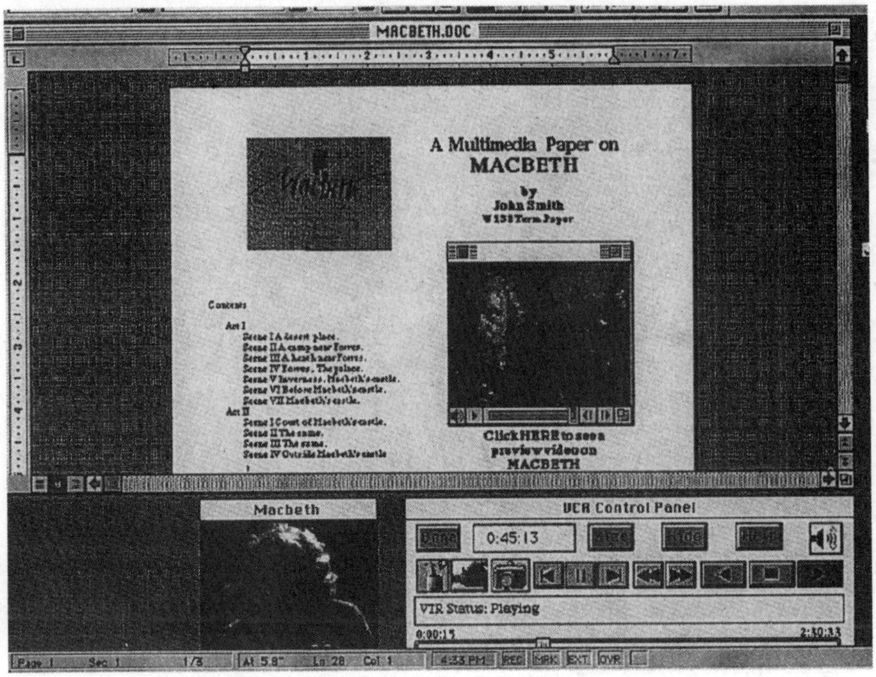

5. MULTIMEDIA

After the paper is written and images or video clips are copied, the multimedia paper may be saved into a personal disk space facility called BookBag (http://www-lib.iupui.edu/toolbox/apps/book-bag.1). The multimedia paper may then be retrieved for further editing, presented in the classroom or delivered to the instructor via the Internet and a file transfer program.

While the IMDS system is very new and unknown to many on the IUPUI campus, some faculty members have already requested that students prepare their term papers in multimedia format using the IMDS and the BookBag resources.

Figure 3: Cut & Paste Video Clips Into Scholarly Papers

■ Application: Advanced Multimedia

The third type of IMDS application is for advanced multimedia applications. The IMDS utilizes a series of powerful and well-defined communication protocols to search, retrieve and control media over the Internet.

Using the IMDS' communication protocol, faculty and students can produce advanced multimedia presentations or instructional packages by using off-the-shelf multimedia authoring software like ToolBook, Director or even HTML language

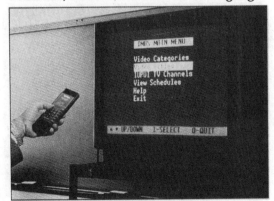

Figure 4: Low-Cost TV Monitors & IR Remotes Can Receive and Control Video Resources

to produce presentations or home pages that include online interactive full-motion video.

This advanced feature of IMDS enables both production and playback of multimedia packages that, in turn, can automatically launch a variety of multimedia resources simply by clicking on a word.

■ Application: Special Classroom Needs

In addition to Mac and PC computers, television receivers can also be used to supply video-on-demand applications to classrooms (see Figure 4). This provides a cost-effective method of distributing video around campus, especially to those rooms where a computer or computer projection system may not be available. The user interface for television configuration is the familiar infrared remote control, supplying easy interactive control capability from any location in the classroom.

Operating the television interface is simple, easily learned in less than five minutes. Press the power button on the remote control to power the TV set and the IMDS Modem, then select a service from a menu screen, and finally, select an archived video or a live education TV channel.

This three-step operation offers an easy-to-use environment while providing many advanced interactive control features, including searching to a specific location on a video in addition to basic play, pause and frame advance. And to place a video title on reserve for future playback, both computers and television receiver systems' onscreen menus may be used.

■ IMDS System Design

Primary design objectives were to architect a system that is easy to use, highly reliable and an extremely useful tool to support teaching, learning and research functions at the university.

From an architectural point of view, the system was designed to adapt easily to emerging digital technologies as they become available. From an application point of view, it was assumed that users would not have more than five minutes to learn how to run the system and thus it should be very easy to use. From an operational point of view, the IMDS was designed as a fully automated online system with 24-hours availability and to be easy to maintain.

IMDS design began with a conceptual design, followed by system design, schematic design, research and development, software engineering, technology specification, and final review and correction of its system architecture.

A conventional design model was used to design the IMDS system, whereby a single "system architect" or a "design engineer" was responsible and accountable for design of the entire system, rather than a school committee or several independent groups or technology vendors. The system architect, therefore, developed and maintained the vision of the system and identified and delegated sub-problems and sub-system design to members of the design team.

Design was based on a set of functional and technical requirements that resulted from a series of brainstorming discussions with groups of faculty, students and staff. One system requirement, defended by the Executive Vice Chancellor and Dean of Faculties, simply suggested that the system should "work." In order to design such a "working" system, the project architect defined the overall system requirement as being easy-to-use, highly reliable and supporting useful applications to facilitate teaching, learning and research.

The main difference between our IMDS system and other, similar merging systems on the market is the fact that IMDS was fully conceptualized, designed and developed *by* educators *for* educators, and its designers fully understood the applications, the technology and the future direction of information systems.

IMDS is not just a new technology gadget to show off technology's wonders; it was designed to "work" as a multimedia tool for better and easier learning, teaching and research.

■ Four Parts to IMDS

The design of the IMDS system consists of four main parts: client workstation and the user interface, the distributed multime-

> It was assumed that users would not have more than five minutes to learn how to run the system.

dia controller system, the media storage and playback system, and multimedia networks. The design and architecture of each of these components are discussed below.

Client Workstation & User Interface

The current IMDS software development provides full support for both Macintosh and PC platforms, in addition to future client applications development for Sun or other high-end workstations. For the computer platform, a graphical user interface facilitates human-computer interaction. A mouse was the primary communication interface to the computer. For television receivers in classrooms, a wireless remote control was the primary communication link to the IMDS system.

Distributed Multimedia Controller System

The Distributed Multimedia Controller System (DMCS) is the brain of IMDS, playing the major role in the system's functionality, reliability, ease-of-use and flexibility.

Totally designed and developed at IUPUI, major design features of DMCS includes modularity, client-server architecture, NetWare NLM, off-the-shelf components, intensive computing and control power, and more. DMCS was designed to support the next phases of IMDS development and emerging technological advances in multimedia, distance education, Internet, and digital storage, retrieval and distribution.

Media Storage & Retrieval

Libraries hold video materials that are, for the most part, in VHS format. The IMDS project uses two TiltRac robotics videotape management systems to automatically load tapes and electronically circulate video in the library and around the campus, making it possible to view tapes on televisions or computer workstations.

A videodisc jukebox provides random selection of video programs from among 72 archived videodiscs. The next phase of the IMDS will include digital video servers that will hold video materials not restricted by copyright limitations.

There are two methods of archiving video information: analog, such as videotapes and videodiscs; and digital, such as compressed video on a video server.

While digital format offers unique characteristics, its major limitations include concerns about the copyright and legal issues of converting existing video materials into digital format. Digital storage of video was seriously considered for the first phase of the IMDS project, but because of copyright concerns, cost and lack of established standards, the digital archive solution was not used for this phase.

Instead, the popular VHS/S-VHS tape format and eight-inch videodisc were selected as primary formats for phase one of the IMDS project.

Multimedia Distribution Networks

Intensive analysis and study were conducted during the IMDS design to choose the best networking solution to distribute video across the campus.

After considering the available and established networks on campus, a combination of three were used for the project. This includes the available star configuration of the fiber optic network in the University Library building, the campus-wide bus topology broadband cable network and IUPUI's local Ethernet network. This combination offered cost-effective and reliable high-quality video distribution all over the campus.

At the University Library, fiber optics connected computer workstations to a central video switch. The Ethernet data network provided two-way interactive control to the media players. A sub-split cable network was used to deliver video and redundant control data across the 285 acres of campus. The coax network currently provides 16 simultaneous users with media playback, in addition to 24 TV and teleconferencing channels over a single coax cable.

The IMDS hardware system is centrally located within the server room at the new IUPUI electronic library.

■ IMDS Usability Study

To improve the overall ease of use and functionality of the IMDS, a usability study was conducted in the summer and fall of 1995. In addition to casual observations and interviews with IMDS users, a selected sample of students, faculty and staff evaluated the IMDS system.

> Already, new R&D projects for the system have been identified.

Main purposes of this study were twofold: (1) to test the user's perception of the media control interface and determine the ease of use of the system and, (2) to specifically test the user's perception and ease of use for the system's Copy and Paste functions in producing a multimedia paper. Results of this study helped to further improve the ease-of-use and functionality of the IMDS. Results of the IMDS usability study will be published in an appropriate scholarly journal in the future.

■ On the Horizon

The current IMDS system was deployed in August of 1995, providing a hardware and software infrastructure to support future campus initiatives in multimedia information technologies.

Already, new R&D projects for the system have been identified. These include remote workstations for faculty offices and student dormitories, interactive videoconferencing via computer, digital video servers to support simultaneous playback of a single video file, distribution of archive video to homes and other campuses using ISDN and ATM networks, and interactive online audio distribution via Internet. These projects are currently in different stages of development. For instance, a test page to demonstrate online audio distribution is on the Internet — http://www.infolab.iupui.edu/imds/audio/audio.html.

Ali Jafari *was the system architect and project leader of the IUPUI Interactive Multimedia Distribution System (IMDS) Project. He is Director of Research and Development and an Associate Professor of Computer Technology at Indiana University Purdue University Indianapolis (IUPUI).* E-mail: jafari@iupui.edu

For more on IUPUI technology planning & projects, contact Dr. Garland C. Elmore, Associate Vice Chancellor for Information Technologies. E-mail: gelmore@iupui.edu

Products & companies mentioned:
ToolBook; Asymetrix Corp., Bellevue, WA, (800) 448-6543
Director; Macromedia, San Francisco, CA, (800) 945-9085
Robotic videotape management system; TiltRac, Inc., Carrollton, TX, (214) 980-6991

Multimedia and Cultural Diversity

DR. MARIA A. PACINO, Associate Professor
Azusa Pacific University
Azusa, Calif.
and JOE L. PACINO, Multimedia Producer
Rancho Santiago Community College
Santa Ana, Calif.

In the next century, a large portion of the United States population will be primarily of Latino and Asian background. This is already the case in many Southern Californian communities. In this environment, responsible educators continue to search for teaching strategies and resources that promote acceptance of cultural diversity and reflect the learning styles of this student population.

New Strategies

At Azusa Pacific University, all education students must enroll in a course on cultural awareness — Diversity in the Classroom. In this course, students identify cultural barriers in terms of socioeconomic status, ethnicity, language, religion and gender differences. They also examine societal issues that impact the classroom, such as racism, prejudice and discrimination. Through reflective thinking and problem solving, students begin to develop strategies for effective multicultural instruction in a pluralistic democracy.

In a similar course — Administration of

> **Students could react openly to dramatized issues and then express personal views.**

Education in a Multicultural Environment — school administrators study ways of designing, implementing and evaluating effective multicultural programs in their school districts.

In courses like these, students often find it difficult to express their feelings and attitudes about those who are culturally different. One of the most effective ways of encouraging student involvement and participation is through experiential activities, such as role playing and simulation. Case studies are often used and become much more effective through interactive media's visual dramatization.

Interactive Media's Role

While searching for a methodology that encourages active learning, I discovered a convincing argument in favor of interactive media.[1]

"Interactive video can provide a medium for observation and, more importantly, it can provide an environment for reflection. Reflection, however, is an inherently social process. It implies a debate of different viewpoints, a challenge to currently held beliefs, and an emotional commitment to resulting conclusions. While all of this can be accomplished by an individual alone, it is more innovative and motivating when alternative viewpoints are provided by others, when others challenge one's current beliefs, and when the commitment to resulting conclusions is expressed in the presence of other people…"

This statement prompted my decision to create a multimedia project (videodisc and CD-ROM versions) that could be utilized by individuals in independent study, but also in a group setting where students could react openly to dramatized issues and then express personal views.

This collaborative project, involved many people: myself, as the faculty expert; a media producer/director and television crew; computer programmers; an instructional designer; graphics artists and student actors.

The videodisc we developed is called Intercultural Communication; the CD-ROM's title is Exploring Cultural Diversity. Both were done at, and copyrighted by, Ball State University.

■ A Courseware Project Is Born

The menu-driven computer program for the titles includes intercultural barriers, cultural variables, universals of culture, a chart of comparative cultural assumptions, a glossary of intercultural/multicultural terminology and other concepts. A prototype lesson plan and reflective questions were designed to engage participants in analysis and discussion after viewing filmclips and scenarios.

Filmclips provide several examples of intercultural interaction, as well as stereotypical portrayals of African-American, Asian, European and Hispanic/Latino cultures. These cultural groups were chosen because they are representative of cultural pluralism in the United States.

In one filmclip, for example, students are asked to identify stereotypes and to explain the historical antecedents of involuntary immigration of African-Americans. Another clip depicts ethnocentric attitudes when an Irishman resents that his daughter is in love with a Chinese man. European hierarchy and class structure are depicted in a scene from the film *Grand Illusion*.

> The experience guides students through essential steps of critical thinking and metacognition.

Specific questions accompany these filmclips. The feature films on public domain were transferred from 16mm to video, then to a videodisc, and finally, to CD-ROM.

Ten videotaped scenarios dealing with intercultural incidents present examples of concepts, like kinesics or proxemics, as well as simulated intercultural conflict. In one, an Italian-American overwhelms his American friend by invading his spatial boundary; slowly, the American male is pushed out of the frame. One portraying two females, one Arab and one American, addresses the role of women in society, as perceived in two different cultures. In another, a Latino student is humiliated when his teacher forbids him from speaking Spanish in class.

■ How the Courseware Works

Specific questions for the scenarios present problematic situations for the user and offer alternative responses. Students are expected to give the most appropriate answer and to reflect upon the choice made. When the improper answer is given, learners are asked to try again by reviewing the clip or scenario and making another selection.

Using the interactive mode of instruction, students assume greater responsibility in the learning process. The instructor becomes more of a facilitator helping learners sort through the information given. Abstract concepts become more meaningful when learners can see realistic applications. Soon, students feel more comfortable in sharing their own intercultural experiences and reactions, thus making the classroom a democratic microcosm of the larger society.

During these experiential sessions, students become engaged in healthy debates regarding the incidents portrayed and the possible answers given. Participants "argue" or rationalize through the problem presented in an attempt to find an appropriate resolution. Regardless of whether or not a solution is achieved, the experience guides students through essential steps of critical thinking and metacognition — the ability to critique and evaluate one's own reflective processes.

■ Colleagues' Critique

While presenting this project at a conference on critical thinking at Sonoma State University in California, an audience of international educators engaged in an in-depth analysis of the case studies and critiqued the various answers/conclusions reached. The session was animated and elicited many personal experiences revealing similarities and contrasts in various cultures.

The group, therefore, related what they saw to their own personal experiences, which led to self-reflection and understanding of cross-cultural issues. This cooperative session also reinforced the fact that teaching and learning are more effective when using a multiple-perspective approach to problem solving.

The multimedia, computer-based pedagogical framework of this project on cultural diversity conforms to the educational needs of our technology-oriented society. It enhances interactive communication among students and instructor, as well as provides opportunities for discovery learning.

Culturally different students are given a comfort zone in which to engage in cooperative learning, a road to self-discovery, acceptance of cultural pluralism, and reflective critical thinking.

Maria A. Pacino, *is an Associate Professor of Education at Azusa Pacific University in Azusa, California. She teaches cultural diversity to pre-service teachers and practicing teachers and administrators. E-mail:mpacino.apu.edu*

Joe Pacino *is an Instructional Media Producer at Rancho Santiago College in Santa Ana, California. He develops multimedia programs for higher education.*

The project -- a laserdisc, "Intercultural Communication" and CD-ROM, "Exploring Cultural Diversity" -- was developed when the authors taught at Ball State University (which owns the copyright) in Muncie, Indiana. Maria provided the multicultural content, while Joe created and programmed the CD-ROM.

References:
1. Hanson, Edmund (Sept. 1990), "The Role of Interactive Video in Education: Case Study and a Proposed Framework," *Educational Technology*, pp. 13-20.

Strengthening the Visual Element in Visual Media Materials

by R. Dwight Wilhelm

Want an eye-opening experience? Try watching a television program or an audiovisual presentation *without* the sound. How much information do you receive from the visual element alone? Often it is very little and/or confusing by itself.

It may seem like stating the obvious to say that television is predominantly a visual medium. Yet much of what appears on the screen is still radio with pictures. We could make the same observation about other materials which combine sound and images. So often on television and in audiovisual presentations, the visual element alone does not provide very clear communication. On other occasions, the narration is saying one thing while the screen is "saying" something different, thereby producing a conflicting message. In both situations, we lose the powerful potential of visual communication. It seems as if those who create visual material still rely strongly on words to which they then add some pictures. How many times have *you* written a script before giving serious thought to the visuals?

One Central Topic

How then can we more fully exploit this potentially powerful visual element in video and audiovisual material? The first step is the identification of one — and only one — central topic. In doing this, we more nearly guarantee a sharply-focused program content.

R. Dwight Wilhelm is Professor of Telecommunications at Ball State University in Muncie, Indiana.

In practice, however, we want to cover several related topics in a single production. While this may save a few dollars, it does so at the cost of effective communication. A production well focused on only one topic communicates much more effectively than a production which is de-focused because it tries to deal with a number of topics.

After having identified a central topic, write it down in one short, concise sentence. "The purpose of this production is to *show*. . ." The key word here is "show," because you are working in a visual medium, and your principal tools are images. (Synonyms such as "illustrate," "demonstrate," "display," etc., may be substituted for "show.") The written central topic will serve as a point of reference to keep you on track throughout the production. Each part must have a *direct* relation to the central topic. If not, it doesn't belong in this production.

Visual Development

You are now ready to begin development of the content—but not with words. Think in terms of a series of sequentially-related images developed in a logical manner. If upon seeing the completed visual development, a person is not able to glean your general message, you have not achieved a logical, coherent visual development. A production which has a clear visual development is one from which a deaf person could glean the general message.

From *TechTrends*, April/May 1996, pp. 24-25. Reprinted with permission from the Association for Educational Communications and Technology, Washington, DC.

Breaking our tendency to think in words alone is not easy. Much of our formal education is directed at developing a progressively more abstract style of thinking. What a fertile imagination children have, full of images! But by the time they graduate from high school, most of that imagination and the ability to think in images is lost. Therefore, you may have to re-orient your manner of thinking. Some people find it useful to close their eyes and try to project the material as a progression of images on the "screen of their mind."

The temptation to revert to the verbal is constantly present. So you may have to continually remind yourself that the reason for having chosen a visual medium was in order to be able to *show* something rather than just talk about it. If words alone were sufficient, you should have chosen an audio recording or the printed page.

After having visually developed your material, the next step is to formalize this process by preparing a storyboard. At this stage, you are interested only in the empty frames, not the corresponding spaces for writing the text. For if you have properly followed our development plan, you haven't even begun to write the script. In the empty frames, sketch each basic camera shot, showing the visual composition desired, the angle from which it is to be taken, and any other factors.

Why bother with a storyboard? One important reason is that it is another way of assuring a *visual* development of the material. You can see concretely the sequential progression you have thus far only imagined. And in so doing, you verify that there is genuine visual communication rather than just a series of images which have little or no logical progression.

There is another important, very practical reason. Many times, the persons planning the material are not the same persons who will be doing the shooting. Therefore, in order to ensure that the images shot are as near as possible to those desired, the camera operator needs something more precise than just a verbal description of what is expected. This can also be an excellent time saver. Getting the right shots the first time eliminates the need to return to the location site to re-shoot.

Before moving ahead, a valuable test of your work thus far would be to show your proposed visual development individually to several persons completely unacquainted with the production. Ask them, "What is the central message of the material?" If they have gleaned the general idea, you have communicated visually and are ready to move ahead. Otherwise, you still have more visual thinking to do before continuing.

The Text

You are now ready to begin writing the script. And you may be surprised how a good visual development can greatly reduce the number of words needed. Just remember that the purpose of the script is not to explain what appears on the screen. A good picture speaks for itself. Neither should the script introduce information which is foreign to the visual treatment or does not relate to the central theme. And certainly, the script should never be talking about something other than what is appearing on the screen.

The script supports the visual material. Words accent and emphasize. But they always play a *supportive* role to the image, enhancing and complementing the communication.

In well-planned visual material, not only are words less necessary, many times they are undesirable. If good visual communication is present, words can distract. If good visual communication is *not* present, no amount of verbiage will create it. Furthermore, periods of silence allow for reflection, thinking, and absorption of information.

Once in a great while, someone creates a good television spot which utilizes very few, if any, spoken words. Usually it is very effective. Why? Most of the time it is because the power of the visual communication has been totally exploited in hitting the target with the message. Therefore, words are superfluous.

Compared with hearing, we receive more than double the amount of information through sight. Therefore, when we produce visual material, if we fail to exploit the image to its fullest potential we lose much of the impact of this powerful medium. The result is much less effective communication.

Special Issues

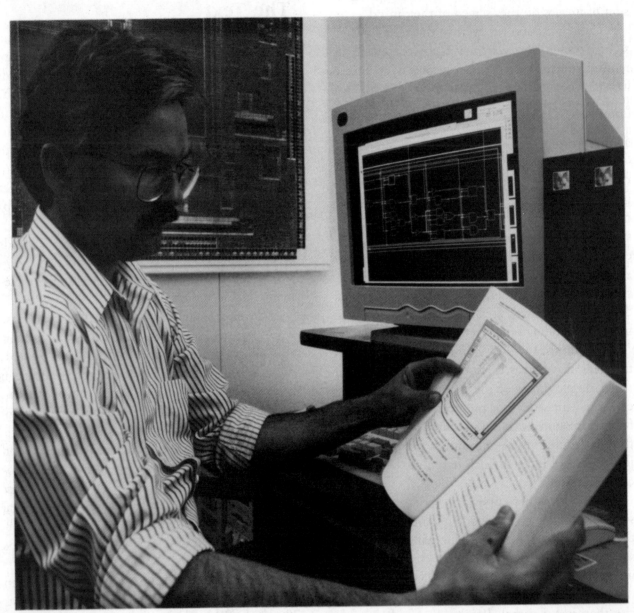

Some of the problems with integrating technology into education are receding due to the spread of technology in our society. During the years 1995 and 1996, the computer moved into the classroom as a mainstream teaching tool. More than 51 percent of college and university professors claim to use the computer as part of their instructional activities. In addition, the use of the computer has become widespread enough to become a basic need similar to automobiles, telephones, and television. In schools, during the year 1994, there was one computer for every 12 students. Now, in 1997, there is one computer for every six students. Today, educators show excited interest in interactive computer-based multimedia applications and the World Wide Web. The computer has become a reference and communication vehicle for the majority of teachers and students. We are raising the level of instruction from skill-based and procedure-oriented to inquiry-based and decision-oriented through the use of teacher/technology-centered learning teams who use the communication and reference tools of the Internet along with multimedia simulated lab and field study modules to spark interest, improve performance, and change attitudes.

The wave of interest in network-based technologies that include communications, reference, and learning tools is rising and is placing a great deal of pressure on the educational software development community to produce high-quality, high-learning-level, student-driven instructional titles that protect privacy as well as copyrights. Large and powerful forces in the publishing/entertainment industry (ABC, Disney, Time Warner, Turner Broadcast Corporation) are building huge, vertically integrated organizations. The big players sense a business opportunity in network-based, interactive digital titles. They anticipate that they can produce products that meet the bright and glittery promises that have heightened the expectations of educators and the public. They believe that they can produce products that will engage and sustain the interest of educators. They also believe that they have a powerful distribution channel in the World Wide Web.

Although the immediate future looks very bright, questions remain. Administrators are concerned with how to measure the productivity factor that technology-based education may provide. Policymakers wonder how to get educators to form consortiums so they can access joint educational facilities and thus increase the usage of the facilities while decreasing the per unit cost of delivery. Teachers wonder how technology can best be used with existing educational programs in a distance learning format. And the public is concerned with the level of the return on investment that will be realized from the new technologies in the home and classroom.

The articles in this unit shed some light on the promises and the areas of concern. In the first report, "Factors Facilitating Teachers' Use of Computer Technology," Warren Hope discusses the problems of implementing technology with teachers who are disinclined to use technology in the classroom.

Next, Steven Gilbert cites 1995 as being the year in which educational uses of information technology began passing from the "early adopters" to the "mainstream faculty" in many colleges and universities. Gilbert believes that "electronic mail and the World Wide Web are bring-ing computing into instruction in the way word processing brought computing into personal use for students and faculty in the 1980s." Then, "The Coming Ubiquity of Information Technology," by Kenneth Green, points out that information technology has finally emerged as a permanent, respected, and increasingly essential component of the college experience. He reports major gains in the proportion of college courses and college faculty using information technology.

In the following article, Paul Starr discusses how the computer revolution of earlier decades has now turned into a communications revolution and opened up important new possibilities for learning. He believes that the entire world of communication and knowledge is being transformed and that education is being assimilated with that transformation. It is clear to Starr that, because of all they make possible, computers must be part of education.

In "Mad Rushes into The Future: The Overselling of Educational Technology," Douglas Noble claims that getting schools to leap onto the Information Highway is just the latest in a series of corporate forays marked by ignorance, self-interest, and marketing madness. He believes that there is a need for cautious planning and teacher training so that education does not become a servant of technology. In the last article, "A Response to Douglas Noble: We're in This Together," David Dwyer responds to Nobel's sharp critique of the emerging instructional technology market. He claims technology adds value to schools when it is an integral part of a comprehensive plan for instructional improvement and when teachers are adequately prepared to use it as one more tool in their arsenal.

Looking Ahead: Challenge Questions

What is the business world's case for providing new ways to learn in today's homes and schools?

What economic factors are causing school administrators and school boards to continually add interactive instructional computing into the nation's classrooms?

Describe how a "technology-enhanced learning environment" could stimulate classroom activity.

What would you say is the key to understanding the effects of graphic aids in electronic texts? Why?

Do you agree that edutainment interactive software programs are high-tech learning tools? Defend your answer.

Factors Facilitating Teachers' Use of Computer Technology

WARREN C. HOPE

Computer technology, many educators believe, represents the solution to a plethora of problems. It promises teachers new ways of accomplishing tasks and of teaching the skills that students need to learn (Kearsley, Hunter, and Furlong 1992). Yet, computer technology has not reached its potential in schools (Senese 1984; Hannifin, Dalton, and Hooper 1987), largely because many of America's teachers are reluctant to make the move from traditional teaching methods to teaching with computers. Principals of schools with teachers who are disinclined to use computers are confronted with a dilemma: whether to impose the use of computers on the teachers or let the teachers decide when to make that shift. The following comments by teachers, overheard in a school's technology committee meeting, illustrate the dilemma:

> You can't leave it to teachers to decide whether or not to use computer technology. . . . I know you're saying teachers always have something thrown at them, but some things you throw at them because they never change. (Hope 1994, 74)

> You can't throw computers down their throats because certain teachers would just have it in the room collecting dust. (Hope 1995, 74)

To impose computer technology on teachers is to create an environment that is not conducive to learning (Gillman 1989). As Willis (1993) and Giannelli (1985) have pointed out, putting pressure on teachers to use computer technology does not correspond positively with use over time and with successful technology projects; teachers who already fear computers may become even more reluctant to use the technology if it is imposed on them. On the other hand, to leave the decision up to teachers is to invite procrastination or, worse, the failure to be involved at all with computers.

Resolution of the dilemma for a school principal lies in recognizing teachers' points of view regarding computer technology and identifying with their feelings about it. The

Warren C. Hope is an assistant professor of middle grades education at Georgia Southwestern College in Americus, Georgia.

literature about computer technology and teachers reveals five factors that, if addressed, will make teachers more likely to adopt computer technology.

Ease of implementation. There are dozens of configurations that computer technology can take—many more than a teacher can master. Configurations relating to teachers' productivity include word processing, computer-managed instruction, and use of databases, spreadsheets, and e-mail. Academic uses include computer-assisted instruction, media integration, simulations, and distance learning. It is not realistic to expect teachers to use all of these configurations. Rather, teachers will embrace computer technology when its configuration is not overly complex (Bauchner et al. 1982) and when they understand clearly what they are to accomplish with the technology (Hope 1995).

Access to computer technology. It is frustrating to be expected to accomplish tasks using computer technology but not to have access to components of the configuration. Teachers' access to the technology is essential for them to become users (Sheingold and Hadley 1990).

Collaboration. Collaborative work among teachers in which they share their expertise about computer technology has a positive impact on their acceptance of computers (Hope 1995). Camaraderie, enthusiasm, and support are all benefits of such collaboration (Sandholtz and Ringstaff 1993). Teachers thereby acquire skills in a nonthreatening environment, and they become a motivating force for other teachers.

Training. Training is a key to teachers' adopting computer technology (Stakenas, Tishken, and Resnick 1992). Teachers themselves realize that training is vital, and they generally expect that school leaders will give them opportunities to practice with new technology. In fact, without sufficient learning engagements, teachers are unlikely to acquire skills to use computer technology as a productivity tool or integrate it in their teaching methods (Thomas and Knezek 1991).

Sufficient time. Teachers introduced to computer technology

From *The Clearing House*, November/December 1996, pp. 106-107. Reprinted with permission of the Helen Dwight Reid Educational Foundation. Published by Heldref Publications, 1319 Eighteenth Street, NW, Washington, DC 20036-1802. © 1996.

recognize immediately the need for significant time to learn and plan its use in the classroom (Fulton 1989). Combining the power of the computer with the intelligence of software to produce desired results does not happen overnight.

It is prudent neither to leave it to teachers to make the decision about using computer technology nor to force them to use it. However, when the factors listed here are present in a school, the likelihood of teachers becoming users of computer technology increases.

REFERENCES

Bauchner, J., J. Eiseman, P. Cox, and W. Schmidt. 1982. *People, policies, and practice: Examining the chain of school improvement*. Volume 3, Models of Change. A Study of Dissemination Efforts Supporting School Improvement. Andover, Mass.: The Network, Inc.

Fulton, K. 1989. Technology training for teachers: A federal perspective. *Educational Technology* 29(3): 12-17.

Giannelli, G. 1985. Promoting computer use in the classroom: The teacher is always the last to know. *Educational Technology* 25(4): 30-31.

Gillman, T. 1989. *Change in public education: A technological perspective*. Trends & issues. (Report No. ISBN 0 86552 0976). Eugene, Ore.: University of Oregon. ERIC Document Reproduction Service No. ED 302 940.

Hannafin, M. H., D. W. Dalton, and S. Hooper. 1987. Computers in education: Ten myths and ten needs. *Educational Technology* 27(2): 8-14.

Hope, W. C. 1995. Microcomputer technology: Its impact on teachers in an elementary school. Ed.D. diss., Florida State University.

Kearsley, G., B. Hunter, and M. Furlong. 1992. *We teach technology: New visions for education*. Wilsonville, Ore.: Franklin, Beedle and Associates.

Sandholtz, J., and C. Ringstaff. 1993. Computers and colleagues. *Apple Education Review* (2). Cupertino, Calif.: Apple Computer.

Senese, D. J. 1984. *Instructional technology: Realizing the potential*. Logan, Utah: Seminar of the Association for Educational Communications and Technology. ERIC Document Reproduction Services NO. ED 298 879.

Sheingold, K., and M. Hadley. 1990. *Accomplished teachers: Integrating computers into classroom practice*. New York: Center for Technology in Education. Bank Street College of Education.

Stakenas, R., D. Tishkin, and M. Resnick. 1992. *Best practices in developing teachers' knowledge and skills in using instructional technology*. Tallahassee, Fla.: Center for Policy Studies in Education, Florida State University.

Thomas, L., and D. Knezek. 1991. Providing technology leadership for restructured schools. *Journal of Research on Computing in Education* 24(2): 265-79.

Willis, J. 1993. What conditions encourage technology use? It depends on the context. *Computers in Schools* 9(4): 13-34.

MAKING THE MOST *of a* SLOW REVOLUTION

By Steven W. Gilbert

Education *can provide the excuse and the means for transforming* ***society****...for better or worse.*

Information technology *can provide the excuse and the means for transforming* ***education****...for better or worse.*

For more than 25 years, I've been involved with information technology and education. During most of that time, I (and many of my colleagues) have believed that "the next 18 to 24 months" would bring revolutionary change in how people teach and learn, through the use of technology or otherwise. Yet we're still waiting for those widespread, dramatic improvements; and we're also still waiting for research results that definitively prove the educational merit of applications of these new technologies. Meanwhile, we have observed a gradual—perhaps accelerating—process in which individual faculty members find, try, discard, rediscover, adopt, adapt, and use applications of information technology to improve teaching and learning. Commitment to change based on accumulated experience is outpacing the availability of conclusive research results.

During each week this past fall, I visited a couple of different campuses, making presentations, consulting, asking ques-

Steven W. Gilbert is Director, Technology Projects, at the American Association for Higher Education.

tions, and listening. I also run AAHESGIT, an Internet online discussion group of more than 3,800 "subscribers" on topics related to teaching, learning, and information technology. What I've seen and heard from these sources suggests that 1995 was the year in which educational uses of information technology began passing from the "early adopters" to the "mainstream faculty" in many colleges and universities, and that for higher education in the 1990s, electronic mail and the World Wide Web are bringing computing into instruction in the way that word processing brought computing into personal use for students and faculty in the 1980s.

Typical *first* educational uses of computer-related technology by mainstream faculty members include the following:

- using a computer-driven projection device as a more powerful version of an overhead projector;
- learning from a colleague how to use a specific application of information technology to teach a specific topic in a specific course better than was possible otherwise;
- almost casually introducing electronic mail into a course as a slight enhancement to student-teacher communication; or
- being invited to teach a course via video telecommunications to a group of students who cannot conveniently attend classes on the main campus.

Evidence is growing that these steps can improve teaching and learning of some topics in some courses with "acceptable"

From *Change*, March/April 1996, pp. 10-23. Reprinted with permission of the Helen Dwight Reid Educational Foundation. Published by Heldref Publications, 1319 Eighteenth Street, NW, Washington, DC 20036-1802. © 1996.

OBSTACLES TO IMPROVING TEACHING AND LEARNING WITH INFORMATION TECHNOLOGY

1. Limited and Uneven Access to Equipment, Software, and Support Services.

Only institutions and student bodies making the greatest investments in direct, comfortable access to information technology can be sure that all who need to use equipment and information resources to improve teaching and learning will be able to do so. Part-time students and faculty usually are the least able to afford the time and money for access to technology. Institutions serving the greatest numbers of poor students tend to be the least able to afford publicly accessible information technology resources—and their students are the least able to take advantage of such options. Faculty who undertake new instructional uses of information technology are likely to be quite disappointed if many of their students have limited access to and experience in using the relevant equipment and media.

2. Fragmented Institutional Planning: Thinking Institutional Plans Can Focus on Technology *Instead of* Teaching/Learning.

Most colleges and universities have one or more groups assigned to some task associated with planning the institution's future with respect to the use of information technology—perhaps even giving some attention to the improvement of teaching and learning. Most often, each group focuses on a piece of the overall picture, and there is no single forum for bringing together all those who are needed for an understanding of overall trends and for the support of major advances. Often, one of these groups is working—without much access to institutional thinking about teaching and learning—on some version of an institutional plan for the development of information technology resources. It is then likely that the technology plan will be completed and adopted without having been shaped by adequate discussion of the institution's educational mission and objectives. The risk is that the technology plan will be adopted and will then limit educational options before the institution's teaching/learning goals with respect to technology have been clearly developed—perhaps eliminating some high-priority educational alternatives along the way.

3. Fragmented Support Services.

On most campuses, there is little communication and coordination among those who provide the support services necessary to enable faculty and students to make the most effective uses of new approaches to teaching, new applications of technology, and other available resources. It is rare that librarians, technology professionals, faculty development experts, and other groups meet together and discuss how best to collaborate to help faculty and students.

4. Distrust and Poor Communication Among Board, Administrative Leadership, Faculty, Computing Professionals, and Staff.

In the absence of clear priorities and a coherent institutional plan for the educational use of information technology, faculty assume the worst. Announcements that major new investments in information technology are under consideration during a period when most departmental budgets are being cut leads faculty to ask, "Will technology be used to reduce the size of the faculty?" Lack of communication about major educational decisions and budget reallocations leads to mistrust between different staff and faculty members and undermines potential collaboration.

5. "Anybody, Anytime, Anywhere": A Misleading Educational Banner.

It is both highly desirable and increasingly plausible that information resources will become more widely and fully accessible via the Internet; however, that accessibility is a necessary—but *not* a sufficient—condition for effective education. Education that is available to anybody, anytime, anywhere may be education that focuses too tightly on access to information and on individual students' narrow self-interest. If "education" is available anytime to any person who wants it, it is unlikely a common group meeting will emerge from uncoordinated, individual time/place preferences. The power and attraction of live participation in a group may be overlooked.

6. Underestimating the Difficulty of Faculty Adoption of New Combinations.

When faculty are asked to adopt new teaching combinations involving technology, they are being asked a lot. Most faculty members are busy people who have never observed others teach effectively using information technology. It is unrealistic to expect any human being to replace—quickly, easily, and without help—habitual behaviors based on years of observing others who have used the same old (teaching) model. When the requested new behaviors are only *described* instead of modeled, a major commitment of time and energy is needed. In addition, asking someone who has become a successful professional teacher to adopt new ways of teaching is to ask that person to return to a subordinate, insecure, learning role. The incentives and support services had better be ample.

7. Lack of Easily Available Information About "Good Practice."

For most faculty members who reach the point of wanting to consider alternative ways of teaching with information technology, there are no obvious sources of information about "good practice." For most colleges and universities, there is usually no easy way to identify other faculty members on campus who have already begun to use technology effectively in their teaching (and in their students' learning). And for most academic disciplines, there is no comprehensive, easy-to-find source of information about relevant instructional applications of information technology that also includes reliable evaluative information. While the number of locally successful models of educational uses of information technology continues to increase, access to good descriptions of those models, training for them, and reports of their strengths and weaknesses are not easy to find.

8. Difficulty of Understanding and Obtaining Legal Use of Intellectual Property.

By its very nature, the process of developing new laws is always behind the development of new technologies. In the case of potential educational uses of recent and anticipated applications of information technology, the gap is becoming significant. First, the pace of arrival of the relevant applications is faster than that of many others in the past. Second, several of them undermine some of the technical limitations on which current legislation depends. (The ease with which intellectual property in digital formats can be identically reproduced, modified, and redistributed challenges the copyright system). Third, ☞

pedagogical trends, educational needs, and technological capabilities (especially multimedia development tools and the Web browsers) are increasing both the attractiveness and feasibility of faculty and student development of multimedia materials. Obtaining the currently required legal permissions to use excerpts of readily available attractive digital material may be more costly and time-consuming than doing the creative and technical-development work.

9. Faculty Reward System.

The formal reward system's policies (tenure and promotion) in most colleges and universities today pay little attention to information technology. Most of the administrators and faculty committees responsible for implementing the policies have little understanding of how to evaluate faculty work that makes extensive use of information technology for instruction, or how to evaluate the development of new educational applications of the technology. There is no peer-review process for the development or use of educational applications of information technology. As more institutions establish policies encouraging faculty to use information technology to improve teaching and learning, it will become even more important to provide faculty members with procedures for effectively communicating and validating the impact of such work.

10. Expectations for the "Products" Are Too High, Too Soon.

After centuries—at least decades—how many excellent books and movies are produced each year? How many lousy ones? Enormous amounts of money and time, and the skills of extremely capable people are still not enough to ensure success. These efforts are too complex to succumb to any formula yet devised. We should expect an even lower success rate for complex, new products in media in which the creators and publishers have had only a few years to develop their craft. Publicity and marketing efforts make unreachable claims for the quality of educational uses of new applications of information technology in new media. The backlash of skepticism and unreceptivity toward new products is all too understandable.

11. If Everyone Is Behind, Who's Ahead?

Most people apologize for what their college or university (or department) is *not* doing with information technology. Most people in higher education feel that they are behind in educational uses of this technology. This lack of understanding of actual comparative status with peer institutions, combined with other external pressures, is more likely to lead to rash decisions or paralysis than to progress. ∾

increases in costs ("acceptable" to individual departments, faculty, and students when the full costs of computers, networks, and so on are spread widely across all the different uses that the institution can find for these technologies).

For many colleges and universities, 1995 was also the year when student and faculty use of electronic mail exploded. I haven't yet found an institution where anyone adequately predicted how fast e-mail and World Wide Web usage would grow once they became widely accessible and easy to use. (Lots of anecdotal reports and some data [see "The Coming Ubiquity of Information Technology," by Kenneth C. Green, *Change,* March/April 1996] suggest that for most other institutions, 1996 or 1997 will be the year for this explosion.)

Along with the e-mail explosion, more faculty members began offering their e-mail addresses to students and inviting them to ask course-related questions via e-mail, as well as during regular office hours. Although neither the faculty nor the students perceive this step as a marked departure from traditional practice, many faculty members report even this simple use of e-mail increases the participation from categories of students usually underrepresented in class discussions (women, minorities, speakers of English as a second language, shy

people, and others). Some faculty report that classroom participation seems to increase along with e-mail participation, and others report that students continue discussing course-related ideas via e-mail even after the course has ended.

Faculty who use e-mail to supplement their communication with students report significant increases in their own workloads, but these reports are usually offered along with expressions of pleasure and pride about the changes in learning that seem to follow, and the improved quality of education. The quality changes even further as faculty and students discover how to use the World Wide Web. And it is difficult to ignore how rapidly that medium is growing in content, availability, and use.

An old idea—distance education—is also attracting new attention as more powerful forms of telecommunications (such as two-way video, electronic mail, and the World Wide Web) make it a more attractive option. However, no form of distance education or any other *widely applicable* educational use of information technology has yet proved so much more effective and/or less expensive than "traditional" forms of teaching and learning as to become a complete replacement for them. Meanwhile, more academic leaders believe they must offer better access to higher-quality information technology to compete for students and faculty. And still other forces (economic, political, philosophical) are pushing colleges and universities toward change. The signs and symptoms of this "slow revolution" are appearing more frequently:

• Among faculty, students, academic leaders, and the general public, there is a growing recognition of the power of information technology to help improve the quality of teaching and learning, improve the motivation and attention of students, and improve students' career preparation.

• At a meeting of the Western Governor's Association in December 1995, the governors of the Western states unanimously endorsed the notion of a "virtual university" to serve the entire Western region and authorized the formation of a design team to create a plan by this June. (See Johnstone and Krauth in the March/April 1996 issue of *Change.*)

SIMPLE TESTS FOR E-MAIL AND WWW

Here is a simple test to see if your institution has "easy-to-use" electronic mail: Is it almost effortless to send through your e-mail system a copy of a document that you prepared using your favorite word-processing software? If you answered yes, you're using "good" e-mail, and your institution either has already experienced the explosion in network usage or is about to. If the answer is no, your "explosion" probably will be delayed.

A similar test for World Wide Web access: Can you usually connect on your first try? Is there usually almost no delay when waiting for the result of a "hop"? ∾

• Legislators and regents are pushing for productivity gains in higher education. For example, the Indiana legislature has been urging the state universities to prepare to serve a growing and more varied body of students, while reducing state funding and allowing only modest tuition increases.

• Faculty organizations are working not only to understand and support new technology options, but also to prevent the loss of jobs and tenure they fear may result from advancing educational uses of information technology.

• Colleges and universities—especially the wealthier ones—are extending their investments in computer- and video-related hardware. (Some of the most selective and best endowed colleges are able to afford these investments while simultaneously continuing their commitments to small classes and face-to-face discussion.)

• Nationwide from 1994 to 1995, according to Kenneth Green's data, the percentage of faculty using several key instructional applications of information technology approximately doubled; the proportion of the faculty with direct personal access to computers grew past 50 percent; and the proportion of entering freshmen who had already had some academic experience with computing was also beyond 50 percent.

• The percentage of students who refuse to buy the required textbooks (new or used) for their courses has grown rapidly in the past few years—now averaging 25 to 40 percent nationwide.

Faculty members are doing what they have always done with respect to improving teaching and learning. Some try new things, figuring out how to incorporate more permanently those that work well and telling each other about the ones that succeed. More and more faculty are using various applications of information technology to help their students through "instructional bottlenecks" in courses; that is, when faculty find new techniques that help their students master topics that have been troublesome to students in the past, they work hard to integrate the new approaches.

Faculty commitment to better learning is the basis for seeking new successes and integrating them along with the old, and faculty experience is the basis for recognizing such instructional improvements. However, in spite of the rapidity with which exciting new computer-related technology applications continue to arrive from industry, the pace of faculty adoption of the most significant changes in teaching and learning is still measured in years or decades rather than months—and depends heavily on the accessibility of equipment, "software" in various media, and support services.

Education is being transformed, but the inertia of the system is enormous, and the costs associated with widespread, "deep" integration of information technology into teaching and learning are significant. In order for institutions to make difficult choices among strategies for change in the absence of conclusive data, each college and university must get the best advice it can from those within its own community who have relevant experience, knowledge, skills, and insights about teaching, learning, and technology. Implementing the best strategies requires institution-wide collaboration involving all key stakeholders. The cumulative impact will be "revolutionary," changing how people teach and learn, and what is taught and learned.

So now I believe that the next decade—not the next 18 to 24 months—will be critical. There seems to be rapidly grow-

ore academic leaders

believe they must offer better access

to higher-quality information technology

to compete for students and faculty.

ing acceptance that the ways in which information technology is used for teaching and learning will be a significant part of this transformation. What can colleges and universities do to prepare for this slow revolution? Can we learn how to participate comfortably and effectively in it—and even to direct it?

Unfortunately, the most common institutional strategy for integrating information technology into teaching and learning is CRISIS, LURCH, CRISIS, LURCH, CRISIS, LURCH.

What follows are 12 recommendations for avoiding this pattern while improving teaching and learning through more effective use of information technology.

1. Fundamental Questions
    Keep asking fundamental questions.
2. Future Vision
    Observe trends; shape the future; build a vision.
3. Permanent Change
    Adjust to new pace and depth of change.
4. Judgment, Reductionism, Trust
    Use judgment; resist reductionism; trust faculty and students.
5. Dichotomies, Combinations
    Reject dichotomies; find good combinations.
6. Intellectual Property, Fair Use
    Understand intellectual property law; help keep "fair use."
7. Guidelines, Policies
    Develop new guidelines quickly; develop new policies slowly.
8. Support-Service Crisis
    Prepare for your support-service crisis.
9. Student Roles
    Extend student roles as assistants, learning colleagues; form Faculty Student Support Service Teams (FSSSTs) and learning communities.
10. Portfolio of Change Strategies
    Develop a portfolio of change strategies.
11. Realistic Expectations: More Time, Money
    Invest more time and money.
12. Institutionwide Collaboration
    Develop institutionwide collaboration to improve teaching and learning.

Early in 1995, someone pointed out that most of what I'd written for the Teaching, Learning, and Technology Roundtable (TLTR) Program was obvious common sense that any institution could use—without our program. That worried me for a few months, but as I visited more campuses and discovered that people appreciated hearing our ideas and receiving our guidelines, I also realized that no one was already implementing them systematically. So now I'm quite comfortable

offering these simple—perhaps obvious—recommendations.
They are the foundation on which the TLTR Guidelines, local
TLT Roundtables, and the national TLTR Program's activities
are built. Developing a local TLT Roundtable is one way—but
not the only way—of implementing several of these points.
The recommendations are not listed in order of priority, except that the first is really the first, the most important, and the
simplest.

1. FUNDAMENTAL QUESTIONS
Keep asking fundamental questions.

Through the inevitable transformation of education...

- What do you most want to gain?
  For yourself? For your institution? For your students?
- What do you most cherish and want not to lose?
- What are the remaining obstacles and how can you reduce
  them?
- Which combinations of face-to-face meetings, independent
  work, and telecommunications are best—and for what
  purposes? How can information technology help most effectively?

These questions need to be asked at least once each year for
the entire institution, for divisions within it, for departments,
and for individuals. The answers should tell whether or not
you're moving in the right direction and suggest how you may
need to correct your efforts. It is the second question that is too
often overlooked and that too many feel is not quite legitimate. People going through major changes need to be conscious of what they can be justifiably proud of from the
past—of achievements and activities that are worth extending
into the future.

I've led many groups on many campuses through these questions during the past year. When faculty members, support-service professionals, administrators, and board members respond
to these questions individually and privately, and then compare
answers, they are often surprised at how consistent the results
are across group boundaries. Concern for the needs of students
and for close relationships between faculty and students often
rise to the top of everyone's list. Faculty may be pleased to learn
that administrators do not care only about cutting costs, and administrators may be pleased to learn that faculty do not always
put their personal research and job security first.

Discovering disagreements and commonalities at this highest
conceptual level is important for effective institutional planning
and implementation. The discovery of widespread convergence
of answers to these questions can unleash and sustain energy for
achieving the goals that emerge from them. Understanding any
underlying differences can be the first step toward achieving the
working consensus needed to move forward.

With respect to the use of information technology in teaching and learning, perhaps the single most important research
question for structuring higher education in the next decade is,
"Which combinations of face-to-face meetings, independent
work, and telecommunications are best—and for what purposes?" I'm sure we will discover that different mixtures of these
three key elements will be optimal for different purposes and
contexts (such as educational missions, kinds of students, kinds
of faculty, and condition of buildings and equipment). I'm also
sure that we have barely begun to understand which dimen-

ADAPTIVE TECHNOLOGY AND DISABILITIES: EASI

Applications of informa-
tion technology are now
available that enable students and faculty—independent of most disabilities—to
participate fully in all types
of academic activities. Efforts to extend the power of
these "adaptive technolo-
gies" will also aid the cause
of matching various forms
of education to the individual needs and abilities of the
widest possible range of students and faculty members.

For more information on
educational uses of information technology for persons
with disabilities, contact
Norman Coombs, EASI
Director: (716) 475-2462 or
nrcgsh@ritvax.isc.rit.edu ✺

---

sions of face-to-face group experiences can be effectively reproduced in telecommunicated participation or recordings.

We are likely to discover that for some kinds of learning
and communications, face-to-face discussion is absolutely essential. For others, it may be more effective for most people to
learn on their own, from books or interactive CD-ROMs, for
example. But I expect we'll find that what is usually best is
some mixture of conventional instructional materials, new applications of information technologies, face-to-face conversations, independent work, telecommunications, and various
pedagogical approaches—matched against the different individual abilities and needs of students and faculty.

Colleges and universities have better resources than any
other kind of institution for doing the research that will help
identify and explain the critical factors in selecting these combinations. Few other institutions have as much to gain or lose
from the results.

2. FUTURE, VISION
Observe trends; shape the future; build a vision.

Too many people seem to focus either on media reports of
the most exciting new educational uses of technology or on reports of the most wasteful expenditures—and accept one or
the other as the norm. Too many people believe that their institution, their department, their own work is far behind "everyone else" in the use of computers. Too many people ask for
explanations of current trends in the educational uses of information technology as if they believe that the future is something that is going to happen to them, rather than something
they can influence.

Instead, it is more useful to observe what is happening in
your own institution and its peers, to find or collect some data,
and to be skeptical about any claims that a particular application of technology can "fix" much of education in a matter of
months. More importantly, learn about and understand trends
in technology and its uses with the purpose of making your
own decisions and taking actions to shape the future into
something worthwhile.

This more confident approach, however, is not enough by itself. To shape the future effectively, people need both a "vision
worth working toward" and the conviction that—with enough
leadership, commitment, and effort—it can be achieved.

Since "an institution is inseparable from its people and its
values," as the Lane Community College Future Faculty Task
Force stresses in its Fall 1995 report, any vision about the role

ny vision about the role

of technology in education should be based on

institutional mission and personal values:

technology must serve the mission and values.

∾

missed. We will be seeking ways to avoid future replication of instances in which technology has damaged valuable elements of social discourse and education. More important, we will be looking for replicable/extendible models of using information technology to advance teaching, learning, institutional missions, and widely regarded human values. Models will be analyzed and judged not only on the basis of their goals and effectiveness, but also on their feasibility and costs.

3. PERMANENT CHANGE
Adjust to new pace and depth of change.

"The operational definition of eternity is 18 months...the length of a product cycle": this quote from Harry Wilker, creative director of Broderbund Software, in a *New York Times* article last September, is typical of—and reflects the reality of—those who live in the world of the information industries. It does not, however, reflect the reality in educational institutions. It is increasingly important for higher education leaders to understand that those who live primarily in other sectors may have a very different sense of time and history—and thus to understand the growing impatience of legislators, board members, funders, students, and some faculty who see urgent societal needs for new educational applications of technology.

Reports from researchers in the information industries confirm that in the next 10 years we will see more new technologies with apparent educational potential than ever before. Who can say today whether or not virtual reality will have a great role in education? Who knows what will arrive after virtual reality? The recent restructuring of the information, entertainment, and telecommunications industries also suggests that new entities will compete in providing some forms of education traditionally offered only by colleges and universities.

But there are also signs of technological change in education. As reported above, over 50 percent of all higher education faculty in the United States now have their own computers, and over 15 percent use information technology in their teaching. The percentage of entering freshmen who have already had some academic computing experience moved above 50 percent in 1995. Students of all ages are now likely to take courses with the expectation that computer-related technology will be made available and used, and to enter college with the expectation that they will leave the institution better able to use the computer-related tools they are likely to need in their chosen careers.

But still, the best estimates reported from a wide variety of campuses are that more than 75 percent of all U.S. undergraduate education consists of traditional lectures, teachers leading

---

---

of technology in education should be based on institutional mission and personal values: technology must *serve* the mission and values. This message is essential to reassure the large number of people worried that information technology is a juggernaut about to squash them and to eliminate from education and society everything they care about most. (See box, above.)

New applications of information technology can be used either to increase the isolation of individuals and fragmentation of our society or to support new forms of collaborative work and sustain more effective communities. Technology can be used either to separate students and researchers further from original source documents and real laboratory experience, or to provide better access, practice, and preparation for more users. A "vision worth working toward" can guide an institution's efforts and increase its likelihood of moving in the positive rather than the negative directions.

To address these concerns directly, the American Association for Higher Education's TLTR Program is developing a track on "Education, Technology, and the Human Spirit" as part of the second annual TLTR Summer Institute in Phoenix in July 1996. As enthusiasm and opportunities increase for using information technology to change the core processes of education—teaching and learning—more people are afraid of losing important elements and of having cherished values dis-

EDUCATION IS ENTERING THE THIRD STAGE OF TECHNOLOGY INTEGRATION: CHANGING THE CORE FUNCTIONS—TEACHING AND LEARNING

One simple interpretation of the progression of what used to be called the "automation" of industries and organizations consists of three stages.

1. Automate Common Business Administrative Operations.

The organization identifies common administrative functions that other businesses have already "automated" and implements similar changes. For example, most colleges and universities have already adopted the practices of other organizations for doing payrolls and purchasing. These adoptions tend to be quick and relatively painless, since others have already figured out how to make the same things work well. Significant productivity gains may result, usually in being able to do old tasks with greater speed and security

and being able to provide additional information about transactions.

There is usually little distress or enthusiasm about these changes, and little impact on the core functions of the organization.

2. Enhance Current Tasks.

Individuals within the organization find applications of information technology from other fields that can easily be adapted and applied to important tasks. For example, faculty find presentation software and computer-driven projection systems to replace the use of chalkboards and overhead projectors. A full accounting of the costs for equipment, software, and training compared with the amount of teaching time saved or the relief of student strain related to reading handwritten materials will most likely show a cost-bene-

fit loss. Transitions occur within a few months.

There is usually little distress or enthusiasm about these changes, and little impact on the core functions of the organization, but small gains are observed in the quality of instruction. *And participants gain valuable preparative experience for deeper changes.*

3. Change Core Functions.

In the third stage, people realize that information technology may enable them to do new kinds of tasks. New applications that achieve objectives essential for—and perhaps unique to—a particular industry are developed. It usually takes from three to 10 years to design and implement changes to the core functions. Large gains are likely to be experienced in quality of results, speed of "production," and capabili-

ties of the organization. Organizations that are advanced in the third stage may find they are not in quite the same business as before—products and services have changed. Conventional calculations of productivity gains become almost meaningless because of the difficulty of comparing new costs and levels of outputs with old ones: too much has changed.

Strong reactions to third-stage changes are likely in education as in no other industry. Because many people believe that education has a significant impact on children's futures and other important elements of society, expectations that the availability of information technology is changing some of the fundamental core processes of education—teaching and learning—can result in strong emotional responses, both hopes and fears. ❧

classroom discussions, students reading textbooks, and so on. Although much of this instruction is good, and the envy of people worldwide, there is plenty of room for innovation. Higher education is entering the third stage of technology integration: changing the core functions—teaching and learning. Given that higher education is at the beginning of a process that takes other industries three to 10 years, and that educational institutions tend to change more slowly than others, we are unlikely to experience the conclusion of third-stage major "automation" in less than a few years, and are more likely to see a decade-long transition—after a 40-year build-up that began in the 1950s. This is truly a "slow revolution."

On the other hand, those who have been expecting that the recent deluge of technological changes will settle down so that we can get back to "business as usual" will be disappointed. No return to the former "stability" is foreseeable. Colleges and universities must develop the ability to live with the frequent arrival of new educational options and new competitive challenges. Faculty members must be supported and encouraged to stay as current with instructional materials and approaches as with research results in their fields. None of this can be accomplished simply through exhortation: equipment, time, incentives, training, and other support services are essential.

4. JUDGMENT, REDUCTIONISM, TRUST
Use judgment; resist reductionism; trust faculty and students.

Resist both the "quantitative reductionism" that denies the

significance of that which cannot be measured, and the "media reductionism" that asserts that audio and video reproductions can capture all that is essential in important human interactions.

Good judgment is what is needed for most significant decisions about allocating resources to instructional uses of information technology. Judgments must be made on the basis of the most plausible estimates available about quality and costs. Is the quality of learning notably improved, or not? Are the costs about the same? A lot more? A lot less? (See "Asking the Right Questions," by Stephen C. Ehrmann, in the March/April 1995 *Change.*) Erwin Boschmann, associate dean of faculties of Indiana University-Purdue University at Indianapolis, reports a slowly growing accumulation of evidence about certain kinds of learning that, under specific conditions, seem to be improved by the use of some applications of information technology. Jack Wilson, dean of undergraduate and continuing education at Rensselaer Polytechnic Institute, has developed a "studio" approach offering new roles for faculty and effectively integrating information technology into the teaching of introductory physics and some other subjects. The data he has collected about student achievement in the courses and about related costs show improvements in learning even by conventional measures—and overall costs held close to previous levels.

However, most decision-making about educational uses of technology cannot be precise. Although much that is important can be observed and judged, it isn't easy—and may not be neces-

<table>
<tr><td>

COLLABORATIVE LEARNING AND GROUPWARE — AN EXCITING CONVERGENCE

Collaborative learning coupled with groupware is an important combination with exciting potential. Collaborative learning is a pedagogical movement closely related to cooperative learning; both are movements slowly gaining momentum in higher education. (See the *Change* articles "Sharing Our Toys: Cooperative Versus Collaborative Learning" by Kenneth A. Bruffee in the January/February 1995 issue and "Building Bridges Between Cooperative and Collaborative Learning" by Roberta Matthews et al. in the July/August 1995 issue.) To oversimplify, these approaches offer both a theoretical basis and specific suggestions for encouraging faculty to guide students to work in small groups as a legitimate part of the learning process.

Meanwhile, based on work that began in universities, the software publishing industry, during the past decade, has begun to produce "groupware"—tools that facilitate collaborative work among groups of people though access to a set of networked computers. Lotus

</td><td>

Notes is the best-known product in this category. (Some software companies and users are now adapting World Wide Web browsers and home pages to perform rudimentary groupware functions.)

A growing number of colleges and universities are beginning to use generic groupware tools from industry (such as Lotus Notes) to support students' collaborative work (beyond the use that has grown on several hundred campuses during the past 10 years of applications designed by the Daedalus Group, W. W. Norton & Co., Inc., and the Houghton-Mifflin Co. specifically for teaching English composition collaboratively in computer-networked environments). This looks like an unusually felicitous convergence of pedagogy and technology. Early reports from campuses like New York University and the Cranfield School of Management in the United Kingdom are that groupware effectively facilitates collaborative learning—especially in cases where regular, face-to-face meetings are inconvenient. ∿

</td></tr>
</table>

sary for decision-making—to produce meaningful numbers describing all that happens in college courses. Consider: What evidence could someone provide that would make your institution abandon word processing and have everyone return to using pencil and paper or typewriters? For most, the answer is "None."

For many examples of effective teaching and learning—both old and new—we do not yet know enough to claim that capturing pictures of the teacher or recording the words exchanged reproduces all or even the most important elements of the educational experience. Our conceptual and observational tools for detecting the important differences between educational options are still crude. Student and faculty analyses of their interactions can provide useful insights.

It is also worth noticing what has really happened with "educational television" since its introduction and the initial excitement (and fear) in the 1950s. Offering a live or taped video of a lecture is—decades later—obviously neither a completely equivalent alternative to live presentations nor a worthless imitation. We are still experimenting and learning which topics,

---

*E*ffective education must be both learner-centered and teacher-centered—and so must educational uses of information technology be both learner- and teacher-centered.

∿

modes of presentation, distribution, and pricing make the most attractive alternatives to live sessions, and for which categories of learners.

Information technology is beginning to enable faculty to teach in new ways, and to enable students to engage with new content, new ways of communicating, and new ways of thinking. These changes may be difficult to quantify, but they can be observed and reported. Listen to faculty and students. Get their observations, interpretations, and conclusions. Trust them. Use your own judgment.

5. DICHOTOMIES, COMBINATIONS
Reject dichotomies, find good combinations.

Unfortunately, some advocates of new educational uses of information technology overzealously compare them with more traditional teaching approaches, claiming to offer clear-cut choices between "right" and "wrong." The implication is that we are all "good guys" if we agree and jump on the new bandwagon and "bad guys" if we don't. Thrusting dichotomies on the faculty and students reflects a lack of understanding of the time and effort required for transitions.

For example, urging a faculty member to replace the entire syllabus and all texts of a course with a new combination of a CD-ROM and access to the World Wide Web in one term is unrealistic. Similarly, some advocates of a single medium for "distance education" (for example, one-way video with two-way audio) may urge the abrupt adoption of their approach as a complete replacement for face-to-face meetings. (See the December 1995 *AAHE Bulletin*, a special issue on distance education.)

A final example of a dysfunctional dichotomy: "learner-centered versus teacher-centered" education. It is often argued—perhaps correctly—that too many colleges and universities have leaned too far toward meeting the needs and interests of the faculty in recent years. The solution, however, is *not* to lean too far toward the needs and interests of students instead. Effective education must be *both* learner-centered *and* teacher-centered—and so must educational uses of information technology be both learner- and teacher-centered. To advocate trying to meet the individual needs and capabilities of students while treating faculty as interchangeable makes no sense.

Most faculty members and educational institutions are much more likely to participate willingly and effectively in a gradual change than in making a sudden, diametrically opposite choice. When you are pressed to make such a choice (to grossly paraphrase Nancy Reagan), "Just say no to dichotomies." The obvious alternative to choosing between two extremes is to find good combinations.

Another common mistake for which combinations are the

remedy is that of advocating a specific application of information technology or trying to judge its educational value in the absence of its instructional context. We must learn to seek effective *combinations* of teaching approach, application of technology, instructional materials, facilities—to use and evaluate the *combination*, not the *application*. Two important combinations of technology and pedagogy well worth extending are instructional uses of e-mail and collaborative learning through groupware. (See box, Collaborative Learning and Groupware—An Exciting Convergence.) As more faculty and students discover more compelling combinations, the need for adequate services to support their efforts to improve teaching and learning keeps growing.

6. INTELLECTUAL PROPERTY, FAIR USE
Understand intellectual property law; help keep "fair use."

The original purpose of intellectual property law in the United States was to *promote* the development, distribution, and use of new ideas. The copyright, patent, and other systems were developed to ensure that adequate incentives went to the originators and publishers of new information to keep them motivated and financially able to continue their work.

In 1976, the copyright law was modified to include the fair use doctrine, which states that certain uses of copyrighted material are permissible without either purchasing the work or obtaining permission or a license from the copyright holder. Academic research and teaching *under certain conditions* are high on the list of "fair uses" of print material (and other types of) excerpts. One of the intended functions of the fair use doctrine is to enable teachers and researchers to use materials for their professional work when it is unlikely that doing so will significantly undermine legitimate sales and related fees. (A workable but tense truce has been achieved between the strongest advocates of free access to information [often led by librarians] and the strongest advocates of fee for access [often led by commercial publishers].)

The copyright system of rendering payment for the acquisition and use of copied material evolved, in part, as a consequence of the difficulty and expense of making a precise duplicate of any representation of information. Unfortunately for the copyright system, among the exciting capabilities of new information technologies are the ease and speed with which information represented digitally can be moved, amended, duplicated, and redistributed. Figuring out how to apply the copyright system—especially fair use—in this new environment has not been easy.

New problems emerge as educators make the transition from using only print media in teaching to also using computer software and seeking to develop their own instructional multimedia materials. For instance, finding out who "owns" all the necessary rights to even a small piece of a movie is far more complicated than finding out who holds the single copyright for an entire book. One of the key determinants of fair use of print works was the duplication of only a small portion of a text; but when a professor demonstrates a computer program even for a few seconds, a complete copy of the software is created automatically within the computer being used. Such distinctions take on considerable weight as faculty and publishers find that getting all the necessary legal permissions may be more time-consuming and costly than the actual tech-

nical production of multimedia. Unfortunately, many administrators, faculty members, and students are neither conscious of nor knowledgeable about the legal requirements and penalties associated with the use and copying of computer software and other multimedia elements.

Higher education may be profoundly affected by the results of the revisions of copyright and other intellectual property laws now under consideration. Failure to extend the fair use concept to new media could both delay the use of attractive instructional options and dramatically increase related costs.

Having students, faculty, or staff caught illegally copying software can undermine an institution's apparent commitment to both intellectual integrity and the rights of authors, as well as result in substantial fines and inconvenience. Colleges and universities should educate all their members about the ethical and legal implications of using information in various media. Any opportunities to advocate extension of fair use to educational and research uses of information technologies should be taken. Consult your librarians for updates on these topics.

7. GUIDELINES, POLICIES
Develop new guidelines quickly; develop new policies slowly.

While intellectual property law and the copyright system have special significance for educational institutions and scholars, even the U.S. Congress seems worried about some of the possibilities for misbehavior in the new information environment, especially the Internet. Recent incidents have raised concerns about the invasion of privacy, rights to free speech, distribution of pornography, hate mongering, misrepresentation of authorship, distortion of others' works, embezzlement of funds, interception of credit card numbers—and who knows what will be next. The environment is changing so quickly that it is not clear how to apply previous rules of conduct, laws, and even ethical principles. The legislative system cannot quickly catch up.

Establishing clear policies in these areas is a worthy effort that is unlikely to have satisfying results for years: there are simply too many complex factors changing too fast. However, some of the issues are so closely related to central academic principles that colleges and universities do not have the option of waiting for federal, state, or local (or international) law to establish the boundaries of permissible and desirable behavior. In the meantime, each institution should soon develop relatively flexible guidelines providing direction for students, faculty, and staff, with the expectation that these will be replaced eventually by more definitive policies based on accumulated experience and emerging patterns.

Such guidelines and policy-making efforts require the best thinking and perspective of a wide range of campus stakeholders in order to avoid missing key implications. Consider the complexity of policy issues raised by one simple, not-so-unusual example: A student uses the college computing network to retrieve a sexually explicit picture from the Internet and send it—unsolicited, and without indicating its source—to another student at a different institution. What are the implications for privacy, free speech, institutional sanction of pornography, and intellectual property?

Working with peer institutions that share the same concerns and have similar needs can speed the process of developing guidelines and policies, and reduce the magnitude of the task. Ironically, the Internet—the source of many new challenges—may be the ideal vehicle for both distributing case studies suggesting the problems that must be addressed and exchanging drafts that can be refined collaboratively within and across institutions.

8. SUPPORT-SERVICE CRISIS
Prepare for your support-service crisis.

Your support-service crisis has already begun if

- the person in charge of academic computing support services has been working 60 to 80 hours per week for several months, looks terrible, and sounds worse;
- there is nasty talk among the faculty and students about the declining quality of support services; and
- the administration is considering firing the person in charge of those services; or
- there is no person in charge; he/she has already quit to take a job in industry at double the salary and half the hours.

Otherwise, your crisis hasn't arrived yet; just wait a few months.

As William Geoghegan of IBM has observed (see "An 'Online' Discussion" in the March/April 1995 issue of *Change* and the articles by Green—with commentaries from Rogers, Geoghegan, Marcus, and Johnson—in the March/April 1996 issue of *Change*), most colleges and universities did reasonably well in the past 10 years at developing support services appropriate to the character and needs of "innovators" and "early adopters"—the first 10 to 15 percent of the faculty to implement educational uses of information technology. However, most institutions have not provided the quantity, mix, or quality of support services necessary to enable the "early majority" and "late majority"—the next 70 percent of the faculty—to make effective use of information technology in their teaching.

In fact, the level and quality of support that was adequate for the first 5 percent of the faculty is probably strained dealing with 15 percent, and will not "scale up" for the next 70 percent. Proportionally more support will be required, and those providing it will need better and more varied skills—including the ability to deal with the easily bruised egos of faculty who have no special propensity for technology.

A pattern of campus crisis is becoming common. An institution manages to get a special grant for computing hardware or revenues from a special bond issue for adding a telecommunications network—but the funds are not allowed to be used for support staff. Then the "hardware meteor" crashes into the campus.

Meanwhile, the need for support service continues to grow. In recent years, the software publishers have been getting more

Any suggestion about new staff or new services seems expensive when stable or shrinking budgets are the norm. However, there is one glimmer of hope in this picture— another old idea: using students as assistants.

effective at producing new products, updates, and upgrades that offer tools or elements that are hard to resist; computer viruses continue to arrive; and the e-mail explosion is either a reality or imminent. The same campus technical support staff is supposed to train users in how to install and make effective use of new packages and features, then to answer questions as the new packages are fitted into a myriad of configurations on old machines; to help the victims of viruses; and to help everyone learn to use e-mail and the World Wide Web.

And that's not all. As more faculty become intrigued with instructional uses of e-mail and presentation tools in the classroom, they begin to ask about more advanced, *deeper* uses of information technology to improve teaching and learning. They need a more diverse combination of support services: technical, library, faculty development, and so on. These faculty members also need people with pedagogical expertise to help them rethink their teaching approaches, and they need librarians' skills to help them find and authenticate course-related materials on the Internet (and librarians who can work with students who want to use the Internet for course-related research).

So, things may get worse before they get better! The technology base is expanding, with faculty and student interest in the use of information technology increasing, and support-staff funding is usually level or shrinking, with technical support people in many regions feeling burned out, unappreciated, and underpaid by industry's standards. In summary, there is increasing demand and decreasing supply at most colleges and universities for support services needed to improve teaching and learning through more effective use of information technology. Any suggestion about new staff or new services seems expensive when stable or shrinking budgets are the norm. However, there is one glimmer of hope in this picture—another old idea: using students as assistants.

9. STUDENT ROLES
Extend student roles as assistants, learning colleagues; form Faculty Student Support Service Teams (FSSSTs) and learning communities.

Student Assistants. Undergraduate students have performed well as assistants in a wide variety of jobs on campus for years. What is new is the recognition that many undergraduates have better skills and knowledge about information technology than most faculty and staff members. Student assistants can help other students, staff members, and faculty members (and even K-12 teachers and students), and most faculty seem to have little problem accepting help from them. Student assistants can help increase the educational use of information technology,

In most academic disciplines, it has become impossible for a faculty member to know every resource a bright beginning student might stumble into on the Internet while doing a research paper.

alleviate the support-service crisis, and save money for the institution.

Most campuses have some librarians or computing staff who are already using student assistants or interns quite successfully. These professionals can be quite helpful in designing an extended program to engage more students in combating the support-service crisis. Phil Long, director of instruction and research technology at William Paterson College, reports great success with student assistants owing to an extensive training program he has developed for them and to the substantial staff time that has been committed to scheduling and supervising their work. Most of those who have successfully used students report the importance of recruitment, training, supervision, and rewards. Students who go to work on the front lines helping their peers or faculty members usually need training and guidance not only on the technicalities, but also on pedagogy and service manners.

Work-study wages are usually quite low. Another alternative, labeling the work an internship, may remove the necessity for paying the students, giving them academic credit instead. If this begins to sound too much like exploitation, it isn't. Most students enjoy this work. In addition, as they acquire technical and people/service skills, they prepare both for higher-paying part-time jobs in the information industries during college, and for entry-level positions in a wide variety of businesses after college. The potential career benefits for these students are real and obvious to them.

Faculty Student Support Service Teams. The AAHE TLTR Program encourages participating colleges and universities to extend the idea of using students as assistants by forming Faculty Student Support Service Teams (FSSSTs). Each FSSST consists of individuals representing key support services—such as library, computing, and faculty development—and includes student assistants. (If it is not feasible to assign people full-time to these teams, an institution can begin by forming one FSSST as a pilot test and assigning something like 20 percent of a person's time from each category.) FSSSTs can provide some faculty members who are trying to improve their teaching and their students' learning through more effective uses of information technology with the full range of support services necessary to make the transition successful.

A by-product of forming an FSSST—or a separate valuable activity in itself—is "cross-training" among key support services: librarians train computing specialists and student assistants; faculty development specialists train librarians and student assistants; technology specialists train faculty development professionals and student assistants; and so on. George Mason University is already having some success with this approach.

Learning Colleagues, Learning Communities. Forming FSSSTs and having students serve as technical assistants can help faculty recognize students' expertise in academic uses of information technology, thus precipitating a movement toward the eventual formation of more collaborative learning communities—communities in which faculty are relied on for leadership, but students participate actively in shaping the goals of instruction and selecting the means for achieving them. The changing structure of information resources—especially those available on the Internet—and changing demographics of students and faculty also may support shifts in this direction. **(See Batson and Bass in the March/April 1996 issue of *Change*.)**

For example, in most academic disciplines, it has now become impossible for a faculty member to know every useful resource that a bright beginning student might stumble into on the Internet while doing a research paper. Consequently, a faculty member cannot always control or evaluate student research in traditional ways, and many faculty are adopting pedagogical approaches in which students are encouraged to take more active roles as learners.

In addition, more undergraduate and graduate students are taking courses part-time while working part-time or full-time. Meanwhile, many full-time employees in industry teach part-time late in their careers. Based on their experience working in teams for their jobs, these "non-traditional" students and faculty may accept a collegial relationship with each other more comfortably than would their "traditional" counterparts.

As "learning colleagues," students accept more responsibility for their own education, including understanding their own needs and abilities and the characteristics of the pedagogies and instructional materials most helpful to them. Eventually this trend may lead to the formation of formally recognized learning communities.

10. PORTFOLIO OF CHANGE STRATEGIES
Develop a portfolio of change strategies.

There is a big difference between wrong decisions and dumb decisions. With respect to planning for educational uses of information technology, no one can be certain of avoiding wrong decisions—too many factors change too quickly and unpredictably. But dumb decisions can be avoided by including key stakeholders and service providers in advisory discussions leading to an overall institutional strategy and a portfolio of change strategies.

Since no college or university can now afford to support all attractive educational uses of information technology, the first step in avoiding dumb decisions is to develop an overall *institutional* strategy. One set of options for participants—to be a "leader, follower, or resister"—is analogous to Everett Rogers' descriptions of individuals as innovators, early majority, and laggards. "Leader" institutions must be able to invest heavily in new opportunities and accept a high likelihood that some will fail. "Followers" need to watch peer institutions carefully and adopt whatever seems to be working well already for at least 20 percent of the others. "Resisters" try to avoid engaging in new activities until it becomes embarrassing not to do so.

After identifying the most appropriate overall strategy, those responsible for institutional planning should develop a

For more than a decade, individual faculty members and educational publishers have been developing educational applications of information technology that permit the teaching and learning of topics otherwise almost inaccessible for most students, including applications to help students through "instructional bottlenecks"—well-known places where many students get stuck and fall behind in courses. A few examples of such "irresistible combinations" of technology and teaching approach follow.

In music, some kinds of ear training are now taught using computer-driven devices that produce tones and respond immediately to students' efforts to identify them. The combination of accurate tone production and immediate response enables learning at a pace and with a quality otherwise almost impossible. The fact that the devices represent an additional expense seems to matter little when the educational value is so obvious; most music departments perceive the expense as "reasonable."

A general class of combinations that fits into the "irresistible" category is the use of computer-driven graphics to permit easy display or manipulation of visual images that would otherwise be quite difficult to demonstrate. For example, the teaching of some advanced mathematical topics depends heavily on manipulating three-dimensional images; this can be done more easily on computer. Likewise, some concepts of relativistic physics cannot be "shown" in reality, but can be offered visually via computer-generated images. Geographic Information Systems also have been developed, which permit the presentation and manipulation of geographic and geological information in ways that are qualitatively superior to paper maps; consequently, in these fields some new approaches to organizing and thinking about information and concepts have evolved and are now being taught. And art historians are finding ways of "mounting" slides of paintings and other works of art on CD-ROMs and projecting them in classrooms with enough acuity to rival 35mm slides—enjoying the ability of jumping from one image to another out of sequence in response to student questions or new instructional ideas. ∾

stream. The goal is a combination of strategies that, in the long run, has the effect of being both wide and deep.

Interesting specific strategies emerging from the TLTR Program that have already been introduced and discussed elsewhere in this article are student assistants, FSSSTs, electronic mail and instruction, collaborative learning and groupware, and internal faculty grants. There is growing recognition that

- using student assistants for information technology is a "win-win" program;
- FSSSTs are attractive in theory and politically difficult to implement;
- using e-mail to extend instruction is an easy way for faculty and students to begin to integrate technology into teaching and learning; and
- "collaborative learning and groupware" is a combination offering some of the "deepest" impact.

Internal faculty grant programs can be established supporting any of these strategies. Brief descriptions of three additional strategies that have emerged from the TLTR Program—faculty mentors, irresistible combinations, and faculty conversions—follow.

Faculty Mentors. Another option for increasing the quality and availability of support services while holding down costs is to engage early adopter faculty as peer mentors. Training and supervision are necessary for this approach and must be handled tactfully. Stipends and release time are the usual means of rewarding faculty mentors. If these faculty members already have tenure or are otherwise secure enough, they can be invaluable to colleagues. For untenured faculty, the benefits of being a mentor are not so obvious, and the time required can jeopardize career progress.

Irresistible Combinations are those combinations of teaching approach, technology, and other factors that are most obviously worthy of support and dissemination—those that prove almost irresistible to faculty and students because they permit teaching and learning that would otherwise be extremely difficult or impossible. (See box, Examples of "Irresistible Combinations.") These combinations can have a progressively deeper impact on the teaching and learning of those who use them, but they remain focused rather narrowly within specific courses. Support for them can move quickly from narrow/shallow to narrow/deep.

Faculty Conversions. Faculty who begin experimenting with information technology in education often undergo "conversion experiences" that leave them better teachers. Their effort to understand what is different about teaching with technology versus teaching without it forces them to reflect more consciously on the teaching and learning processes, and often leads them into discussions with colleagues—and perhaps students—about the relative merits of various teaching approaches. These "converts" become aware of pedagogical issues likely to influence their teaching forever, whether or not technology is involved. (See Alley and Repp in the March/April 1996 issue of *Change.*)

Identifying faculty members who are already in the early stages of these conversion experiences and supporting them—perhaps through small grants—is a narrow/deep strategy. There is still much to be learned about how to help faculty move into these early stages.

"portfolio" of specific change strategies that includes a combination of a few "narrow/deep" and a few "wide/shallow" change strategies that can be readily explained and justified. The "narrow" versus "wide" dimension refers to the proportion of all faculty and students involved in using the new technology; the "shallow" versus "deep" dimension refers to the level of impact on those whose teaching and learning experiences are affected. (In the March/April 1995 *Change* and in other TLTR materials, four categories of change from shallow to deep are explained: 1) increase personal productivity, 2) enhance teaching, 3) change pedagogy, 4) change epistemology and content.) The narrow/deep options tend to be expensive and should enable the institution to keep some early adopter faculty motivated and moving forward. The wide/shallow strategies should be more affordable and reach enough faculty and students to sustain the emerging participation of the main-

11. REALISTIC EXPECTATIONS: MORE TIME, MONEY
Invest more time and money.

Colleges and universities are under great pressure to
1. improve the quality of undergraduate education;
2. increase access to education—geographically and for those with disabilities or with demanding work schedules; and
3. reduce the cost of education.

Some state legislatures, regents, boards of trustees, and institutional leaders have been leaping toward investments in information technology as one of the more obvious options for meeting these three goals in the near future. Unfortunately, most of the experience of those who have worked hardest and most successfully at using information technology to improve teaching and learning suggests that we can achieve the first two goals, but that costs go up initially as we do so. Just because many institutions need to meet the three goals simultaneously—and in the near future—does *not* mean that it is possible. It is extremely unlikely they can be achieved together in just a few years.

Necessity may be the mother of invention, but the gestation period can be very long. Major transformations take major amounts of money and time. The divestiture of the Bell System and establishment of the "new" AT&T took 10 years, and now another major reorganization has begun. Distance education is an old idea with a new imperative—and new telecommunications capabilities to achieve it—but all the evidence suggests that it takes years, not months, to build effective distance-education programs. Digital libraries are still being defined, and many believe that the role of print on paper in libraries—as well as costs—will be reduced dramatically; but clarifying and achieving this goal has just begun and will take a lot of time and money.

Higher education institutions need to organize for continual reinvestment in educational uses of information technology for the foreseeable future—to recognize that newer technologies that serve specific teaching and learning needs even better than the previous ones will keep arriving from the information industries, and that computers that still function perfectly are considered obsolete in two or three years. Traditional educational budgeting and accounting systems don't take these computer obsolescence cycles into consideration or recognize that cumulative costs of software, maintenance, and other support services may be larger than the price of the computer. Colleges and universities need to learn how to treat computing-related expenses as annual operating expenses, and adjust budgets accordingly—and painfully. (See "Paying the Digital Piper," by Kenneth C. Green, in the March/April 1995 issue of *Change*.)

Many academic leaders believe that all revenue sources are already working at full capacity and that a net increase in budget for educational uses of information technology must be offset by decreases elsewhere. On campuses where budget cuts have been common in recent years, this will be a painful process and one difficult to justify. That pain can be reduced or mitigated by engaging representatives of widely diverse stakeholder groups within the institution in deliberations focused on the teaching/learning gains that appear increasingly to be within the reach of technology, and on the competitive pressures from peer institutions.

12. INSTITUTIONWIDE COLLABORATION
Develop institutionwide collaboration to improve teaching and learning.

Institutionwide, collaborative efforts to improve teaching and learning through more effective uses of information technology are necessary for the following reasons:

- Educational uses of information technology are improving student learning.
- Information technology and information resources are becoming key assets in the increasingly intense competition for students, faculty, and funding.
- No institution can afford *all* attractive options for using information technology to improve teaching and learning; choices must be made.
- No individual faculty member can find or know *all* teaching options using information technology that might be relevant for a particular course; mechanisms for sharing valuable information among faculty and others must be provided.
- Fragmented planning efforts fail to harness the insights of all those who can help understand current patterns of change in teaching, learning, and technology and help shape a "vision worth working toward."
- Fragmented policy-making always fails to identify and address some important implications of the changing information environment and the new options for behavior in it.
- Fragmented support-service activities fail to meet the needs of most faculty and students seeking to improve teaching and learning.

To create a climate that fosters and supports long-lasting, widespread, significant instructional change, most colleges and universities need to "de-fragment" the usual campus planning, policy-making, and support activities. One approach that is gaining acceptance and seems effective is to form a Teaching, Learning, and Technology (TLT) Roundtable or an equivalent forum. (More than 100 institutions have already begun participating in the American Association for Higher Education's TLTR Program).

This advisory group, which includes representatives of all key stakeholders, facilitates communication, coordination, and collaboration within the institution—with a focus on teaching and learning first, technology second. The TLTR Program also encourages participants to exchange information with those conducting similar efforts at peer institutions nationwide. A long-term goal is for each college or university to achieve a balance among individuals' expectations, institutional priorities, and the availability of resources.

THE COMING UBIQUITY *of* INFORMATION TECHNOLOGY

BY KENNETH C. GREEN

Academic pundits frequently comment that the pace of innovation in higher education can be measured by the 40 years it took to get the overhead projector out of the bowling alley and into the classroom. The (few) pundits who know something about both bowling and technology often add that faculty are now far more likely to find computerized projection systems in bowling alleys than in college classrooms.

But something significant is happening. Fueled by more than four decades of aspirations and a dozen years of sustained (if often ad hoc) experimentation, information technology has finally emerged as a permanent, respected, and increasingly essential component of the college experience. New data from the annual *Campus Computing* survey, now in its sixth year, indicate a major gain in the proportion of college courses (and by extension, college faculty) using information technology as an instructional resource. These data reveal that the use of information technology in instruction is finally breaking past the innovators

Kenneth C. Green (cgreen@earthlink.net), director of the annual Campus Computing *survey, is a visiting scholar at the Claremont Graduate School in Claremont, California.* © *Kenneth C. Green, 1995, 1996.*

and early adopters and into the ranks and experience of mainstream faculty.

A rapidly rising minority of *all* of college students and faculty—some 16 million people—now have some sort of recurring instructional experience with information technology resources and technology-based learning activities. These are technology activities that go beyond the broad use of word processing (at one end of the continuum) and the technical skill of computer programming (at the other); rather, these are experiences that extend the content of the curriculum, enrich the classroom discourse, and enhance learning opportunities.

Although the technology experience may not be universal, the presence of technology in the learning environment is increasingly common: an e-mail address on a course syllabus; electronic mail as a supplement to office hours; class sessions held in computer labs; desktop computers in faculty offices; commercial software and simulations as part of the resources provided by textbook publishers; and course assignments that send students to World Wide Web (WWW) sites in search of information resources (published articles, conference papers, digitized images, and just-released data files). These examples and others reflect the new significance of information technology in the instructional domain—across almost all disciplines (from art history to zoology) and in virtually all types of campus contexts, from elite research

universities to community colleges to distance-education programs.

Admittedly, there is great variation across academic programs and institutions. Students and faculty in research universities and elite institutions are far more likely to own and use computers than their peers in community colleges. But the growing use of information technology in instruction indicates significant change. It reflects more than the aggregated impact of rising levels of computer ownership among college students (now at about 33 percent, but approaching 80 percent or more at some institutions) and faculty (over 50 percent across all of academe, but close to 100 percent on some campuses). And it extends beyond prior exposure as reflected a) by the growing numbers of U.S. families that have a computer in the home (approaching 40 percent) or b) by the secondary school experience of the majority of entering college freshmen who report having received a half-year or more of some sort of computer training during high school. It demonstrates the diffusion of information technology across *all* sectors of higher education, rather than increased use in those institutions with a strong technology base and long institutional history of support for instructional innovations and technology experiments.

As noted above, the 1995 *Campus Computing* data reveal dramatic recent changes in the use of information technology in instruction. As shown in

6. SPECIAL ISSUES

The proportion of college courses using some form of information technology resource rose significantly between 1994 and 1995, increasing by at least one-half and in some cases doubling.

Chart 1, the proportion of college courses using some form of information technology resource rose significantly between 1994 and 1995, increasing by at least one-half and in some cases doubling. The dramatic one-year gains shown in Chart 1 represent important changes in the way growing numbers of faculty across all types of institutions and in all disciplines develop their courses, select content for the syllabus, present material in class, structure course assignments, and evaluate student performance.

Admittedly, not all faculty are passionate (or even frequent) computer users, and not all courses have a technology component. Moreover, some of the technology applications that are common in many courses today are decidedly "low-tech," such as the use of word processing for preparing class papers. Yet one "low-tech" tool—electronic mail—is quickly becoming an important resource in instruction: on many campuses e-mail has become an important supplement to office hours and class discussion, allowing students to communicate with faculty and one another outside of the classroom.

Indeed, the rapid spread of electronic mail over the past year represents a major innovation: it reflects a new level of

CHART 1
PERCENTAGE OF COLLEGE COURSES USING VARIOUS KINDS OF INFORMATION TECHNOLOGY, 1994 AND 1995

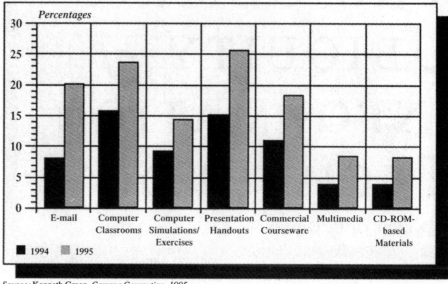

Source: Kenneth Green, *Campus Computing, 1995.*

CHART 2
USER SUPPORT ISSUES

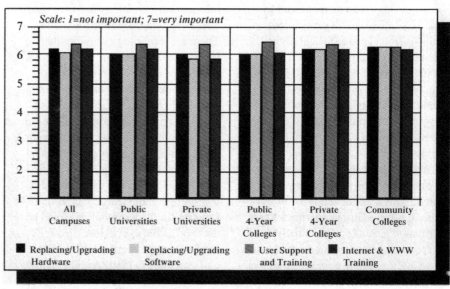

Source: Kenneth Green, *Campus Computing, 1995.*

technology utilization by faculty (and students) that moves the computing and technology experience off of the desktop, out of the office, and into a rich and networked world where faculty are "connected"—to one another via e-mail, to the Internet and to resources on the Web, and to disciplinary colleagues for scholarly communication and professional correspondence (not to mention a little bit of academic gossip!). Although word processing and e-mail may not be

hallmarks of technological skill and sophistication, they have become, nonetheless, core tools.

Other "low-tech" tools are also being adapted to instruction. For example, the growing use of presentation handouts has been aided in large part by the software industry's transition to software "suites" that bundle several applications such as a word processor, spreadsheet, database, and graphics tool into an aggressively priced package. The dis-

166

CHART 3
PERCENTAGE OF COLLEGE COURSES USING COMMERCIAL COURSEWARE

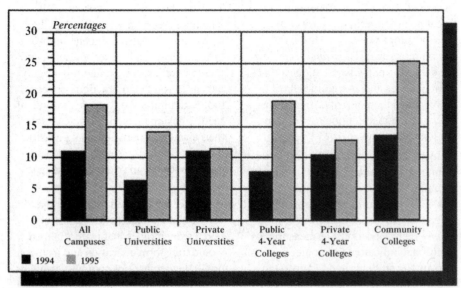

Source: Kenneth Green, *Campus Computing, 1995.*

CHART 4
PERCENTAGE OF COLLEGE COURSES USING COMPUTER LABS FOR TEACHING AND INSTRUCTION

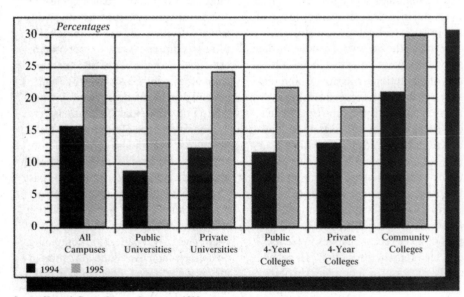

Source: Kenneth Green, *Campus Computing, 1995.*

ture fosters innovation. Even though the level remains low, the instructional use of CD-ROM-based materials and multimedia resources doubled over the past year, in large part a direct result of new multimedia-capable computers in homes, student dorms, campus labs, and faculty offices. (The percentage of computers with CD-ROMs in student-accessible campus labs more than doubled between 1994 and 1995, from 6 percent to 15.4 percent.) On many campuses, recent infrastructure enhancements reflect the replacement of obsolete equipment rather than a net gain in the total number of computers in campus labs and faculty offices. Similarly, the growing use of commercial courseware and computer simulations is directly linked to the role of textbook publishers and other firms creating these materials for the college and university market.

Taken together, these data point to the importance of *infrastructure*—multimedia-capable computers, commercial interest in the campus market, technical assistance, and user support—as critical catalysts for innovation and for the integration of technology in instruction. Too, the data suggest that instructional use will continue to rise, accompanied by growing demand for expanded and enhanced infrastructure resources and services—more and more powerful computers in campus labs and faculty offices; more support personnel to assist and train faculty and students; richer and more sophisticated instructional software and multimedia products from commercial developers and publishers.

Indeed, user support issues represent a major financial, operational, and technical challenge for most institutions. Replacing aging equipment, updating obsolete software, and supporting the exploding student and faculty interest in the World Wide Web are top institutional concerns according to the 1995 survey (Chart 2).

Yet the survey data also suggest that some aspects of user support have not expanded to meet growing demand. For example, although the use of instructional technology resources in courses has increased dramatically in recent years, the proportion of colleges and universities that have expanded their in-

counting involved with software suites, especially for campuses with site licenses, has made the suites very attractive products; once installed, the software (such as Freelance from Lotus, or PowerPoint from Microsoft) is readily available to large numbers of faculty who may have had little initial interest, but who eventually experiment with the new tool out of curiosity and collegial encouragement. Many faculty like what they experience, finding that presenta-

tion software provides a good way to organize and update their class materials and also to incorporate various kinds of graphics into their class presentations. Moreover, student response is often very positive. On many campuses, the faculty experience with presentation software has led to increased demand for classrooms equipped with computer projection facilities.

In other instances, the gains shown in Chart 1 reflect the fact that infrastruc-

vestment in instructional development (that is, providing assistance to faculty eager to use technology in their instructional activities) has remained flat over the past six years. Several factors explain the "demise" of instructional development:

• *Learning curve.* Developing really good, really useful instructional "stuff" is far more complex than originally anticipated.

• *Sustained investment.* Institutions have learned that instructional development is not a static activity. Rather, it requires sustained investment. Most campuses (and even many enthusiastic faculty) have not been prepared to make the sustained investment of time, personnel (faculty and technical support), and financial resources need to develop "market-quality" instructional resources.

• *Patron support.* Foundations and technology vendors provided much of the early money that helped many institutions launch ambitious, widely publicized instructional development programs in the 1980s. But the campus initiatives often did not deliver on their promises, and the changing fortunes of (and profit margins in) the technology market mean that vendors such as Apple, Digital, IBM, and others can no longer provide truckloads of equipment and other goodies to support campus efforts.

• *Pressing demand for more traditional user training.* Although technology use has moved to the mainstream, campuses have been under great pressure to control their technology expenditures. Over the past five years, many campuses have shifted their user support from instructional development to serving the growing numbers of students, faculty, staff, and administrators who need assistance and training.

Taken together, these factors help explain the demise of instructional development, even as demand for instructional resources has been growing.

These data also indicate that the use of information technology has reached what diffusion theorist Everett Rogers calls *critical mass:* "the point at which enough individuals have adopted an innovation so that the innovation's further rate of adoption becomes self-sustain-

ing." Rogers' widely acclaimed work suggests that critical mass typically occurs when about 15 or 20 percent of a target population (in this case college faculty) adopt a new innovation (see box on next page). The *Campus Computing* data shown in Chart 1 suggest that most colleges and universities have finally passed the point of critical mass affecting the instructional use of information technology.

Interestingly, the use of information technology resources is often greater in community colleges than in other sectors. To some this may be surprising, given that the technology infrastructure in two-year institutions, as measured by traditional indicators (computer ownership among students and faculty, status of the campus network, the number of technology support staff), is generally less well developed and less well funded than in elite institutions and research universities. But as shown in Charts 3 and 4, community colleges take the lead in certain measures reflecting the use of information technology in instruction.

Perhaps the best way to view the data shown in Charts 3 and 4 is in the context of institutional mission. Community colleges have a focused teaching mission; consequently, the broader use of certain kinds of information technology resources is consistent with that mission, even absent significant financial resources to support an in-depth or high-tech implementation effort.

How should faculty, administrators, and campus committees assess the impact of these recent changes in the use of technology in instruction? Have we really witnessed a "computer revolution" or experienced the "technology transformation" of higher education?

Alas, it is still premature to talk about a technology-driven *transformation,* as academe is still in the early stages of adapting and incorporating various kinds of information technology into its instructional functions. And it is hyperbole to discuss a technological revolution, which implies a sudden and dramatic departure from past practice. Information technology, as a function and as a resource, has in fact entered the pedagogical mainstream. But information technology has not radical-

ly transformed classrooms or the instructional activities of most faculty. The transformation, if it occurs, will take time—certainly another decade. Curriculum enhancement and innovation, however, will be a continuing and incremental process, remaining largely dependent on the interaction between individual initiative (the way individual faculty design the syllabus and structure their classes) *and* institutional infrastructure (the hardware, software, and support services available to students and faculty).

Unlike the demand for film and television—other once-heralded instructional technologies that many claimed would transform education and instruction—the demand for computing and information technology resources remains strong, is broad-based, and continues to expand. Students often want and expect an IT component in their courses; growing numbers of faculty are using various kinds of information technology resources in their instructional and professional activities; and the institutional infrastructure necessary to support the effective and wide use of information technology continues to improve and expand despite the financial problems confronting individual institutions.

The emergence of information technology as a curriculum component (or experience) is a significant innovation in higher education. The events of the past 15 years suggest a steady migration of information technology into instruction and other aspects of the learning experience. The arrival of desktop computing on college campuses ("the new computing" is what Steve Gilbert and I called it in a 1986 *Change* article) fostered broad hopes and great aspirations for the eventual integration of computing and information technology into the curriculum. Technology in this context is not a goal or an outcome; rather it is an enabling resource intended to supplement, enhance, and extend the learning experience. The potential of technology to provide new tools and information resources has long been the great expectation that fueled institutional investments and individual experimentation; the potential and the possibilities remain as appropriate and attainable goals.

THE DIFFUSION OF INNOVATION— AND INFORMATION TECHNOLOGY

Everett M. Rogers is the individual most often associated with the diffusion of innovation literature. The descriptors of innovation he created some 30 years ago—innovators, early adopters, laggards, change agents, and opinion leaders—have migrated into the common language routinely used to describe events, individuals, and organizational behavior. (See Rogers, *Diffusion of Innovations*, 4th ed., New York: The Free Press, 1995.)

Rogers' S-shaped diffusion curve—a statistician's bell curve with a twist—charts the diffusion of all types of innovations: agricultural practices, cellular phones, medical technology, microcomputer technology, clothing styles, and more. It even helps to explain the change in George Bush's position on Medicare over 25 years: as a first-term congressman in 1963, Bush denounced President Kennedy's proposal

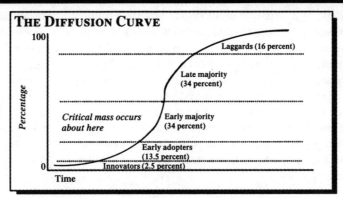

THE DIFFUSION CURVE

Laggards (16 percent)

Late majority (34 percent)

Critical mass occurs about here

Early majority (34 percent)

Early adopters (13.5 percent)

Innovators (2.5 percent)

Percentage

Time

Source: Based on Everett Rogers, *Diffusion of Innovations,* 1995 (pp. 262, 314)

to create Medicare as "socialized medicine." As the concept of Medicare moved into the political mainstream between 1963 and 1980, Bush, as vice president and president, came to accept and support it.

In the context of the instructional use of information technology, a number of campuses (Carnegie Mellon, Michigan, Stanford, Reed, and Drexel, among others) became nationally known as technology innovators by virtue of early institutional commitments and investments intended to inte-

grate computing and technology into instruction. Similarly, faculty who invested time in desktop technology often were tagged as "early adopters" by colleagues on their campuses and in their disciplines.

Drawing on the work of both Rogers and Geoffrey Moore (*Crossing the Chasm*, 1991), William Geoghegan of IBM has described a "gap" that separates the early technology adopters from other faculty on college campuses. On Rogers' innovation curve, "Geoghegan's gap" occurs exactly at

the point Rogers identifies as critical mass—"the point at which enough individuals have adopted an innovation so that the innovation's further rate of adoption becomes self-sustaining" (Rogers, 1995, p. 314). Crossing the gap, says Geoghegan, means recognizing that "the deployment of instructional technology has to do with the social and psychological factors that underlie the spread of any innovation...and the way these factors have combined to create a veritable chasm between the early adopters of educational technology and [other faculty]." (Geoghegan's 1994 article, "What Ever Happened to Instructional Technology: Reaching Mainstream Faculty," was published by IBM and is available on the IBM Higher Education Home Page: http://ike.engr.washington.edu. The article is posted in the White Paper area of the News section.) ∾

IN RESPONSE
Four Viewpoints

BY EVERETT M. ROGERS

Those of us in academe (and elsewhere) ultimately owe much to the bright young people who labored at Xerox PARC (Palo Alto Research Center) in the 1970s. While others had conceived of the computer as a communication de-

vice, the PARC researchers did the influential early work designing software and systems that gave initial form to those visions. The key elements of the PARC design work (personal computers, windows, mouse, and graphic user interface) were initially popularized by Apple in the early 1980s with the Lisa and Macintosh systems. These design elements are now imbedded in the inter-

face of virtually all computers and have done much to expand the concept of the computer to include both computational *and* communications functions, and more recently, instruction and learning.

Have we crossed the point of critical mass for instructional use of information technology in higher education, as Green suggests in this useful and readable article? Probably so. The dramatic gains in the rate of adoption of these technologies that he reports are undoubtedly related to the growing public awareness of the Internet, as well as the expanding access to, and use of, personal computers across broad parts of American society: growing numbers of elementary and secondary school students have access to computers at school and in their homes; growing numbers of adults routinely use (personal or desktop) computers at work.

Green's use of the idea of critical mass and, more broadly, the diffusion of innovations framework, seems natural; he accurately and appropriately applies these concepts. One important implication of his work is the demand (or rate-of-adoption) curve that follows after passing the point of critical mass. The rate of adoption is quite likely to continue to shoot upward over the next several years, creating financial and infrastructure needs that university campuses will be forced to address: new equipment, more user training, new kinds of courses, and more. Infrastructure, as he correctly notes, can drive innovation. In this instance, it also creates still more demand for still more infrastructure and support as growing numbers of faculty across all disciplines and institutions adopt and adapt information technology resources in their instructional activities. ∾

Everett M. Rogers is professor and chair, Department of Communication and Journalism, University of New Mexico. He is known for his book, Diffusion of Innovations *(NY: Free Press, 1995), recently published in its fourth edition.*

By William H. Geoghegan

The findings coming out of Green's latest *Campus Computing* survey are tremendously exciting. Not only is there extraordinary raw growth in the classroom use of information technology—increases on the order of 50 percent to 100 percent in just a year—but there are also important changes in the types of technology being used, and critical thresholds in usage levels are being crossed.

While the use of computer-generated presentation material leads the list by a narrow margin, other technologies that hold the potential for deeper and more transformative integration into the curriculum are also approaching or exceeding the 15 percent to 16 percent adoption figure that has been a critical barrier separating the early adopters of instructional technology from the mainstream (led by Rogers' "early majority"). The use of simulations, software specifically designed for instruction, and even e-mail falls into this category; and the rapid growth in their use is to me an extremely encouraging sign.

In fact, data on e-mail and Internet use (the latter are not shown in Green's charts in this article) lead me to think that these may be the real driving force behind much of the upswing. The explosive growth of the World Wide Web over the last two years—not to mention the richness and variety of resources that it provides—has clearly excited and engaged faculty across the disciplinary spectrum. The use of customized Web pages to support specific courses is already running around 6 percent. And the Web provides a gentle, "high-touch" approach to multimedia that may turn out to be the real key to wider use of this technology in the classroom. The pedagogical benefits of class-related e-mail have been widely promoted on the Internet in recent months (through e-mail-based conferences, I might add); and its growth is very likely to keep pace with—or exceed—the steady improvements we see in access to campus networking and the Internet.

What this bodes for the long term is less certain. Growth of the type and magnitude that Green's data suggest could cause immense problems for campus technology budgets and for support organizations, which in the majority of cases are not well positioned to deal with a mainstream population whose needs differ in both extent and kind from those of the innovators and early adopters the organizations have served in the past. This is perhaps the next "crisis" we have to face.

While some campuses have begun to recognize the need for major changes in the extent and type of faculty support, and are taking steps to address the problem before it gets out of hand, the general signs are not that encouraging. In looking back over the previous five years of Green's *Campus Computing* survey, which began in 1990, it is surprising how little movement can be discerned in the proportion of campuses offering the "softer" forms of instructional technology support. There has been no significant change, for example, in the proportion of campuses providing any of the following:

• a formal plan for integrating computers into the curriculum (now about 26 percent)

• formal projects for developing courseware (around 32 percent)

• support for faculty developing courseware (about 46 percent)

• a policy for rewarding courseware development (around 14 percent)

• a royalty-sharing agreement (down a few points over the years to about 13 percent)

Even if we interpret the "courseware" term narrowly to exclude activities such as developing Web pages for the distribution of course materials or for guided access to external sources of relevant information, or efforts to integrate e-mail into the teaching and learning process, we still see no appreciable change in instructional technology planning, or in support via the academic incentive and reward system.

The long-term issue, I think, is sustainability: can we sustain the rate of growth that typifies the "take-off" portion of Rogers' diffusion curve, and can we sustain the involvement of those new adopters who are still in the process of confirming their decision to integrate information and communications technology into the instructional process? This will certainly require thorough and extremely well-informed planning, a clever refocusing of existing support services, and probably more in the way of added resources than many schools will feel they can afford.

Now that we have finally breached those metaphorical barricades, we have to confront what awaits us on the other side.   ∾

William H. Geoghegan is an academic consultant for IBM North America's Higher Education organization.

BY JANE MARCUS

Whether you view it as a blessing or a curse, we are indeed living in interesting times. In the last 10 years, as Casey Green points out, word processing and electronic mail have become the new "core tools" of academe. Many in higher education anticipate that use of the Internet, spurred by innovations like the World Wide Web, will increase at an even faster pace.

For those who have not yet begun to explore the Web, or those who have explored and have found little there of value, there are lessons to be learned in looking at the adoption of the now ubiquitous core tools at Stanford.

Almost 20 years ago, when mainframes—now the dinosaurs of computing—were the only tools around (and with Everett Rogers as my advisor and mentor), I studied the diffusion of word processing among Stanford's non-technical faculty. I tested a model of adoption on a group of faculty and administrators who were being encouraged to trade in their typewriters for an innovative WYSIWYG (what-you-see-is-what-you-get) mainframe-based text editor.

An added feature used to promote that system was the ability to share files with colleagues and to send and receive electronic messages both at Stanford and across ARPAnet, the precursor of today's Internet.

Though many early adopters made the leap to text processing, few of the faculty made use of the system's communication capabilities. All they really wanted to do was write articles. They were wary of sharing their work with others for fear of getting "scooped." They rarely communicated with Stanford colleagues, who usually had different research interests, and few of their colleagues at other institutions even knew what e-mail was.

Without a critical mass of others with whom to communicate, the combined word processing *and* communication system proved more costly and less valuable than the new IBM stand-alone personal computers (a.k.a. "fancy typewriters") that appeared on campus in the early 1980s. The non-technical faculty didn't return to e-mail until the early 1990s when local area networks could connect their desktop machines to the Internet, easy-to-use e-mail packages became available, and the faculty began to find colleagues and students who were eager to communicate with them online.

The concept of critical mass is an important one to consider as we look at the future of the Internet and the World Wide Web. In this case, the critical mass is not one of people but of information. The Web will not become a core tool for scholars until a critical mass of credible information becomes available online.

Stanford computer scientist Terry Winograd often refers to today's Web as the Wild West, a place where anything (and everything) goes. This is because the technology has not yet had time to settle down. As the technology stabilizes, what will be important is not the amount of information available but its relevance and quality. Winograd believes that providing methods for establishing the credibility of electronic information is an area to which experts should give more attention.

Some progress is being made with scholarly information, particularly in the sciences. A Stanford biochemist recently mentioned that the five scholarly journals to which he subscribes (*Science, Nature, Journal of Biological Chemistry, Protein Science*, and *Journal of Molecular Biology*) are now available online. While only three of the journals are currently available in full text, all plan full text by the end of this year.

Two of these online journals, the *Journal of Biological Chemistry* (http://www-jbc.stanford.edu/jbc/) and *Science* (http://science-mag.aaas.org/science/) are delivered across the Internet by the High-Wire Press (http://highwire.stanford.edu/), a network publishing project of the Stanford University Libraries and Academic Information Resources. Working with a small number of scholarly societies and university presses, the High-Wire Press is attempting to provide new models for the publication of scholarly literature.

According to John Sack, director and associate publisher of HighWire, daily feedback from online readers indicates that the vast majority are enthusiastic about the Internet editions. Because the *Journal of Biological Chemistry* project has been so successful, many authors have now made publishing in the *JBC* a higher priority than they did before an online version was available.

Experiments like HighWire are the leading edge of innovations that will change scholarly communication. It will be some time before things settle down, and we should expect some reinvention along the way. Reinvention is defined by diffusion scholars, such as Rogers, as the degree to which an innovation is changed or modified by a user in the process of adoption and implementation. Blessing or curse, we're in for some very exciting times as we continue to adapt to this fundamental shift in the way we receive information and interact with it and with each other. ∾

Jane Marcus is manager of School and Departmental Support, a part of the Customer Assistance Group within Information Technology Systems and Services (ITSS) at Stanford University.

BY LARRY JOHNSON

The annual *Campus Computing* survey, always enlightening, is especially so when Green juxtaposes this year's results with Rogers' work on the diffusion of innovation. Now that college use of information technology for teaching and learning is poised at Rogers' point of "critical mass," the fuel that will propel information technology past that point into mainstream use will be the ways information technology brings people together.

Green downplays electronic mail as a low-technology application of information technology, but it may well be the "killer app" that provides the compelling rationale mainstreamers need to begin experimentation in their own right, for teaching and learning are interactive processes that occur between people. Electronic mail can extend and amplify traditional instructor-to-student and student-to-student interactions in significant ways that add value easily recognized by the most reticent of faculty. Only a small leap remains for an instructor familiar with electronic mail to begin to tap into the resources available on the World Wide Web.

In this context, Green's observation that infrastructure fosters innovation is especially compelling. It may seem an easy matter to add an e-mail address or Web-based activity to a syllabus, but it makes sense to do so only if the instructor—and the student—have easy access to a network providing the necessary tools. As colleges consider how to leverage the considerable investments already made in information technology and where to put their limited resources for new technology, expanding and enhancing network resources and infrastructure should be at the top of their lists.

Larry Johnson is associate director of the League for Innovation in the Community College.

COMPUTING OUR WAY TO EDUCATIONAL REFORM

BY PAUL STARR

There is little talk in America these days of bold new public initiatives; public money is scarce, and faith in public remedy even scarcer. One notable exception is new technology and education. Bill Clinton's challenge to connect all of America's schools to digital networks by the end of the 1990s is the only initiative today that echoes, if only faintly, John F. Kennedy's call to put an American on the moon by the end of the 1960s. Like the moon shot, linking America's classrooms to computer networks appeals to a technological nationalism that seems beyond partisan politics: Everyone—almost everyone—likes the idea of putting the U.S. first in the race to the future. Thus in the same legislation widely heralded as deregulating telecommunications, the Republican Congress and President Clinton were able this year to agree on regulatory requirements for universal service that for the first time include affordable connections for schools.

Yet past efforts to improve education with better technology have generally not lived up to the promises made for them. In the eyes of skeptics, the current enthusiasm for computers is the triumph of hope over experience—or worse, it reflects a persistent infatuation with technological fixes for deeply rooted social problems. It would be a mistake, however, to dismiss the new initiatives on the basis of such a reading of the past. The new media are different from the earlier technologies, even from computers as they were introduced into education, and these differences improve the odds of substantial change. The computer revolution of earlier decades has now turned into a communications revolution and opened up important new possibilities for learning. The new media, moreover, are becoming essential to intellectual and artistic expression and scientific work. As the entire world of communication and knowledge is transformed, it becomes inconceivable to leave education out.

Of course, computers are now integral to work of all kinds, and public support for educational technology reflects an appreciation of that inescapable fact. Many parents want the schools to use computers for the same reason that often influences their purchases at home: They believe that computers will help prepare children for good jobs and careers. In fact, workers with computer skills do enjoy higher earnings. Instead of deploring the interest in computers—"I know a false god when I see one," the critic Neil Postman writes of computers in his recent book, *The End of Education*—reformers should regard the popular support for new technology as an opportunity for positive change.

The question is what form innovation may take. Some critics—such as Lewis J. Perelman, the author of *School's Out*, a 1992 book popular in Newt Gingrich's high-tech, free market circles—believe that the new technology demands the end of school as we know it. The new media and schooling are incompatible, they say, and schooling must go. This is a setup for failure; Americans are not ready to abandon the very idea of school, nor should they. But there are important changes in schools worth making, some of which have been on the agenda of reformers ever since progressive educators first proposed them early in the twentieth century. Ironically, the continued diffusion and evolution of the new technologies may finally help to bring those reforms about.

THE RIPENING OF TECHNOLOGY

Forecasts of technological change often fail, Anthony Oettinger observes, because an innovation is not yet "ripe." Failed predictions may convince many people it will never work, but then it ripens—its costs fall, its limitations are overcome, it suddenly matches the demands of a market or the needs of an institution—and everything changes.

The history of education in the twentieth century is littered with mistaken forecasts of technological revolutions in education. In 1913, Thomas Edison predicted that books would "soon be obsolete in the schools" because of motion pictures. Similar predictions of epochal change in education accompanied the diffusion of radio in the 1920s and '30s and television in the 1950s. In *Teachers and Machines*, published in 1986, the educational historian Larry Cuban argues that these expectations were repeatedly disappointed, despite effort and investment, not for the reasons that advocates usually cited— poor implementation, insufficient money, resistance by teachers—but because of a more fundamental obstacle: the logic of the classroom.

Every day teachers confront enormous problems in accomplishing their objectives, including just managing their students. "The tools that teachers have added to their repertoire over time (e.g., chalkboard and textbooks) have been simple, durable, flexible, and responsive to teacher-defined problems in meeting the demands of daily instruction," Cuban observes. In contrast, movies, radio, and television typically required a lot of setup work and advance scheduling and did not necessarily mesh with lesson plans. Administrators and reformers also initiated change from the top down without engaging teachers as active participants. As a result, except for a few enthusiasts, teachers have tended to use movies and broadcast media only to supplement regular classes and break up routines of instruction.

Computers originally seemed destined to go through the same cycle of enthusiasm and disappointment, eventually to be relegated to the margins of education. Broadly speaking, educational computing has gone through three phases. In the first, from the mid-1950s to the early 1980s, the principal interests were the development of computer-assisted instruction (CAI) and the teaching of computer programming. Though often ridiculed as mere "electronic flashcards," CAI had a more sophisticated conception as an approach

> The new technologies may help realize ideas that progressive educators have long advocated.

that could customize instruction according to individual needs and allow students to pace themselves. After stirring initial excitement, the approach drew increasing criticism in the 1960s and '70s and had relatively little impact on the educational mainstream. As of 1980, according to a review by the Educational Testing Service, most computer education in secondary schools "consisted primarily of teaching white middle-class males to write programs in the BASIC language."

The impetus for CAI originated primarily outside of the schools. As was generally true of computers and computer science, the military was the chief sponsor of research, contributing three-fourths of all the research funds for educational technology up through the early 1980s. Perhaps the most highly publicized project that grew out of defense research was PLATO ("Programmed Logic for Automatic Teaching Operations"), based at the University of Illinois and owned by the Control Data Corporation, which hoped to build a business educating students all over the world from its central computers. By 1981, Control Data had 115 "learning centers" in the United States, making it the largest computer-based instructional system. Because of its cost, however, PLATO was rarely used by schools; the orientation was chiefly toward technical training. Control Data ultimately lost nearly a billion dollars on PLATO, a failure that became emblematic of dashed hopes in computer-based education.

The second phase of development began roughly in the early 1980s with the spread of personal computers, graphical user interfaces, and general applications software. Between 1981 and 1991, the proportion of schools with computers rose from 18 percent to 98 percent, and the number of students per computer fell from 125 to 18. Instead of just offering specialized courses in programming, schools incorporated computing into many subjects and activities. Still, computers were typically located only in special laboratories (as most still are today), and student time on computers averaged only slightly more than an hour per week or about 4 percent of instructional time. At the secondary level, most such instruction took the form of courses in "computer literacy"; at the primary level, computers were typically used for "integrated learning systems" that provided drill-and-practice in basic skills. None of this much affected the core curriculum or general educational experience. In an article called "Computers Meet Classroom; Classroom Wins," Cuban could still argue in 1993 that computers were likely to continue to have limited impact and might be expected to become more significant only in primary schools because of their greater flexibility in classroom structure.

By this second phase, however, computers were already deviating significantly from the pattern followed by earlier technologies. Much of the interest in computers was coming bottom-up from teachers and students, not merely top-down from administrators. PCs and general applications software made computing more flexible and easily adapted to different subjects and styles of teaching. Unlike motion pictures, radio, and TV, computers were far more susceptible to both student-centered and teacher-defined activities. And as computers began to be used for communication and the development of new learning communities, they took on an entirely different character from the earlier technologies.

These possibilities are all being extended in a third phase of development that has begun in the 1990s with the advent of multimedia, the explosive growth of the Internet and the World Wide Web, and the transformation of computing from a segregated activity into a ubiquitous part of the everyday work, school, and home environment. If, as Cuban argues, teachers adopt tools that are "simple, durable, flexible, and responsive to teacher-defined problems in meeting the demands of daily instruction," computers now increasingly meet those minimum requirements—but, obviously, they can also do much more.

THE COMMUNICATION REVOLUTION IN LEARNING

To some critics, the problem with computers has not been the obstacles to their adoption, but the effects on education if they are adopted. Computer-based education, critics have worried, would value "calculation" and "instrumental reason" over the emotional, aesthetic, and critical faculties. It would mechanize education, reduce its personal character, and lead students to become engrossed in relations with machines instead of developing relations with teachers and other students.

The first phase of educational computing with its emphasis on teaching machines gave some reason for this concern. But alongside the model of the computer as tutor there grew up another paradigm of educational computing that emphasized creative, student-centered learning. As the former reflected the didactic tradition of education, so the latter reflected the approach advocated by John Dewey and other exponents of progressive education, which views students as actively shaping their own understanding and teachers as facilitating that process. During the 1980s, this constructivist approach to computing, best exemplified in the work of Seymour Papert of MIT, became more prominent.

In addition, the culture that grew up around Apple's Macintosh computer offered humanist critics a more comfortable aesthetic that celebrated creativity, self-expression, and individuality—not calculation. The Mac's graphical user interface reversed the whole premise of "computer literacy"; instead of making students sophisticated enough to use computers, it made computers simple enough for students to use. The predominance of Macs in schools may have resulted from Apple's corporate strategy, but it also fit with a preference for dealing with the computer, not as an analytical engine, but as a tool useful for a variety of tasks, projects, and activities. Feared originally as an educational straightjacket, the computer turned out in many of its uses to be a new medium of expression—like writing or painting.

Of course, one virtue of the computer is that it can become, as computing pioneer Alan Kay writes, "any and all existing media, including books and musical instruments." And with the advent of multimedia, the computer has evolved into a distinctive medium that is uniquely capable of juxtaposing text, images, audio, and video. Multimedia permits an extraordinary flexibility in conveying concepts—through words, pictures, and sounds, as something that can be built or played as well as read or watched. The connections change old genres and make possible new ones. The traditional dictionary had a cumbersome and inadequate method to describe the pronunciation of words; the multimedia dictionary pronounces them. New genres, such as simulation games, are emerging that challenge the user or player to build some complex creation—a city, species, business, or world—out of some given set of resources, or that put the student into a simulated environment or through a scenario to meet a challenge or learn a skill. The computer thereby turns the passive reader into a participant; it cues the student of a need to do something, but not necessarily what to do. With multimedia the computer draws on more of the senses, and more dimensions of intelligence, enlarging the opportunity to learn for those who have been less able to learn from conventional teaching materials. And as the tools for creating multimedia become less expensive, students will make multimedia fully their own by creating work that exploits its new aesthetic and intellectual possibilities.

Multimedia has such stunning possibilities that it invites a fascination with technical virtuosity and surface effects that can become a distraction from learning. New software that combines learning and play has blurred the boundaries between them in a new hybrid variety, "edutainment." The very term expresses perfectly both the opportunity to turn education into play and the danger of learning being lost amid the games and the glitter. It is one thing to play at something; another to reflect upon it and acquire a discipline. Software that is good for play may not be good for learning in the full sense. Much educational software also just renders on a computer screen what is already available in books and merely adds gimmickry. But some uses of the new media are genuinely inspired, provocative, and engaging, and these examples suggest that we have opened an important chapter in the history of the imagination—and of education.

The transformation of computers into a medium of two-way communication also advances the creative and exploratory uses of the technology. Access to the Internet and the Web puts students in reach of resources and people that schools could never before provide. Even if the Internet consisted only of texts and images, it would be of immense value as it becomes the world's largest library. But it also increasingly provides access to audio and video archives, which conventional libraries generally do not offer. Hypertext links offer pathways that allow the novice to find connections among different sources, and the growing search capacities on the Web make it an increasingly powerful instrument of research.

And, of course, the Internet provides not simply published resources, but also cyberspaces—news groups and other forums for discussion; MUDs for role playing and simulation; and new learning networks that help connect students, teachers, and others for a widening variety of purposes. Electronic networks enable students and teachers to combine resources and communities and to work with one another in novel ways. Groups of students at different schools, even in different countries, work together on collaborative projects, comparing the results of environment studies or cross-cultural surveys and thereby learning not only the subject at hand but also other skills in social relationships—just the kind of learning that the early critics of teaching machines were afraid computers would stifle.

Through distance learning, both students and teachers can take courses in special subjects not locally available. In a recent article in the *American Journal of Physics* (December 1995), Edwin F. Taylor and Richard C. Smith—two physicists who since 1986 have been teaching online courses on relativity to a mix of students and teachers from high schools and colleges—report that they have equally good results teaching online as in person. Their first two conclusions contradict the usual expectations:

1. The computer conference setting can be personal, friendly and inclusive. The medium is largely race-neutral, location-neutral, status-neutral, age-neutral, income-neutral, disability-neutral, and would be gender-neutral except for the clue of first names. Student participation in the discussion (in part forced by our course format) is greater than in any of our face-to-face classes. Some kinds of personal warmth appear to be more freely exchanged in the absence of bodies.

2. Computer conference classes bring instruction to a range of students for whom enrollment in

> The term "edutainment" expresses both the opportunity and the danger.

conventional courses is difficult or impossible. Participation can occur conveniently at any time in a busy daily schedule. Some students blossom when in front of a computer screen and accomplish tasks that they otherwise would avoid. . . .

Taylor and Smith also recognize some drawbacks in the online format—for example, students don't receive visual cues from teachers—and they are not suggesting that online instruction will replace ordinary teaching. Their online students are a special, self-selected group. But many students and teachers have special interests; schools traditionally have just had little way of meeting them.

Long before computers, progressive educators called for strengthening the contact between school and the society beyond. Computer communications make such contacts, at whatever physical distance, easier and less costly. For example, students now take electronic field trips to enter into discussions with people in specialized fields of work, to view exhibits, even to use the cameras and other physical instruments that are now being connected to the Web and that will increasingly enable students in real time to enter into events at a distance and to participate in scientific experiments.

The Web is beginning to transform the practice of scientific research as it becomes a system for publishing not only scientific literature, but also scientific data. Genetic, meteorological, geographic, and census data are readily available to be downloaded and analyzed. Some journals are linking articles, data, and bibliographies, enabling a reader to jump back from the text to the original data or sources on which they are based. With the benefit of "applets"—software programs available on the network usable for specific purposes—readers will increasingly be able to redo the analysis or to extend it. Thus, an article about supernovas can include a simulation of a supernova explosion, along with tools that allow the reader to see the simulation run under different assumptions. In short, the Web is emerging not simply as a digital library, but also as a digital laboratory—a genuinely revolutionary development in science.

In the light of these developments, the history of educational computing takes on a different significance. Evaluations of the "effects of computers," whether in education or other areas, have had a short half-life because the very nature of computing has changed so fundamentally with the development of PCs, the introduction of graphical user interfaces, the advent of multimedia, and the explosion of computer communications. Cost-benefit analyses of educational computing compared to conventional teaching have been particularly prone to obsolescence because of the declining costs of computing, especially relative to teaching. And the value of early efforts in educational computing was not measurable in the short run because the benefits did not only involve what students learned. They also involved what everyone else learned. The early efforts helped American software designers and developers as well as schools and teachers to begin climbing a learning curve far ahead of other societies. Today educational software is largely an American industry. The Internet and the Web, while global in scope, also reflect America's distinctive edge.

Some evidence suggests that current technology already offers benefits in the narrow sense of measured student learning. The "Kickstart Initiative," the final report by President Clinton's Advisory Council on the National Information Infrastructure, cites studies showing that "technology supporting instruction [has] improved student outcomes in language arts, math, social studies and science"; that "multimedia instruction—compared to more conventional approaches—[has] produced time savings of 30 percent, improved achievement and cost savings of 30 to 40 percent" and demonstrated "a direct positive link between the amount of interactivity provided and instructional effectiveness"; and that "remedial and low-achieving students" have registered "gains of 80 percent for reading and 90 percent for math when computers were used to assist in the learning process." I would not stake my life on these numbers. But even approximately equal results for computer-based education would amply justify further investment given the trajectory of costs, and in any event the more important uses of technology now extend and enliven education and discovery in ways that such studies do not capture.

The skeptics are surely right, however, that the "learning revolution," as the magazines call it, still has not had any general influence on schools. The many high-end uses of the new technology, like online courses in relativity, are appropriate for advanced secondary and college work but do not address the general needs of primary and secondary education. The market for educational software is growing rapidly, but many students, especially from middle-class families, are more likely to use it at home than at school, while students from low-income families never use it at all.

New educational sites on the Internet appear daily but don't affect most classrooms. The challenge now is to go from scattered initiatives to more comprehensive changes. And that is what many reformers are trying to do by combining new technology with an educational reform agenda—one that progressives of the 1920s would have no trouble recognizing.

> The challenge now is to go from scattered initiatives to comprehensive changes.

PROGRESSIVE EDUCATION REBORN?

Reports and commentary on education now often argue that as our current system of schooling reflects the industrial age, so we need a new approach to learning in the information age. Thus a report published in 1995 by the National Academy of Sciences, *Reinventing Schools: The Technology Is Now!*, says postindustrial society "calls for a new, postindustrial form of education" — one that puts students in a more central, active role in their own learning, helps them learn "to ask many questions and to devise multiple approaches to a problem" instead of forcing them to come up "with one right answer," and encourages "critical thinking, teamwork, compromise, and communication." Similarly, the Clinton administration's "Kickstart Initiative" foresees innovation that "brings the world to the classroom," "enables students to learn by doing," and "allows educators to become guides and coaches to students, rather than be 'the sage on the stage.'" On the right, Lewis J. Perelman, the author of *School's Out*, wants to empower students to seek out instruction individually in the electronic marketplace. While significantly different, all these proposals call for use of technology to advance student-centered, project-based approaches to learning.

To anyone familiar with the history of educational reform, such ideas will have a familiar air. For example, in the opening pages of *The Child-Centered School* (1928), one of the classics of progressive education, Harold Rugg and Ann Shumaker decry traditional schooling as a product of the industrial age and "mass mind." They use two photographs in the book's frontispiece to represent the contrast between "the new and the old in education." One photo shows a class of students at their desks ("Eyes front! Arms folded! Sit still!"), which Rugg and Shumaker call the old "listening" regime. A second photo shows students in small groups busily working on different projects ("Freedom! Pupil initiative! Activity! A life of happy intimacy . . ."). This was the image of the future in the 1920s, and though the tools and terminology have changed, it is still the image of the educational future that many reformers hold up today.

Perhaps the absence of acknowledgments by today's reformers is understandable. For those who claim to be anticipating a new era, old antecedents are embarrassing. Moreover, what progressive education achieved in the first half of the twentieth century—the expansion of the curriculum, addition of extracurricular activities, greater flexibility and mobility in elementary school classrooms, improved teacher training, child study teams, changes in school architecture to provide for more varied activities, and much else—is now taken for granted, and the movement is better remembered for its failings. Progressive education collapsed during the 1950s because it had lost its way and then ran into a storm of distorted charges. Taken over by professionals, it became encrusted as an ideology of the teachers colleges. From one direction, conservatives accused progressivism of subversive tendencies on the basis of its old entanglements with the left; from another direction, liberal critics accused it of promoting conformity and anti-intellectualism. Perhaps progressive education had to die to be shorn of all the extraneous baggage it had accumulated.

In their concern for active, student-centered learning and communication with the wider world, today's technological neoprogressives have revived an old and worthy tradition. And by connecting progressive ideas with computers, they may have finally found a way not only to present them in an appealing, updated form, but also to make them work. For the difficulty with the ideal of active, student-centered education was not simply the opposition it aroused, but the demands it imposed on teachers and schools. The new technology may help manage those demands.

A growing body of evidence suggests that the introduction of computers into classrooms promotes a greater emphasis on projects, with teachers acting as guides and students taking on a central role in their own learning. Alan Collins, head of educational technology at BBN Corporation, an internet services company for businesses, identifies eight major shifts that research suggests computers bring about in education—all of them moving in the direction of progressivism. Among these are a "shift from whole-class to small-group instruction" and "from lecture and recitation to coaching." When computers are introduced, Collins argues, teachers find it hard to keep students in "lockstep" and so adopt more "individualized" approaches. A study of the Apple Classrooms of Tomorrow found that teacher-led activities dropped from 70 percent in classes without computers to less than 10 percent in classes with computers, and that activities facilitated by teachers, rather than directed by them, increased from about 20 percent to 50 percent of class time. Other trends, according to Collins, include shifts "toward more engaged students," "from a competitive to a cooperative social structure," "from all students learning the same things to different students learning different things," and "from the primacy of verbal thinking to the integration of visual verbal thinking."

The new technology alone does not determine these effects. Schools with different cultures and philosophies will make use of computers, like other tools, in different ways. A school wedded to the didactic approach can use integrated learning systems to reinforce conventional teaching methods. A constructivist approach isn't easy; it requires a great deal of institutional support. In a recent study of nine sites pursuing an educational reform agenda emphasizing "student-centered, curriculum-rich, technology-based projects," Barbara Means and her colleagues at SRI, a California research organization, found that the key factor in determining success was a coherent, school-wide instructional vision.

One factor that in the long run may help advance this approach is cost. For the immediate future, the cost of technology is an obstacle to large-scale plans for change. The National Academy report says the technology is "now"—but, alas, the money is not. The fundamental trends, however, are implacable. The cost of labor only goes up, while the costs of computer power and telecommunications go down—steadily and sharply. Computers will become extremely cheap in the next century, and thus student-centered projects based on computers will be far less expensive than today. The obstacle to more individualized instruction and smaller classes has always been the cost of employing additional teachers. But if additional teaching comes inexpensively from computers, individualized education is more feasible. By occupying some of the students, computers can reduce the number of students teachers need to supervise at any given moment. This amounts to a reduction in *effective* class size. Moreover, according to Collins, unlike teachers in conventional classes, who tend to call on stronger students, teachers in classes with computers spend relatively more of their time with weaker students.

The use of computers can also help address another obstacle to change—standardized achievement tests. The new technology may encourage some change in assessment methods, but the present system will likely remain for such critical purposes as college admissions. To prepare students for those tests, schools can make use of the more didactic forms of computer-based education without organizing their whole program on that basis.

As technology may help create effectively smaller classes, so it may also strengthen the case for *smaller schools*. Empirical studies indicate that students in large schools take part in fewer school activities, identify less with the school, and have lower scores on achievement tests than do students in modest-sized schools. Deborah Meier, a principal in East Harlem and an advocate of smaller schools, argues that small size permits closer relations among administrators, teachers, and students and thereby fosters the kind of unified educational vision that researchers have repeatedly identified as a key to successful schools. In a small school, students are less likely to be lost amid the throng. The creation of little schools within the framework of public education makes diversity and school choice accessible on an equal and local basis.

Of course, modest-sized schools can be created from big ones without any help from technology. But the new media may help mitigate some of their shortcomings and improve the trade-offs. Many parents are concerned that smaller schools may not be able to offer as great a diversity of courses. Computer learning networks can provide them. As a small school can create a strong local learning community, so online communities can help students widen their contacts and affiliations—offering the best of both worlds. And just as computers help small businesses by enabling them to perform complex services that used to require large bureaucracies, so the new technology can help small schools manage their affairs.

Computers and computer communications may also have particular value for alleviating some sources of inequality. Computer communications enable people with disabilities to gain access to resources otherwise unavailable and to take part in groups without hindrance or stigma. Similarly, computer networks improve access to educational resources for those in small communities and rural areas. For the same reason, they may be especially valuable for those who seek to continue their education while working at a job. Members of racial and ethnic minorities may learn more through interactive software or online services because they sense no stigma or disapproval. Social psychologists Lee Sproull and Sara Kiesler have found in experimental research that lower-status participants in electronic discussions are less inhibited and more likely to speak up than when communicating face-to-face. Thus, the very groups that now lag in the use of computers and computer communications may especially benefit from access to them.

Of course, nothing guarantees that computers will be used for progressive purposes. Conservatives would like nothing better than to use the technological limitations of schools as a rationale for privatizing the schools or substituting a kind of high-tech home schooling. Inevitably, choices about technology become entangled in larger choices about politics.

THE POLITICS OF THE COMPUTER TRANSITION

The use of computers and the Internet is now expanding rapidly, but with marked disparities between rich and poor school districts. In 1995, according to a U.S. Department of Education survey, half of public schools had at least some internet access, up from 35 percent in 1994; and while only 9 percent of classrooms were connected, that was up from 3 percent a year earlier. A student in an affluent community is roughly twice as likely as one in a poor community to attend a school with internet access.

Students are now using computers differently from in the past. The computer laboratory, typically set up for computer literacy and programming courses, is evolving into general-purpose computer work area where students can do projects of all kinds, including internet work. For most schools, according to the SRI study, concentrating computers in a laboratory is still the most efficient way to provide maximum access to a limited number of machines; distributing computers through classrooms optimally requires at least 6 to 8 computers for a class of 25 to 35 students. At present rates of growth, the average school in the United States should approach that roughly one-to-four ratio around the turn of the century.

The 1996 Telecommunications Act made it a matter of national policy that schools receive "affordable" access to telecommunications. The legislation sets a new precedent by linking communications policy and education; the Federal Communications Commission (FCC) will now determine the exact obligations of the telecommunications industry in the subsidy of school connections. Cost estimates vary, depending on the assumed level of access and whether the estimates include the cost of the computers themselves. There is a wide range of possibilities between providing a school with a dial-up account for one computer and creating a high-bandwidth network linking computers on every student's and teacher's desktop. As platforms change, the standard for universal school service is likely to evolve. In the near term, if every school were to have a local area network, 60 new computers, a router, and a local server—with every district, or 4 to 6 schools, having a high-bandwidth (T-1) connection to the Internet—such a system, according to a 1994 Department of Education study, would run between $9 billion and $22 billion in onetime costs (about half of which would pay for the initial purchase of computers) and $1.75 billion to $4.61 billion annually. Of the annual costs, roughly a quarter would go for the telecommunications lines and internet service; so if only those are cross-subsidized, the schools would still be left with very large costs indeed. The FCC is exploring whether to set aside spectrum to provide schools wireless connections, which could particularly help to minimize indirect costs, such as asbestos removal, from retrofitting school buildings.

Schools in affluent districts may be able to raise these costs in local taxes. Some districts (such as my own in Princeton) have already benefited from partnerships with universities and businesses in making the transition to networked schools. But even with the most supportive telecommunications policies and voluntary support, schools in low-income communities will almost certainly need additional financing from the states or federal government to shoulder the required investments. Otherwise there seems little prospect that inequalities among schools or communities will soon diminish.

In principle, the falling cost of computers and bandwidth should increase opportunities for lower-income groups and communities. So far, however, possession of computers (and of network connections) has continued to grow more rapidly among high-income than among low-income households, thus widening the disparities, according to a recent RAND analysis of changes in computer ownership from 1989 to 1993. Eventually, if histories of the telephone, radio, and television are accurate precedents for the computer, the diffusion of computer communications will tend toward universality. But the transition could take a long time—decades. In the meantime, many groups will be disconnected from a communication network of growing value, and we will all lose the benefit of "network externalities"—the increased value of a network to each user as others are connected. For example, the value of computer communications to schools increases as teachers are able to reach more of the parents of their students and as more students can use the systems from home. Hence the rationale for using public policy to accelerate the transition to universal electronic communication for both community institutions and households in low-income areas. Schools and libraries seem to be the only institutions for which such support is now politically obtainable; they may take on larger significance by opening up access for families as well as the children themselves.

The schools need not only cheap connectivity, but also low-cost access to content. Currently, the Web provides free access to enormous amounts of information, but many sources are likely to be available only on a fee basis as commercial transactions become customary. To be sure, governmental sources, many nonprofit organizations, and schools themselves will continue to offer publications and other resources for free. So will companies interested in fostering long-term business. But many journals and other sources will be available only at a price, and students will lose access to such sources unless there are affordable site licenses and other arrangements for schools. The development of online libraries providing free access to work in the public domain and low-cost access to copyrighted material of educational value should be a priority for both public and philanthropic support. What Carnegie did a hundred years ago can now be accomplished more efficiently, for the entire world.

As the cost of computers declines, schools will likely move from computer laboratories to desktop computers distributed through classrooms and then, in a further stage, toward more mobile forms of computing. Voice activation will often obviate the need to sit down at the keyboard; wireless will liberate the networked computer from its place on the desktop. Increasingly, students and teachers may scarcely even think of computing as a distinctive activity. Drawing an analogy with electricity, Marc Weiser of Xerox PARC (Palo Alto Research Center) suggests that a truly powerful technology "disappears" from awareness and that the computer of the future will assume diverse forms (tablets, pads, badges, whiteboards) and be a ubiquitous but taken-for-granted part of the built environment. Weiser envisions computers becoming so cheap that some would be left around like scratch pads, the very opposite of the "personal" computer. Thus, a computerized classroom in the future might not have students sitting at keyboards and monitors; it could be a classroom where computing was both ubiquitous and incidental, allowing students freedom to play and work with one another while using the technology's extraordinary capacities.

But, of course, none of this will answer the truly important questions about learning. Here Postman and the other skeptics are right. Ultimately, the qualities of education that we care most about are not technological; they are matters of educational philosophy and practice and in turn depend on broader moral and political judgments. In thinking about education, we ought not to be preoccupied with computers at all, and if the technological transition is successful, we will not be. Because of all they make possible, we must make computers part of education. Then they should "disappear."

MAD RUSHES INTO THE FUTURE:

The Overselling of Educational Technology

Getting schools to leap onto the Information Highway is just the latest in a series of corporate forays marked by ignorance, self-interest, and marketing madness.

Douglas D. Noble

School technology is big business again, given a shot in the arm recently by government and corporate leaders. President Bill Clinton, appearing with the heads of media giants Disney, Time Warner, and Turner Communications, announced a major federal initiative of public-private partnerships to equip the nation's classrooms with computers and to link every school to the "information highway" (West 1995b). The nation's governors, meeting with business leaders at IBM headquarters for their Education Summit, have requested hundreds of millions of dollars for new school computers and telecommunications (West 1996).

This "technology fever" sweeping the nation's executive suites and board rooms is not the result of new insights or widespread success in school technology use. Most observers agree that, despite promising experiments, the billions already spent on technology have not had a significant impact on school effectiveness. Research results remain ambiguous, with thoughtful experts calling for cautious planning and extensive teacher training, not necessarily additional or more advanced technology (Office of Technology Assessment 1995).

So how, then, do we explain this most recent explosion of interest in state-of-the-art educational technology displayed by the moguls of newly merged corporate giants in computers, media, and communications? Can we really trust the improvement of education to them and their expensive new technology, as government officials (and some educators) seem so ready to do?

I suggest instead that we learn from some sobering experiences of the past. For several years I have been researching the political history of computer-based education, including its military roots (Noble 1991), its early commercialization, and its widespread adoption. I have been especially interested in recurring corporate high-tech ventures into schools, usually at government invitation and expense. The information I've gathered can be distilled into three lessons about the educational technology market.

Business Leaders' Illusions

Lesson 1. Business leaders often do not know what they are doing. Market fantasies and intense competition, rather than good business sense or a concern for education, typically drive corporate decisions in educational technology.

What I have found above all is that big business often has not known what it was doing in school technology. Again and again, major firms with little knowledge of education have exploited political opportunities to break into the schools, marketing their technology according to the latest education fashion, trying to make the killing they had mistakenly convinced themselves was there for the taking.

Repeatedly, leaders of major firms have blindly believed their own illusions and followed the predictions of information age fortune-tellers, despite the skepticism of their own lieutenants. The hubris of these corporate leaders in their self-appointed role to "save" education, to pursue the holy grail of electronic teaching, and to come up with the "killer application" for their gadgetry has sometimes driven their firms to destruction. At the same time, this high-tech sideshow has created an appalling distraction for educators, who have been taken for an expensive ride on the roller coaster of computer madness.

In the 1960s, federal education officials solicited private defense contractors to enter into a partnership to revolutionize education with warmed-over

Can we really trust the improvement of education to corporate giants and their expensive new technology as government officials seem so ready to do?

military hardware and systems. Massive federal expenditures created a new, "unnatural" educational technology market, one that was producer-driven rather than consumer-driven (Gandy 1976). Francis Keppel (1967), who as U.S. Education Commissioner first opened the federal coffers to business enterprise and eventually headed the General Learning Corporation, a joint venture of General Electric and Time Warner, explained later that "a billion dollars looking for a good, new way to be spent does not ordinarily turn the American businessman into a shrinking violet." Also, once some major firms entered the market, others felt compelled to enter as well; they couldn't afford to "remain aloof in the midst of a technological revolution . . ." (Ellis 1964). Lyle Spencer (1967), who led the first charge into school technology with his firm, SRA, linked to giant IBM, marveled at the parade of Fortune 500 firms soon entering the market and exclaimed, "They probably assumed we knew what we were doing."

Eventually all the major technology and media firms dove headlong into the school technology market, long before they had any viable educational technology and with wildly exaggerated estimates of market size. Their leaders eagerly believed futuristic rhetoric about a "knowledge industry" explosion and invested millions in "resoundingly premature ventures" (Solberg 1984), trying to market rudimentary technology that was "somewhere between bland and downright insulting" (Bowen 1965). In a 1983 interview, Keppel explained that "in

the middle 1960s, . . . there was then as there is now again, an enthusiasm, a euphoria for what modern information technology, computers, etc., could do for education. . . . This was going to be the great system of changing education. It flopped. All the companies flopped." Their efforts had been "put together out of idealistic dreaming and very little hard business sense" (Reichek 1970), instances of "those mad rushes into the future that big corporations do now and then" (Prendergast 1986)—taking schools, teachers, and students along for the ride.

In the 1970s, William Norris, head of computer giant Control Data Corporation (CDC), fantasized about revolutionizing education with his PLATO system, "the biggest thing since the beginning" (Pantages 1976). After a decade and more than a billion dollars invested in increasingly desperate strategies to market PLATO in the public schools, so much of CDC had become wrapped up in PLATO that the company disintegrated. In 1986 Norris was forced to step down, but it was too late to save the company. The lesson here is this: Don't count on high-profile corporate leaders to know where they're going, much less where education should go.

One recent example of a company being taken to the brink of disaster by its leader's "mad rush into the future" is the sell-off in 1993 of Jostens Learning Corporation, the largest educational software firm in the country. H. William Lurton, chairman of Jostens, Inc., vendor of school graduation products

such as class rings, yearbooks, and school photographs, decided to diversify into multimedia education. Although Lurton knew nothing about interactive educational software, he rationalized that Jostens was already in the educational market, so it would not be too great a stretch. Besides, Lurton saw a huge potential K–12 market for Jostens Learning products.

Lurton rushed into a hot business he knew nothing about, "a cropper chasing a fad," according to an account in *Forbes* (Schifrin 1994). In 1988, he purchased a 25 percent stake in Broderbund Software. Then he bought Education Systems Corporation, an interactive software company, and hired its entrepreneurial chairman to become chief executive of the new subsidiary, Jostens Learning. From 1986 to 1991, Jostens Learning grew merrily, and in 1992 Lurton bought Wicat Systems, Inc., its biggest educational software competitor. This gave Jostens Learning more than 60 percent of the market in "integrated learning systems," focused on sophisticated multimedia presentation with sound, animation, and video. Lurton and Jostens Learning seemed exceptionally well placed within the education business.

But Jostens was actually heading for disaster. Jostens software could run only on its own expensive computer systems, and educators were starting to choose software that could run on different computers, preferably those already in their schools. Jostens did not know enough about such trends, and its market share began to erode. By mid-1993, Lurton was unceremoniously ousted after 22 years as head of Jostens, and Jostens sold Jostens Learning to an investment group with its own illusions about the educational technology market.

Marketing's Supremacy

Lesson 2. Schools are typically sold a bill of goods, not the goods themselves. Penetration of the education market with computer-based technology has depended more on effective conditioning of the market through a barrage of advertising and ideology than on the effectiveness of the technologies themselves.

6. SPECIAL ISSUES

Marketing is the name of the game in the educational technology business. One Control Data vice president lamented that "potential customers do not share our sense of urgency for the implementation and use of computer-based education" (Morris 1977). A General Learning executive insisted that ". . . we must act with agonizing care in picking not only the right materials to present but also the moment and method of presentation, so that . . . the whole American community feels that the materials we produce are what the community wants, badly needs, and must have" (Bowen 1964). Participants in early ventures typically blamed their failure on the fact that the education market was not yet "ready" for their technology. This is partly true, but not because the technology itself was ahead of its time; rather, the ideological leavening of the education market had not yet set. Although the glamor of technology captivated some, the rhetoric of the Information Age had not yet fully conditioned the schools to welcome the gadgetry into classrooms.

The first real inroads came with the campaign for computer literacy and thinking skills ("mindstorms") and Apple's tax-deductible donations of microcomputers to schools (an effort labeled "Kids Can't Wait"). By 1984, with the computer as *Time* magazine's "Man of the Year" and the *Nation at Risk* report calling for computer literacy—even programming—as a "new basic skill," the Information Age had seemingly arrived, and the schools opened up to a flood of computers. States invested heavily to bring computer literacy to their students and to prepare them for the Information Age.

The term "computer literacy" had been coined with just that scenario in mind. Andrew Molnar, director of the Office of Computing Activities at the National Science Foundation (NSF), later recounted that educational technophiles at the foundation were deeply concerned about the scattered, uncoordinated programs in computer-based instruction that a skeptical NSF was reluctantly funding. They wanted a coordinated effort to bring computer-

based education into the schools. "We spent . . . something like a half a billion dollars on technology in education, but they were so uncoordinated that you either had to be a liar, a thief, or corrupt in order to pull all of these things together to do a program that would involve technology in any significant way" (Aspray 1991).

Molnar and his colleagues took just such a route. "We started computer literacy in '72," Molnar recollected. "We coined that phrase. It's sort of ironic. Nobody knows what computer literacy is. Nobody can define it. And the reason we selected [it] was because nobody could define it, and . . . it was a broad enough term that you could get all of these programs together under one roof" (Aspray 1991). Molnar and others held prestigious national conferences on computer literacy, and eventually, in the early 1980s, the term took on a life of its own, resulting in millions of computers in schools.

Hundreds of thousands of computers also entered the schools amidst the exaggerated claims by Seymour Papert and Bolt, Beranek, and Newman that their LOGO software would bring thinking skills and "powerful ideas" into the classroom through child-centered computer programming. In fact, LOGO was conceived as a means to teach grammar and then elementary mathematics. The idea that LOGO would teach generalized thinking came **later, as an extremely marketable afterthought (Lawler 1987), one that has never been demonstrated. Still, the image of a child at a computer came to symbolize intense intellectual inquiry akin to that depicted by Rodin's famous statue.**

The LOGO-inspired movement to enable children to think and have

Information "hypeway" is but the latest, and potentially the most costly, bill of goods sold to the schools.

powerful ideas using computers inundated the schools with new hardware and software, which now remain in some classrooms even though their exaggerated rationale has long since been abandoned. At a recent restrospective on LOGO,[1] its apologists and proselytizers, now reduced to an insular cadre at MIT's Media Lab, conceded that they had been "naive" and that once "realism . . . set in," they realized that the "LOGO culture" was drastically—and prematurely—oversold to the nation's schools. Only a handful of schools still use LOGO, typically as a vehicle for science and mathematics exploration. Talk of "enhanced thinking" or "powerful ideas" has disappeared.

The recent term "Information Highway" also serves to saturate schools with computer technology, this time bringing in fiber-optic cable and online services at an estimated eventual cost of $10 billion. A recent comprehensive report on the Information Highway notes that no two educators, technologists, or telecommunications experts define the term the same way or "agree on exactly how [its] development will affect education" (West 1995a). This information "hypeway" is but the latest, and potentially the most costly, bill of goods sold to the schools in the name of a computer-based educational revolution.

Corporate strategies for the marketing of computer-based education are chameleonlike, changing colors to meet the needs of every educational fad or government invitation or technological innovation that comes along. A report on educational technology released in April 1995 by the Office of Technology Assessment recounts how "the advice of experts in education technology has changed dramatically over the past decade."

In 1983 teachers were told to use computers to teach students to program in BASIC, because "it's the language that comes with your computer." In 1984 they were told to teach students to program in LOGO in order to "teach students to think, not just to program." In 1986 they were told to teach with integrated drill-and-practice systems in computer labs to "individualize instruction and increase test scores." In 1988 they were told to teach word processing because children should "use computer tools as adults do." In 1990 they were told to teach with curriculum-specific tools, such as science simulations, history databases, and data probes, to "integrate the computers into the existing

Education as Technology's Servant

Lesson 3. Computer-based education is more about using the education market in the service of technological product development than it is about using technology in the service of education.

Much of the experimentation with computers in schools in the 1950s and 1960s was only marginally about education. The defense industries were aggressively pursuing new, diversified markets for developing and implementing their military technology, and federal education funds filled the bill. "The entertainment industry is now the driving force for new technology, as defense used to be," said a *Business Week* article (Mandel et al. 1994). So in the 1990s, with the expansion of the Information Highway into the schools,

ment are coming together, there's not going to be a future" (Hill 1993).

The merger frenzy now dominating the mad dash to the Information Highway is surprisingly reminiscent of the mid-1960s' flurry of mergers between hardware and software companies. "There seems to be no end in sight to the coupling of the entertainment and communications giants. The cable and phone companies are the infrastructure guys; and the entertainment companies have the content needed to fill those pipelines" (Clarkin 1995). The difference this time is that education is just one lucrative niche in the coming interactive media deluge: "Somebody's 'big wire' is going to be in every school," notes one executive, "and that presents a [huge] opportunity" (West 1995a). Once again, corporate moguls are betting their companies on mad rushes into the future. The competitive jockeying for position to build and fill the Information Highway, whose ultimate shape or marketability no one can yet predict, lies behind the latest push for educational technology.

One recent example is the promotion of CD-ROM multimedia technology that began in the late 1980s. Competition among computer hardware makers and software publishers drove firm after firm to leap into a consumer and school CD-ROM market that was, in fact, "mainly wishful thinking" rather than a real market based on consumer demand (Losee 1994). Corporate marketers have thrust CD-ROM capabilities, built into personal computers, on school and home consumers because companies have seen the CD-ROM market as a competitive strategy; not because an abundance of quality CD-ROM-based multimedia software exists or because CD-ROM technology is the wave of the future. One executive identifies it as "a low-risk way to practice making content for interactive television (ITV)."

Corporate executives admit that CD-ROM is merely a "bridge technology," a stopgap on the way to the Information Highway: "CD-ROMs are the Quonset hut of media—temporary structures that have a way of becoming permanent," explains one executive. "You're

The implementation of computer-based technology in schools is still highly experimental, despite the billions spent annually.

curriculum." In 1992 they were told to teach hypertext multimedia programming because "students learn best by creating products for an audience." In 1994 they were told to teach with Internet telecommunications to "let students be part of the real world."

These rapid-fire changes in the prevailing wisdom of educational technology experts indicate that still, after 30 years, the implementation of computer-based technology in schools is highly experimental, despite the billions spent annually. More important, they reflect powerful, unrelenting pressure from corporate marketers and their government ideologues to get computers into the schools, one way or another. Even most research on educational technology, such as Apple's high-minded "Apple Classrooms of Tomorrow," is really long-term marketing and product development masquerading as education reform.

educational technology arguably serves the interests of the entertainment/telecommunications industry rather than the interests of education.

Corporate America now views educational material as a category of "software" or "content" on the Information Highway, alongside computer games, electronic mail and bulletin boards, news, books, magazines, movies, pornography, television shows, interactive TV, consumer advertising, and gambling and home shopping capabilities. "What's clear," notes one Bell Atlantic executive, "is [that] this is not so much an info highway, but an entertainment highway" (Scwartz 1995). Education is simply a variation of consumer entertainment services, and educators are "at best, peripheral players in the game" (West 1995a). According to the leading marketer of educational videodisks, "For companies that don't recognize that education and entertain-

Education is just one lucrative niche in the coming interactive media deluge.

not going to get to participate in ITV unless you get in early . . . It's a warmup." One industry observer says that "Companies view CD-ROM as a competitive advantage," and this competition to position firms for the Information Highway has resulted in untold quantities of CD-ROM drives and "a proliferation of ill-conceived and sloppily executed CD-ROM [software]" being discounted or given away to schools in the wake of "seller-fed hysteria" (Losee 1994). Competitive advantage, not educational benefit or consumer demand or even careful business sense, is what is driving the technology into an already bewildered school market.

Skewed Predictions

Educators need to understand that high-tech corporate moguls and marketers, despite their government supporters, are scrambling to predict the future, are seduced by their own high-tech fantasies, and are locked in treacherous, high-stakes gambles. Education for them has typically been a sideshow, a proving ground, or a long-shot investment. Their state-of-the-art technologies have not in the past been products with direct or immediate applications for education, nor will they be in the future. Further, their skewed predictions about education and technology are no better than our own.

Educators, therefore, need not keep abreast of every innovation for fear of losing ground or falling behind. Leave the experiments to the technophiles. The rest of us, unashamedly and with renewed integrity, should follow our own sense of sound educational practice, using proven technologies when applicable. There is no need to join the mad rush into the future or to gamble with our students' education.

[1]"Rethinking the LOGO Culture: What Lessons Have Been Learned?" (April 18, 1995). Symposium at the Annual Meeting of the American Educational Research Association, San Francisco.

References

Aspray, W. (September 25, 1991). "Interview with Andrew Molnar," OH 234. Center for the History of Information Processing, Charles Babbage Institute, University of Minnesota.

Bowen, E. (January 9, 1964). Memo to Norm Ross and J. Handy on Education R&D. Carl Solberg Papers, Box 1. Special Collections, Millbank Memorial Library, Teachers College, Columbia University.

Bowen, E. (February 1, 1965). "Proposal to Task Force." Carl Solberg Papers, Box 1. Special Collections, Millbank Memorial Library, Teachers College, Columbia University.

Clarkin, G. (May 11, 1995). "Giants' Mad Dash to Find Partners." *New York Post*, Business Section, 29.

Ellis, R. (December 9, 1964). "Position Paper: Time Inc.–General Electric Talks." Carl Solberg Papers, Box 1. Special Collections, Millbank Memorial Library, Teachers College, Columbia University.

Gandy, O. H. (1976). "Instructional Technology: The Reselling of the Pentagon." Unpublished doctoral diss., Stanford University.

Hill, M. (May/June 1993). "Textbook, Technology Publishers Meet on Common Ground." *Electronic Learning* 12: 12.

Keppel, F. (January 1967). "The Business Interest in Education." *Phi Delta Kappan*, 48.

Keppel, F. (1983). Interview. Spencer Foundation Oral History Project. Oral History Research Office, Columbia University.

Lawler, R. W. (1987). "Learning Environments: Now, Then, and Someday." In *Artificial Intelligence and Education, Vol. 1*, edited by R. W. Lawler and M. Yazdani. Norwood, N.J.: Ablex.

Losee, S. (September 19, 1994). "Watch Out for the CD-ROM Hype." *Fortune*, 127.

Mandel, M. J., M. Landler, and R. Grover. (March 14, 1994). "The Entertainment Economy." *Business Week*, 60.

Morris, R. (May 10, 1977). Memo to J. R. Morris. Control Data Corporation Archives, Box 149752. Center for the History of Information Processing, Charles Babbage Institute, University of Minnesota.

Noble, D. D. (1991). *The Classroom Arsenal: Military Research, Information Technology and Public Education*. London: Falmer Press.

Office of Technology Assessment. (April 1995). *Teachers and Technology: Making the Connection*. Superintendent of Documents Stock #S/N 052-003-01409-2. Washington D.C.: U.S. Government Printing Office.

Pantages, A. (May 1976). "Control Data's Education Offering." *Datamation*, 183.

Prendergast, C. (1986). *The World of Time, Inc., Vol. 3*. New York: Atheneum.

Reichek, M. A. (May 2, 1970). "High Marks in the Teaching Business." *Business Week*, 32.

Schifrin, M. (July 18, 1994). "Look Before You Leap." *Forbes*, 80–81.

Scwartz, E. (February 1995). "Ray Smith: The I-Way, My Way." *Wired*, 114.

Solberg, C. (May 30, 1984). Cover letter to David Ment, Archivist. Carl Solberg Papers. Special Collections, Millbank Memorial Library, Teachers College, Columbia University.

Spencer, L. (June 27, 1967). Speech to IBM Board of Directors. Lyle M. Spencer Papers, Box 1, University of Chicago Archives.

West, P. (January 11, 1995a). "Logged On for Learning." *Education Week*, 1–28.

West, P. (October 18, 1995b). "Clinton Pushes School-Technology Campaign." *Education Week*, 18, 23.

West, P. (March 13, 1996). "Many Governors Touting Technology as a Magic Bullet." *Education Week*, 1, 22, 23.

Author's note: For a full account of the research discussed here, see my chapter, "A Bill of Goods," in *The International Handbook of Teachers and Teaching*, edited by Bruce J. Biddle, Thomas Good, and Ivor Goodson. Dortrecht, The Netherlands: Kluwer Academic Publishing (in press). The research was conducted with the support of a National Academy of Education Spencer Postdoctoral Fellowship. A longer article by the author on this subject appeared in *Afterimage* (March/April 1996).

Editor's note: See next article for a response from David Dwyer on Noble's critique of the instructional technology market.

Douglas D. Noble is the author of *The Classroom Arsenal* (Falmer 1991) and numerous articles on the history and politics of educational technology. He is cofounder and currently Teacher Coordinator at Cobblestone School in Rochester, New York, and Learning Specialist at the Rochester Institute of Technology. He may be reached at 76 Westland Avenue, Rochester, NY 14618; (716) 442-3383.

A Response to Douglas Noble

WE'RE IN THIS TOGETHER

Along with technology's promise come inevitable problems. But educators can't afford to leave the solutions to others, nor to pretend that this revolution is not happening.

David Dwyer

In "Mad Rushes into the Future: The Overselling of Educational Technology" (see previous article), Douglas Noble offers a sharp critique of a young industry and new market; but he reveals old themes: avarice, hyperbole, insensitivity, and egomania. In the light of the dawning millennium, these ignoble behaviors sadly but stubbornly persist among us. Noble's words sound an always useful buyer-beware alarm, but his message projects a bunker mentality—an ill-advised us-against-them way of thinking.

We are experiencing one of the great transitions in human history. With all the uncertainty it engenders, a global community is emerging, born largely of digital communications and jet-powered transportation. The optimism around new social and economic possibilities stands in stark contrast to the realities we face today.

Browsing the World Wide Web recently (one of those globe-shrinking technologies), my wife encountered a poignant illustration of our global plight. The anonymous author asked us to imagine that the world had been distilled down to a village of just 100 people. In that village, half of all material goods would be in the hands of 6 people. Each of those people would be U.S. citizens. Eighty members of the community would live in substandard housing, 50 would be malnourished, 70 would be unable to read, and only 1 would have enjoyed a college education.[1]

If we considered all U.S. citizens and focused on education, we'd encounter a real-life version of this scenario. We would see that 74 percent of adults over 25 years of age have completed high school, and 19 percent have completed college (Cremin 1990). Laudable facts. But at the same time, more than 3,000 children in the United States drop out every school day, according to the Children's Defense Fund (1996). And half the children between the ages of 10 and 17 engage in behaviors that place them at a serious risk of alienation from their society—or even of death (Carnegie Council on Adolescent Development 1989). In short, we have a long way to go to forge a more humane and equitable world, and we are all in this together.

Mounting Evidence of Gains

Many of us — in both the U.S. and other global villages — ardently believe that schools and their communities have a significant role to play in building a better future. In the crucible of experimentation and debate, educators, researchers, parents, policymakers, and corporate partners who believe in this vision have sought to create more productive and engaging **learning environments for our children. Part of the debate has been about technology and schools; and today, we know a great deal about the role computers can play and the difficulties that universal deployment of technology entails.**

Beyond the self-evident fascination children display toward technology, significant and mounting evidence shows that technology improves students' mastery of basic skills, test scores, writing, and engagement in school. With these gains come decreases in the dropout rate and decreases in attendance and discipline problems.[2] The acquisition of 21st century work skills— communication, collaboration, technology use, and problem solving—have been demonstrated, as well (Tierney 1996).

Are these improvements entirely the result of adding computers to classrooms? Certainly not. Technology adds value to schools when it is an integral part of a comprehensive plan for instructional improvement and when teachers are adequately prepared to use the technology as one more tool in their arsenal. Along with staff development, of course, relevant software is required, as well as enough technology to give students routine access.[3]

Significant and mounting evidence shows that technology improves students' mastery of basic skills, test scores, writing, and engagement in school.

A Quiet Revolution

While evidence is slowly mounting about technology's positive impact in schools, it is already clear that digital technologies are well on the way to becoming a permanent part of the educational arena at all levels and in countries all around the world. U.S. President Clinton last February issued a challenge to schools to ensure technological literacy for all children. Inherent in the challenge was the provision of appropriate training for teachers, modern multimedia computers in classrooms, connections to the Internet, and effective software and online learning resources. The expectation is that by the year 2000, there will be a three-student-to-one computer ratio in our schools.

Throughout the Pacific Rim, many countries have robust plans for integrating technology in schools. Among the leaders are Singapore, South Korea, Canada, Australia, Malaysia, Brazil, and Mexico. Howard Mehlinger (1996) describes this growing use of technology in schools as a quiet revolution, unlike any other he has seen in

education. He characterizes the revolution as slow and steady; eclectic and largely devoid of ideology; and sparked, not by business interests or policymakers, but by teachers and principals who are simply trying to make their schools better.

Other pressures lend a sense of inevitability to this revolution. Our schools have been, and always will be, microcosms of their societies. They evolve over time to reflect values and processes. Our society has undergone a technological revolution in the past 5 to 10 years. Digital technologies now underlie the way we communicate, the way we conduct business, industry, and science, and even the way we entertain ourselves. Further, parents are well aware of the pace of technological change and how it has affected their work places. They want their children to master the knowledge and skills that rewarding work will require in the new millennium.

Problems and Promise

The promise of technology is that it will greatly improve the efficiency and effectiveness of our institutions and evolve as an avenue for lifelong learning and universal communication. But along with that promise come inevitable problems: How will schools keep up with the pace of change? How will we ensure equitable access to everyone? How will we deal with information complexity and quantity? What

about standards for quality? And what about privacy? How do we protect the intellectual work of our writers, artists, scientists, and engineers? Where in our curriculum do we help children navigate this new world? How do we make the minimum number of mistakes that we will surely make as we open school doors to this exotic future?

Noble expounds on the villainy and blundering of business leaders, policymakers, and technologists, and frets over their conspiracy to "use" schools. He concludes that educators should leave the experiments to the "technophiles among us." He recommends that the rest of us "unashamedly and with renewed integrity follow our own sense of what is sound educational practice."

I conclude differently. The serious questions about the use of technology in schools must be answered with care and forethought. In many instances they will only be answered through trial and error—we have not traveled this path before. But above all, they must be answered by all stakeholders in our children's futures, working in concert. Educators cannot leave these questions to others; they must be the salient voices, the designers of experiments, the risk takers, and the critics of results.

Technology, whether we like it or not, is changing the face of the planet.

Technology adds value to schools when it is an integral part of a comprehensive plan for instructional improvement and when teachers are adequately prepared to use it as one more tool in their arsenal.

It is changing our notion of who we are as citizens of that planet. We can pretend that this is not happening and hold onto the past for as long as we can. Or we can grab this opportunity to build a world of peace, prosperity, and understanding. ■

[1] I traced this work to Cornell University, but lost the digital trail there.

[2] These results are found in a number of studies: For example, in his meta-analysis studies, James Kulik of the University of Michigan's Center for Research on Teaching and Learning found trends indicating that when children studied basic skills using technology, their achievement scores rose 10–15 percent and their productivity, 30 percent. See also Barbara Means, (1993), *Using Technology to Support Education Reform*, (Menlo Park, California: SRI International); Alice W. Ryan, (May 1991), "Meta-Analysis of Achievement: Effects of Microcomputer Applications in Elementary Schools," *Educational Administration Quarterly* 27, 2: 161–184; Joan Herman, (1994), *OTA-Testing in American Schools: Asking the Right Questions*, (Los Angeles: National Center for Research on Evaluation, Standards, and Student Testing); J. Sivin-Kachala and Ellen Bialo, (1994), *Report on the Effectiveness of Technology in Schools, 1990–1994*, (New York: Interactive Educational Systems Design, Inc.). Also, the work of J. Dexter Fletcher of the Institute of Defense Analysis, Arlington, Virginia, and John Pisapia and Stephen Perlman of the Metropolitan Educational Research Consortium, Virginia Commonwealth University, Richmond.

[3] *Getting America's Students Ready for the 21st Century: Meeting the Technology Literacy Challenge* (U.S. Department of Education 1996) provides research-based and experience-based plans for developing technology resources in schools and school districts. It is an excellent compendium of case studies and state and federal initiatives.

References

Carnegie Council on Adolescent Development. (1989). *Turning Points: Preparing American Youth for the 21st Century*. New York: Carnegie Corporation of New York.

Children's Defense Fund. (1996) *Facts and Figures: Every Day in America*. World Wide Web: http://www.childrensdefense.org.

Cremin, L. (1990). *Popular Education and Its Discontents*. New York: HarperCollins.

Mehlinger, H.D. (1996). "School Reform in the Information Age," *Phi Delta Kappan* 77, 6: 400–408.

Tierney, R. (1996). "Redefining Computer Appropriation: A Five-year Study Of ACOT Students." In *Education & Technology: Reflections on Computing in Classrooms*, edited by C. Fisher, D. Dwyer, and K. Yocam. San Francisco: Jossey-Bass and Apple Press.

David Dwyer, a former middle school and high school teacher, is Vice President of Advanced Learning Technologies, Computer Curriculum Corporation, 1287 Lawrence Station Rd., Sunnyvale, CA 94089 (e-mail: ddwyer@cccpp.com).

The Internet and Computer Networks

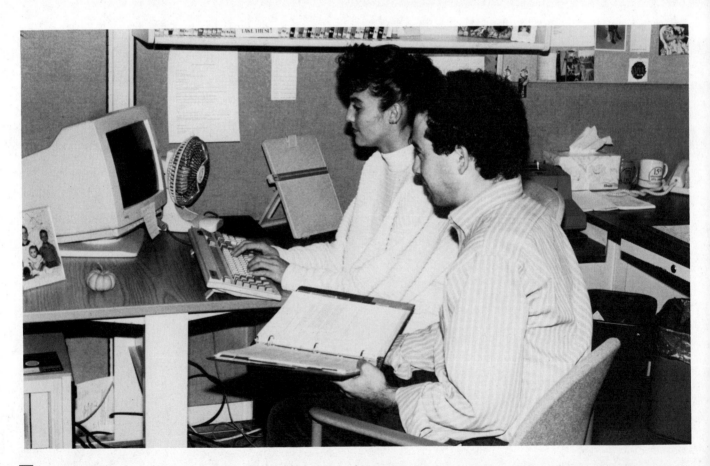

The history of humankind has been tied closely to the tools of each age and the conditions shaped by those tools. Throughout the last century the United States and enlightened countries in Asia, Europe, and Latin America have looked to breakthroughs in machinery and systems design as the practical means for realizing gains in productivity. Productivity has come about by replacing the strength of human and animal muscle with machine speed, strength, and communication facilities.

During the last years of the twentieth century, enlightened countries are looking toward increasing the strength of human thinking and communication using the speed and power of computers on the Internet. These countries are expanding power by bringing intelligent power to the masses. Networked computing is enabling people to acquire, shape, produce, and distribute information faster, more powerfully, more accurately, and more quickly than at any period in history.

However, the torrential hype that has surrounded the Internet and the World Wide Web has created expectations high above its current capabilities. We are not yet at the moment when we can have 500 interactive channels at our fingertips. However, if we turn our attention away from interactive video and focus on what the Internet is now, there is much to be excited about.

The articles in this section address several questions about what the Internet means to educators today—how we plan for it, how it is used, what the resources are, and what current and future benefits it will bring.

In the first article, "Journey into the Unknown," the authors describe an electronic, highly interactive, hands-on field trip entitled MayanQuest. Students virtually peer over the shoulders of scientists, read data, and engage in meaningful dialogue with experts on location. The article also includes a list of resources that can be used by teachers to locate electronic field trips.

Next, Fan Fang tells the story of how Chinese bilingual studies use the Chinese language to communicate in Chinese around the world and to publish an online student newspaper in Chinese. The program allows Chinese students to become conversant in all academic activities in their primary language, and to make significant progress in learning English.

The following article, "Ready Reference on the Internet: A Beginning List of Sources," addresses selection of Internet ready-reference sources for home page or bookmark lists. The author suggests that teachers and students should participate in the selection process and provides activities for students to make their own evaluation criteria.

In "Monster Job!" Laughon and Kurshan describe how some K-12 teachers became moderators of educational telecommunication projects and present results of a survey of 100 moderators who describe their roles. Tables list expressions that describe moderators and World Wide Web project sites.

Finally, "Tips & Tricks for K-12 Educational LANs" offers guidelines for school districts planning to add computer technology, especially local area networks (LANs). Topics include electricity for laboratories, networkable software, hard drives, file servers, facilities, inservice training, budget issues, and much more.

Looking Ahead: Challenge Questions

What do you believe is the future of the Internet within education? What effect will it have on education in the last years of this century?

What is the role of telecomputing in the classroom, the library, the administration, or the home?

Journey into the Unknown

Now you can take your class to places you never dreamed possible. Antarctica and the Yucatán peninsula are just a few seconds away with electronic field trips!

Doug Mason/Earthtrek

School children in Belize ask kids in the United States questions with Dan Buettner.

By Dan Buettner and Cathy de Moll

Last April 24 at 10:52 A.M., 12-year-old Sierra Gaitan was on hand as archaeologists uncovered an important hieroglyphic text at Caracol, a Maya site deep in the Belize Jungle. Sierra studied the glyphs, conversed with the archaeologists, offered her interpretations, and then left in a hurry. The bell had rung, signaling the end of her fourth-hour class at Como School in St. Paul, Minnesota. She logged off the computer and let the next class connect to Central America.

A whole world of information

Electronic field trips have been around since the late '80s. It's become de rigueur for explorers, adventurers, and even scientists to link school kids to the remotest regions of the world via satellite dishes and computers. The first electronic field trip was The Jason Project, conducted by scientist Bob Ballard. This electronic journey is still in existence today. Students travel to an area museum to observe scientists on their journeys to parts of the world.

Today, electronic field trips are highly interactive and offer a wide variety of resources to supplement the trips. Even the teacher who is in a school that is woefully underequipped with computers can take advantage of this rich experience.

When Sierra participated in the electronic field trip known as MayaQuest™, she went a step beyond the long-distance observation of a few years ago to a more hands-on participation in one of the most compelling mysteries of our time—the disappearance of the ancient Maya civilization. Not only was Sierra able to follow where the explorers were going, but she could

- analyze photographs fed by satellite from the Peten Jungle via the Internet,
- email her opinion of the content of the glyphs to the scientists in the field,
- use her research skills to decide where the explorers should go next.

All of this happened on location through a portable satellite dish as the glyphs emerged from the dirt. Discoveries that would have taken years to reach the classroom in the past now travel in a dizzying number of hours.

Better yet, Sierra became empowered by the process of investigation itself. She learned about inquiry and conjecture, the value of research, and how to ask questions and formulate opinions. She learned history, geography, math, language, and art—all through a real-world and real-time vehicle. This, indeed, is a learning adventure. Sierra's teacher joined the chorus proclaiming that MayaQuest provides the best teachable moments ever.

What kinds of electronic adventures are available?

There's more and more variety in the learning adventures being devised. Some of them offer excellent value; others have more glitz than substance.

Be sure to collect as much information as possible about the field trip before signing up. Field trips vary greatly in their interactivity.

The most expensive trips (up to $295 per site per event) typically are television based, offering video and online programming, supported by written material or teacher training or both. The components work best in tandem but can be used separately. With a cable television hookup, teachers can join live field trips to Costa Rica's rain forest (Turner Education's Science in the Rain Forest), the Florida Everglades (The Jason Project), or NASA's Kuiper Airborne Observatory (Live from the Stratosphere).

The increased use of email through Internet services to schools now makes it possible for electronic field trips to produce exciting and extremely rich text and graphic materials that are much more interactive. As in MayaQuest '96, students on the Internet have the capability to peek over the shoulders of professional scientists, read data, and engage in meaningful dialogue with experts on location.

In other Internet-based programs, students can track and report migrating animals (Journey North), take a field trip to Antarctica (Blue Ice™: Focus on Antarctica), or follow a car journey around the world (Global School Net's Where on the Globe Is Roger?). Such programs tend to be less expensive than television-based programs, they last longer, and they fit better into a teacher's schedule.

One of the emerging leaders in the adventure learning field is MECC. In addition to the company's growing library of disk and CD-ROM titles, MECC is clustering a group of interactive education adventures on the Internet in its new MECC Inter@ctive Explorer Series™. This program includes two highly interactive programs mentioned above—Blue Ice: Focus on Antarctica and MayaQuest '96. Both give students and scientists the ability to communicate back and forth over the Internet.

What if I don't have an Internet hookup?

If you don't have access to the newer technologies, you won't be left out. The printed study materials from most of the above programs offer a wide range of activities and resources which can serve as stand-alone supplementary materials.

MayaQuest pulls together the best of the above interactive elements and provides other services for teachers without computers or Internet hookups. (See "Get Started on the Journey.")

Get Started on the Journey

In March and April 1996, the four MayaQuest '96 bicyclists will travel to Mexico and Central America to explore new Maya sites. Numerous resources are available that will give colorful reports on this biking and learning adventure; they can be used at all grade levels.

Poster and newsletter. This 24- x 36-inch color poster tells how to get started on the journey. *Cost:* free. *Contact:* MayaQuest, 529 S. Seventh St., Ste. 320, Minneapolis, MN 55415 (send self-addressed, $1.24-stamped, 9- x 13-inch envelope).

Live satellite telecasts. Three live cable programs highlighting the team's adventures. Students may interview Maya experts and see how the field trip is being incorporated into the classroom. Satellite capabilities or cable access viewing required.

Beginning March 1996. *Cost:* free. *Contact:* Tvlive@informns.k12.mn.us.

Video updates. Offered via *CNN Newsroom*. These live reports from Central America track the team adventure. Available for classroom viewing. Beginning March 1996. *Cost:* free. *Contact:* (800) 344-6219.

MECC's Inter@ctive Explorer Series: MayaQuest '96 Explorer Program. Designed for grades 4–12. Includes a teacher resource guide, MECC's MayaQuest interactive CD-ROM, weekly lesson plans, extended photograph library, direct access to the team in the field, and email voting rights to team destinations. *Cost:* $85. *Contact:* (800) 375-0055.

MayaQuest '96. Offers biweekly updates, postings by a team archaeologist, guest appearances by the world's top archaeologists, photograph library, list serves, news groups, and more. *Cost:* free. *Contact:* http://www.mecc.com/mayaquest.html or MayaQuest@mecc.com.

MayaQuest: The Interactive Expedition. Explores the Maya, both ancient and contemporary. Written by Dan Buettner, this book offers the best of more than 22,000 photographs and 850 pages of online contributions. *Cost:* $39.95. *Contact:* (800) 888-1220.

Other electronic field trips

Science in the Rain Forest
(800) 639-7797

The Jason Project
(800) 923-5548

Live from the Stratosphere
(800) 626-LIVE

Blue Ice: Focus on Antarctica
(800) 375-0055

Journey North
(800) 965-7373

Are electronic field trips just a fad?

The Internet continues to grow at a nearly unimaginable rate of 10 percent each week, while more and more classrooms are being wired with cable and fiber optics. New technologies also allow the delivery of video email and digital audio. Educators now have the capacity—and responsibility—to develop an alternative to expensive and dry textbooks. Our children can visit and take·part in the rest of the world, directly from their classrooms. Programs like MayaQuest '96 and Blue Ice: Focus on Antarctica

- strive to meet national teaching standards to make the subjects kids learn more relevant;

- make the material manageable for a block of class time;

- ensure the interaction is efficient, real, and satisfying so students enjoy learning;

- provide a field trip that is cost effective and user friendly so teachers need not fear the technology.

And as the integration of electronic learning is harnessed to serve the curriculum goals of the classroom teacher, adventure learning is finally poised to meet its full potential. For, as Sierra will tell you, her encounter with archaeologists in MayaQuest was one of the "awesomest" things she ever did in school.

Dan Buettner, leader of the MayaQuest '96 expedition and author of MayaQuest: The Interactive Expedition *and* SovieTrek, *has traversed five of the earth's seven continents by bicycle, breaking several Guinness World Records along the way. Cathy de Moll has participated in electronic learning adventures for over seven years. Their current endeavor, MayaQuest, was recently cited on National Public Radio's* Talk of the Nation *as the best online education program and received an A+ rating by the new Internet publication,* the net.

Traveling the Internet in Chinese

For Chinese bilingual students, a ride on the Information Superhighway renewed cultural connections and boosted academic prowess, language skills, and self-esteem.

Fan Fang

It was spring 1996 in San Diego. At the Bilingual Project Institute, a group of bilingual educators was listening to a speaker explain why shifting bilingual students to English-only classes was inevitable. "As more and more students are using the Internet in the classroom, they will have to master English because all information on the Net is in English."

In the crowd, a teacher raised her hand: "I'm afraid that may not be true. A teacher and his students in San Francisco are navigating the Internet using Chinese characters."

Photo courtesy of Fan Fang

*B*efore I received a $1,000 check from the San Francisco Education Fund, I never believed my project, which enables Chinese bilingual students to use Chinese on the computer, would be funded. Of course I had no idea that in two years my students would become the first U.S. students to communicate in Chinese with people around the world and to publish what is probably the world's first online student newspaper in Chinese.

Losing the Chinese Students

Horace Mann Academic Middle School is a regular public school in the heart of the mission district in San Francisco. The school shares the common characteristics of most public inner-city schools in California: 54 percent of the students are classified as educationally disadvantaged youth, and more than 40 percent are limited English proficient or non-English proficient. As a Consent Decree school, Horace Mann Middle obtains generous funding from the state and federal governments. As a restructuring school, Horace Mann's teachers have more opportunities to introduce innovative teaching strategies to better serve the diverse student population.

In 1993, when I first came on board at Horace Mann, I was surprised to find the substitute Chinese bilingual teacher using Chinese to teach English and English to teach science. The 8th graders who were newcomers were just copying the missing words from their textbooks to their worksheets; they had no understanding of what they were

> **"Because most of their Chinese pen pals expected them to be good English tutors, they became highly motivated to learn."**

doing even though they were working on the 3rd grade science curriculum.

The job was tough. Compared to the Latino student population, the Chinese student population in California is relatively small. (San Francisco is an exception. Chinese students are the most populous group in the San Francisco Unified School District.) While our Spanish bilingual science and social studies teachers used the Spanish version of the regular 8th grade textbook, our Chinese bilingual teachers had few Chinese materials that fully supported the content of the regular English textbooks.

My Chinese bilingual students were lost, both academically and emotionally. Having been taught the babyish stuff repeatedly, they became bored; having been cut off from their connection with their language and culture,

"I had no idea that in two years my students would become the first U.S. students to communicate in Chinese with people around the world."

to communicate with others who speak Chinese.

3. Students would be able to produce their computer projects or electronic portfolios in Chinese.

The proposal was soon approved.

The students were enthusiastic about learning the new technology. They launched a pen pal request in three of the Chinese language newsgroups and received some 300 e-mail messages from Hong Kong, Taiwan, Singapore, England, the United States, and even

learning English. He thought it was too hard to learn, and he also found it embarrassing to speak a foreign tongue in front of his peers. To help his pen pal, however, Tien became the hardest worker in his English-as-a-second-language class. He even went to a school tutorial center to learn more.

Stories like Tien's were common among our students. Because most of their Chinese pen pals expected them to be good English tutors, they became highly motivated to learn.

鯨魚是不會生蛋的。請改正您在⋯中⋯頁的描述。

Translation: "Whales don't lay eggs. Please correct your description on page 3 of the book."

they became depressed and had low self-esteem.

Translating the Curriculum

As a bilingual teacher, I believe that we should provide equal education opportunities to limited-English-proficient and non-English-proficient students. They should not be deprived of the right to access the same core curriculum as the English-speaking students. Being a science teacher, I thought of technology as a solution.

In 1994, I drafted a funding proposal to the San Francisco Education Fund for my Information Superhighway in Chinese project. We planned to achieve three goals the first year:

1. By using a Chinese translation software program, within minutes students would be able to translate any English materials into Chinese.

2. With the help of the translation program, a subscription to America Online, and a digitized writing pad, students would be able to use e-mail in Chinese to do research and

mainland China, where only the top scientists had access to experimental Internet services. For the most part, students picked pen pals who were near their age level, although some preferred to write to college students or to scientists. The lost cultural connection was suddenly restored.

The impact of this global networking in Chinese was greater than we had expected. Tom, a 7th grader, was surprised to learn that a scientist in China also was once a student in the U.S. and that he had faced the same struggle in adjusting to a new culture. Mary, an 8th grader, sent an e-mail message to a science fiction author in Hong Kong to challenge him:

Tien received e-mail from Taiwan in both English and Chinese. His pen pal asked him for help: "My English essay is terrible. My dad grounds me whenever I get an F. I have never met an American who writes Chinese. Could you help me with my English?" Tien had come to this country only five months earlier. He had no interest in

One chilly winter day, the classroom was as warm as it is in the spring. Twenty pairs of eyes stared nervously at the computer screen. We logged on to a private "Chinese chat room" in America Online. "Here they are!" someone yelled excitedly. One, two, three screen names popped up in the upper-right corner box. Wen, our fastest Chinese typist, quickly wrote two Chinese characters on the digitized writing pad:

您好！

Translation: "How are you!"

In response, these characters appeared from one of the screen names: "Yes!!" the students cheered. Yes, we succeeded! We became the first students ever to conduct a live chat in Chinese through America Online.

The Information Superhighway in Chinese project drew wide attention. The world's largest Chinese newspapers, *Sing Tao Daily* and *World Journal,* reported our story several times. Many companies, universities, and agencies contacted us for information on how to realize telecommunication in Chinese. America Online chief executive officer Steve Case honored us

San Francisco Education Fund, we are able to expand it to more schools. Working with more students, we are publishing the first online student newspaper in Chinese—one of nine global electronic newspapers in Chinese. Each day, 1,102 people down-

您好！荷雷斯曼的筆友嗎？

Translation: "How are you! Penpals from Horace Mann?"

in one of his e-mail messages for our "dedication and commitment in realization of Chinese online." And the president and chief executive officer of a trading company in Hong Kong thanked us in one of his e-mail messages "for preparing future business partners for us. I see the future of global communication from your project."

Witnessing a Transformation

By the end of the year, my students not only participated fully in all academic activities in their primary language, but also made tremendous progress in learning English. Their achievement was reflected in both their Comprehensive Test of Basic Skills scores and the grades on their report cards.

Our project is now in its third year. As we obtain more funding from the

load our newspaper from three newsgroups. We are also maintaining the world's first student Web site in both English and two different coded Chinese characters (http://user.aol.com/ishchinese/ishmpage.htm).

Students have started to branch out from their foundation in e-mailing in Chinese to live conferences and some specialized areas, such as news reporting, researching, interviewing, editing, desktop publishing, and such recent Internet developments as Chinese HTML (hypertext markup language) and Web authoring.

Above all, the students no longer feel academically inferior as a result of not being proficient in English. Our project has restored their self-esteem, which in turn has helped them master English faster while further developing

"They launched a pen pal request in three Chinese language newsgroups and received some 300 e-mail messages from Hong Kong, Taiwan, Singapore, England, the United States, and even mainland China."

their primary language skills. They are opening their minds by communicating with other Chinese-speaking people around the world. And they're coming to realize what a gift it is to be truly bilingual and bicultural.

Fan Fang is the ESL/Bilingual Department Head at Abraham Lincoln High School, San Francisco Unified School District. He can be reached at 2162 24th Ave., San Francisco, CA 94116-1111 (e-mail: ffang@muse.sfusd.k12.ca.us).

Ready Reference on the Internet: A Beginning List of Sources

by Barbara Ripp Safford

Barbara Ripp Safford is Assistant Professor of Library Science at the University of Northern Iowa in Cedar Falls. She has been a middle school and elementary school library media specialist in Maryland, a high school library media specialist in Ohio, and a public library director in Pennsylvania.

Choosing ready-reference sources for your homepage or bookmark list presents interesting new selection issues. As with most things, you will find you are making choices among items depending on price (mostly "free"), recency, ease of use, reliability, dependability, and even appearance. There will be trade-offs: *Bartlett's Quotations* is available online for no subscription cost; it is key word searchable—much better and faster than using the index in the paper copy—but because of copyright issues, it is the 1901 edition. The *Britannica* is online; it has a wonderful search engine; it is the latest edition, updated; it comes with *Webster's Dictionary;* but it costs a hefty annual fee to access.

It will be easier for your students and teachers to participate in selection. We have always wanted to involve teachers and students in selection—it says so in your selection policy. Remember how you tried to get your science teachers to look through issues of *Science and Children* to identify items for you to order? Remember their lack of enthusiasm? Remember how you finally wrote out the order cards and gave them to teachers to prioritize? With a selection of web sites, you will have more help than you want. Show the list of web sites in this article to people who use the Internet and they will all have suggestions of additional and/or better sites to add to the list. You will constantly be bombarded with suggestions. So get ready to really share selection decision making.

Criteria for my suggestions include the usual sorts of things. I looked for quality and importance in a collection, but I also looked for reliable sites that should be around a while, I looked for direct links, and I looked for good directions or ease of use. A good activity for students is for them to list criteria they think important for a ready-reference web site.

Students can also compare typical book-reference source information with that found on the web sites, and begin to make their own comparisons of preferred information-finding sources—whether paper or electronic.

Last month, I suggested some categories for ready reference on your homepage. I have not ventured into special subject ready-reference sources here, although there are several good sources for science, history, health, and so on. It is also not the purpose of this list to lead to extended data sources for reports and research, although many links to such data can be made from some of the sources listed.

Following then, are some suggestions of sites with their URLs and comments about using the sites. (All URLs are subject to change at any time!)

Geographic Information
The CIA World Fact Book
http://www.odci.gov/cia/publications/95fact/index.html

Popular since the text-only days of telnet and gopher, this is a quick source of essential information about countries of the world. Published every July, the versions listed on many web sites are a year or two old. Going straight to the publication source on the web guarantees the most recent edition available soonest. Information is easily accessible by first-letter links to country lists and then links to the country file. Data include location, size, geographic features, environmental issues, demographics, government, economics, and transportation. Appendices include regional reference maps and United Nations and other international organization facts.

CityNet

http://city.net/

A database of upwards of about 2000 places (updated daily), this attractive and easy-to-use web site performs a service of quickly locating local information sites. Several search choices are available—by region, country, index, or word search. Hits will take users to the local homepage—often multiple homepages will be listed for any specific place. Because the actual page is locally published, it varies from place to place, but usually includes historical and tourist data.

Census Bureau Data Maps

http://www.census.gov/ftp/pub/statab/
www/profile.html

Fast maps of states that show counties with links to county information. Click on U.S. map to go to state map; click on state map to get county information. Other Census Bureau information at http://www.census.gov/is both useful and addictive. Students will love finding the 1990 frequency rank of their first and last names.

An Incomplete Collection of World Flags

http://www.adfa.oz.au/CS/flg/index.html

This is one of those trade-off choices. The problem here is reliability of the site, which seems to be a neglected one recently. However, the searching is easy and the flags are available in color and in multiple sizes ranging from small to huge. Another bonus is that there are links from the country and its flag to a version of the World Fact Book.

Dictionary Hypertext Webster Interface

http://c.gp.cs/cmu.edu:5103/prog/webster?

The advantage of this site is that it provides a keyword search capability for searching the dictionary at other site(s). Searching some misspellings results in suggestions of correctly spelled words; prefix truncation is also available. An automatic link to one of the *Roget's Thesaurus* gopher sites is also provided.

Current Events CNN Interactive

http://www.cnn.com

The choices for current events are many; this is just my favorite. It is fast, updated often, colorful, easy to move around in, full of audio and video clips. It has a good balance of news and features, including sports.

National Weather Service

http://www.noaa.gov/nws_intro.html...

Weather information is usually available through a local web site, which is a better choice for many users. But this is a good way to find your regional forecasting center web site, which can be loaded on your ready-reference homepage in addition to any other local information source. Here, too, are reliable reports on storm information, climate data, and many other related issues.

Directory U.S. Postal Service Address and ZIP Code Information

http://www.usps.gov/ncsc/

When in doubt, go directly to the source. This one works by searching mailing address for correct ZIP and by searching ZIP for matching city. Just as with the paper copy of the ZIP Code Directory, the homepages offer other useful mailing information. Lots easier to use than the paper copy! Several librarians have "confessed" that this is the web reference tool they use the most.

AT&T Toll-Free 800 Directory

http://www.tollfree.att.net:80/index.html

Of all the directories, this one is easy to search by category or keyword and results in numbers that won't lead to huge phone bills! The various "white and yellow" page directories that are also available are so incomplete as to be meaningless.

Government Information
The United States Government Manual

http://www.access.gpo.gov/nara/
nara001.html

Fast and sophisticated Boolean search en-

Ready Reference Hunt

One way to introduce your students to your new ready-reference WWW list is to have a contest. These sample questions with answers found in the sources listed here will be a good start.

1) Where is Christmas Island?

2) Describe the flag of Slovakia.

3) Who said, "There is now less flogging in our schools...but less is learned."

4) What time will the sun rise in Indianapolis on July 27, 1997?

5) What is the population density (per square mile) of Prairie County, Montana?

gine makes this important document and its information easily available.

Online Library The Internet Public Library
http://ipl.sils.umich.edu

This great site, a service of the School of Information and Library Studies at the University of Michigan, can serve as an extension of your ready reference library and as a gateway to subject area information. It offers many other services intended especially for children and young adults.

The Iowa Official Register (as a sample of state government manuals)
http://www.sos.state.ia.us/register/register.htm

Most states now have their own government manuals available in one electronic form or another. Your state homepages may feature government, tourist, and historical information that is more up to date than even CityNet knows about.

The process of building your ready-reference list will serve as a learning process for you. The sites you find that you won't include on a ready-reference list may give you suggestions for other lists to compile. You will be entertained and amazed at the material available on the WWW. And you will begin to become an important guide for your students and teachers as they begin to explore the resources of the Internet.

P.S. Please send me your good site finds! Barbara.Safford@uni.edu

Monster Job!

Sally Laughon and Barbara Kurshan

Roanoke, Virginia

"My monster has pitchforks for hands, and spatulas, knives, forks, and spoons all around his head. He is the utensil monster," wrote the 5th grader. The class in Virginia was preparing to exchange paragraphs using email with another class in New York, as part of the Monster Project moderated annually by a teacher at Brunner Elementary School in Scotch Plains, New Jersey (http://www.intac.com/~brunner/bhp.html). As the moderator of this project, the teacher has a Herculean task to identify what would bridge the connections among the children, the network, and the project.

WHAT THEY DO

A moderator coordinates, or sometimes directs, the flow and nature of the communications through online activities. These activities, also known as projects, are designed to bring distant participants and classes together for collaborative exchanges of information. As educators embrace the use of telecommunication activities in the classroom, students are learning from and with others around the world, independent of time and distance. These activities encompass projects that use the Web, LISTSERVs, email, or independent commercial networks. Depending upon the list or the project, the moderator could be a volunteer with a loosely self-defined role or an "official" moderator with a structured, well-defined role.

As the Internet has expanded beyond the scientific community and as more teachers come online, telecommunication projects are evolving from amorphous or self-regulated entities to highly structured curriculum-based programs such as The Global Schoolhouse or National Geographic Kids Network. This change was implemented because often classroom teachers could not fulfill all the time-consuming moderator tasks. As one teacher said in response to an online moderator survey we conducted, "I do all that the job calls for, helping a steady stream of new users learn their way around the Internet." Other participants noted that they work "on an as-needed basis." This attitude reflects the extensive volunteer nature of the position and the need for moderators to do whatever is necessary for successful projects.

THE PROJECT ENVIRONMENT

Moderators have been described in many different ways. Table 1 provides a scheme for understanding some of the other expressions that have been used to describe a moderator. For each term, synonyms, the origin of the term, a brief description of the prominent responsibilities, and an example of where this term is used in educational telecommunications are listed.

Sometimes the moderator's role is defined by both the tasks performed and the environment in which the project is conducted. There are a number of different types of networks where telecommunication projects can be found. Networks can be divided into categories based upon their capabilities, which include geographic boundaries, purpose, and function. We have grouped them into six categories based upon those defined by Roy Tennant and other online pioneers. Within each category we have provided an example that illustrates the definition of that online learning environment.

1. Bulletin board or distributed network. A bulletin board system (BBS) is normally locally oriented. Bulletin

Table 1
Expressions Describing a Moderator

Term	Origin	Description	Example
circle leader	education	lead teacher for a group of teachers	l*Earn
chair	professional committees	mediator and teacher participant	TERC Star Schools Project
curator	museum	a collector, guardian	Virginia's PEN state network
host	online conferences	a greeter	America Online, IRIS
moderator	broadcast media	supervisor of discussion	Internet, Usenet
SysOP	systems operator	technical manager of system	bulletin board systems

Reprinted by permission from *MultiMedia Schools*, January/February 1996, pp. 12-18. MMS is published by Information Today, Inc., 143 Old Marlton Pike, Medford, NJ 08055; 800-300-9868; www.infotoday.com.

boards assemble email messages into areas of interest, often called conferences. The moderator, also known as the system operator (SysOp), owns, manages, maintains, and often modifies the programs of a BBS. (*Example:* Newton BBS; http://www.newton.dep.anl.gov or modem connection 708/252-8421

2. State or regional network. A state network is a telecommunications system that is partially or fully operated and funded by a state agency or outside organizations to support instructional and administrative activities in K–12 classrooms across the state. These networks connect every school or every school district in a state. They provide moderated projects in which users can participate. (*Example:* The Texas Education Network, TENET; http://www.tenet.edu)

3. Internet lists. A list, sometimes called a LISTSERV, is an electronic mailing list managed by specialized computer software housed on a machine that is directly connected to the Internet. Messages sent to this type of computer program are distributed to every member's mailbox, making it a convenient way to reach hundreds or thousands of people with one message. Usually these lists are moderated. (*Example:* Kidlink; http://www.kidlink.org/general.html)

4. Commercial educational networks. These commercial networks were developed specifically to provide quality curriculum projects and moderated activities. These services often include complete communications software and supplementary software for analyzing data, unlimited phone connections, and curriculum materials. Most projects include moderator functions as an integral part of the design (*Example:* Scholastic Central; http://www.scholastic.com/)

5. Commercial networks. These networks provide educational conferences or forums as part of their numerous features and services. Some of the features available are current news, financial information and services, encyclopedias and reference works, assistance from major software and hardware vendors, games and entertainment, travel, and shopping. On these networks, a plethora of projects are provided for educators. (*Example:* America Online; http://webcrawler.com/AOL/)

Moderators are pioneers in the information age who ask for the position or find themselves volunteering because they originated the project they manage.

---

6. World Wide Web (Web). The Web provides a graphical interface to the Internet. With the extensive use of home pages, projects are available to the educational community and the creator becomes the de facto moderator of the project. These projects blend the best from commercial, educational, and community projects. (The Hotlist is a place to explore educational sites and resources; http://sln.fi.edu/tfi/hotlists.html. See Table 2 for other K–12 project Web sites.)

ONLINE PIONEERS

In order to glimpse behind the scenes, we surveyed over 100 network moderators during 1993, with follow-up in 1994. We found that moderators play a variety of roles and perform numerous online and offline tasks as they facilitate projects or activities. They are pioneers in the information age who ask for the position or find themselves volunteering because they originated the project they manage.

• Moderators work on their projects from 7 to 18 hours a week. Overwhelmingly, they indicate that personal satisfaction and enjoyment are the primary rewards for their work, not compensation in any other form. The volunteer spirit is pervasive. Moderators often reiterate that their jobs are essentially whatever is needed for a successful project or activity. Further, moderators indicate they are collectors of information, which they disseminate to participants in projects. This task is one way; moderators facilitate and encourage members.

• When moderators work with projects, the structure of the network determines how their time is allocated. For example, on commercial networks, if several projects are running concurrently in a forum, one moderator may be responsible for all of them. However, if a moderator is working on a list, time is more likely to be expended on one project at a time. Bulletin board systems are similar to lists by encouraging successive projects rather than concurrent projects for moderators. These managers do not work alone. Duties are shared with other moderators or with the participants in the projects themselves. If moderators work on the Web, they spend time updating their home pages to ensure that the information is accessed on a regular and repeated basis.

• When they counted the hours online, moderators were spending more time than they had originally thought they were working. They were surprised to learn how much time they actually spend online, but noted that it is difficult to distinguish between personal time online and time spent moderating projects.

• Moderators spend extensive time online with little formal evaluation or feedback. They rely on their own evaluation or on feedback from the members of their projects more often than surveys or written evaluations. Other moderators indicate that they view increased participation as a measure of successful projects.

Moderators have the power both to ensure the successful integration of telecommunications into the classroom or to destroy a network because of costs and work overload.

• Moderators enjoy the community that develops during a project. This enjoyment as well as a sense of responsibility propels them to provide as much technical support and training assistance as possible. Whether such support is defined in the role or not, the camaraderie that develops

Table 2
World Wide Web Project Sites

Academy One
http://yn.la.ca.us

This site is a virtual school with centers for student interests as well as for adults. Many projects are available with archives of information from past projects. Often projects are so popular they become annual events.

ArtsEdge
http://artsedge.kennedy-center.org

ArtsEdge is a cooperative agreement between the John F. Kennedy Center for the Performing Arts and the National Endowment for the Arts. It combines an online magazine, a collection of What's New In Arts and Education, resources for developing curricular activities that link national and state standards, and a Cafe for sharing information, ideas, and problem solving with colleagues.

Children's Museum Hotlist
http://www.win.com/~deltapac/ocean_od.html

Take an ocean odyssey without getting wet at this site. Learn about nautical signal flags and whales; explore aquatic images and touch the sea animals and plants in the Safari Touch Tank.

EdWeb
http://edweb.cnidr.org:90/

EdWeb is sponsored by the Corporation for Public Broadcasting and the Center for Networked Information Discovery and Retrieval (CNDIR.) This site is designed for exploring technology and school reform. Resources include policy information as well as resources for assisting schools that want to develop home pages and discussion on how to incorporate the WWW into education.

Global Schoolhouse
http://k12.cnidr.org/gsh/gshwelcome.html

The Global Schoolhouse links schools and students nationally and internationally to conduct collaborative research. A variety of tools are utilized, including live video conferences using personal computers.

Hotlist
http://sln.fi.edu/tfi/hotlists.html

The Hotlist is an organized list of educational sites and resources. Each hotlist is divided into three main groups: Topics, Science Resources, and Teacher Resources. You can read about each group before trying a hotlist.

Intercultural Email Classroom Connections (IECC)
http://www.stolaf.edu/network/iecc

These archives and mailing lists are maintained by St. Olaf College to help teachers and classes link with partners in other countries for email pen-pal and classroom project exchanges.

Kid Pub
http://www.en-garde.com/kidpub

This site provides a publishing forum for kids of all ages. Classes can also submit their stories for viewing by all who visit this page.

K–12 Cyberspace Outpost
http://k12.cnidr.org/janice_k12/

Janice and John's electronic newsletter gathers together project ideas and resources for education. It changes frequently and archives are available.

Megamath
http://www.c3.lanl.gov/mega-math/

Megamath is a project site for having fun with math. Topics include The Most Colorful Math of All, Untangling the Mathematics of Knots, Games on Graphs, Machines that Eat your Words, Algorithms, and Ice Cream for All.

Midlink Magazine
http://longwood.cs.ucf.edu/~Midlink

Middle School Electronic Journal's next issue is due next month. Have you ever wondered what kids in other countries like to read? Students at Vitebsk School 37 in Vitebsk, Belarus want to share their favorite books with you. You can join the fun by sending a paragraph about your favorite book.

NASA Ames Research Center K–12
http://www.arc.nasa.gov/index.html

Scientific Research Resources provides information about the facilities and the ways in which they contribute to national programs in aeronautics and space, including the Shuttle and the International Space Station.

The NASA K–12 Initiative
http://quest.arc.nasa.gov/

This site provides educational experiences from NASA. You can be in touch with NASA scientists, researchers, and engineers, and also participate in exciting Online Interactive Projects.

Yazone
http://www.spectracom.com:80/yazone/ Here you can meet and greet Generation Xers; those who are evolving can have their voices heard. Places are available for people ages 8–14, and parents too.

compels moderators to become vital assistants, especially to newcomers.

HERCULEAN OVERLOAD?

Moderators serve a valuable role in leading and perpetuating educational telecommunication projects. Indeed, online moderators are like Hercules—with remarkable strength and conviction, they contribute significantly to the development and implementation of online projects and educational networks.

Numerous coordinating tasks can be alleviated or simplified through the development of online tools for moderators and training. Tools should include templates for creating and distributing newsletters to project participants; tools for creating, conducting, and reporting online surveys and polls; tools for developing training courses; and tools for developing Web home pages. Tools should also provide simplified mail creation and distribution, as well as a database for information gathering and management. Today, these interfaces and tools are being developed and implemented by commercial services, the Internet through the World Wide Web, and network projects from National Geographic Kids Network and The Global Schoolhouse. But, many would-be online participants do not yet have the required hardware or connections.

As more teachers integrate telecommunications projects into their classrooms, moderator demand will rise and will require more clearly defined roles. Although moderator roles are being defined daily, the issue needs further exploration to ensure that networks do not collapse from the demanding support and maintenance required. Moderators have the power both to ensure the successful integration of telecommunications into the classroom *or* to destroy a network because of costs and work overload. It is time to address this pivotal issue.

Sally Laughon has used the Internet in the classroom in grades 4–12 for the last seven years. She currently teaches Telecommunications in Education at Virginia Tech, where she will receive a doctorate in Instructional Technology this year. Her interests include all phases of integrating technology, especially telecommunications, into the curriculum.

Dr. Barbara Kurshan has been actively involved with technology in education for almost 20 years. Since receiving her doctorate in Computer Science and Education from Virginia Tech, she has developed her expertise in the areas of computer literacy, educational telecommunications, virtual reality, and multimedia interactive curriculum product development. She has written numerous articles and texts on these topics and has designed software and networks to address these areas.

Communications to the authors should be addressed to Sally Laughon at laughon@vt.edu or to Dr. Barbara Kurshan, ECC, 10 E. Church Avenue, Roanoke, VA 24011; 703/345-1429; email—bkurshan@aol.com.

Tips & Tricks for K-12 Educational LANs

PHILIP HESS, Computer Technician
North Hills School District
Pittsburgh, Pa.

For the past several years, I've been employed as a computer technician in an elementary school and worked with my district's administration to develop the labs in our schools into functional computer learning centers. Along the way, I've developed a good grasp of what has worked and what could be improved. For those districts planning to add computer technology to their instruction, these suggestions and ideas are offered as a guide.

■ Some Hardware Basics

Let's start with some basics. Use multiple circuits for the lab. If you have a lot of computers you'll need to distribute the load on the circuit breakers. Consider having three separate circuits. One for the monitors (shut off the monitors to get children's attention or clear the room at the end of class), one for computers (start up the lab with the flip of a switch), and one for things that should never be turned off like the file server and printers.

To do this you'll need to know the amount of electricity that the computers will draw. It will be expressed in a figure called *amps* and is often on the back or bottom of equipment. When in doubt, check with the manufacturer. Always round this figure up.

> If your file server has "mission critical" applications consider an external SCSI drive for all the network files.

For example, if the computer, monitor and CD-ROM drive together draw 4.3 amps, round up to 5 amps.

Place wires and power cords on the back side of computer tables, not along the ledges. Small children, whose feet won't reach the floor, like to prop them up on those ledges. Many a network has gone down by someone accidentally pulling out the plug to the file server. The same holds true for any other networking hardware as well. If anything supporting the network loses power, down it all comes.

It's also a good idea to protect the server with a UPS (uninterruptible power supply) so that if the power fails you can shut down the system properly. If the room will be staffed all the time, one of those $100 models will suffice. Otherwise look for a "server" model that has software to shut down the system if power is not restored within several minutes.

Don't overlook having up-to-date start up and maintenance disks ready to go in the event of hardware problems. Macintosh users can get these[1] by an anonymous ftp: *ftp.support.apple.com/pub/apple_sw_updates/ US/Macintosh/System%20Software/System_7.5 _Update_1.0/.* Keep multiple copies of start-up disks and utilities handy; if one disk goes bad, you'll have another ready to go.

Reprinted with permission of *T.H.E. Journal*, L.L.C., from the April 1996 issue, pp. 84-87.

As a precaution, locate the file server away from the rest of the room, preferably in another room located next to the lab, like a locked closet. A file server sitting next to printers or computers that students use invites curious eyes and hands. Whatever you do, *don't* use this closet as a storage room. Allow the room's air to circulate. And don't pile supplies, like boxes of paper, around it. Later, when you need access, you don't want to have to move a lot of other things out of the way.

If you can't keep the server physically away from children then use a password-protected screen blanker. Make sure it's something simple; the animated graphics in most commercial screen savers will tie up the CPU and eat into network performance.

Use a *big* hard drive for the server. I like to have applications load off the server. It makes the computer "universal" so any child can run any application from any computer.

While networkable software may cost more initially, as the network grows, you can add additional users at no additional cost. In all cases check your software license to see how many computers can legally use it. The Administrator function of networks makes it easy to lock applications to a certain number of users.

Others prefer loading applications onto the local hard drive for speed reasons. In my lab, I use a mixture of both. I try out the application on the network and if it doesn't work or is too slow I load it onto local drives.

If you can, buy only networkable software. It lets you use less expensive computers as workstations, and they won't need a large hard drive since only the files needed to start the workstation and networked programs are loaded.

Set up applications to install *over* the network even if you can't run them *on* the network. Every application I've ever tested on the Mac can be setup to install over AppleShare. This saves you from having to drag around a bunch of floppies to each machine.[2] When installing software, particularly new system software, install it on only one machine and monitor that machine for problems for several days.

Use SCSI hard drives in the file server. SCSI can queue multiple read/write requests for greater speed. Also, SCSI drives are available in greater capacity and higher RPM speeds. The faster the platters rotate on a hard drive, the more information can

Savvy graduate students make good onsite technical support people.

be put down or pulled off it. Another plus to SCSI is that it is as close to a universal expansion bus as you can get; one can connect up to seven devices to each SCSI card. With this configuration you can add additional hard disks, CD-ROMs, tape backup units, scanners and a variety of other devices to the server for just the cost of the device and a cable.

If your file server is going to be used for "mission critical" applications like an administrative network or students records, consider an external SCSI drive for all the network files. This way you can remove the drive from the file server, in case of a fatal system crash, and plug it into another machine. While your network may work slowly in this configuration, at least it's working. Test this setup before you really need to use it. Another technique is to have applications on a write-protected/read-only disk or partition and have documents stored on a read/write disk or partition. This way you can backup applications once and documents as frequently as needed.

■ Get Others Involved

Start a computer club at the school. This shifts learning the mechanics of a computer to non-instructional time. Then, when the children come to the lab for a classroom assignment, they don't have to be taught how to use a mouse, etc. Also, students can help out their teachers with the in-classroom computers, which they are proud to do. Look for fun projects for the children.

Have an after-school keyboard class if state education laws prohibit teacher keyboarding/typing without a business teacher/typing teacher present.

You may want to consider evening classes for parents as well. Frequently, parents are at a loss when it comes to finding quality computer instruction for their family. College courses are often out of a working family's price range, although community colleges sometimes offer low-cost classes in popular software programs. Instruction at computer stores is often just as expensive. And all of those options are likely to have full enrollment. Local schools have a unique ability to offer instruction to families of students at affordable rates. Depending on your district, computer facilities and ambition, you could have a self-supporting computer program by offering computer classes at night in your labs.

Have an onsite technical person if possible. Look for that unique combination of people skills and computer expertise. If you can't find both, go with the people skills first as these are more difficult to come by. Many districts cannot fund a teaching position to run the lab, so by hiring a technician or network manager they get the onsite support for teachers and students. Ensure everyone is comfortable with the setup. Include the teachers' union, if there is one, in discussions. Everyone should know that this person is there to provide support, not to do the teacher's job. In the best arrangements of this type, the computer person gets a lot of support from the administration. Strive to achieve a peer-to-peer relationship between the computer support person and teachers.

The best people for this position, in my opinion, are computer-savvy graduate students. Undergraduate students are too close in age to students at middle or high schools, and frequently will have classes that prevent them from being in the lab for part of a day. Graduate students, on the other hand, often have classes after school hours or on weekends.

All prospective lab technicians should go through a screening process and receive clearance from the state police or FBI. In Pennsylvania this is known as Act 33/Act 34 clearance. Remember that these people will be working with your students and should behave accordingly.

Finally, a telephone in the lab is essential for reaching vendors' customer support staffs and for modem communications. If your school or district is concerned about costs, have the phone line restricted to prevent calling unauthorized numbers. With a phone in every lab, technicians in other buildings in your school district can help one another out.

■ Facilities Considerations

Allow room for other materials on computer tables. My tables are six feet long by two feet in depth. These are too small; the children have no room for their papers and the depth does not allow for connections on the back of the computers.

I've found that a 30-inch by 30-inch work area per computer works best in a lab situation. One way to decide how deep tables should be is to measure the size of the computer and add 18 inches to the depth.

Use a whiteboard instead of a blackboard — computers and disk drives don't like chalk dust. A whiteboard can function as a

> **The curriculum should drive the computer program, not the other way around.**

projection screen as well, although I prefer to use a video adapter that displays a computer's output on a television set. With that set up, teachers can show the whole class how to do a new procedure or skill during class. Such adapters can also send output to a VCR to make instructional videotapes, which can then be played back in class *before* going to the lab, allowing children to see how to do what the teacher is asking.

Don't forget training for specific software packages. Show teachers how to fully utilize the programs they will be using with students. Whatever you do, don't assume that they'll just "get it."

Whenever your school gets new software, it's the job of the computer support person to install it, learn it and train teachers on its use. But don't overlook the training of your support staff as well, which should be the responsibility of veteran technicians. With new software or hardware, negotiate for training in the purchase.

Inservice training programs should be continual, not a one-shot deal where, if a teacher misses it, they're out of luck. Training needs to be on a yearly schedule to account for changes in professional staff. Always evaluate a training program to ensure the skills taught were mastered.

Notebook computers can be an effective tool for teacher training. Load the software they are interested in learning and teachers can take the computer home to learn at their leisure. During the day, with network monitoring software, technical support staff can perform diagnostic work on the network using the same machine.

■ Access Issues

If there will be several labs in a school district, connect them together for cooperative learning activities. This can be as simple as a modem on the lab's phone line, ISDN connection or as complex as a fiber optic link or T1 data line between all schools.

Include access to the Internet in your lab. Depending on your needs and goals, this could take the form of a dedicated Internet connection or several shared modems. Internet access is an issue all to itself, so I'll leave the subject by saying you need to have a mechanism in place that limits students access. You don't want children to use this resource without some sort of checks and balances. Two programs of potential benefit are SurfWatch and Net Nanny, offered in Mac and Windows versions. Other programs and approaches are available as well.

Sponsor a parents/community night after

the lab is up and running and let both students and teachers show off their skills for visitors. Some members of the community, especially those without children in your schools, will view computers as an unneeded expense. Make sure the lab is open and operational during Open House. Have plenty of examples of student work on hand — maybe some of the most skilled students can demonstrate their knowledge. Invite the media when you show off your lab; they love this kind of human interest stuff.

■ Planning & Budget Issues

Eight megabytes of RAM is essential to run today's software and operating systems. Minimum memory requirements listed on software boxes are typically for stand-alone machines, not a network, and networking software always takes up some memory. If memory is tight some packages won't run or will exhibit odd behavior. Having 8MB in the computers also saves you from having to resort to using virtual memory, a technique that uses a portion of the computer's hard drive to simulate memory. While it does work, performance takes a major hit.

When preparing a yearly budget, don't overlook the inevitable software upgrades. Evaluate upgrades as you would any other software purchase. If the application is a major part of your program then it's worth upgrading as older versions cannot usually read files created by newer versions. If a program is not integral, then sticking with an older version may be fine.

Use only Ethernet or other high-speed networking systems. LocalTalk (for Apple Macintosh) and other low-cost networking systems are just too slow to use with anything except small classroom clusters of computers or for printer sharing.

If you're extending your lab to classrooms, pull additional runs of network cable to each location. This has several advantages, the first being reduced labor costs. Indeed, 65% of the investment you make in wiring will be for labor, the rest will be for the cable. It will cost no more in labor to run four network cables into a classroom than it will to run two. In case you need to expand your network or a cable gets damaged, there is already a backup in place.

With Ethernet use only Category 5 wiring; while this will be more expensive than Category 3, you won't have to replace it to switch to a faster speed network.

Involve the professional staff early on. They will take ownership of the computer

> To track down network problems, the "divide & conquer" approach works with or without test equipment.

lab and network and want it completed. During planning, listen to what the teachers want. Make it clear that the district or school is behind this 100% and wants them to provide input as to direction and purpose. If teachers want small clusters in classrooms, give it to them. Remember that the purpose of a computer lab is to enhance the students' education. Whatever you do, it should be educationally sound. The curriculum should drive the computer program, not the other way around.

When planning, divide the budget into four broad categories: computers, networking, software and training. Use these figures to see where you will need to raise additional money or perhaps implement your program in stages. While every situation is different, this assures that essential items won't be overlooked.

■ Troubleshooting

When making changes, change only one thing at a time. That way you know what went wrong and can easily restore it back to the way it was.

Carefully document changes to the network and allow proper time to evaluate the impact. Once set up, most networks will run without needing any changes.

Performance can almost always be improved by judicious tweaking of certain parts of the networking software. Always record all settings before you begin and make backup copies of critical network files.

One way to improve network performance is to increase the memory allocated to the cache on the file server. However, be alert for the "plateau effect," where the server and network's performance plateaus and increasing memory to cache gains very little. Once you reach this, reduce the amount of memory allocated to the cache down to when the plateau begins to occur.

Often you will have no test equipment to help track down network problems. A tried-and-true method is the "divide & conquer" approach, which works with or without test equipment. Divide your network into smaller and smaller segments until the problem is isolated. Once the problem is solved, reconnect everything in reverse order that you took it apart and you're done.

A related technique is to drop machines off the network one by one until the problem goes away. The machine you just took off the network is usually the culprit. Look for loose connections, cards not properly seated or breaks in network cables, especially around connections. Substitute the suspected faulty part with a known working one to determine if your prognosis is correct.

Use the Groups function of the networking software to cluster your users. On the Macintosh network at my school, there is a Children's Group (all computers in the lab) and a Teachers Group (all teachers in the building). Each teacher has their own private folder into which they save work. They can log into the LAN from any computer and work with their files.

Don't forget to set up a user for yourself and include it in each group. This way you can log in as a member of that group without having to ask someone to reveal their password. On my school's network, I made several users for myself that allow me to access different resources. If I'm working on

a problem and get called away, the network is protected from "exploring" by students.

Philip Hess *was computer technician for Seville Elementary School in North Hills School District in Pittsburgh, Pa. He is now student teaching at McIntyre Elementary, in the same district, and will earn his masters in Elementary Education in May 1996 from Duquesne University.*
E-mail: philip@nauticom.net
Home page: www.nauticom.net/www/philip/

References:
1. Taken from Tidbits #266, a Macintosh newsletter delivered by Internet e-mail, published by Adam C. Engst. For more info, send e-mail to: info@tidbits.com
2. Call (800) 505-0171 and request document # 20702, Apple's "Software Installation Over a Network" sheet.

Products mentioned in this article:
SurfWatch; SurfWatch Software, Inc., Los Altos, CA, (800) 458-6600, www.surfwatch.com
Net Nanny; Trove Investment Corp., Vancouver, BC, (800) 340-7177, netnanny@netnanny.com

Distance Learning

One of the primary concerns facing distance learning today is finding ways to increase the amount of student involvement and thus maintain their interest in what they are learning. Fortunately, technology that can solve this thorny problem has become available. Over the past decade, several technologies have emerged that can be used in distance learning—audio-, video-, and computer-conferencing, CD-ROM, and other forms of interactive computer-based multimedia are a few that offer immediate help. However, when using these more sophisticated technologies, it becomes essential that an adequate infrastructure be constructed and high-quality technical support be made available when students and instructors need it. Technology's role in high-quality interactive distance learning is to create an environment that will promote active learning using higher-order thinking skills such as evaluation, analysis, and synthesis, rather than simply rote learning and memorization. In addition, the technology can be used to promote individual and social interaction for the student during the construction of knowledge and problem-solving skills.

Within a technology-driven distance learning environment, there are two kinds of interaction with regard to learning. One is a student individually interacting with content. The other is social activity, a student interacting with others about the content. Both types of interaction are necessary for efficient, effective, and affective learning. In distance education, it is particularly important to

provide an environment in which both kinds of interaction can occur.

Technology advances such as phone mail systems, the Internet, bulletin boards, teleconferencing systems, and interactive networked multimedia systems provide an effective means for facilitating faculty/student, student/content, and student/student communication, interaction, and involvement. Today's technologies provide an electronic pipeline to reach students at a distance with an instructional delivery system that will involve and interest those who are using it.

The articles in this unit demonstrate how educators are riding the crest of current technology and instructional design to meet the need for interaction and involvement in a distance learning environment.

The unit begins with Sandra Kerka's article that provides readers with an overview of the newest methods of distance learning using the Internet and the World Wide Web. Kerka also mentions the disadvantages, such as limited bandwidth, slow modems, reduced media, student loneliness and many others. In the next report, Rita Laws focuses on "Distance Learning's Explosion on the Internet." The article is divided into three sections: introduction to the world of distance learning; nine different distance learning applications found on the Internet; and a bibliography of useful distance learning books, journals, and software catalogs.

Jacquelyn Tulloch, in "Seven Principles for Good Practice in Distance Learning," focuses on seven principles and practices to guide initial program development. The paper also discusses several low- and high-tech solutions to consider when implementing distance learning.

Next, Hirschbuhl, Jackson, and Bishop report on the effects of a self-paced interactive multimedia computer simulation on teaching, learning, motivation, and costs.

The focus is on methods and tactics for fostering learner interaction and engagement in a distance learning environment.

Cambre, Erdman, and Hull then describe a distance learning environment that includes avenues for interacting, such as telephone, e-mail, live teleconference call-in, regular exchange of course assignments, and postcard feedback. The authors also report potential obstacles in developing and delivering instruction and in securing interaction between students and faculty.

Finally, Barker and Dickson present a series of questions that they believe hold the answers to the question, "Is your school ready to include distance learning as part of its instructional program and what direction should be taken in implementing distance learning?" The article is directed to rural school administrators who are interested in distance learning.

Looking Ahead: Challenge Questions

What will be the role of interactive technologies within a distance learning environment during the remainder of the twentieth century?

To what extent will higher education provide distance learning to business and the community?

Is the intent of distance learning to allow students to work alone, or is it to bring them closer together? Provide reasons for your answer.

Distance Learning, the Internet, and the World Wide Web

Sandra Kerka

In the beginning was the word—the printed word. In its earliest form, distance education meant study by correspondence, or what is now called "snail mail." As new technologies developed, distance instruction was delivered through such media as audiotape, videotape, radio and television broadcasting, and satellite transmission. Microcomputers, the Internet, and the World Wide Web are shaping the current generation of distance learning, and virtual reality, artificial intelligence, and knowledge systems may be next. Some define distance education as the use of print or electronic communications media to deliver instruction when teachers and learners are separated in place and/or time (Eastmond 1995). However, others emphasize distance *learning* over education, defining it as "getting people—and often video images of people—into the same electronic space so they can help one another learn" (Filipczak 1995, 1995, p. 111), or "a system and process that connects learners with distributed resources" (ibid., p. 113). These two definitions imply learner centeredness and control.

Typical audiences for earlier generations of distance education were adults often seeking advanced education and training at home, on the job, or in the military whose multiple responsibilities or physical circumstances prevented attendance at a traditional institution (Bates 1995). Now anyone is potentially a distance learner, a concept that has implications for the organization of educational institutions and for teaching. This *Digest* focuses on some of the newest methods of distance learning (DL) using the Internet and the Web. It highlights some of the issues that could profoundly change the delivery of adult, career, and vocational education.

Distance Learning in Cyberspace

Perhaps more than any other distance media, the Internet and the Web help overcome the barriers of time and space in teaching and learning. Educational uses of the Internet are burgeoning. The University of Wisconsin-Extension's Distance Education

Clearinghouse lists numerous institutions offering online instruction <http://www.uwex.edu/disted/home.html> and corporate training is featured on AT&T's Center for Excellence in Distance Learning website <http://www.att.com/cedl/>. *Internet World*'s October 1995 issue gives examples of "The Internet in Education," including online degree programs offered by traditional institutions such as Penn State and Indiana University as well as nontraditional entities such as University Online and the Global Network Academy. DL on the Internet usually takes one of the following forms (Wulf 1996): (1) electronic mail (delivery of course materials, sending in assignments, getting/giving feedback, using a course listserv, i.e., electronic discussion group); (2) bulletin boards/newsgroups for discussion of special topics; (3) downloading of course materials or tutorials; (4) interactive tutorials on the Web; (5) real-time, interactive conferencing using MOO (Multiuser Object Oriented) systems or Internet Relay Chat; (6) "intranets," corporate websites protected from outside access that distribute training for employees; and (7) informatics, the use of online databases, library catalogs, and gopher and websites to acquire information and pursue research related to study.

Examples of the use of these modes include the following. High school students with disabilities in Project DO-IT (Disabilities, Opportunities, Internetworking, Technology) connect with the University of Washington (UW) to receive instruction via e-mail, join worldwide discussion groups, and access online resources (Burgstahler 1995). Also at UW, rehabilitation therapists learn about adaptive computer technology through videotapes and an Internet class discussion group (ibid.). The Distant Mentor project pairs workplace experts with school-to-work "apprentices" online; they can also simulate work environments through desktop software with an audio channel connected through the Internet (Dede 1996). At Carnegie-Mellon University, the Virtual Corporation simulates a work setting for business students (ibid.). A career counselor offers group and individual online conferences, a listserv, and a database of resumes and resources for clients (Sherman 1994). CUSeeMe software enables technology teacher education supervisors to observe student teachers using a desktop video-

ERIC Clearinghouse on Adult, Career, and Vocational Education, Center on Education and Training for Employment, College of Education, The Ohio State University, 1900 Kenny Road, Columbus, OH 43210-1090

conference through the Internet ("Agricultural Education" 1996).

Advantages of delivering distance learning on the Internet include the following (Bates 1995; Eastmond 1995; Wulf 1996): (1) time and place flexibility; (2) potential to reach a global audience; (3) no concern about compatibility of computer equipment and operating systems; (4) quick development time, compared to videos and CD-ROMs; (5) easy updating of content, as well as archival capabilities; and (6) usually lower development and operating costs, compared to satellite broadcasting, for example. Carefully designed Internet courses can enhance interactivity between instructors and learners and among learners, which is a serious limitation of some DL formats. Equity is often mentioned as a benefit of online learning; the relative anonymity of computer communication has the potential to give voice to those reluctant to speak in face-to-face situations and to allow learner contributions to be judged on their own merit, unaffected by "any obvious visual cultural 'markers' " (Bates 1995, p. 209). The medium also supports self-directed learning—computer conferencing requires learner motivation, self-discipline, and responsibility.

As with any medium, there are disadvantages. At present, limited bandwidth (the capacity of the communications links) and slow modems hamper the delivery of sound, video, and graphics, although the technology is improving all the time. Reliance on learner initiative can be a drawback for those who prefer more structure. Learner success also depends on technical skills in computer operation and Internet navigation, as well as the ability to cope with technical difficulties. Information overload is also an issue; the volume of e-mail messages to read, reflect on, and respond to can be overwhelming, and the proliferation of databases and websites demands information management skills. Access to the Internet is still a problem for some rural areas and people with disabilities. Social isolation can be a drawback, and the lack of nonverbal cues can hinder communication. Although the Internet can promote active learning, some contend that, like television, it can breed passivity (Filipczak 1995). The next section takes a closer look at distance learning processes.

Distance Learning Processes

Multimedia/hypermedia contexts such as the Web support constructivist approaches to learning, which are based on the belief that individuals construct their own understanding of the world as they acquire knowledge and reflect on experiences. Dede (1996) describes how carefully designed online learning can assist the construction of knowledge by showing learners the links among pieces of information and supporting individual learning styles.

When Wiesenberg and Hutton (1995) conducted a continuing education program using computer conferencing, they found it necessitated two to three times more delivery time. Learners appreciated the convenience of asynchronous communication, but many were anxious about putting their written words "out there." The course was more democratic but less interactive than expected, and the instructors recommended giving learners a better orientation to the online learning environment, providing technical support, and fostering self-directed learning and learning-to-learn skills.

Eastmond (1995) highlights the ways that computer discussion both requires and facilitates learning-how-to-learn skills, such as locating and accessing information resources, organizing information, conducting self-assessment, and collaborating. Adult learners in his study found the following strategies critical to success in electronic learning: becoming comfortable with the technology, determining how often to go online, dealing with textual ambiguity, processing information on or off line, seeking and giving feedback, and using one's learning style to personalize the course.

The Social Nature of Distance Learning

A common stereotype is "the loneliness of the long distance learner" (Eastmond 1995, p. 46). Learning at a distance can be both isolating and highly interactive, and electronic connectedness is a different kind of interaction than what takes place in traditional classrooms: some learners are not comfortable with it. Lack of nonverbal cues can create misunderstanding, but communications protocols can be established and relationships among learners developed. Because humans are involved, social norms do develop in cyberspace, but they require new communications competencies (ibid.). Online courses often feature consensus building and group projects, through which learners can develop skills in collaborating with distant colleagues and cooperating with diverse individuals. Such skills are increasingly needed in the global workplace (Dede 1996).

Answering charges that computer learning environments cannot duplicate the community of the classroom, Cook (1995) argues that the assumption of a sense of community in traditional classrooms may be false. If community is defined as shared interests, not geographic space, electronic communities are possible. Wiesenberg and Hutton (1995) conclude that building a learning community is of critical importance to the creation of a successful virtual classroom. Dede (1996) agrees that, "to succeed, distributed learning must balance virtual and direct interaction in sustaining communion among people" (p. 199).

Strategies for Distance Learning

Filipczak (1996) notes that DL on the Internet can be cheaper, faster, and usually more efficient than other learning modes, but not necessarily more effective. As Dede (1996) puts it, "access to data does not automatically expand students' knowledge; the availability of information does not intrinsically create an internal framework of ideas" (p. 199). To help learners make effective use of distance learning methods, skilled facilitation is essential. Rohfeld and Hiemstra (1995) suggest ways to overcome the challenges of the electronic classroom: (1) establish the tone early in the course; (2) to overcome the text-based nature of online discussion and to build group rapport and cohesion, introduce participants to each other, match them with partners, and assign group projects; (3) offer training and guidelines to help learners acquire technical competence and manage discussions; (4) provide a variety of activities, such as debates, polling, reflection, and critique; and (5) use learning contracts to establish goals for participation. The following strategies are intended to make distance learning more effective (Bates 1995; Dede 1996; Eastmond 1995; Filipczak 1995):

- Understand the technology's strengths and weaknesses
- Provide technical training and orientation
- Plan for technical failures and ensure access to technical support
- Foster learning-to-learn, self-directed learning, and critical reflection skills
- Develop information management skills to assist learners in selection and critical assessment
- Mix modes—e.g., combine e-mail discussion with audio/video methods to enhance the social aspect
- Structure learner-centered activities for both independent and group work that foster interaction

In the end, the word is still with us. The way it is transmitted and received is changing. Educators can play a role in the development of a "vital form of literacy" (Dede 1996, p. 200): the transformation of information into knowledge. The choices they make can also help determine which of these possibilities come to pass: (1) distance technologies as an add-on to existing institutions; (2) "knowledge in a box," impersonal, individualized, and socially isolating; or (3) a networked learning society that keeps human relationships at the center of learning (Bates 1995).

References

"Agricultural Education and Distance Education." *Agricultural Education Magazine* 68, no. 11 (May 1996): 3–18, 21–23.

Bates, A. W. *Technology, Open Learning and Distance Education.* London: Routledge, 1995.

Burgstahler, S. E. "Distance Learning and the Information Highway." *Journal of Rehabilitation Administration* 19, no. 4 (November 1995): 271–276.

Caudron, S. "Wake Up to New Learning Technologies." *Training and Development* 50, no. 5 (May 1996): 30–35.

Cook, D. L. "Community and Computer-Generated Learning Environments." *New Directions for Adult and Continuing Education* no. 67 (Fall 1995): 33–39.

Dede, C. "Emerging Technologies in Distance Education for Business." *Journal of Education for Business* 71, no. 4 (March–April 1996): 197–204.

Eastmond, D. V. *Alone but Together: Adult Distance Study through Computer Conferencing.* Cresskill, NJ: Hampton Press, 1995.

Filipczak, B. "Putting the Learning into Distance Learning." *Training* 32, no. 10 (October 1995): 111–118. (EJ 511 253)

Rohfeld, R. W., and Hiemstra, R. "Moderating Discussions in the Electronic Classroom." In *Computer Mediated Communication and the Online Classroom, vol. 3,* edited by Z. L. Berge and M. P. Collins, pp. 91–104. Cresskill, NJ: Hampton Press, 1995.

Sherman, D. "Career Counseling in Cyberspace." *Journal of Career Planning and Employment* 55, no. 1 (November 1994): 29–32, 62–63. (EJ 497 318)

"The Internet in Education." *Internet World,* October 1995, pp. 38–85.

Wiesenberg, F., and Hutton, S. "Teaching a Graduate Program Using Computer Mediated Conferencing Software." Paper presented at the Annual Meeting of the American Association for Adult and Continuing Education, Kansas City, MO, November 1995.

Wulf, K. "Training via the Internet: Where Are We?" *Training and Development* 50, no. 5 (May 1996): 50–55.

Developed with funding from the Office of Educational Research and Improvement, U.S. Department of Education, under Contract No. RR93002001. Opinions expressed do not necessarily reflect the position or policies of OERI or the Department. *Digests* may be freely reproduced.

Distance Learning's Explosion on the Internet

ABSTRACT

DISTANCE LEARNING (DL) is education's gold rush. Many adults need convenience if they are to initiate or finish college degrees. This article, focusing on Distance Learning and the Internet, is divided into three sections. The first section consists of an introduction to the world of DL On-line and includes a four-step road map of success for DL students. The steps are: self-education about DL issues; defining personal, career, education, and financial needs; choosing a DL program; and finding and keeping DL resources and support. The second section deals with the nine different DL applications found on the Internet, the international computer network with over 50 million users. These include: DL Newsgroup discussions; World Wide Web DL information home pages; Financial Aid Web Sites; DL University Home Pages on the Web; Electronic Mailing Lists and Listservs, E-mail Resources; On-line Services; Tutoring On-line; and MOOs (Mud Oriented Object) known as "virtual classrooms." The final section contains a bibliography of useful DL books, journals, and software catalogs for people who are interested in learning more about DL. *(Keywords: distance education, distance learning, innovation, Internet, on-line, external degrees, World Wide Web, Booklist, adult education, Information Highway, alternative learning)*

Rita Laws

Moderator, Prodigy's D.L. Guidebook

INTRODUCTION

YOU SEE THEM ALMOST EVERY DAY on the international electronic discussion group called alt.education. distance: universities asking for information about developing a Distance Learning (DL) program. DL is education's gold rush, with good reason. In a fast moving world, what could be more convenient and appealing than earning college credits on all degree levels from the comfort of your home?

Distance Learning, or DL, is simply studying from a distance, usually from home or from a conveniently located off-campus site. DL is part of all degree types from the A.A. to the Ph.D. DL involves finding alternative ways to earn college credits through challenge examinations and credit for life and work experience.

DL remains primarily a books and paper proposition, but it is made more convenient with the delivery of information via the Internet, on-line services, telephone, TV, cassette tapes, radio, and CD-ROM. As Jill Ellsworth, Ph.D., author of the book, "Education on the Internet," puts it, "Most often distance education is delivered through a hybrid of these techniques, for example, television supported by print materials delivered through correspondence. The Internet has been used very successfully in such hybrid situations."

A FOUR STEP DL ROAD MAP

THE FOLLOWING FOUR STEPS are just one road map to a college degree through home study. The four steps include: Educate yourself about DL issues; Define your career, educational, and financial needs; Choose a school; and Find and keep DL resources. Each is followed by suggestions for implementation.

EDUCATE YOURSELF ABOUT DL ISSUES

DL issues (degree acceptance in different career fields, regional accreditation, state approval, federal regulations, credit for life experience, tuition costs, the Internet's role, future trends, and others) must be studied before you can make an effective choice of schools. There is a wide range of content and cost among both accredited and state approved colleges and universities. If you don't understand these issues, you may end up spending far more money than necessary or spending

From *Journal of Computing in Higher Education*, Vol. 7, No. 2, Spring 1996, pp. 48-64. Reprinted by permission of the author and the *Journal of Computing in Higher Education*, Amherst, MA.

215

too little for a degree that turns out to be worthless in your field. *Resources: Booklist, Newsgroups, E-mail*

DEFINE YOUR CAREER, EDUCATIONAL AND FINANCIAL NEEDS

Understanding your own specific needs is not as easy as you think, especially if you plan to use a U.S. school. The reason is accreditation, an American institution, which no other nation has. Foreign colleges are licensed or chartered by their respective governments. Obtaining a degree from a legally existing international university is usually seen as having the equivalent of an accredited U.S. degree.

Many people new to the newsgroups express shock that any American would even consider a nonaccredited, but high quality, state approved university. In fact, such a route is not a viable option for people in certain professional fields and for young people seeking entry to prestigious graduate schools. An accredited degree is not necessary, however, for some mature adults who need a graduate or postgraduate degree to fulfill a job requirement, for older adults wishing to finish a degree, and for many people in business. Further, since financial aid is less available for mature adults and for those in DL programs, many people cannot afford the double and triple cost of accredited institutions.

There are three types of American schools, the regionally accredited, the state approved, and the degree mill. Regionally accredited schools are accredited by an organization, CORPA, or are recognized by the U.S. Education Department. Relatively few full DL schools exist in this category because regional accreditors have traditionally turned thumbs down on degree programs that are completely nonresidential. In the second category are many high quality universities, operating legally, which do not choose to go through the accreditation process. The savings realized from this decision is passed on to the student. The savings can be dramatic. There are cases where students saved 20,000 dollars in tuition this way.

Degree mills are unaccredited schools which are not operating legally under the laws of the state where they exist. They do not require work or certified work equivalents for their degrees, only money. Degree mills do not exist in the high numbers that they once did, thanks in part to the work of law enforcement agencies, like the FBI, to shut them down. However, they can make a convincing sales pitch. Some even claim accreditation that they do not have. The diplomas from degree mills are not worth the cost of the paper used to print them.

Each potential DL student must decide which type of degree is best: regionally accredited or quality state-approved. Each student needs to question future job and educational needs as well as current ones. You should question whether you need an accredited B.A. now so that you can apply for admission to accredited graduate schools later? Do licensing or certification requirements mandate accredited school or is there some flexibility? Are these requirements under review and, if so, how are they likely to change? Millions of Americans have found out through this self-study process that a state-approved, non-resident DL degree-program can meet their needs and save

money. The important thing is to know what you are doing before you spend any money.

While it is not as easy to find scholarships, grants, and loans for schools that are not regionally accredited, it is not impossible. Many state-approved universities offer no-interest monthly payment plans with payments as low as $100 per month. A few even offer textbook loaner libraries which not only save money but also save time. It can be a time-consuming process in tracking down the latest edition of some textbooks. *Resources: Newsgroups, Web*

CHOOSING A SCHOOL

Choosing a school should only be done once you have selected the type of school, regionally accredited or state-approved, which best meets your individual needs. This may be the easiest part of the four steps. Simply call or write for information packets and start reading. Pay close attention to any survey information about alumni satisfaction. If the alumni are happy and find jobs in your field, that is a good sign. Do not hesitate to investigate your choices with a phone call to the state departments of education and to the Better Business Bureau.

Mature adults usually find that they do not need to apply to many colleges. A high percentage of DL students gain acceptance to the college of their first choice. *Resources: the Web, Booklist*

FIND AND KEEP DL RESOURCES

Mature adults are the most self-directed of all students. They are highly motivated—usually by the need to get a job, keep a it, or earn a promotion or a raise. However, even highly self-disciplined adults can find it difficult to stay motivated, especially in the summer when warm-weather activities beckon.

This is a time when the need to find and keep a support system becomes important. A little encouragement, understanding and socializing provide just the medicine most people need to get back on track toward their degrees. On-liners are fortunate because the same newsgroups, forums and web sites that helped them learn about DL, their needs and the available schools, are the same places they can turn to for support. These electronic gatherings are also the place to pass on helpful DL experiences to those who are just starting. *Resources: On-line services, newsgroups*

THE INTERNET: NINE DIFFERENT DL APPLICATIONS

THERE is no instructional tool that saves more time and effort for DL educators and students than cyberspace, because it is an effective aid in all aspects of DL learning, from finding money for college to joining alumni associations. Here's what the Net has to offer:

1. DL Newsgroups (Discussion groups) on the Internet

Interpreting the names of the world's more than 20,000 different Usenet Newsgroups involves understanding the purpose behind their three parts. Take alt.education.distance for example. The first part designates the type of group. Alt is alternate, or unmoderated—a kind of free-for-all discussion. The second part represents the category, in this case, education. The final part of the name specifies the kind of education: distance education.

Reading and posting at the following Usenet Newsgroups contributes to an understanding of critical DL issues such as degree acceptance in different career fields, regional accreditation, state approval, federal regulations, credit for life experience, tuition costs, the Internet's role, future trends, and others.

alt.education.distance (By far, the best-known DL discussion)
alt.education.research

These two discussion groups have the most traffic. Several DL experts post regularly at alt.education.distance and help match individuals to the best programs in their respective career fields. Once a month, I post an updated "Getting Started in DL" booklist on this newsgroup. Misc.education (misc being shorthand for miscellaneous) encompasses a wide variety of topics in addition to DL, including home schooling and K–12 issues. Heated arguments called "flames" are rare, and neither newsgroup is moderated, making for an informal atmosphere.

alt.education.alternative
misc.education
misc.education.adult

2. World Wide Web DL Information Sites

The Web is a popular part of the Internet and resembles a kind of massive collection of mini-electronic libraries. There are dozens of DL information sites on the Web. There are a few that stand out because they have essential information or because they have grouped some of the best links together in one place.

- Peterson's Education Center is maintained by the famous college guide publisher of the same name. With detailed information about their traditional and DL guides and links to other DL resources, this is an especially useful site for DL students who are just getting started.

  http://www.petersons.com

- The Distance Education Clearinghouse is an informational database maintained by the University of Wisconsin. The searchable gopher index can be found at:

  gopher://gopher.uwex.edu/77/distanceed/.waisindex/ind

- London's Open University maintains the International Centre for Distance Learning (ICDL), a collection of DL resources from around the world.

  http://acs-info.open.ac.uk

- The DL Booklist is a "getting started" in distance learning bibliography updated monthly by Rita Laws and posted at various locations around the Internet. It contains a list of helpful DL books, journals, and software catalogs. This web page can be accessed from anywhere on the net.

  http:pages.prodigy.com/(OK/ritalaws/ritalaws2.htm/

3. Financial Aid Web Sites

To find a certain type of Web page, people use searching programs called search engines. A search engine called "Yahoo" at http://www.yahoo.com is very popular right now because it is very easy to use. Just type in your subject, such as "scholarships," press the enter key, and Yahoo offers several scholarship sites to try. Student Services Incorporated, http://web.studentservices.com:80/search, is an excellent example. It is a database of more than 180,000 scholarships and grants for U.S. students and is very easy to use. Just type in your major, and the search is on. The Scholarship Foundation of America, a nonprofit corporation at http://cen.cenet.com/sfa/sfahome.html, awards merit-based scholarships and matches gifted students to corporate sponsors.

Since most financial aid is targeted at young adults in traditional residential programs, DL students, most of whom are mature adults, can have a difficult time finding scholarships. Experts John and Mariah Bear (see #6, E-mail Resources) have written a book about Financial Aid with a special emphasis on assisting DL Students.

4. DL University Home Pages on the Web

The Web is host to hundreds of university home pages. Those listed here are a representative sampling. Athabasca, Canada's Open (DL) University, has 25 years experience. UNISA is the largest DL university in the English-speaking world. American students like its low tuition fees.

City University, the University of New Mexico (UNM), and the University of Phoenix represent popular American DL universities. City University is private and nonprofit. The UNM Home Page contains a comprehensive collection of links to many other American university home pages. Phoenix has an on-line presence on Prodigy and is especially popular with MBA students.

- Athabasca University, Canada's Open (DL) University for 25 years, is a popular choice for DL students.

  http://www.athabascau.ca

- City University EDROADS (Education Resource and On-line Academic Degree System) is a vehicle for students to complete select courses over the Internet. Located in Bellevue, Washington, City University is a private, nonprofit university.

  http://www.cityu.edu/index.html

8. DISTANCE LEARNING

- California Coast University, "serving mid-career professionals" and other mature adults, is a completely nonresidential university and is an example of a state-approved (not regionally accredited) DL university with an excellent reputation on the Internet and in the business world.

  http://www.iwy.com: 80/ccu

- University of New Mexico Home Page contains information about UNM and has a wonderful list of links to many other American university home pages.

  http://www.unm.edu

- University of South Africa (UNISA) is the largest DL university in the English-speaking world. American students like its low tuition fees.

  http://www.unisa.ac.za

5. Electronic Mailing List and Listservs

Another resource on the Internet are the e-mail mailing lists, an electronic version of the printed newsletters you may find in your mailbox. Pennsylvania State University and The American Journal of Distance Education are the forces behind the e-mail newsletter, DEOSNEWS (Distance Education Online Symposium News), edited by Melody M. Thompson (MMT2@PSUVM.PSU.EDU). DEOSNEWS contains the latest DL news from the Net and from academia. It has over 3,000 subscribers in 59 different countries. It is very easy to access back issues. To subscribe to DEOSNEWS and DEOS-L (a discussion forum), post the following commands to:

LISTSERV@PSUVM or to LISTSERV@PSUVM.PSU. EDU:

SUBSCRIBE DEOSNEWS (or DEOS-L), skip one space, and type your first and last names.

6. E-mail Resources

For people who only have e-mail access, there is still a wealth of information to be found. Here are the IDs of a few people with helpful information to share.

- John B. Bear, Ph.D. (johnbbear@aol.com)

In addition to dispensing free advice of the most expert variety on the newsgroup alt.education.distance, Dr. Bear is soon to have a Web page to sell his best-seller (coauthored with daughter Mariah): *Bears' Guide to Earning College Degrees Non-Traditionally,* now in its 12th edition with 250,000 copies sold. This book is considered by many to be the "bible" of DL. Here's a sample from the detailed e-mail prospectus on the book: "It is possible to earn an accredited legal, legitimate, prestigious Bachelor's, Master's, Doctorates, even Law degrees, without ever taking a single traditional course." The same two authors have another book called *Finding Money For College.*

- Ken Brownson, Ed.D., Ph.D. (VHCD25A@prodigy.com)

Dr. Brownson offers a free pamphlet describing his services as a paid DL consultant. He has helped many people find the school best suited to their individual needs and graciously offers a great deal of DL information gratis in e-mail, on forum discussions at AOL and Prodigy, and on alt.education.distance.

- Jill H. Ellsworth, Ph.D. (je@world.std.com)

Dr. E's Compendium of Electronic Resources for Adult/Distance Education, compiled by Dr. Jill Ellsworth, is a valuable collection of on-line DL resources. You can get a free copy on request through e-mail. Dr. Ellsworth will also be happy to e-mail you information about her 590 page book called "Education On The Internet" which contains a chapter about DL.

7. On-line Services

On-line services are not part of the Internet but are commercial services for people with modems. All of them now feature gateways to the Internet. Prodigy has developed its own collection of Web pages. From on-line classes to chat rooms, on-line services offer a little bit of everything to the DL student.

AOL. Use the keyword command EUN, an acronym for the Electronic University Network, and take a noncredit course free to try it out. While in EUN, look for the DL Forum. This will connect you to the DL Conference and the DL Message Board. The EUN Conference Hall at the Student Union contains chat rooms, and there is a large library of informational files to download.

CompuServe. Several different forums on CompuServe offer on-line classes; ask the Education Forum Sysop for a list. The EdForum is the home of Section 11, called SchoolNet/Distance Learning. The files area has everything from a DL bibliography to educational shareware. CIS offers a massive array of general educational choices—too many to list here.

Delphi. The Delphi forum called Education Ideas debuted in early 1995 for the discussion of on-line educational services of all types. Go REF and then choose EDUCATION IDEAS. In addition to Delphi's complete Net access, you can also go CUSTOM from the Main Menu to look at the current Custom Forums list. These member-maintained discussion groups include several with educational themes.

e-World. "Building a Distance Learning Community" is the slogan of The Education Coalition; shortcut TEC. It contains chat, files, a calendar of events, forum, and information about major on-line DL resources. EEC is another shortcut. It takes you to the e-World Educator Connection. Do not forget to e-mail ID Merle Marsh (no spaces) on e-World and ask to be put on the mailing list for their excellent educational newsletter called EEC Notes.

GEnie. At the Top Menu, look for Education Services which will take you to features such as Peterson's College Guide, Peterson's Graduate School Guide and the Education Round Table (RT). The RT offers files, chat, college Aid Resources, RT News, and discussion areas which include topics for nontraditional students. GEnie, like CompuServe, has excellent research features and databases in many different fields.

Prodigy. Jump EDUCATION BB for the Distance Learning Topic, COLLEGE BB for the Non-Traditional Topic, and UNIV PHOENIX for the University of Phoenix's on-line degree program. MEU is the jump word for Mind Extension University, a collection of DL resources. The Distance Learning Guidebook is a Web Page currently accessible only through Prodigy. Jump WEB PAGES and then look for the INTEREST AREAS to find this Prodigy web page: http://antares.prodigy.com/dlcoi.htm

MSN. Microsoft Network debuted in August, 1995. While it is expected to grow rapidly, no DL areas were identified as of this writing.

8. Tutoring On-line

They are not part of the Internet, but on-line services hook into and serve as easy-access commercial onramps. The three largest in the pack all offer tutoring in the form of homework help. On CompuServe, "Go" EDUCATION and look for the STUDENT FORUMS. You will see several homework Help areas. On America Online, use the keywords ACADEMIC ASSISTANCE CENTER to look for a virtual homework help "classroom" and a "teacher paging" system. Prodigy has the massive database at GoTo or Jump command words HOMEWORK HELPER. Students can also find help at almost any subject on the Education BB. All three of these services have lots of on-line reference "books," multimedia encyclopedias, and chat rooms where kids can talk "live" to people through their keyboards. Chat features should be used with parental supervision, however, for some on-line people are not as nice as others.

9. Classrooms MOOs

Virtual classrooms called MOOs are starting to increase in number as people explore their potential. MOO is an acronym for Mud Oriented Object and is a type of electronic discussion called a MUD (Multi-User Dimension). Most MUDs are role-playing games. MOOs are a social type of MUD and may include on-line classrooms.

In a MOO classroom, the instructor imports the text of the lesson to the computer screen and the students, sitting in front of computers at many other locations, raise their hands to ask questions. To raise your hand in a MOO, the student types a question mark or some other prearranged symbol, and your name and the question mark shows up on the screen for all to see. The professor then calls upon each student, in turn, who has a question. When called upon, the student then types his or her question and waits for an answer.

The University of Pennsylvania is a pioneer in virtual classrooms, which is all just another way of saying on-line classrooms. English and Latin are two of the MOO classes.

GETTING STARTED IN DL

BECAUSE DL is such a new idea to many Americans, getting started can be the most daunting step in the process. In 1994, this writer began compiling a list of books that are particularly well-suited for learning about DL and choosing the best school to meet individual needs. This booklist is now updated monthly as a service to DL students and is posted all over the Net.

Distance Learning "Getting Started" Essential Reading Booklist and Software Catalog List. UPDATED NOVEMBER, 1995.

1. Dr. John Bear and his daughter, Mariah P. Bear, have written several helpful books: *College Degrees By Mail*, BEARS' *Guide To Earning Non Traditional College Degrees* (12th Edition), and *Finding Money For College*. The first two list and profile DL schools, accredited and nonaccredited, national and international, and is very easy to use. Just as important, they offer expert information about the major DL issues and answer common questions, such as how to obtain college credits through life and work experience. Call 800-841-BOOK (Ten Speed Press, PO Box 7123, Berkeley, CA, 94707, USA).

2. *The Independent Study Catalog* by Peterson's lists accredited schools that offer DL courses, as does *The Electronic University*. Financial issues are covered in *Paying Less For College 1995* and *USA Today Financial Aid For College*. It is not specific to DL. Many people use their book called *Colleges With Programs For Students With Learning Disabilities*. Call Peterson's at 609-243-9111 or 800-338-3282 or check out their web page at http://www.petersons.com.

3. *The Internet University—College Courses By Computer* by Dan Corrigan describes more than 600 accredited courses and 30 schools along with 1,500 Internet sources of free study. Write to: Cape Software Press, P.O. Box 800, Harwich, MA, 02645, 508-432-2435.

4. Informative brochures, including some about life experience credits, are available from the Distance Education and Training Council, which is recognized by the U.S. Department of Education. Call DETC at 202-234-5100.

5. Oryx publishes *The Oryx Guide To Distance Learning: A Comprehensive Listing Of Electronic and Other Media-Assisted Courses,* and *The Adult Learner's Guide To Alternative and External Degree Programs* by Eugene Sullivan. These are a bit expensive but are very thorough if you are interested in accredited degrees. Call 800-279-6799 or 602-265-2651.

6. *Education on the Internet* (Sams Publishing, 201 West 103 Street, Indianapolis, IN, 46290, USA. Call. 800-428-5331) by Dr. Jill H. Ellsworth is 590 pages of everything you want to know about electronic educational resources from kindergarten through graduate school. It is designed for teachers, students and parents with teaching ideas, research help, and cool on-line places like virtual museums. There is also information about taking classes on-line and distance learning. This is a super-overall resource.

7. You can actually earn a B.A. (accredited) simply by taking GRE/CLEP tests. For more information, call Regents College in Albany, N.Y. or try this book that describes the process in detail: *How to Earn a College Degree in Only 4 Months* (Educational Awareness Publications, Tustin, CA. Call 714-832-1157.) Also, read *The Distance Learning Funding Sourcebook*, 3rd Edition, by Arlene Krebs and published by Kendall Hunt. 800-228-0810.

8. Following is a list of distance learning journals.
   a. Open Learning, Longman group UK Limited Subscriptions (Journals) Department, Fourth Avenue Harlow, Essex CM19 SAA UK
   b. *Journal of Distance Education*, CADE Secretariat, 151 Slater Street, Ottawa, Ontario, KIP SN1 CANADA
   c. The *American Journal of Distance Education*, American Center for the Study of Distance Education, College of Education, The Pennsylvania State University, 403 South Allen Street, Suite 206, University Park, PA 16801-5202, USA

9. Here are a few education software catalogs you may find useful. Some of these companies have won awards for their service and low prices. I have not tried them all. Assure yourself of the company's integrity before ordering. SURPLUS SOFTWARE (very inexpensive), 800-753-7877; SCI-TECH (math, science, statistics, and technical), 800-622-3345; MAC WAREHOUSE, 800-255-6227; EDUCORP, 800-843-9497; EDUCATIONAL RESOURCES, 800-624-2926; CD-ROM WAREHOUSE, 800-237-6623; KIDSOFT, 800-354-6150; ENHANCE, 800-777-3642; COMPUTABILITY, 800-554-9948; McGRAW-HILL SCHOOL SYSTEMS, 800-663-0544; and PC ZONE, 800-258-2088.

SUMMARY

ONE OF THE MOST ENDURING MYTHS about DL is that it is a new idea. It is not! DL has been a completely accepted and popular method of earning college degrees for hundreds of years in Europe and in other parts of the world. People in England do not question the value of DL degrees earned at legitimate universities. UNISA, the University of South Africa, where President Mandela once studied, is the largest DL university in the English speaking world with an enrollment of about 200,000!

DL is only a new idea in America. The oldest state-approved totally DL university in California was founded in 1974. However, as late as America was in embracing this method of study, it is making huge strides now.

"The adult learner has indeed been a neglected species," says Malcolm Knowles, Ph.D., an educator who is considered to be the "Father of American Distance Learning." Nowadays, mature adults need college degrees as much as young people in order to obtain and keep their jobs and to earn promotions. Cyberspace is fueling the growth of DL and DL schools at an enormous pace. Many of the most well-known state-run and private universities in the country have or are instituting DL programs of some kind, complete with matching WWW home pages.

The future of education is DL, because it is the only way millions of adults can ever hope to have a college education. College work, however, is not any easier via correspondence and on-line. But DL is a convenient way of getting an education without commuting. It only requires some instructional materials, a computer with a modem and the necessary communication software, a printer, and the determination to achieve personal goals.

ABOUT THE AUTHOR

Rita Laws, a former schoolteacher, works as a webmaster on the World Wide Web, and as a free-lance writer/columnist for *On line Access* magazine. Her web page, accessible through the Prodigy service, is called The Distance Learning Guidebook. The URL, or web page address, is http://antares.prodigy.com/dlcoi.htm. She also maintains the DL Booklist web page, accessible from any place on the Internet (http://pages.prodigy.com/ritalaws/ritalaws2.html). Dr. Laws completed her first college degree in the mid-70's using a traditional route and later completed two graduate degree programs in the nineties through distance learning, including a doctorate in 1995. She is currently coauthoring a book about support for DL students. Author's present address: 5150 North Harrah Rd. Harrah, OK 73045-9718. Internet: paum88a@prodigy.com

SEVEN PRINCIPLES FOR GOOD PRACTICE IN DISTANCE LEARNING

Jacquelyn Tulloch

Director, Instructional Telecommunications, Dallas County Community College, Dallas, TX

As enrollments level or decline in community colleges, many institutions rush to implement distance learning programs which enable them to attract and serve new populations. While accrediting associations and state agencies frequently provide guidelines for the development of such programs, these are often crude or address administrative or organizational policies and procedures in the absence of what are often significantly different instructional processes. Establishing "good practices" in a distance learning program requires understanding instruction in terms of desired outcomes, design issues, and appropriate use of technology. Principles of good practice in initial program development include:

1. The program has **purpose, direction, leadership,** and clearly identified **target audiences.**
2. Course objectives are **clearly defined** and are **comparable to campus based, traditional classes** in terms of learning objectives, requirements, and rigor.
3. Faculty **participation** and **leadership** is encouraged and supported by administrators and others in the institution.
4. Faculty and administrative **roles** are **clearly defined** and can be **appropriately evaluated.**
5. Faculty are **expert in the discipline content** as well as in the **technologies** available to support the instructional process.
6. Choices regarding **technologies** are based upon the **content matter, learning objectives,** and **availability to students.**
7. **Students** are provided with **information** about the **nature of distance learning** and the **skills required for success. Support** in developing learning skills is **provided** for those who need it.

Paper Presented at the Fifth Annual International Conference for Community & Technical College Chairs, Deans and Other Organizational Leaders, February 14–17, 1996, Phoenix/Mesa, Arizona

In addition to building on these principles as the basis for a distance learning program, formulating responses to each of the Seven Principles of Good Practice in Undergraduate Education[1] can be a useful point of departure for faculty and administrators as they begin development of courses and services for learners.

HOW WILL WE . . .

- **Encourage student-faculty contact?**
- **Support cooperation and collaboration among students?**
- **Provide prompt feedback?**
- **Encourage Active Learning?**
- **Emphasize time on task?**
- **Communicate high expectations?**
- **Respect diverse talents and ways of learning?**

The following discussion provides some direction in terms of the use of a variety of "high" and "low" tech solutions to these questions. While it is not a comprehensive look at all of the possibilities, hopefully it serves as a place to begin the process.

TELEPHONY:

In addition to **telephone** conversations and **answering machines,** the creative use of **voice mail systems** can provide support to distance instruction in a variety of ways. If there is a voice mail system at your institution, find out if the system is large enough to accommodate all of the students in the distance learning program. If not, there are relatively inexpensive software packages, such as *The Total Communicator,* which operate through a PC and provide enough mailboxes for 100 students. This type of system allows both group and individual messages for faculty and students to access when convenient. For example, students might be reminded of an upcoming text

---

[1]Compiled in a study supported by the American Association for Higher Education, the Education Commission of the States, and The Johnson Foundation.

review, provided with a correction to the syllabus, or receive individual feedback on an assignment or test. Voice mail systems have also been used successfully as a part of the instructional process in courses which require oral testing or collaborative writing, such as foreign languages or English composition.

In addition to providing communication between and among students and faculty, a voice mail system may be designed to provide potential students with consistent and detailed information regarding course objectives, materials, and requirements. Thus voice mail can help to establish realistic expectations on the part of students prior to enrollment.

Added to your telephone system, an **audio "bridge"** supports multiple callers talking together in a conference mode. This type of technology provides a means for conducting "on air" office hours, test reviews, and discussion sessions, with students participating from different locations. In addition, students are able to collaborate in small groups at times convenient to themselves.

FAX:

In addition to providing a means for the exchange of assignments and completed work in a timely fashion, "fax on demand" systems permit student acquisition of documents related to the course or the program, such as the syllabus, ancillary materials, or brochures.

SNAIL MAIL:

Time permitting, course newsletters and/or postcards with feedback on assignments and tests keep students informed. Faculty may also require students to submit postcards of introduction at the beginning of the course or at regular intervals throughout the course.

COMPUTER NETWORK SYSTEMS:

The use of an electronic bulletin board (BBS) with electronic mail, live teleconferencing, and asynchronistic discussion forums is invaluable to any distance learning program. It allows not only timely, flexible communications between students and faculty but also permits students to collaborate and work together in small groups while being separated by time and space.

Sophisticated systems such as *Galacticomm, First Class,* and *Wildcat!* provide a connection to the Internet which may be used as a means for research as well as for linking with other classes or interest groups in other parts of the world. The technical support personnel at your institution will be able to provide information about the variety of computer-based options that are available at your location. If purchasing the necessary hardware and software is not an option, investigate the cost of leasing from a commercial vendor or cost sharing with another institution.

COMPUTER SOFTWARE PRODUCTS:

In addition to using computers for communication, software programs may also deliver portions of the instruction over a network or through an independent PC. Publishers now frequently provide programs such as practice tests, interactive exercises, and other learning aids on diskette or CD Rom along with the course textbook. In addition, electronic files containing course information produced locally, such as a multimedia lecture or chapter notes and outlines, may be put on diskettes for student use.

AUDIO TAPES:

Audio tapes may be used for a variety of purposes, such as providing a review checklist or an alternative explanation of a particularly difficult concept. Tapes may be placed in a Learning Resource Center for students to duplicate or check out. In addition, material may be dubbed and mailed to students. Distance learners are often quite willing to pay a fee to get additional support materials in a more convenient manner!

TELEVISION, CABLE, AND VIDEO:

Consider using a local cable channel to show locally produced video (live or recorded), which may not be a part of the required materials. Examples include orientations or test review sessions. In addition, incorporate relevant PBS, C-Span, or other cable programming into course assignments. If the production is live and in-house, provide a number for students to call in and ask questions. If material is commercially produced or airing over an outside network, consider an audio bridge conference call-in after the airing. If such options are not available due to lack of equipment or funds, locate or lease a home video camera to record a review or presentation and arrange for check-out or lease through the library, bookstore, or other organization.

MEETINGS:

If students are not at a physical distance, orientations, discussion groups, test reviews, and individual conferences can be used to encourage active student involvement in the learning process. However, because scheduling is often a problem for some students, it is suggested that another, more flexible option for any meetings always be provided, if possible.

PRINT MATERIALS:

Clear, detailed, and error free print materials continue to be important to any distance learning program, but are critical when few other technologies are being used. Publicity efforts such as brochures and class schedules, as well as course syllabi, homework activities, and examinations all need to be carefully constructed and tested with students for clarity.

As indicated previously in the discussion of the basic principles for developing a sound distance learning program, the choices around the particular technologies to be integrated into courses and services must hinge upon the learning objectives, the discipline, and the students to be served. Attention to these factors should, by definition, address many of the *Seven Principles for Good Practice for Undergraduate Education.* However, the principles add an important dimension to decision making and ensuring effective responses to them is a task requiring both faculty and administrators to think creatively about the meaning and impact of distance in the teaching/learning process.

Jacquelyn B. Tulloch

Jackie is currently the Director of Instructional Telecommunications Services at the LeCroy Center for Educational Telecommunications, part of the Dallas County Community College District (DCCCD). In her current role she manages the faculty and student support services for the District's distance learning program which includes telecourses, modem based courses and live televised classes. The program has annual enrollments of approximately 10,000. Before becoming Director, Jackie was with the Educational Computing Division of the Center as content expert for the CASES computer project. Jackie also served as a Director of Counseling and Division Chair for Human Development/Physical Education at Brookhaven College in the DCCCD for seven years. Before coming to Dallas in 1982, Jackie worked in the Virginia Community College system as an Associate Professor and Coordinator of Counseling. Jackie completed her undergraduate work at Salem College (N.C.) and her M. Ed. and Ed.D. at the University of Virginia.

Despite a somewhat ridiculous workload (common to most community college administrators), Jackie is an avid golfer and ice dancer.

Teaching at a Distance: Student Involvement Through Interactive Multimedia

John J. Hirschbuhl,
Jim Jackson, and
Dwight Bishop

John Hirschbuhl *is currently an Assistant to The Associate VP. of Information Services and is Professor of Education at The University of Akron.*

Jim Jackson *is an Associate Professor of Geology Emeritus at The University of Akron.*

Dwight Bishop, *Leader Developer, Information Services, University of Akron, has been the primary developer of the Environmental Science: Field Laboratory program.*

INTRODUCTION

One of the primary concerns facing distance learning today is finding ways to increase the amount of student involvement and thus maintain their interest in what they are learning. At a remote site, involvement is measured by the amount of participation and inclusion students believe they experience (Do they feel they are part of the teaching/learning environment?). Student interest is measured by the amount of appeal, attention and enthusiasm students have for how and what they are learning. Distance learning can be delivered through the use of computers, networks, interactive TV, teleconferencing, telecourses, televised instruction, and other technologies. The selection of the proper combination of these technologies, greatly enhances the potential for effectively providing an in-structional delivery system in which all students are involved and interested. Passive, single mode delivery systems do not provide enough instructional power to ignite the student's interest because they fail to provide student involvement. Student involvement aids student achievement (Berger, 1991; Kay, 1991).

PROJECT/PRODUCT DESCRIPTION

Over the past two years the University of Akron has been engaged in the development of an interactive distance learning series entitled *Environmental Science: Field Laboratory.* The series provides multimedia simulations based on actual field studies. In each program module, the student takes the role of an investigator. Each module presents a different environmental problem which the students investigate by using the tools of an environmental scientist. During each investigation the students collect and evaluate real environmental data, and write summary research reports. The students choose data collection sites, collect samples using computer simulated instruments, conduct record searches for data recorded by previous studies, and keep a modeling book of their findings. These hand-on field experiments are made possible through the use of audio, photographs, video, animation, maps, charts, and text windows. In addition, students use on-line messaging to ask questions, challenge the computer's analysis of their study, or send their reports to the instructor.

While the students are allowed to structure their own investigation using any of the tools available, guidance is accessible at every point in the program. The program evaluates each student's methods and conclusions, and provides a post-test. All students write a final report of their investigation's findings. The program keeps records for each student, including the performance (sampling and conclusions), post-test scores and final essay scores.

PROGRAM CONTENT

The program's topics presently include:
* Introduction to Environmental Science
* Legal Control of the Environment
* Geology of Homesite Selection
* Minerals for Society
* Radiation in the Environment
* Energy from Coal
* Streams and Floods
* Stream Pollution

PRELIMINARY INVESTIGATION

During the academic year 1993–94, student success in an interactive multimedia course was studied by Jim Jackson and Dave Massaro. Differences in teaching, learning and productivity that could be attributed to the interactive multimedia program were evaluated. The course was designed for non-science majors at the University of Akron and included in excess of 400 students.

RESULTS OF THE STUDY

The data suggest that student use of the interactive multimedia program is an effective instructional delivery system that produces increased student performance. In addition, student attitudes appear to be

Teaching at a Distance: Student Involvement through Interactive Multimedia, pp. 1-6, from the 11th Annual Conference on Distance Teaching & Learning Proceedings, August 9–11, 1995. Reprinted by permission.

more positive when using the simulated field studies. The cost effective implications are that the interactive multimedia treatment reduced the failure rate from 36% to 22% hence increasing potential student fees by at least 14%. As a result of this dropout reduction, retention rates for freshmen improved. Computer simulations also reduced certain risk factors inherent to scientific field studies (Chen, 1989).

One of the purposes of the course is to develop problem solving abilities without heavy use of mathematical exercises. The best predictor of student success in this course, however, appears to be the amount of mathematics beyond algebra 1 that students took in secondary schools. The course develops the inferential thinking skills nurtured by mathematics, by means of its investigative exercises (Bitner, 1986; Cox, 1986; Dede, 1989).

Comments made on evaluation instruments indicated the technology increased student awareness of proper environmental management. In addition, students said they felt comfortable using the program. Students reported feeling a sense of responsibility and control over what they were learning. University counselors stated that student advisees who had difficulty in the course blamed themselves for their poor performance. Students indicated that they liked using the field simulation modules because:

1. **They were in control of when they worked and the pace of their lab work.**
2. **The self initiated one-on-one interactions with the program were helpful.**
3. **The problem solving method of instruction held their interest.**
4. **They immediately knew the results of their efforts.**

IMPLICATIONS AND FINDINGS

Students who used the simulated field studies felt they took an active part in learning by means of navigating, accessing and manipulating the data through the program. They all indicated they had high interest in what they were learning because of the way they were able to access and manipulate the data.

In short, the study indicates the students felt highly motivated because they were actively engaged in learning the material through an interactive multimedia environment which permitted them to access a variety of resources on an on-demand basis at their own pace (Lawson, 1991).

RECOMMENDATIONS

Faculty development
Faculty should receive adequate training in the development and use of interactive multimedia instructional programs before engaging in staff supported instructional development.

Training should include how to:

1. Identify an instructional problem.
2. Determine terminal and supporting objectives which lead to the solution of an instructional problem.
3. Select the appropriate medium to fit the instructional requirements of each instructional objective.
4. Work with instructional designers and developers.
5. Increase one's knowledge of the proper utilization of interactive technologies when teaching at a distance.

Expand Faculty Reach
Too many of our students today cannot be present in the classroom when instruction is being delivered. Therefore, instruction must become accessible from a distance asynchronously. We can no longer be constrained by walls, times or by the faculty's location. We must be able to provide sound, interesting, interactive instruction to students where and when they are able to use it (Kearsley, 1993; Skolnik, 1993).

Improve the Instructional Design
The basic problem with current distance learning delivery systems is they are designed for students in a classroom and ignore the needs of the distant student . . . flexibility, interest and involvement. Part of the problem stems from faculty having only themselves and an occasional graduate student to rely on for design, creativity and expertise. Today's well designed instruction incorporates the work of several skilled people, such as instructional designers, educational

technologists (developers), and quality assurance specialists (Arnheim, 1991).

Use Current Technologies
Technological advances such as phone mail systems, the internet, bulletin boards, teleconferencing systems and interactive, networked, multimedia systems provide an effective means for facilitating faculty-student communication and involvement. Today's technologies provide an electronic pipeline to reach students at a distance with an instructional delivery system that will involve and interest the students who are using it (Van Horn, 1991).

Ride the Back of Current Technologies
We live in an age of diminishing astonishment and rising expectations. The only way to satisfy this volatile environment is to ride the back of current technology by managing and reporting the real time achievements that result from interaction and involvement.

REFERENCES

Arnheim, Rudolf. (1991). Learning by looking and thinking *Education Horizons 69*, 94–98.

Berger, Carl. (1991). Ann Jackson and the four myths of integrating technology into teaching. *Syllabus, 21*, 2–7.

Bitner, B.L. (1986, March). The GALT: A measure of logical thinking ability of eighth grade students and a predictor of science and mathematics achievement. Paper presented at the annual meeting of the National Association for Research on Science Teaching, San Francisco, CA.

Chen, J. Wey. (1989). From work stations to teacher support system: A tool to increase productivity, *Educational Technology*, 34–37.

Cox, Dorothy A., Berger, Carl F. (1986). The importance of group size in the use of problem-solving skills on a microcomputer. *Journal of Educational Computing Research, 1*, 459–468.

Dede, Christopher. (1989). Planning guidelines for emerging instructional technologies. *Educational Technology, 29*, 7–12.

Kay, Alan C. (1991). Computers, networks and education. *Scientific American, 265*, 138–148.

Kearsley, Greg. (Autumn/Winter, 1993). Education @ Internet *Ed-Tech Review*, pp. 43–45.

Lawson, A.E. (1991). Hypothetico-deductive reasoning skills and concept acquisition: test a constructivist hypothesis. *Journal of Research in Science Teaching, 28*, 953–972.

Skolnik, Racquel, Mith, Carl. (Winter 1993). Educational technology: Redefining the American classroom. *Foundation for advancement in science and education*, 1–8.

Van Horn, Royal. (1991). Educational power tools: New instructional delivery systems, *Phi Delta Kappan 73*, 527–533.

The Challenge of Distance Education

Marjorie A. Cambre
Barbara Erdman
Leslie Hall

An awareness of potential obstacles in delivering a distance education program can help staff developers address complications before they occur.

I n an effort to provide opportunities for Ohio's low-wealth school districts to learn about integrating technology into K-12 schools, the state legislature funded Project Equity grants through each of the state's eight public television stations. In the autumn of 1992, the producers from WOSU-TV/WPBO-TV in Columbus, Ohio, met with a group of administrators and teachers representing the low-wealth districts in their viewing area.

The outcome of that meeting was the request that WOSU-TV/WPBO-TV use their Project Equity grant to create a graduate-level course focusing on the integration of technology in the K-12 curricular areas of math, science, the arts, social studies, and language arts. The producers requested that the College of Education at The Ohio State University, and specifically the program area of Instructional Design and Technology, collaborate with them on this project.

This began a year-long partnership which resulted in "Technology in the Curriculum: A Telecourse for K-12 Educators" being aired during the autumn quarter of 1993. This article describes some of our experiences and insights into staff development at a distance.

Staff Development Delivery Approaches

As Lieberman (1994) observes, there is a continuum of staff development delivery approaches: "Technology in the Curriculum" falls under her heading of "direct teaching." While approaches such as peer coaching (Leggett & Hoyle, 1987), action research (Bennett, 1994), reflection (Schoenbach, 1994), and networking (Lieberman & McLaughlin, 1992), which are more embedded in school settings and the daily lives of teachers have been found to be more satisfying for many teachers than direct teaching methods, the geographic size (160 miles by 60 miles) of the WOSU-TV/WPBO-TV viewing area and the accessibility of public airwaves made a broadcast format the most feasible means of reaching our target population of educators in low-wealth school districts.

Other components of the course were used to address the need for more job-embedded experiences. For example, responses to reading assignments required enrollees to reflect on their own teaching practices. Final project options provided opportunities, individually or in groups, for participants to engage in proposal writing, thematic unit development, or outlining a building or district technology integration plan. A course reflector bulletin board, set up through the university's mainframe computer, gave participants a chance to network.

It was our hope that the teachers and administrators who requested this course would encourage their peers to enroll in the course with them, watch 12 half-hour preproduced telelessons and four live teleconferences together, and collaborate on final projects. Many did so. However, there were also students who were the lone enrollees in their schools or districts.

The Telecourse

"Technology in the Curriculum" required no campus visits by those enrolled. Participants registered through the U.S. mail and the computerized telephone registration system in place at the university. Registrants were mailed the course manual, which included all of the instructions necessary to fulfill the requirements of the course.

Direct instruction was profiled through 12 half-hour preproduced programs and four hour-long live teleconferences (two-way audio, one-way video) that aired on the public television station, and through a 163-page course manual which included readings. Readings were followed by written assignments which were faxed or mailed to the authors, who were course instructors. Feedback to participants was returned on formatted postcards.

Instructors kept office hours for call-in questions. An e-mail forum was set up

From *Journal of Staff Development*, Vol. 17, No. 1, Winter 1996, pp. 38-40. Reprinted with permission of the National Staff Development Council, P.O. Box 240, Oxford, Ohio 45056; 513-523-6029.

for the electronic exchange of ideas. As the final project for the course, students prepared a technology plan designed for a classroom, school, or district; group work was encouraged in the preparation of this final project.

Demographic Profile

Enrollment from the school community was recruited through brochures and announcements in district newsletters, although one did not have to be a practicing educator to enroll. One hundred seventy five people signed up for the course; of those, 169 actually completed it for credit. A profile of course participants revealed that most of the enrollees were female (128), between the ages of 45-50 (94), and classroom teachers (94).

Twenty four participants were library media specialists, and 14 were school administrators. The remaining 37 were education specialists. Most were frequent technology users, with 77 indicating they used some form of media or technology in their classrooms or media centers daily, and 43 using it several times a week.

Demographically, the group seemed to be fairly representative of teachers and school administrators. In response to questions asking for self-ratings of technology use and confidence levels, respondents rated themselves a bit above the norm. This suggests that those with some technology interest and experience were more persuaded to sign up for this course than those with little or none.

Instructor's Observations

Instructors (the authors) and their assistants kept a close watch on the progress of the course. Avenues for interacting, namely the telephone during office hours, e-mail, and live teleconference call-in were rarely utilized. The most successful form of interaction was the regular exchange of course assignments and postcard feedback, which progressed on schedule six times during the quarter. Several hypotheses for the low level of student/instructor interaction are offered in the discussion of the following means of communication.

Telephone Office Hours. An instructor was available nine evening hours a week for calls; however, there were only about six calls per week. Some students may not have wanted to pay for a long distance call, or they may have felt uncomfortable chatting with course instructors that they

did not know. Most calls were for assignment clarification or about logistical difficulties such as taping programs. To the instructors' disappointment, few calls were to discuss course content.

E-mail. Electronic mail was provided as a means of networking for participants. However, access to e-mail proved to be complicated and plagued by technical difficulties; only the most experienced technology users succeeded in communicating.

While we feel that e-mail is a viable option in distance learning, in our case its use was, perhaps, a bit premature because most teachers are not yet equipped at school or home to take advantage of electronic mail. If it were more easily accessible, e-mail could have been a very useful way for participants to communicate mutual interests and exchange ideas.

Live Teleconference Call-ins. Again, few participants called the studio during live teleconferences, which were aired from 3:30-4:30 p.m. An 800 number was provided so long distance charges would not be a deterrent. However, it seemed clear after two teleconferences that many participants were not watching live, but were taping them just as they taped the preproduced programs. We have concluded that teachers' after school professional duties or family obligations were a major impediment to their live participation.

Live teleconferences can be a worthwhile component of distance learning. Given the technical limitations of a teleconference, however, one must remember that a limited number of callers can get through in one hour, that continuity is difficult to maintain, and that responses tend to be superficial. In distance education, teleconferences are perhaps best used to motivate participants to use other methods of interaction.

Final Projects. The telecourse called for

a major final assignment designed to help participants synthesize and apply what they had learned. While some were very successful, many projects were disappointing. Several factors may have contributed to this poor performance: (a) teachers ran out of "steam" and time, as their own grades at school were due just about the time the final projects were to be turned in, (b) teachers were uncomfortable with this type of assignment and needed more guidance than was provided, and (c) the lack of interaction with classmates and instructors put many at a disadvantage.

In a regular, on-campus course, students acquire ideas from each other and from the instructor, refine their work as they go along, and produce projects that reflect a collaborative and interactive effort. If students are expected to produce the same level of work through distance learning, their isolation must be addressed.

Mail/Fax Assignments and Feedback. In terms of interactions between participants and instructors, mailed or faxed assignments and postcard feedback worked very well. From the timely responses on the five reading assignments, it was clear that teachers were doing the assigned reading with thoughtfulness and care. Final course evaluations showed that the prompt and personal feedback by postcard was much appreciated.

Pre-produced half-hour programs. Course evaluations indicated that the 12 half-hour programs which formed the heart of the instruction for this course also worked very well. One of the most popular features was that the programs could be taped off air and watched at a convenient time. Another popular aspect was that they featured local talent—that is, teachers and students from the viewing area, using technology in actual classrooms.

Course Manual. The 163-page course manual provided logistical information, summaries of the programs, readings and

---

In a regular, on-campus course, students acquire ideas from each other and from the instructor, refine their work as they go along, and produce projects that reflect a collaborative and interactive effort. If students are expected to produce the same level of work through distance learning, their isolation must be addressed.

assignments, e-mail instructions, and numerous resources and references. This was by far the most familiar component of the course to teachers who are accustomed to receiving instruction in print form. Course evaluations indicated that the course manual was highly regarded.

Evaluation Results

A three-page evaluation form was included in the course manual and about 90% (n=153) of the forms were returned. Those aspects of the evaluation that shed light on the success or failure of this venture as an inservice vehicle are summarized here.

Participants' strongly felt that the course met its stated objectives. They rated highly the information presented about planning for the use of technology; they were less satisfied with the lack of "tools" for doing so. E-mail was clearly our least successful effort for reasons already discussed.

Participants were asked to rate how well each of the components of the course worked for them. Teachers most appreciated those aspects of the telecourse that were most traditional and familiar in the following order: print, reading and written assignments, television, teleconferencing, and electronic mail. One way to think about these data is to compare them on a hypothetical scale of comfort; teachers are most comfortable learning with print and least comfortable learning with e-mail. One might also conclude that the course instructors were better at providing those things with which they themselves had most practice.

The "comfort hypothesis" was corroborated in part by several other questions. As stated earlier, teachers indicated a relatively high satisfaction with the postcard feedback aspect of the course. Participants were also asked to rate their comfort with each of the interactive components of the course. It is no surprise that the newer technologies of teleconferencing and electronic mail were considered to be less comfortable to use. The only contradictory aspect of these data is that participants for the most part did not use the telephone for interactions with instructors despite an anticipated high comfort level with it.

The evaluation elicited suggestions regarding changes in the telecourse. Suggestions were offered about (a) scheduling (b) topics for tele-conferences; (c) focusing readings, programs, and teleconferences more closely; and (d) ways to facilitate involvement in e-mail and teleconference call-ins. Open-ended comments suggested an overwhelming sense of satisfaction with the course. Participants felt it was beneficial and that they would consider taking another distance learning course. Convenience came up time and time again as a major factor in their positive reactions.

Discussion

We undertook this project with a question: Are convenience and availability of technologies justification enough for delivering graduate-level staff development by distance, or is the trade-off of face-to-face interactions too much to sacrifice? We would like to emphasize the following key points about our experiences.

1. It takes some practice for instructors and students to effectively use distance learning. Our most successful components were those with which instructors and students were most familiar—in this case a course manual, paper and pencil exchanges, and lecture-based instruction, albeit over television.

This confirms the findings of other researchers. Bland (1992) found that the most effective instructional strategies were those less affected by the limitations of the distance learning environment, notably a well-designed lecture supported by planned visual aids. The lack of experience by both providers and participants with electronic mail and with active involvement in live teleconferences may have resulted in less satisfaction with these elements of the distance learning experience.

Traditional roles of "instructor" as the fountain of knowledge and "student" as receiver need to be reexamined in the distance learning setting, just as they are being challenged in the classroom.

---

2. The traditional roles of "instructor" and "student" need to be reconsidered in the distance learning setting to enable students to be active learners. Traditional roles of "instructor" as the fountain of knowledge and "student" as receiver need to be reexamined in the distance learning setting, just as they are being challenged in the classroom. Power (1993) reports that, in comparing three models of distance education for teacher inservice in Hawaii, in all cases the greater the attenuation (i.e., the more diffuse the connections) between instructor and teachers the greater the need to structure the class to maintain active involvement.

This may mean that instructors must become facilitators, enabling students to construct knowledge in a contextualized and therefore more meaningful way. Researchers studying the four-year experiment known as the *NEA School Renewal Network* report that there was an observable progression in the use of the electronic network from concentration on technical issues the first year to substantial small-group project development in the fourth year (Watts & Castle, 1992).

3. A professional production crew greatly enhanced the quality of this telecourse. The preproduced programs formed a major instructional component of the telecourse. Had these programs failed as productions, the course as a whole would have been much less successful. This is not to say that staff development programs need to rival commercial products. Indeed, in this case the on-camera "talent" were university professors, school teachers, and other school personnel inexperienced in television appearances. What made the programs successful was the professionalism behind the scenes provided by television station personnel.

4. The issue of convenience versus live interactivity needs to be carefully weighed in designing distance education for staff development. With the exception of e-mail, those elements of the telecourse that participants could do at their convenience (i.e., doing assignments, watching taped programs) were judged to be successful by participants and faculty alike. Those elements that required live "attendance," notably the teleconferences and telephoning faculty during office hours, worked less well. While the relative success or failure of each of these components cannot be reduced to one factor, convenience and availability are certainly part of the equation.

5. Fostering meaningful interaction is perhaps the most difficult challenge of distance learning. We believe the course would have provided stronger student-to-student interactions if participants had been provided with the means to *conveniently* network among themselves through improved electronic networking and through additional aids such as the exchange of personal data sheets that would have identified subgroups with similar interests and needs. Course participants would then have experienced the richer learning potential of live interactions along with the convenience of distance education.

Recommendations for Staff Development

The following practical suggestions are offered for staff developers considering distance learning as a method of delivery.

1. Offer the course in the winter. Due to legislative constraints, "Technology in the Curriculum" had to air during the autumn quarter just as teachers were beginning a new school year. We suggest that others consider winter as the air time for distance courses. This schedule would allow for publicity to be conducted in the autumn after teachers have returned to school. We were forced to publicize our telecourse in the spring when many teachers were busy wrapping up one school year and not ready to think about the next year. This affected enrollment at the front end and later had teachers trying to wrap up the telecourse while being faced with the rush and distractions of the impending holidays.

2. Offer training sessions to use the Internet. Using the Internet is not easy and can be very intimidating for novices attempting to use it alone. Several small-group training sessions scattered around the viewing area before or during the first few weeks of a telecourse would help novice users get on-line.

3. Provide direct experience, consultation, and observation. Shedd & Bacharach (1991) identified direct experience, consultation with peers, and observation of other teachers as three main sources of teaching knowledge and skill. The half-hour preproduced programs gave our students opportunities to observe their peers using technology in the classroom and reflecting on those experiences in the interview.

> We believe the course would have provided stronger student-to-student interactions if participants had been provided with the means to *conveniently* network among themselves through improved electronic networking and through additional aids such as the exchange of personal data sheets that would have identified subgroups with similar interests and needs.

The students frequently remarked that it was encouraging to see "someone like me" using technology successfully in the classroom. They also appreciated the candidness of the on-screen teachers who discussed their fears in attempting to integrate technology into the curriculum. Because teachers value other teachers' experiences, more live demonstrations of teaching with technology could be included in teleconferences as well as in the pre-produced programs.

To build rapport, we suggest that course instructors initiate telephone interactions with the participants, especially those with no e-mail access or those who are isolated by building, district, or region. It would also be beneficial to set up a means whereby participants could communicate electronically with teachers featured in the on-screen demonstrations.

4. Schedule live teleconferences in the early evening. While no time is ideal for busy teachers with home and school responsibilities, in light of our experiences with the 3:30-4:30 p.m. teleconferences, we propose that teleconferences be scheduled in the early evening. It is more likely that participants watching from home would have a telephone at hand to call in. If the personnel are available, we also recommend clustering participants at local sites with facilitators who could encourage both on-site and call-in participation. This would provide participants with opportunities for networking. Teleconferences could also be videotaped for reference during follow-up discussions.

Inservice at a distance offers educators the convenience of fitting a course such as "Technology in the Curriculum" into their busy schedules. An awareness of the potential obstacles can assist staff developers in addressing complications before they occur.

References

Bennett, C.K. (1994). Promoting teacher reflection through action research: What do teachers think? *Journal of Staff Development, 15*(1), 34-38.

Bland, K.P. (1992). *Student attitudes toward learning link: A distance education project.* Paper presented to the Mid-South Educational Research Association, Knoxville, TN (ERIC Document Reproduction Service No. ED 356 766).

Leggett, D., & Hoyle, S. (1987). Peer coaching: One district's experience in using teachers as staff developers. *Journal of Staff Development, 8*(1), 16-20.

Lieberman, A. (1994, Dec.). *Staff development at the crossroads: Building community, capacity, and collective inquiry.* Paper presented at the meeting of the National Staff Development Conference, Orlando, Florida.

Lieberman, A., & McLaughlin, M.W. (1992). Networks for educational change: Powerful and problematic. *Phi Delta Kappan 73*(9), 673-677.

Power, M.A. (1993). *Interactive ESL in-service teacher training via distance education.* Paper presented at the Annual Conference of Teachers of English to Speakers of Other Languages, Atlanta, GA. (ERIC Document Reproduction Service No. ED 359 844).

Schoenbach, R. (1994). Classroom renewal through teacher reflection. *Journal of Staff Development, 15*(1), 24-28.

Shedd, J., & Bacharach, S. (1991). *Tangled hierarchies.* San Francisco: Jossey-Bass.

Watts, G.D., & Castle, S. (1992). Electronic networking and the construction of professional knowledge. *Phi Delta Kappan, 73*(9), 684-689.

About the Authors

Marjorie A. Cambre is an associate professor of instructional design and technology, and Leslie Hall is a graduate teaching assistant and Ph.D. candidate, all at The Ohio State University, College of Education, 29 W. Woodruff Avenue, Columbus, Ohio 43210. Barbara Erdman is an assistant professor of library media education at Western Kentucky University, College of Education, Bowling Green, Kentucky 42101.

Factors in Determining Rural School Readiness To Use Distance Learning

Bruce O. Barker
Michael W. Dickson
Western Illinois University

Educational readiness to begin using distance learning delivery systems is a question facing many rural school administrators at the building and district level. In looking at distance learning as an educational alternative, administrators are faced with several key questions. These fall chiefly into three categories: (1) program need or purpose, (2) resource assessment at the school (human resources, facilities, and equipment); and (3) selecting a distance learning technology system (Karim, 1994). Listed below are a series of questions, if answered by school administrators will help them assess their readiness to include distance learning as a part of their instructional program and the direction they should take in implementing distance learning at their school.

Program Need or Purpose

• *Why does the school need a distance learning program?* Is the purpose to provide elementary enhancement, expand secondary curriculum offerings, offer staff development for faculty, provide community programs, etc.? Administrators should identify their specific distance learning programming needs. For example, most national providers (satellite vendors, some cable vendors, etc.) focus chiefly in providing advanced placement or advance level high school courses for college students. Others provide extensive enrichment or enhancement programs for elementary students. Others might have a large array of staff development programs for faculty and staff or graduate degree oriented programming (Beckner and Barker, 1994). In any event, administrators must first determine exactly why they want to invest in distance learning at their school.

Note: This manuscript has been adapted from material originally produced by the authors for the North Central Regional Laboratory (NCREL) at Oakbrook, Illinois.

• *Should programming be locally controlled or purchased from a national provider?* Compressed video, fiber optic, small cable networks, or computer-networked systems (audiographics) might be locally controlled by a small number of schools joined in a cooperative effort to share resources, control programming, and manage the cooperative network. National providers of distance education programs are chiefly satellite based. They typically provide a "turn-key" operation, offering an extensive array of program offerings and service to subscribing schools (Barker, 1992).

Resource Assessment at the School

• *Staffing – what kind of staffing is available to work with the distance learning program adopted by the school?* A turn-key program (eg. satellite, large cable network) will require limited if any additional staffing needs. Whereas a locally controlled system (eg. audiographics, compressed video, or fiber optic network) will typically require extensive administrative effort to work with participating schools, hire distance learning teachers, maintain and trouble shoot technical problems associated with the system, maintain record keeping, etc.

• *Room Space and Power – where will the distance education rooms be located; are there sufficient power outlets in the room?* An adequate room is needed for those students who will be taking distance learning courses and for the equipment items which will be part of the technology delivery system. Sufficient electrical outlets are needed for equipment items generally associated with distance learning such as televisions, VCRs, computers, printers, facsimile machines, etc. Furthermore, room security should be considered. The distance learning room will usually house expensive computer and/or telecommunications equipment.

- *Telecommunications Connections – does the room include video, telephone inputs, or other telecommunications connections?* Facsimile machines and computer modems operate on a direct telephone line which does not go through a switch board. Satellite and cable programs require a video cable connection. Fiber optic and compressed video systems require specialized fiber, ISDN, T1, Switch 56, or DS3 lines.

- *What technologies/facilities are currently available for distance learning?* Besides power outlets and telecommunications connections for the distance learning room, administrators should assess availability of equipment items which could be dedicated to the distance learning room. Items might include a television, telephone, facsimile machine, computer, modem, VCR, etc.

Resource Assessment at the School

- *What kind of program delivery is desired at the school?* The technologies used in distance learning offer a variety of program formats. Satellite, cable, microwave and ITFS (Instructional Television Fixed Services) systems are typically one-way video, two-way audio. Fiber optics and compressed video are typically two-way video, two-way audio. And audiographic or computer-linked networks are usually two-way computer conferencing with audio interaction (Barker, 1992; Withrow, 1990). Equipment and transmission costs vary widely depending on the system chosen. The cost of installation, equipment, and transmission of fiber optics, compressed video, microwave, or ITFS systems can be high. Without help from external funding sources (grants, foundations, etc.) or legislative initiative, such systems have remained cost prohibitive for a large number of rural schools. A satellite downlink dish and video equipment to receive the TV signal has proven affordable for many rural schools. The same has been true in regards to cable TV systems. The cost of installing and operating an audiographic system is typically limited to the cost of a standard computer, specialized program software, purchase of a facsimile machine, and access to a direct telephone line (OTA, 1989).

Once a distance learning delivery system ha been selected, administrators will need to determine what equipment items – not already owned by the school– should be acquired. In addition, electrical wiring, video and telecommunications connection needs, and room modifications should be considered. Deciding on the system that best meets local needs or falls within budgetary limits may not be as simple and as one might think. Listed below are brief explanations of the more common distance learning technologies currently being used in the United States (Barker, 1992; Barker and Hall,

1994). These are presented to help inform administrators of the specific equipment, cabling, and connections requirements associated with each system; and to help administrators assess which system is best suited for their school's needs.

Interactive Satellite Systems

Interactive satellite systems currently utilize C Band and/or Ku Band frequencies. Although most current systems are analog based, providers are increasingly turning to digital compression technology as a means to improve signal quality and reduce delivery costs. This is occurring even though there are very few digital receivers available at present and the fact that digital reception does not lend itself to steerable muti-purpose receive dishes. Major satellite providers are Westcott Telecommunications TI-IN Network, Dallas, Texas; Satellite Telecommunications Educational Programming (STEP), Spokane, Washington; Arts and Sciences Teleconferencing Service (ASTS), Stillwater, Oklahoma; and Satellite Education Resources Consortium (SERC), Columbia, South Carolina (Beckner and Barker, 1994).

Format: (Half-Duplex) one-way video, two-way audio (return audio via telephone), two-way data (some providers).

Basic Equipment: Satellite receiver (C and/or Ku Band), satellite receive dish (steerable), coaxial cabling, television monitor, telephone and circuit.

Enhanced System: Digital receiver (if required by program provider), VCR, facsimile machine, computer and modem, large screen television.

Special Considerations: Programming source and costs, scheduling, placement of receive dish, reception (based on geographic location), equipment security (receive dish), equipment and liability insurance. Most of the current satellite providers are large centralized systems which provide turn-key services to subscribing schools.

Site Considerations: Does the school or community have an existing satellite receiver and dish; location? Does the local cable system have downlink capability and interconnections to schools? Do schools have internal cabling for delivery to individual rooms; television monitors and VCRs for multiple use.?

Cable Television Systems

Cable television systems have been technologically available for some time. The recent scrutiny of the cable industry by both regulators and users has enhanced cable television's viability as a delivery mechanism. The most visible current example of a cable television system is Mind Extension University (MEU). The most viable current use of cable television systems may be to receive and redistribute interactive satellite programming (TI-IN, STEP, ASTS, SERC, etc.) via cable to schools in urban and/or rural areas served by a cable carrier. Another potential for many users is represented by the existence of local access channels and studios maintained by some community cable companies. These public access channels allow for local production and transmission to the school and community. Future trends include the movement by cable companies into both partnerships and competition with telephone companies which will eventually open more possibilities.

Format: (Half-Duplex) one-way full-motion video, two-way audio (return audio via telephone), two-way data (some providers).

Basic Equipment: Cable access (control box), coaxial cabling, television monitor, telephone and circuit. Local program origination would require a local access channel and broadcast equipment (cameras, etc.).

Enhanced System: VCR, facsimile machine, computer and modem, large screen television.

Special Considerations: Programming sources and costs; the only current truly cable-based service is Mind Extension University which is primarily for college level and is not live nor interactive. However, cable systems can and are carrying programming from K-12 interactive satellite providers. Most networks are centrally controlled, providing turn-key service to subscribing schools.

Site Considerations: Does the commercial cable system and school district have a current or existing relationship (dedicated channel)? Does the local cable system have downlink capability and interconnections to schools? Do schools have internal cabling for delivery to individual rooms; television monitors and VCRs for multiple use?

Microwave Systems

Microwave systems have been in existence for some time and in many cases, particularly with recent digital enhancements, continue to be viable. It should be noted that microwave systems require substantial investments in engineering, equipment, licensing, and operation. However, there are many microwave delivery systems currently in operation and often the investment required to access an already functional system is minimal. Microwave signals have a range of 20-40 miles with most systems centralized in large urban centers.

Format: (Full-Duplex) two-way full-motion video, two-way audio, two-way data (some providers).

Basic Equipment: Transmitter/receiver tower(s), transmitters, receivers, cameras, microphones, coaxial cabling, and television monitors. In addition to basic equipment, Federal Communications Commission (FCC) licensing is required.

Enhanced System: Digital transmitter/receiver, VCR, facsimile machine, computer and modem, large screen television.

Special Considerations: Cost is a prime concern.

Microwave systems require towers for both transmission and reception as well as extensive equipment investments. The operation of these system require and FCC license and an FCC licensed operator. Systems are usually centrally controlled at a regional or large district level.

Site Considerations: Is there any microwave based systems in operation within 40 radius? These systems need not be a video system. Microwave systems might include telephone systems, gas and oil pumping companies, cable companies, government or military systems. Do schools have internal cabling for delivery to individual rooms; television monitors and VCRs for multiple use?

Instructional Television Fixed Service (ITFS) Systems

Instructional Television Fixed Service is actually a variation of commercial broadcast television that is specifically allocated and licensed by the Federal Communications Commission. Utilizing a fairly narrow broadcast frequency and low power transmission, ITFS has been utilized for many years and there are a number of systems in operation. ITFS has recently gained the attention of both potential educational users and regulators as a result of the efforts and activities of rural cable television entrepreneurs (Rural Vision, etc.). Throughout rural America, cable companies have attempted to form partnerships with school districts utilizing their exclusive access to ITFS frequencies to deliver both commercial programming and educational programming. The FCC has considered these partnerships on a case by case basis and granted a sizable number for operation.

Format: (Half-Duplex) one-way full-motion video, two-way audio (return audio via telephone), two-way data (some providers).

Basic Equipment: Transmitter and tower, receivers and antennas, satellite receive system (for rebroadcast) coaxial cabling, and television monitors. In addition, FCC licensing is required.

Enhanced System: Cameras, microphones, VCR, facsimile machine, computer and modem, large screen television.

Special Considerations: Cost is a prime concern. ITFS systems require towers for transmission and special receivers and antennas for reception as well as extensive equipment investments. The operation of these systems require an FCC license and an FCC licensed operator. Most systems are centrally controlled either by a large district or central region.

Site Considerations: Are there any towers available locally? These towers need not be a dedicated television broadcast towers. Administrators must determine distance between potential sites and evaluate potential transmission range based on topography. Do participating schools have internal cabling for delivery to individual rooms; television monitors and VCRs for multiple use?

Compressed Television Systems

One of the most exciting and perhaps least understood developments in the field of distance education is compressed digital television. Generally these systems are digital transmission over terrestrial telephone circuits (either fiber optic or copper). It is a misconception that compressed digital video (television) can only be transmitted via fiber optic circuits or fiber optic lines. Compressed video systems require the transmission of a large amount a data and thus require a fairly large amount of circuit capacity (often referred to as bandwidth) whether fiber or copper. Recent advances in the technology have allowed video transmission over increasingly less circuit capacity or bandwidth. Increasing access to fiber optic circuits has also begun to drive down costs for operation. Most compressed TV systems are cooperative networks of anywhere from two to 10 or more schools linked together. An audio/video bridge is needed whenever three or more schools are linked together for simultaneous audio/video interaction.

Format: (Full-Duplex) two-way compressed video, two-way audio, two-way data (some providers).

Basic Equipment: CODEC (Compression/Decompression Transmitter/Receiver), cameras, microphones, television monitors, access to high capacity telephone circuits (384 kilobits per second minimum up to DS3 capability).

Enhanced System: Remote controlled cameras, microphones, VCR, facsimile machine, computer, large screen television, an audio/video bridge if more than two schools are linked to the network.

Special Considerations: Cost is a prime concern. Currently CODEC prices are declining and many equipment vendors offer integrated systems containing cameras, microphones, monitors, and computer interfaces. However, classrooms must still be modified and have access to high capacity telephone circuits. Perhaps the most costly component is the recurring monthly expense of these telephone circuits. These costs vary according to the circuit capacity and distance covered. Ultimately circuit capacity determines the quality of transmission and thus it may be desirable to sacrifice a small degree of picture quality to lower operating costs. Most systems are small cooperatives locally controlled by participating members.

Local Considerations: Careful study of local telephone system which includes availability and quality of switching and bandwidth (ISDN, T1, Switch 56, DS3, etc.). Also attention should be given to number of local service providers involved as well as long lines carriers and the location of their POP. Because of FCC regulation it will be necessary to check latta lines as well as tariff rates for service.

Audiographics Public Switched Telephone Network (PSTN)

Audiographics technology links microcomputers between school sites. The image on the computer screens whether text or graphics is seen on each machine simultaneously. Audio interaction is usually via speaker telephone thereby leaving the hands free to operate the computer. Neither students nor the teacher can see each other, but they do share a common visual reference on the computer screen and can speak freely in real-time. This technique has been a popular low-cost approach for working with very small groups. As compressed technologies become more advanced and cheaper, it is expected that telephony applications with small cameras at each site will permit compressed video interaction in real-time between participating sites.

Format: (Full-Duplex) two-way fixed image video exchange, two-way audio, two-way data exchange.

Basic Equipment: MS-DOS or Macintosh computer; audiographics/telecommunications software, computer modem, printer, facsimile machine, access to direct telephone lines for computers, speaker telephones, and facsimile machines.

Enhanced System: Video telephones, LCD panel and overhead projector for enlarged projection of computer screen, an audio bridge to link three or more sites together, video cameras and telephony software.

Special Considerations: Audiographics networks lend themselves to small cooperatives of two to four or five schools linked together to share courses. Inasmuch as the computer screen is the visual medium, class size at each site is typically limited to no more than four or five students. Control of the system/network is maintained by the schools which partner together. Most systems required two direct telephone lines – one for the computers to "talk" to each other and one for the speaker telephones at each site.

Local Considerations: Careful study of local telephone system. This study should include availability and quality of switching and bandwidth (ISDN, T1, Switch 56, DS3 etc.). Also attention should be given to number of local service providers involved as well as long lines carriers and the location of their POP. Because of FCC regulation it will be necessary to check latta lines as well as tariff rates for service.

Obtaining Additional Information

Distance learning, a relatively new concept only a few years ago, is now regarded as not only an acceptable, but indeed a desirable means to deliver instruction to students in remote or isolated locations. In rural schools, this approach to learning has helped broaden educational opportunities for students and increased staff development options for teachers.

The information presented in this article is directed to rural school administrators who are interested in adding distance learning as a part of their school's instructional program. The intent has been to pose questions and present options that might promote thinking and discussion among decision makers. Decisions on what kind of technology system to install or national provider with whom to contract should be made only after gathering input from other key players who would be part of the network and after conducting a thorough investigation of what best meets local needs and falls within budgetary guidelines. To gather additional information, school administrators should contact the technology department in their state office of education. Educational technology specialists at the state level should be knowledgeable about specific technologies, their costs, and their potential for local use. Furthermore, specialists at the state level should have names and addresses of successful on-going projects within the state that might be contacted or visited in order to gain added insights. They should also have the names of program providers at both the national and regional level who might be contacted for more information.

References

Barker, B.O. (1992). *The Distance Education Handbook For Rural And Remote Schools: An Administrator's Guide.* Charleston, West Virginia: ERIC Clearinghouse for Rural Education and Small Schools, Appalachia Educational Laboratory.

Barker, B.O. and Hall, R.F. (1994). Distance education in rural schools: Technologies and practice. *Research in Rural Education*, 10(2), 126-128.

Barkner, W. and Barker, B.O. (1994). *Technology in Rural Education.* PDK Fastback #366. Phi Delta Kappa Educational Foundation: Bloomington, Indiana.

Karim, G.P. (1994). *Distance Education in Indiana: Opportunities and Challenges for Rural and Small Schools.* NCREL: Oakbrook, Illinois.

U.S. Congress, Office of Technology Assessment, (1989). *Linking for Learning: A New Course for Education*, OTA-SET-430. U.S. Government Printing Office: Washington, D.C.

Withrow, F. (May, 1990). Star schools distance learning: The promise. *Technological Horizons in Education Journal*, 17(9), 62-64.

Bruce O. Barker is Professor and Chair, Department of Instructional Technology and Telecommunications; Michael W. Dickson is Director, Satellite Education and Interactive Technologies, both with College of Education and Human Services, Western Illinois University, Macomb, Illinois.

This glossary of computer terms is included to provide you with a convenient and ready reference as you encounter general computer terms that are unfamiliar or require a review. It is not intended to be comprehensive, but, taken together with the many definitions included in the articles, it should prove to be quite useful.

Alphanumeric. Data that consists of letters of the alphabet, numerals, or other special characters such as punctuation marks.

Applications software. Software designed to accomplish a specific task such as accounting, financial modeling, or word processing.

Acquisition. Refers to software that is purchased from an outside source such as a vendor or publisher.

Archive. Storage of infrequently used data on disks or diskettes.

Artificial intelligence. Hardware or software capable of performing functions that require learning or reasoning (e.g., a computer that plays chess).

ASCII. American Standard Code for Information Interchange. (The acronym is pronounced "as-key.") An industry standard referring to 128 codes generated by computers for text and control characters (for example, A = 65, Z = 90, a = 97). This code permits the computer equipment of different manufacturers to exchange alphanumeric data with one another.

Authoring language. A high-level language, usually created expressly for use by educators, that allows a user to program with minimal knowledge of computer languages. PILOT.

Automatic Teller Machine (ATM). A machine that provides 24-hour banking services.

Auxiliary storage. A storage device in addition to the core or main storage of the computer. (Includes magnetic tape, cassette tape, floppy disk, and hard disk.) Sometimes called external storage or secondary storage.

Babbage, Charles. Frequently considered the father of the modern computer; in the early 1800s he outlined the ideas that have become the basis for modern computational devices.

Backup. An extra copy of information stored on a disk. If the program or other data stored on the first disk is damaged, it is still available on the backup copy.

Bar code. A code that consists of numerous magnetic lines imprinted on a label that can be read with a scanning device. Often used in labeling retail products.

BASIC. Beginners All-purpose Symbolic Instruction Code. A high-level computer language, considered by many authorities to be the easiest language to learn, and used in one variation or another by almost all microcomputers.

Batch processing. An approach to computer processing where groups of like transactions are accumulated (batched) to be processed at the same time.

Baud rate. The speed of serial data transmission between computers or a computer and a peripheral in bits per second.

Binary. The base-two number system in which all alphanumeric characters are represented by various combinations of 0 and 1. Binary codes may be used to represent any alphanumeric character, such as the letter "A" (100 0001), the number 3 (000 0011), or characters representing certain computer operations such as a "line feed" (000 1010).

Bit. Binary digIT. The smallest unit of digital information. Eight bits constitute one byte.

Bit-mapped. Any binary representation in which a bit or set of bits corresponds to an object or condition.

Board. Abbreviation for printed circuit board. Can also refer to any of the peripheral devices or their connectors that plug into the slots inside a microcomputer.

Boolean. An expression that evaluates to the logical value of true or false (e.g., 1 + 1 = 2 or 3 < 2).

Boot. (Short for Bootstrap.) To start the computer; to load an operating system into the computer's main memory and commence its operation.

Buffer. A temporary memory that is capable of storing incoming data for later transmission. Often found on printers to allow the printer to accept information faster than it prints it.

Bug. An error in a program that causes the computer to malfunction. *See also* Debugging.

Bus. A collection of wires that transmit information in the form of electrical signals from one circuit to another.

Byte. The sequence of bits that represents any alphanumerical character or a number between 0 and 255. Each byte has 8 bits.

CAI. Computer-Assisted Instruction or Computer-Aided Instruction. An educational use of computers that usually entails using computer programs which drill, tutor, simulate, or teach problem-solving skills. *See also* CMI.

Card. Refers to a peripheral card that plugs into one of the internal slots in a microcomputer.

CAT Scanner. A diagnostic device used for producing a cross-sectional X ray of a person's internal organs; an acronym for computer axial tomography.

Cathode-ray tube (CRT). *See* Display screen.

CBT. 1. Computer-Based Testing. Refers to the use of computers to present, monitor, or correct examinations. 2. Computer-Based Training. *See also* CAI.

CD-I. Compact Disc-Interactive. A format available to personal computer users that allows access to picture databases and large text; a compact disc standard that includes music compact discs (CD audio), static data (CD ROM), and graphics.

CD-ROM. Compact Disk Read Only Memory. An auxiliary storage device that uses a rigid disk to store information capable of being read by a computer. These disks have tremendous storage capacities. A single CD-ROM can store up to 680 MB of text, stills, sound, and video.

Central Processing Unit. *See* CPU.

Chip. An integrated circuit used inside a microcomputer and on boards. They contain such electronic devices as transistors, capacitors, and circuits.

CMI. Computer-Managed Instruction. An educational use of computers that usually entails the use of computer programs to handle testing, grade-keeping, filing, and other classroom management tasks.

COBOL. COmmon Business Oriented Language. A high-level language, used mostly in business.

Compatibility. 1. Software compatibility refers to the ability to run the same software on a variety of computers. 2. Hardware compatibility refers to the ability to directly connect various peripherals to the computer.

Compiler. A program that translates a high-level computer language into machine language for later execution. This would be similar to a human translating an entire document from a foreign language into English for later reading by others.

Computer. Any device that can receive, store, and act upon a set of instructions in a predetermined sequence, and one that permits both the instructions and the data upon which the instructions act to be changed.

Computer Bulletin Board Service (CBBS). A computerized data base that users access to post and to retrieve messages.

Computer literacy. Term used to refer to a person's capacity to intelligently use computers. May also be used to refer to programs in schools designed to help students acquire this capacity.

Computer program. A series of commands, instructions, or statements put together in a way that permits a computer to perform a specific task or a series of tasks.

Computer-Aided Design (CAD). An engineer's use of the computer to design, draft, and analyze a prospective product using computer graphics on a video terminal.

Computer-Aided Instruction. *See* CAI.

Computer-Aided Manufacturing (CAM). An engineer's use of the computer to simulate the required steps of the manufacturing process.

Computer-Assisted Instruction. *See* CAI.

Computer-Based Testing. *See* CBT.

Computer-Based Training. *See* CBT.

Configuration. The components that make up a computer (referred to as hardware—a keyboard for text entry, a central processing unit, one or more disk drives, a printer, and a display screen).

Control key. A special function key found on most computer keyboards that allows the user to use the remaining keys for other specialized operations.

Copy protected. Refers to a disk that has been altered to prevent it from being copied.

Cost benefit. A technique or method for assessing the relationship between results or outcomes and the costs required to produce them.

Courseware. Instructional programs and related support materials needed to use computer software in the classroom.

CPU. Central Processing Unit. The "brain" of the computer consisting of a large integrated circuit that performs the computations within a computer. CPUs are often designated by a number, such as 6502, 8080, 68000, and so on.

Crash. A malfunction of a computer's software or hardware that prevents the computer from functioning.

Crossfooting. The ability of a computer to total numeric amounts that have been arranged in columns and rows, and then placing the answers at the end of each row or bottom of each column.

CRT. Cathode-Ray Tube. *See* Display screen.

Cursor. The prompting symbol usually displayed as a blinking white square or underline on the monitor that shows where the next character will appear.

Data. All information, including facts, numbers, letters, and symbols, that can be acted upon or produced by the computer.

Data base. A collection of related information, such as that found on a mailing list, which can be stored in a computer and retrieved in several ways.

Data base management. 1. Refers to a classification of software designed to act like an electronic filing cabinet, which allows the user to store, retrieve, and manipulate files. 2. The practice of using computers to assist in routine filing and information processing chores.

Data processing. Also known as electronic data processing (EDP), it is the mathematical or other logical manipulation of symbols or numbers, based on a stored program of instructions.

Debugging. The process of locating and eliminating defects in a program that causes the computer to malfunction or cease to operate.

Default format statement. Formatting instructions, built into a software program or the computer's memory, which will be followed unless different instructions are given by the operator. (A common default format is a 6.5-inch line, with 1.5-inch margins.)

Design. Refers to the goals and job/task analysis information used to construct objectives of a proposed software product. An objective hierarchy is developed, which specifies the sequence of development activities based on software and hardware requirements.

Desktop publishing. The system that processes text and graphics and, with page layout software and a laser printer, produces high-quality pages that are suitable for printing or reproduction.

Development. Refers to the building of a program according to the requirements of a design document. This includes programming, documentation, and auxiliary program materials.

Directory. A list of files that are stored on a disk.

Disk, Diskette. A thin plastic wafer-like object enclosed in a plastic jacket with a metallic coating used to magnetically store information. The standard size on microcomputer is 5 1/4 inches in diameter, though many are beginning to use smaller 3 1/4 inches or 3 1/2 inches diameter diskettes that are stored in more rigid jackets.

Disk drive. A peripheral device capable of reading and writing information on a disk.

Disk envelope. A removable protective paper sleeve used when handling or storing a disk; must be removed before inserting in a disk drive.

Disk jacket. A nonremovable protective covering for a disk, usually black plastic or paper, within which the disk spins when being used by the disk drive.

Disk Operating System. *See* DOS.

Display screen. A peripheral that allows for the visual output of information for the computer on a CRT, monitor, or similar device.

Documentation. Instructional materials that describe the operations of an individual computer program or a piece of system hardware.

DOS. Disk Operating System. (The acronym is pronounced to rhyme with "boss.") Refers to the program that enables a computer to read and write on a disk.

Dot-matrix. A type of printing in which characters are formed by using a number of closely spaced dots.

Downtime. Any period of time when the computer is not available or is not working.

Dumb terminal. Refers to a terminal that can be used to input information into a computer and to print or display output, but which lacks the capacity to manipulate information transmitted to it from the host computer. *See also* Intelligent terminal.

Dump. Mass copying of memory or a storage device such as a disk to another storage device or a printer so it can be used as a backup or analyzed for errors.

Duplexing. The procedure that permits two computers to transmit data to each other simultaneously.

DV-I. Digital Video-Interactive. Optical storage media that delivers full-motion, full-screen video, three-dimensional motion graphics, and high-quality audio capabilities.

Electronic Funds Transfer System (EFT). A system that eliminates the exchange of cash or checks by automatically transferring funds from one account to another.

Electronic mail (E-mail). Sending and receiving information by computer.

Electronic spreadsheet. *See* Spreadsheet.

Electronic worksheet. *See* Spreadsheet.

Elite. Any typeface that allows the printing of 12 characters to an inch.

ENIAC. Electronic Numerical Integrator and Calculator. The first electronic digital computer produced in the United States.

EPIE. Educational Products Information Exchange. A nonprofit group associated with Consumer's Union, which, among other things, evaluates computer hardware and software.

Error message. A message displayed or printed to notify the user of an error or problem in the execution of a program.

Expert systems. Software packages designed to copy how expert humans in a certain field think through a problem to reach the correct solution.

Exponential notation. Refers to how a computer displays very large or very small numbers by means of the number times

10 raised to some power. For example, 3,000,000 could be printed as 3E + 6 (3 times 10 to the sixth power).

Fan fold. A type of paper that can continuously feed into a printer (usually via tractor feed).

Fax. (n.) Short for the word facsimile. A copy of a document transmitted electronically from one machine to another. (v.) To transmit a copy of a document electronically.

Field. Group of related characters treated as a unit (such as a name); also the location in a record or database where this group of characters is entered.

First-Generation Computers. Developed in the 1950s; used vacuum tubes; faster than earlier mechanical devices, but very slow compared to today's computer.

Fixed disk. *See* Hard disk.

Floppy, Floppy disk. *See* Disk.

Format. (n.) The physical form in which information appears. (v.) To specify parameters of a form or to write address codes on a blank disk in preparation for using it to store data or programs. *See also* Initialize.

FORTRAN. FORmula TRANslation. A high-level language used primarily for mathematical computations; though FORTRAN is used by some microcomputers, it is mainly used by mainframe computers.

Function keys. Computer keyboard keys that give special commands to the computer (for example, to format, to search text).

GIGO. Garbage In, Garbage Out. Serves as a reminder that a program is only as good as the information and instructions in the program.

Global. The performance of any function on an entire document without requiring individual commands for each use. For example, a global search-and-replace command will allow the computer to search for a particular word and replace it with a different word throughout the text.

Graphics. 1. Information presented in the form of pictures or images. 2. The display of pictures or images on a computer's display screen.

Hard copy. A paper copy of the computer's output.

Hard disk. A magnetically coated metal disk, usually permanently mounted within a disk drive; capable of storing 30 to 150 times more information than a floppy disk.

Hardware. Refers to the computer and all its peripheral devices. The physical pieces of the computer.

HDTV. High Definition TV. A television with quality resolution that is higher than current international standards.

Head. Refers to the component of a disk drive or tape system that magnetically reads or writes information to the storage medium.

Hex or Hexadecimal. A numbering system based on 16 (digits 0–9 and letters A–F) rather than on 10. Most computers operate using hex numbers. Each hexadecimal digit corresponds to a sequence of 4 binary digits or bits.

High-level language. An English-like computer language (BASIC, Pascal, FORTRAN, Logo, COBOL) designed to make it relatively convenient for a person to prepare a program for a computer, which in turn translates it into machine language for execution.

Hypermedia. Refers to the random access and use of multimedia to construct real/artificial situations that emulate the thinking process. It usually involves the use of more than one media window on a screen.

Hypertext. A technique that organizes and connects information in a nonsequential or nontraditional manner.

IAV. Interactive Video. The merger of two electronic media, computers and television, and two design areas, instructional and visual.

IC. Integrated Circuit. *See* Chip.

ICAI. Intelligent Computer-Assisted Instruction. A type of CAI on which the interaction between the computer and learner is subject to a complex algorithm that uses student responses to questions to determine subsequent interaction (level of problem difficulty, remedial work, etc.).

Icon. Refers to the use of a graphic symbol to represent something else. Its use is central to the use of advanced computers such as the Macintosh and Amiga.

Indexing. The ability of a computer to accumulate a list of words or phrases, with corresponding page numbers, in a document, and then to print out or display the list in alphabetical order.

Inference engine. Software that accesses a knowledge base, and includes navigation, access, and manipulative facilities. It enables users to build models from multimedia objects stored in a knowledge base. The models can be used to draw inferences needed for problem-solving.

Initialize. 1. To set an initial state or value in preparation for some computation. 2. To prepare a blank disk to receive information by dividing its surface into tracks and sectors. *See also* Format.

Ink jet printer. A dot-matrix printer in which the characters are formed by using a number of closely spaced dots that are sprayed onto a page in microscopic droplets of ink.

Input. Information entered into the computer.

Instructional design. A systematic process for designing, developing, and evaluating software. It includes procedures for identifying instructional goals, conducting instructional analysis, identifying entering behaviors and learner characteristics, performance objectives, test items, instructional strategies, formative and summative evaluation, and a revision process.

Integrated circuit. *See* Chip.

Intelligent terminal. A terminal that is capable of doing more than just receiving or transmitting data due to its microprocessor. *See also* Dumb terminal.

Interactive multimedia. Back-and-forth dialogue between user and computer that allows the combining, editing, and orchestrating of sounds, graphics, moving pictures, and text.

Interface. (v.) To connect two pieces of computer hardware together. (n.) The means by which two things communicate. In particular, it refers to the electrical configuration that allows two or more devices to pass information. *See also* Interface card.

Interface card. A board used to connect a microcomputer to peripheral devices.

I/O. Input/Output. Refers usually to one of the slots or the game port in a microcomputer to which peripheral devices may be connected.

Joy stick. An input device, often used to control the movement of objects on the video display screen of a computer for games.

Justification. A method of printing in which additional space is inserted between words or characters to force each line to the same length.

K. Abbreviation for kilo, or 1000. In information processing, K stands for kilobyte (1024 bytes) and is often used to describe a computer's storage capacity.

Keyboard. The typewriter-like keys on a microcomputer. Each microcomputer will have basically the same keyboard as a typewriter, with major differences limited to special function keys such as ESCape, RESET, ConTRoL, TABulate, etc.

Kilobyte. *See* K.

Knowledge base. A collection of information in a variety of formats such as audio, video, stills, graphics, and text. All of the objects in the knowledge base can be accessed by means of an inference engine or database manager.

Language. Characters and procedures used to write programs that the computer is designed to understand.

Large-Scale Integration (LSI). Refers to a generation of integrated circuits that allowed the equivalent of thousands of vacuum tube switches to be installed on a single chip.

Light pen. An input device, shaped much like a mechanical pencil, which, when touched to a display screen, can be used to select or execute certain computer functions.

LISP (LISt Processing). Programming language primarily used in artificial intelligence research.

Local Area Networks (LAN). The linking together of computers, word processors, and other electronic office equipment to form an interoffice network.

Log on. To execute the necessary commands to allow you to use a computer. May involve the use of a password. More common on mainframe systems.

Logo. A high-level language specifically designed so that it may be used by both small children and adults. It involves a "turtle"-shaped cursor for much of its operation.

M. *See* Megabyte.

Machine language. A fundamental, complex computer language used by the computer itself to perform its functions. This language is quite difficult for the average person to read or write.

Macro. Refers to the use of a simple command to execute a sequence of complex commands while using a computer program. The use of macros can save the user a considerable amount of time and reduce the chance of typing an incorrect key when executing a sequence of commands.

Magnetic Ink Character Recognition (MICR) devices. Computer hardware capable of reading characters imprinted with magnetic ink, such as on checks.

Mainframe. Refers to large computers used primarily in business, industry, government, and higher education that have the capacity to deal with many users simultaneously and to process large amounts of information quickly and in very sophisticated ways. *See also* Time share.

Management Information System (MIS). A systems approach that treats business departments as integrated parts of one total system rather than as separate entities.

MB. *See* Megabyte.

Megabyte. 1,048,576 bytes.

Memory. Chips in the computer that have the capacity to store information. *See also* PROM; RAM; ROM.

Menu. The list of programs available on a given disk to guide the operator through a function.

Menu driven. Refers to software in which the program prompts the user with a list of available options at any given time, thus eliminating the need to memorize commands.

Merge. A command to create one document by combining text that is stored in two different locations (e.g., a form letter can be merged with a mailing list to produce a batch of personalized letters).

Microcomputer. Refers to a generation of small, self-contained, relatively inexpensive computers based on the microprocessor (commonly consists of a display screen, a keyboard, a central processing unit, one or more disk drives, and a printer).

Microprocessor. The CPU. It holds all of the essential elements for manipulating data and performing arithmetic operations. A microprocessor is contained on a single silicon chip.

Microsecond. One millionth of a second.

MIDI. Musical Instrument Digital Interface. A protocol that allows for the interchange of musical information between musical instruments, synthesizer, and computers.

Millisecond. One thousandth of a second; abbreviated "ms."

Minicomputer. Refers to a class of computers larger than micros but smaller than mainframe computers, many of which support multiple keyboards and output devices simultaneously.

Mnemonics. A computer's system of commands, which are structured to assist the operator's memory. Abbreviations are used for the command functions they perform (e.g., C for center, U for underline).

Modem. MOdulator/DEModulator. A peripheral device that enables the computer to transmit and receive information over a telephone line.

Monitor. The display screen of a computer.

Motherboard. The main circuit board of a computer.

Mouse. A hand-operated device that is used to move the cursor around on the CRT screen.

Multimedia. Refers to the combination of text, sound, and video used to present information in ways that bring pages of information or ideas to life.

Nanosecond. One billionth of a second; abbreviated "ns."

National Crime Information Center (NCIC). A computerized information center maintained by the FBI that serves agencies throughout the United States.

Network. A structure capable of linking two or more computers by wire, telephone lines, or radio links.

Nibble. 1. Half a byte. 2. Refers to copy programs that copy small portions of a disk at a time, often used to copy otherwise copy-protected programs.

Nonvolatile memory. Memory that retains data even after power has been shut off. ROM is nonvolatile; RAM is volatile.

Numeric keypad. An input device that allows the user to input numbers into a microcomputer with a calculator-like key arrangement.

Off-line. An operation performed by electronic equipment not tied into a centralized information processing system.

On-line. An operation performed by electronic equipment controlled by a remote central processing system.

Operating system. A group of programs that act as intermediary between the computer and the applications software; the operating system takes a program's commands and passes them down to the CPU in a language that the CPU understands; application programs must be written for a specific operating system such as DOS 3.3, Pro-DOS, MS-DOS, TRS-DOS, and others.

Optical Character Reader (OCR). Also called an optical scanner, it is a device that can read text and automatically enter it into a computer for editing or storage.

Output. Information sent out of the computer system to some external destination such as the display screen, disk drive, printer, or modem.

Parallel. A form of data transmission in which information is passed in streams of eight or more bits at a time in sequence. *See also* Serial.

Pascal. A high-level language, with a larger, more complex vocabulary than BASIC, used for complex applications in business, science, and education; named after the seventeenth-century French mathematician.

Password. A code word or group of characters required to access stored material. A protection against unauthorized persons accessing documents.

PC. Personal Computer. *See* Microcomputer.

Peripheral. Hardware attachments to a microcomputer, (e.g., printer, modem, monitor, disk drives, or interface card).

Peripheral card. A removable printed-circuit board that plugs into a microcomputer's expansion slot and expands or modifies the computer's capabilities by connecting a peripheral device or performing some subsidiary or peripheral function.

Pica type. Any typeface that allows the printing of 10 characters to an inch.

PILOT. Programmed Inquiry, Learning, or Teaching. A high-level language designed primarily for use by educators, which facilitates the wiring of computer-assisted instruction lessons that include color graphics, sound effects, lesson texts, and answer checking.

Pitch. A measurement that indicates the number of characters in an inch (e.g., pica yields 10 characters to an inch; elite yields 12 characters to an inch).

Pixel. PIXture ELement. Refers to the smallest point of light that can be displayed on a display screen.

Plotter. A printing mechanism capable of drawing lines rapidly and accurately for graphic representation.

Port. An input or output connection to the computer.

Printout. *See* Hard copy.

Program. A list of instructions that allows the computer to perform a function.

PROM. Programmable ROM. A ROM that is programmed after it has been made.

Prompt. A message given on the display screen to indicate the status of a function.

Protocol. A formal set of rules that governs the transmission of information from one piece of equipment to another.

RAM. Random Access Memory. The main working memory of any computer. In most microcomputers, anything stored in RAM will be lost when the power is shut off.

Read Only Memory. *See* ROM.

Retrieve. The transfer of a document from storage to memory.

RF Modulator. Radio Frequency Modulator. Refers to a device that converts video signals generated by the computer to signals that can be displayed on a television set.

RISC. Reduced Instruction Set Computer. A computer architecture requiring assemblers and compilers to generate a limited series of instructions to perform complex functions.

Robotics. The science of designing and building robots.

ROM. Read Only Memory. A memory device in which information is permanently stored as it is being made. Thus, it may be read but not changed.

RS-232. Industry standard for serial transmission devices.

Run. 1. To execute a program. 2. A command to load a program to main memory from a peripheral storage medium, such as a disk, and execute it.

Save. To store a program on a disk or somewhere other than a computer's memory.

Scanning. Examining text on a display screen for editing purposes.

Screen. A CRT or display screen.

Search and replace. Locating a character string in a document and replacing it with a different character string.

Second-Generation Computers. Used transistors; smaller, faster, and had larger storage capacity than the first-generation computers; first computers to use a high-level language.

Serial. A form of data transmission in which information is passed one bit at a time in sequence.

Software. The programs used by the computer. Often refers to the programs as stored on a disk.

Sort. To arrange fields, files, and records in a predetermined sequence.

Speech synthesizer. Refers to a peripheral output device that attempts to mimic human speech.

Split screen. A type of dual display that allows some computers to view two or more different video images on the screen at the same time. *See also* Windowing.

Spreadsheet. A program that provides worksheets with rows and columns for calculating and preparing reports.

Stack. A list used to keep track of the sequence of required program routines.

Store. Placing information in memory for later use.

System. An organized collection of hardware, software, and peripheral equipment that works together. *See also* Configuration.

Telecommunication. Transmission of information between two computers in different locations, usually over telephone lines.

Terminal. A piece of equipment used to communicate with a computer, such as a keyboard for input, or video monitor or printer for output.

Third-Generation Computers. Refers to the present generation of computers based on microchips. Compare to first generation (tubes) and second generation (transistors).

Time share. Refers to the practice of accessing a larger computer from a remote location and paying for services based on the amount of computer time used. *See* Mainframe.

Tools. Refers to software needed to build applications or perform activities that are required by other software or training programs.

Tractor feed. A mechanism used to propel paper through a printer by means of sprockets attached to the printer that engage holes along the paper's edges.

TTD. A TTY communications device used by the deaf.

TTY. A TeleTypewriter.

Turning test. A person asks questions and, on the basis of the answers, must determine if the respondent is another human being or a machine.

Typeover. Recording and storing information in a specific location to destroy whatever had been stored there previously.

Universal Product Code (UPC). A bar code that appears on virtually all consumer goods; can be read by a scanner or wand device used in point-of-sale systems.

User friendly. Refers to hardware or software that is relatively easy for a new operator to learn, and which has features to help eliminate operator error.

User group. An association of people who meet to exchange information about computers or computer applications.

Very Large Scale Integration (VLSI). *See* LSI.

Video-capture board. Refers to a computer board that can be used to capture still-video images from a display and store it as a file on a disc.

Videodisc. A laser disc player used to store motion video, audio, stills, and software. Storage capacity is 10 GB, which provides about thirty minutes of motion video.

Virtual reality. Refers to simulations or reconstitution of data into three-dimensional representations that are lifelike. The simulations can include sound, touch, feel, etc. It gives one the feeling and experience of "being there" or "doing it."

Voice Recognition System. A system that allows the user to "train" the computer to understand his or her voice and vocabulary.

Volatile. Refers to memory that is erased whenever the power is removed, such as RAM.

WAN. Wide-Area Network. The movement of data between computers in various areas through high-speed links.

Windowing. The ability of a computer to split a display screen into two or more segments so that several different documents can be viewed and several different functions performed simultaneously.

Word processing. Refers to the use of computers as electronic typewriters capable of entering and retrieving text, storing it on disks, and performing a wide range of editing functions.

Wraparound. A computer's ability to automatically move words from one line to the next or from one page to the next as a result of margin adjustments, insertions, or deletions.

Write protected. A disk in which the write-enable notch is either missing or has had a write-protect tab placed over it to prevent information from being written to the disk.

Write-enable notch. A notch in a floppy disk that, if uncovered, allows a disk drive to write information to it, and which, if covered, prohibits such writing.

Write-protect tab. A small adhesive sticker used to write-protect a disk by covering the write-enable notch.

Sources for the glossary include:

Apple Computer Incorporated, Apple IIe Owner's Manual, Cupertino, CA, 1982.

"Apple II New User's Guide"; B. Gibson, "Personal Computers in Business: An Introduction and Buyer's Guide," *MECC,* Apple Computer, Inc., 1982.

Computer-Based Training Start Kit, Department of Treasury, Internal Revenue Service, Document 6846 (5–83).

Craig W. Copley and Stephen J. Taffee, Minnesota Educational Computing Corporation, St. Paul, MN, 55126.

"Glossary of Computer Terms," *Printout,* April 1983.

"Glossary of Computer Terms," S. Richardson, *Noteworthy,* Winter 1982, pp. 27–29.

"Glossary of Computer Terms," William A. Sabine, *Gregg Reference Manual,* 1992, pp. 480–490.

Softalk, January 1983, January 1982.

Stephen J. Taffee, Department of Education, North Dakota State University.

"Using the Computer in the Classroom," *Today's Education,* April–May 1982.

"VisiCalc Glossary," *Apple Orchard,* July–August 1982.

—1993

Index

Credits/Acknowledgments

Cover design by Charles Vitelli

1. Introduction
Facing overview— Apple Computer, Inc.

2. Curriculum and Instructional Design
Facing overview—Tom Way, IBM Microelectronics.

3. Classroom Applications and Software Evaluations
Facing overview—J. Wilson/Woodfin Camp.

4. Teacher Training
Facing overview—Jim Gerberich, AP/Wide World Photo.

5. Multimedia
Facing overview—Tom Way, IBM Microelectronics.

6. Special Issues
Facing overview—Tom Way, IBM Microelectronics.

7. The Internet and Computer Networks
Facing overview—Pamela Carley, Dushkin/McGraw-Hill.

8. Distance Learning
Facing overview—Apple Computer, Inc.

ANNUAL EDITIONS ARTICLE REVIEW FORM

■ NAME: _____ DATE: _____

■ TITLE AND NUMBER OF ARTICLE: _____

■ BRIEFLY STATE THE MAIN IDEA OF THIS ARTICLE: _____

_____

■ LIST THREE IMPORTANT FACTS THAT THE AUTHOR USES TO SUPPORT THE MAIN IDEA:

_____

_____

_____

_____

■ WHAT INFORMATION OR IDEAS DISCUSSED IN THIS ARTICLE ARE ALSO DISCUSSED IN YOUR
TEXTBOOK OR OTHER READINGS THAT YOU HAVE DONE? LIST THE TEXTBOOK CHAPTERS AND
PAGE NUMBERS:

_____

_____

_____

_____

■ LIST ANY EXAMPLES OF BIAS OR FAULTY REASONING THAT YOU FOUND IN THE ARTICLE:

_____

_____

_____

_____

■ LIST ANY NEW TERMS/CONCEPTS THAT WERE DISCUSSED IN THE ARTICLE, AND WRITE A SHORT
DEFINITION:

_____

_____

_____

_____

*Your instructor may require you to use this ANNUAL EDITIONS Article Review Form in any
number of ways: for articles that are assigned, for extra credit, as a tool to assist in developing
assigned papers, or simply for your own reference. Even if it is not required, we encourage
you to photocopy and use this page; you will find that reflecting on the articles will greatly
enhance the information from your text.

We Want Your Advice

ANNUAL EDITIONS revisions depend on two major opinion sources: one is our Advisory Board, listed in the front of this volume, which works with us in scanning the thousands of articles published in the public press each year; the other is you—the person actually using the book. Please help us and the users of the next edition by completing the prepaid article rating form on this page and returning it to us. Thank you for your help!

COMPUTER STUDIES: COMPUTERS IN EDUCATION, Eighth Edition
Article Rating Form

Here is an opportunity for you to have direct input into the next revision of this volume. We would like you to rate each of the 43 articles listed below, using the following scale:

1. **Excellent: should definitely be retained**
2. **Above average: should probably be retained**
3. **Below average: should probably be deleted**
4. **Poor: should definitely be deleted**

Your ratings will play a vital part in the next revision. So please mail this prepaid form to us just as soon as you complete it.
Thanks for your help!

Rating	Article	Rating	Article
	1. School Reform in the Information Age		22. Converting a Traditional Multimedia Kit into an Interactive Video CD-ROM
	2. System 2000: If You Build It, Can You Manage It?		23. The 21st Century Classroom-Scholarship Environment: What Will It Be Like?
	3. The Modern Land of Laputa: Where Computers Are Used in Education		24. Video to the Desktop and Classrooms: The IUPUI IMDS Project
	4. Education Wars: The Battle over Information-Age Technology		25. Multimedia and Cultural Diversity
	5. 21st Century Classroom		26. Strengthening the Visual Element in Visual Media Materials
	6. Unfilled Promises: Can Technology Help Close the Equity Gap? Maybe—But It Hasn't Happened Yet		27. Factors Facilitating Teachers' Use of Computer Technology
	7. Interactivity and Computer-Based Instruction		28. Making the Most of a Slow Revolution
	8. The Relevance of HCI Guidelines for Educational Interfaces		29. The Coming Ubiquity of Information Technology
	9. Designing Interactive Learning Environments		30. Computing Our Way to Educational Reform
	10. Design and Application of Teaching Software		31. Mad Rushes into the Future: The Overselling of Educational Technology
	11. NAEYC Position Statement: Technology and Young Children—Ages Three through Eight		32. A Response to Douglas Noble: We're in This Together
	12. Children's Computers		33. Journey into the Unknown
	13. Software Evaluation		34. Traveling the Internet in Chinese
	14. Where Computers Do Work		35. Ready Reference on the Internet: A Beginning List of Sources
	15. Instructional Applications of Computer Games		36. Monster Job!
	16. Structuring Telecommunications to Create Instructional Conversations about Student Teaching		37. Tips & Tricks for K-12 Educational LANs
	17. Six Stages for Learning to Use Technology		38. Distance Learning, the Internet, and the World Wide Web
	18. Dimensions of a Knowledge Support System: Multimedia Cases and High Bandwidth Telecommunications for Teacher Professional Development		39. Distance Learning's Explosion on the Internet
	19. Interactive Video Cases Developed for Elementary Science Methods Courses		40. Seven Principles for Good Practice in Distance Learning
	20. Stage a Well-Designed Saturday Session and They Will Come!		41. Teaching at a Distance: Student Involvement through Interactive Multimedia
	21. Interactive Multimedia: Cost Benefit Analysis Issues		42. The Challenge of Distance Education
			43. Factors in Determining Rural School Readiness to Use Distance Learning

(Continued on next page)

ABOUT YOU

Name _____ Date _____

Are you a teacher? ❏ Or a student? ❏

Your school name _____

Department _____

Address _____

City _____ State _____ Zip _____

School telephone # _____

YOUR COMMENTS ARE IMPORTANT TO US !

Please fill in the following information:

For which course did you use this book? _____

Did you use a text with this *ANNUAL EDITION*? ❏ yes ❏ no

What was the title of the text? _____

What are your general reactions to the *Annual Editions* concept?

Have you read any particular articles recently that you think should be included in the next edition?

Are there any articles you feel should be replaced in the next edition? Why?

Are there any World Wide Web sites you feel should be included in the next edition? Please annotate.

May we contact you for editorial input?

May we quote your comments?

COMPUTER STUDIES: COMPUTERS IN EDUCATION, Eighth Edition

BUSINESS REPLY MAIL

First Class   Permit No. 84   Guilford, CT

Postage will be paid by addressee

Dushkin/McGraw·Hill
Sluice Dock
Guilford, Connecticut 06437

No Postage
Necessary
if Mailed
in the
United States

‖‖‖….‖.‖.‖.‖.‖‖.‖‖.‖.‖.‖.‖.‖.‖.‖‖.‖.‖‖.‖